The Origins of Moral Theology in the United States

MORAL TRADITIONS & MORAL ARGUMENTS
A SERIES EDITED BY JAMES F. KEENAN, S.J.

The Evolution of Altruism and the Ordering of Love
STEPHEN J. POPE

Love, Human and Divine: The Heart of Christian Ethics
EDWARD COLLINS VACEK, S.J.

Bridging the Sacred and the Secular:
Selected Writings of John Courtney Murray, S.J.
J. LEON HOOPER, S.J., editor

The Context of Casuistry
Edited by
JAMES F. KEENAN, S.J. and THOMAS A. SHANNON

Aquinas and Empowerment:
Classical Ethics for Ordinary Lives
Edited by
G. SIMON HARAK, S.J.

The Christian Case for Virtue Ethics
JOSEPH J. KOTVA, JR.

The Origins of Moral Theology in the United States

Three Different Approaches

Charles E. Curran
Elizabeth Scurlock University Professor of Human Values
Southern Methodist University

GEORGETOWN UNIVERSITY PRESS / WASHINGTON, D.C.

Georgetown University Press, Washington, D.C.
© 1997 by Georgetown University Press. All rights reserved.
Printed in the United States of America

10 9 8 7 6 5 4 3 2 1   1997

Library of Congress Cataloging-in-Publication Data

Curran, Charles E.
    The origins of moral theology in the United States : three different
approaches / Charles E. Curran.
        p.   cm.
    Includes bibliographical references.
    1. Sabetti, Aloysius—Ethics. 2. Bouquillon, Thomas, 1842–1902—Ethics.
3. Hogan, John (John Baptist), 1829–1901—Ethics. 4. Christian ethics—
United States—History—19th century. 5. Christian ethics—Catholic
authors—History—19th century. I. Title.
BJ352.C87   1997
241'.04273'09034—dc21   96-46601
ISBN 0-87840-634-4
ISBN 0-87840-635-2 (pbk.)

To Friends and Colleagues at S.M.U.

Contents

Preface

This book analyzes and criticizes the beginnings of Catholic moral theology in the United States. The volume will study in depth the approaches of Aloysius Sabetti, Thomas J. Bouquillon, and John B. Hogan who taught and wrote in the United States near the end of the nineteenth century. Why a book about the beginnings of Catholic moral theology in the United States? Three reasons strongly support and buttress this project.

First, the study of moral theology's historical development has an important meaning in itself. The quest for knowledge in any discipline seeks to find out the development of the discipline itself. But comparatively few studies have been done in the history of moral theology. There is no definitive and well-accepted history of the discipline as it developed in the Western world. Very little attention has been paid to the historical development of moral theology in the United States. Without doubt moral theology found its primary home in Europe before Vatican II, and even many of the textbooks used in Catholic seminaries in the United States were written by Europeans. Contemporary writings in moral theology in this country almost never refer to the work that has been done earlier, especially in the late nineteenth century. The impression persists that nothing of great importance happened in moral theology in the United States at that time. A reader of this volume for Georgetown University Press, who enthusiastically recommended the publication of the volume, pointed out that the three authors studied here are comparatively unknown even to professors in the field. The name of Sabetti would be known to some older moral theologians because the manual of moral theology that he wrote was subsequently reedited many times until just before Vatican II. However, very few would have bothered reading Sabetti and many trained professional Catholic moral theologians in the United States have never even heard of Thomas J. Bouquillon or John B. Hogan, let alone read their writings.

In discussing the change that has occurred on particular positions in moral theology, John T. Noonan, Jr., who has written significant historical studies on particular issues,[1] points out that no study of the theory of development in moral theology has been done, although many such studies of development exist with regard to dogmatic or so-called systematic theology.[2] One can legitimately enlarge that thesis to say that the history of theology has frequently been written from the perspective of dogmatic theology and not from the perspective of moral theology. However, the history of moral theology might be somewhat different. As a result there is even more reason for a student of moral theology to be concerned about the history of moral theology in general and the earlier development of this discipline in the United States.

Is the impression that nothing of importance or interest occurred in Catholic moral theology in the United States in the latter part of the nineteenth century true? What really did transpire in Catholic moral theology at that time? Was the development of moral theology different from the development of dogmatic theology?

Second, studying the history of moral theology may help us evaluate and criticize the present and the future development of moral theology. One studying the past naturally brings to it the questions and perspectives of the present. What can the past tell us about the present and the future?

In the Catholic ambiance different theological disciplines at different times and places become the focus of attention. In the early part of the twentieth century with the controversy over Modernism, scripture and dogmatic theology shared the spotlight. In the late 1950s and 1960s attention focused on scripture. Today moral theology is in the spotlight. In September 1993, Pope John Paul II issued his long-awaited encyclical, *Veritatis splendor*, dealing with contemporary moral theology. The pope referred to a new situation and "a genuine crisis" in moral theology today created by those who question traditional Catholic moral teaching even in seminaries and theologates.[3]

Cardinal Josef Ratzinger, the prefect of the Congregation for the Doctrine of the Faith, had earlier made a fascinating comment about Catholic moral theology in the United States today. Cardinal Ratzinger pointed out the contrast between the values and style of life proposed by Catholic teaching and the lifestyle in the United States. In this context it becomes difficult if not impossible to present Catholic teaching as reasonable. "Consequently many moralists (it is above all the field of ethics in which North Americans are involved, whereas in the fields of theology and exegesis they are dependent upon Europe) believe that they are forced to choose between dissent from society or dissent from the magisterium. Many choose this latter dissent. . . ."⁴ I disagree with many aspects of Cardinal Ratzinger's remarks. Dissent in moral theology is by no means limited to the United States but appears in many different parts of the world especially in Europe. I recognize aspects of North American culture (e.g., individualism and materialism) that are opposed to the gospel ethos and Catholic teaching. Yet other aspects of American culture (generosity of spirit, compassion, concern for others) seem to be greatly in accord with Catholic teaching.

Pope John Paul II and Cardinal Ratzinger give a very negative picture of Catholic moral theology today. Even those like myself who disagree with such an assessment recognize that Catholic moral theology in the post-Vatican II era differs greatly from preconciliar moral theology. A pluralism of approaches and methodologies now exists. Preconciliar moral theology appeared to be quite monolithic in its method and scope. Moral theologians today occasionally disagree with specific teachings of the hierarchical magisterium. Is the postconciliar development the aberration? Did the preconciliar understanding of the discipline represent the true tradition of moral theology? A knowledge of the historical development of moral theology should be able to shed some light on what is happening in Catholic moral theology today.

Third, I personally have had an interest in the historical development of moral theology although I cannot claim it as my primary area of research or expertise. I have written some summary histories of moral theology for different publications including the *Encyclopedia of Religion* and the *Encyclopedia of Bioethics*.⁵ In the early 1980s I did research in the area of Catholic social ethics in the United States and studied some of the more significant figures in the historical development of Catholic social ethics in this country.⁶ I was the first contemporary moral theologian to analyze and criticize in detail the social ethics of John A. Ryan, the primary figure in Catholic social ethics in the first half of the twentieth century. Since that time I have been deeply gratified by the attention that moral theologians have given to Ryan, including an excellent study by the Protestant ethicist, Harlan Beckley.⁷ Ryan said in his autobiography that his most fortunate experience in student life was his association with Bouquillon.⁸ Through Ryan I became interested in Bouquillon. Then the project broadened and I determined to do something in fundamental moral theology corresponding to what I had done in Catholic social ethics. This development explains my personal interest in the present project.

One cannot understand and evaluate Catholic moral theology in the United States in the late nineteenth century without some knowledge of the history of moral theology in general and of the circumstances of the nineteenth century. Part One of this volume will develop these historical antecedents while the remaining three parts consider in detail the work of Sabetti, Bouquillon, and Hogan.

In keeping with my own expertise, this volume is primarily a work in moral theology in its historical development and does not pretend to be a history of Catholic moral theology in the United States. The three authors studied here propose three somewhat different approaches to moral theology as it developed at that time in the United States. Thus the book focuses on three methodologies. Aloysius Sabetti represents the typical manualist approach with its aim of providing a textbook for seminarians with special emphasis on preparing them to be judges in the sacrament of penance. Sabetti's textbook was not the first manual of moral theology published in the United States. Francis Patrick Kenrick, later archbishop of Baltimore, wrote the first manual of moral theology in the United States in the early 1840s. Part Two will briefly discuss Kenrick's manual and others written at this time but concentrate on the work of Sabetti. Sabetti's compendium has had a greater influence than any of the other manuals written in the United States in the nineteenth century because of its many subsequent editions in the twentieth century.

Part Three will analyze the fundamental moral theology of Bouquillon who wrote from the setting of a university and not a seminary, criticized the manuals of moral theology, and espoused in theory a neoscholastic approach to theology. Hogan, who spent his life training future priests, never wrote a textbook or a monograph in moral theology but developed his understanding of moral theology primarily in his book *Clerical Studies* which dealt with all areas of ministerial preparation. Part Four will analyze and criticize Hogan's approach, which by its very nature lacks the depth and detail of the other two authors considered. Hogan's approach proposes a very different historically conscious method which rejects the dominant neoscholasticism.

To better appreciate and understand the approach to moral theology of all three authors, I have examined their other writings and materials written about them. However, since I am not writing a history as such and am not a historian, I have limited myself to published sources and done no archival research.

I am most grateful to all who have facilitated my work on this volume. My first thanks go to Jack and Laura Lee Blanton who have endowed the chair I hold—The Elizabeth Scurlock University Professorship of Human Values (named after Mrs. Blanton's mother) at Southern Methodist University. Colleagues and librarians have assisted me in many ways especially Laura Randall, reference librarian at Bridwell Library. Carolyn Lee, formerly of the Mullen Library at Catholic University, was most helpful in my search for sources. I have received critical advice and counsel from many others including the late John Ciani of Georgetown with regard to Sabetti; C. Joseph Nuesse, Provost Emeritus of Catholic University, with regard to Bouquillon; and Christopher Kauffman, Catholic Daughters of America Professor of Church History at Catholic University, with regard to Hogan. John P. Boyle of the University of Iowa and James F. Keenan of Weston School of Theology read the entire manuscript, made helpful suggestions, and encouraged the publication of this volume. Jane Cross, my associate, who on a day-to-day basis continues to assist me in her competent and cheerful way, has painstakingly prepared the manuscript for publication. Rosemarie Gorman skillfully composed the index.

NOTES

1. For an overview and analysis of Noonan's work, see John T. Noonan, Jr., M. Cathleen Caveny, and William Joseph Buckley, "John T. Noonan, Jr.: Retrospective," *Religious Studies Review* 18, n. 2 (1992): 111–121.

2. John T. Noonan, Jr., "Development in Moral Doctrine," *Theological Studies* 54 (1993): 669.

3. Pope John Paul II, "*Veritatis Splendor*," *Origins* 23 (1993): nn. 4–5, pp. 301–302.

4. Vittorio Messori, *Colloquio con il Cardinale Josef Ratzinger, "Ecco Perché La Fede e in Crisi," Jesus* (November 1984), p. 77.

5. Charles E. Curran, "Christian Ethics," in *Encyclopedia of Religion*, ed. Mircea Eliade, 16 vols. (New York: Macmillan, 1987), 3, pp. 340–348; "Counter-Reformation Moral Theology," and "Modern Roman Catholic Moral Theology," in *The Westminster Dictionary of Christian Ethics*, ed. James F. Childress and John Maquarrie (Philadelphia: Westminster, 1986), pp. 133–135; 388–393; "Roman Catholicism," in *Encyclopedia of Bioethics*, ed. Warren T. Reich, 4 vols. (New York: Simon and Schuster Macmillan, 1995), 4, pp. 221–231.

6. Charles E. Curran, *American Catholic Social Ethics: Twentieth Century Approaches* (Notre Dame, Ind.: University of Notre Dame Press, 1982).

7. Harlan Beckley, *Passion for Justice: Retrieving the Legacies of Walter Rauschenbusch, John A. Ryan, and Reinhold Niebuhr* (Louisville, Ky.: Westminster/ John Knox, 1992).

8. John A. Ryan, *Social Doctrine in Action: A Personal History* (New York: Harper and Brothers, 1941), p. 63.

PART ONE

The Historical Antecedents

1

Moral Theology before the Nineteenth Century

To understand Roman Catholic moral theology in the United States of America in the nineteenth century, it is necessary to have some understanding of the development of moral theology in general.[1] This chapter does not attempt to develop a comprehensive history of Catholic moral theology but to present aspects of this history which are helpful for understanding how it was practiced in the United States in the nineteenth century.

The church has always had a significant interest in morality. The church as the community of the disciples of Jesus strives to live out the new life received in Christ Jesus through the Holy Spirit. Christianity involves both faith and morals. One of the early names given to the community of the followers of Jesus was "the Way."[2] Living and teaching morality constitute essential elements of the Christian church.

An important distinction exists between morality on the one hand and moral theology or Christian ethics on the other. The discipline of moral theology (the terminology common among Roman Catholics) or Christian ethics (the terminology common among Protestants) attempts to study Christian morality from a scientific, systematic, reflexive, and thematic perspective. Moral theology involves what is often called second order discourse. Morality refers to what people decide and do about moral life and action; moral theology studies this reality in a thematic and systematic way. The moral theologian deals with issues of justification and the grounding of moral teachings and judgments and tries to develop coherent and consistent understandings of all aspects of the moral life. Many people have never read or studied moral theology but are exemplary Christians who lead virtuous lives and make good moral decisions. One does not have to study moral theology to be a good Christian.

Perhaps an analogy with psychoanalysis will be helpful to understand the nature of second order discourse. The psychoanalyst studies human emotional maturity and behavior in a systematic, thematic, and reflexive way. Many people who have never read Freud or any psychoanalytic literature live very mature, well-balanced lives. All would agree (without denigrating a particular profession), that psychoanalysts are not necessarily the most emotionally mature, well-balanced human beings in the world. Psychoanalysis, like moral theology, involves second order discourse and steps back to study in a systematic and thematic way human emotional maturity. One does not have to know all the different theories that have been proposed about emotional maturity and psychoanalytic development to be an emotionally mature individual.

Despite the great significance of the difference between morality and moral theology reality presents a great deal of gray areas. Once an individual stands back to examine life in a more consistent, coherent, and systematic way the reality of moral theology has begun, at least at an incipient level. Different levels of thematization and systematization exist with the deeper levels of moral theology calling for an explicit knowledge of the sources of the discipline, the models used in describing the moral life, the relationship between the different levels of the moral life (e.g., fundamental orientation, virtues, values, decision making) and the consistency and coherence on and across all these different levels.

Moral theology involves ecclesial and academic aspects but at times one aspect is more prominent. The academic aspect of moral theology is quite prevalent at the present time with the discipline being taught not only in seminaries but also in colleges and universities and in dialogue with other types of ethics and with many other disciplines. In its historical development the ecclesial aspect has often predominated and thus influenced how moral theology was developed and treated.

THE EARLY CHURCH

In the early church, as might be expected, the church aspect predominated and the greater systematization associated with the academy was not that important. The first seven centuries, and often more, were generally referred to in the past as the patristic period but these years are better known today as the period of the early church.[3] The teachers of morality in those days were often the same people who were leaders and bishops in the church. They taught morality both orally and in their writings. Epistles, sermons, and homilies often addressed moral issues. More controversial and apologetic writings also discussed morality usually in an attempt to prove the superiority of the Christian approach. Particular questions or issues were often addressed, for example, martyrdom, military service, wealth, and sexuality. Despite the practical and pastoral orientation of most of the literature, some systematization occurred. The *Didache* or Teaching of the Twelve Apostles (probably written as early as the middle of the first century) summarized the Christian moral life under the umbrella of the two ways— the way of life and the way of death.[4] Clement of Alexandria (d. ca. 215) and the Alexandrian school proposed a more truly systematic moral theology. Clement maintained there was no conflict between faith and reason and used his broad knowledge of classical literature and philosophy to explain and defend Christianity. Clement attempted to portray the ideal of the Christian life.[5] Ambrose, the bishop of Milan (d. 397), considered some of the duties of ministers using the format employed by Cicero in his work with the same title *De officiis*.[6]

Augustine of Hippo (d. 430) stands as the most significant theologian in this early church period. Although Augustine did not write a systematic treatise on moral theology, his work has continued to exert a powerful influence on the church. Augustine dealt extensively with fundamental themes in moral theology—free will, grace, sin, law, the reign of God, and human history. His emphasis on grace coincided with his pessimistic view of the human especially in sexuality. The bishop of Hippo also addressed a plethora of practical questions— marriage, sexuality, concupiscence, lying, patience; and the virtues, especially faith, hope, and charity which came to be known as the theological virtues.[7] Augustine also emphasized what is today called a teleological ethical model. Union with God is the ultimate end of our lives and we are to choose the means that lead us to that end. The famous phrase of Augustine is that God has made us for God's self and our hearts will not rest until they rest in God.[8] Gregory the Great (d. 604) in his *Liber regulae pastoralis* dealt with the virtues and ministry of the pastors of souls. His *Moralia in Job* constituted a voluminous commentary, thirty-five books, which deals primarily with pastoral issues in moral theology and shows his knowledge, wisdom, and prudence in discussing the Christian life.[9]

From early times the ecclesial side of moral theology has often been associated with the sacrament of penance. A major change in the structure and celebration of penance occurred in the sixth century in

Ireland. The older process often called public penance could be celebrated only once in a lifetime and reconciliation with the church occurred only after a long and arduous penance. As a result, many people put off the sacrament until they were near death. In Ireland a new practice developed that grew out of the monastic situation common in that country with its tradition of spiritual direction and the manifestation of one's conscience and faults to a superior. This new form of penance, despite opposition from authorities in the church, spread throughout Europe and the Catholic world. The sacrament could now be received more than once. The individual confessed one's sins to a priest, received an appropriate penance, and was reconciled to the church and to God through God's gracious mercy and forgiveness mediated by the priest.[10]

The *Libri paenitentiales* or penitential books were tariff books listing the penance that should be assigned by the confessor for particular sins. The aim of the penance assigned was medicinal—to use the opposite virtue to cut out the vice. Penances consisted mostly of fasting and abstinence (including sexual abstinence), although prayers and almsgiving or good works were also included. Attempts were made to make distinctions based on culpability (ignorance or fear would reduce culpability) and also to take account of one's station in life— whether one were, for example, a cleric or a lay person.[11] Today some people have criticized these books for their crude, mechanical, legalistic, and wooden approaches, but these books illustrate the first attempts within the church to develop a nuanced understanding of the moral life and its relationship to sin and the sacrament of penance.[12]

These following examples illustrate the approach and character of the penitentials:

> If anyone has started a quarrel and plotted in his heart to strike or kill his neighbour, if [the offender] is a cleric, he shall do penance for half a year with an allowance of bread and water and for a whole year abstain from wine and meats, and thus he will be reconciled to the altar.
>
> But if he is a layman, he shall do penance for a week, since he is a man of this world and his guilt is lighter in this world and his reward less in the world to come. . . .
>
> If any layman through ignorance shall communicate with the Bonosiacs or other heretics, let him take his place among the catechumens, that is, separated from other Christians, for forty

days, and for two other forty-day periods, let him wash away the guilt of the mad communion in the lowest rank of Christians, that is among the penitents. But if he shall have done this from contempt, that is, after he has been warned by the priest and has been forbidden to defile himself by communion with this perverse sect, let him do penance for a whole year and the three forty-day periods, and for two other years let him abstain from wine and meat, and thus, after the imposition of the hand by a Catholic bishop, let him be joined to the altar.[13]

MEDIEVAL PERIOD

The academic aspect of theology came to the fore in the twelfth and thirteenth centuries and had a great impact on the development of theology as a discipline. Even before the thirteenth century began the church under the papacy emerged with greater independence, centrality, and authority, and claiming greater power. Three significant factors abetted the more academic interest in theology and the development of theology as a discipline or science—the flourishing of universities, the dialogue with Aristotelian thought, and the founding of religious orders interested in scholarship.[14] Universities began to flourish at this time under the auspices of the church.

The University of Paris which has been called the mother and model of all the universities of Europe (Bologna was the oldest university) came into existence about the year 1200. Schools had been established earlier in Paris with masters and students. At the end of the twelfth century the teachers and scholars worked individually without any organization. At the beginning of the thirteenth century the teachers decided to form a corporation or corporate body which became known as a university of teachers and scholars. Thus the university was founded from below by the people involved although kings and popes soon became its patrons. By 1215 the teachers grouped themselves according to the nature of their discipline and these groupings were called faculties. The original four faculties were theology, jurisprudence (canon law), arts, and medicine, although medicine was not that significant. In this university context the discipline of theology with its emphasis on systematization grew and developed.[15]

A second historical reality contributing to the academic development of theology in general and what would later be known as the separate discipline of moral theology was the introduction of Aristotelian thought through new translations into Latin. In the twelfth century Christian opposition to Aristotle was strong, but gradually various works of Aristotle were used by Christian thinkers. However, in 1210 the Council of Paris decreed that neither the works of Aristotle on natural philosophy nor commentaries thereon could be read at Paris in public or in private. Later Pope Gregory IX changed that decree and corrected versions of Aristotle's work became quite popular. Within fifty years a radical change had occurred with regard to the works of Aristotle, but controversies continued to flare up about the proper interpretation of Aristotle. The acceptance of Aristotle into Catholic thought with its insistence that faith and reason cannot contradict one another opened the way for a more systematic overall approach to theology.[16]

The third factor was the founding of new religious orders, especially the Dominicans and the Franciscans, who were interested in theology and its teaching. The Dominicans, known officially as the Order of Friars Preachers, received papal approval as a religious community in 1216. The motto of this community, "to contemplate and to give to others the fruit of contemplation," well explains both the charism and the direction taken by the Dominicans. In 1252 seven chairs out of twelve in theology at the University of Paris were held by religious priests with the Dominicans holding two chairs. The Dominicans tended to have the leading role and the most influence in the University of Paris at that time.[17] In this historical context the academic study of theology flourished. Albert the Great (d. 1280) and Thomas Aquinas (d. 1274) represented the Dominican school. The Franciscan school included Alexander of Hales (d. 1245), St. Bonaventure (d. 1274) and John Duns Scotus (d. 1305).

Significant differences exist among these approaches, but Thomas Aquinas has emerged as the most significant figure in the history of Catholic theology.[18] Aquinas was canonized as a saint in 1323 and made a doctor of the church in 1567. In the fifteenth century the *Summa theologiae* of Aquinas replaced the *Sentences* of Peter Lombard as the textbook of theology in the universities. In the nineteenth and twentieth centuries the popes made Thomas the patron of Catholic philosophy and theology and decreed that these disciplines should be expounded according to the method, the doctrine, and the principles of Thomas Aquinas. The insistence on Thomism as *the* Catholic approach to theology and philosophy by these popes gave a contemporary prominence to the work of Aquinas.

There was, however, a darker side to the papal approbation of Aquinas as the only approach for Catholic theology and philosophy. Thomas Aquinas well deserves his important role in Catholic theology, but church leaders in the nineteenth and twentieth centuries imposed his teaching in an authoritative manner and thereby downplayed the work of other Catholic theologians in the past and prevented any dialogue with contemporary thought. Ironically the genius of Thomas Aquinas in his own day was to employ the newly translated work of the Greek philosopher Aristotle to better understand and explain the Christian faith.

Thomas Aquinas constructed a synthesis of all theology including what is now moral theology although he did not use that term.[19] Only later did moral theology emerge as a separate discipline and lose its relation to the whole of theology. In the systematization of theology in the *Summa*, Aquinas followed the *exitus-reditus* model.[20] Part one of the *Summa* treats of God and how all things came forth from God. Part two describes the return of the creature to God, and Part three develops the christological aspect of this coming forth from God and returning to God. What is today called moral theology is found in the second part of the *Summa* which deals with the return of the rational creature to God. But even here a problem exists in taking a part out of its whole. The action of the later tradition in equating the second part of the *Summa* with all of moral theology meant that the christological aspect found in part three of the *Summa* is missing in this approach to moral theology.

The second part of the *Summa* in general builds on the principles of image and participation. The first part discusses God while the second considers the human being who is an image of God and participates in the being of God precisely because like God the human being is the principle of one's own actions, having free will and the power of self-determination.[21] The natural law, although not the primary ethical reality for Aquinas, illustrates this same approach because the natural law is the participation of the eternal law in the rational creature.[22]

The principle of finality serves as the systematic organizing principle of the second part of the *Summa*.[23] Aquinas begins his discussion with the question of the ultimate end of human beings. For Aquinas the ultimate end of human beings is happiness. Happiness occurs when the basic powers or faculties of human beings attain their proper and full end. The intellect and the will constitute the two highest powers or faculties that human beings possess with the intellect seeking the truth and the will seeking good. In the final union with God our intellect comes to know perfect truth and our will loves the perfect good. This approach is similar to the Augustinian understanding that God has made us for God's self and we will not be happy until we rest in God.

Aquinas then develops the way by which we come to happiness. The *Summa* first discusses the general way, as distinguished from the particular types of virtues or acts, by which human beings come to their ultimate end. Aquinas treats the principles or the basic sources guiding our actions. The intrinsic principles of human action are the powers from which the act comes. For example, the eye is the power or faculty of the acts of seeing. Habits are stable qualities of acting that incline the faculty or power to act in a certain way. Good habits are virtues, whereas bad habits are vices. The virtue of generosity, for example, inclines a person to act in a generous way, whereas the vice of intemperance inclines one to act intemperately. Habits are very important moral realities because they shape the character of the person and influence the particular actions that one does.

The extrinsic principle of human acts is God who guides us by grace and by law. The word *extrinsic* here refers to the fact that grace and law unlike powers and habits exist outside ourselves. However, they are not extrinsic in the sense of being heteronomous because grace and law guide us to our own perfection and happiness. Grace brings the human being to its perfection. Law, according to Aquinas, involves an ordering of reason for the good. Aquinas understands the eternal law as the ordering of reason or as God's plan for the world and the natural law as the participation of the eternal law in the rational creature. Human reason reflecting on the human nature that has been given us by God can determine how God wants us to act. Human law is based on the natural law either by restating the natural law (e.g., murder is wrong) or by specifying what the natural law leaves undifferentiated (vehicles should drive on the right hand side of the street). All these aspects are developed systematically in what is called the first part of the second part of the *Summa*.

The second part of the second part of the *Summa* treats particular actions under two main categories.[24] The first and by far the largest section treats the particular acts that pertain to all people and all states of life using the virtues as the model of development. The theological virtues of faith, hope, and charity are discussed first with their opposite vices and the actions corresponding to these virtues and vices. The cardinal virtues of prudence, justice, fortitude, and temperance include all the other virtues of the moral life and the acts corresponding to these virtues. Again, the contrary vices and acts corresponding to these vices (i.e., sins) are discussed. The comparatively short second section discusses actions that pertain to some people in a special situation because of the office one holds or the gifts that one has been given.

Although Aquinas never fully finished his *Summa*, the academic quality of his work stands out. The *Summa* involves an attempt at a systematic, coherent, consistent explanation of all aspects of theology in general including the moral life. Notice some significant characteristics of how Aquinas discusses the moral life. The fundamental model for moral theology is teleological—determine what the end is and something is good if it brings one to that end and bad if it prevents one from arriving at this end. Thomistic teleology is intrinsic as distinguished from the extrinsic teleology of utilitarianism since it is based on the finality of the human being and her powers and faculties. The other most common model—the deontological model—understands the moral life primarily in terms of duty, law, or obligation. In this understanding obedience becomes the primary and most important virtue. Yes, Aquinas does speak about law, but law comes at the very end of his discussion of general moral theology, is integrated into the model of finality, and coheres with an intrinsic approach to morality. Law is not primarily an act of the will of the legislator but an act of reason directing all things to their proper end. In this understanding something is commanded because it is good and never the other way around.[25] Thomistic thought strongly rejects an extrinsic morality which claims something is good because it is commanded. Grace and law prompt us to do what is ultimately good for ourselves. Thus morality is intrinsic and synonymous with what is truly good for the individual, and morality ultimately leads one to one's final fulfillment and happiness. Some contemporary Catholic theologians criticize the Thomistic approach for its lack of historical consciousness, its failure to highlight the person as subject, its overemphasis on faculties and powers, and a tendency at times to equate the human and the moral with the physical and the biological.[26] However, all recognize that Thomas Aquinas is a university theologian writing for a university audience and attempting to propose a coherent and consistent understanding of all theology and of moral theology in the light of a total theological vision.

Louis Vereecke, the acknowledged contemporary expert on the history of moral theology, points out that William of Ockham (d. 1350) proposed a nominalistic theory that criticized the approach of Aquinas and greatly influenced theology in the universities in the fourteenth and fifteenth centuries. For Ockham the good is not determined by ontological reality, but by the arbitrary will of God. Something is good because God commands it. Morality consists in obedience to law and thus a deontological model replaces the teleology of Aquinas. Such an approach opened the door to a greater emphasis on casuistry and was congenial with the later development of the manuals of moral theology. However, a Thomistic renewal swept through the growing number of universities in Europe beginning in the early sixteenth century. The *Summa* of Aquinas became the textbook for theology. The school of Salamanca in Spain became a center of what we now call moral theology with eminent theologians such as Francisco de Vitoria commenting on the second part of the *Summa* and discussing many contemporary questions of justice in the light of new developments such as the colonization of America.[27] This vibrant moral theology found its home in the universities.

MANUALS OF MORAL THEOLOGY

The manuals of moral theology, which served as the textbooks of moral theology until the Second Vatican Council, began in the light of the pastoral needs of the church, did not primarily exist within a university context, and had no major academic purpose or orientation. These manuals began in the sixteenth century and developed within the same basic framework and parameters until the Second Vatican Council. The incentive for these manuals came from the sixteenth-century Council of Trent which reformed the Catholic church in response to the Protestant Reformation. Two reforms in the Council of Trent greatly affected the development of moral theology as a separate discipline in Catholic theology with the aim of preparing confessors as judges in the sacrament of penance—the legislation on the sacrament of penance and the establishment of seminaries.

The fourteenth session of the Council of Trent dealt with the sacrament of penance and the decree on penance was issued on November 25, 1551.[28] In 1215 the Fourth Lateran Council had required that every member of the faithful who has come to the use of reason should faithfully confess all her sins once a year to her proper priest. The priest should diligently inquire about the circumstances of the sins and of the sinner so that he might know what counsel and remedies to provide so that the spiritually sick person may be healed.[29] At this time the *Summae confessariorum* came into existence to help the priest in his role in the sacrament of penance. Often the arrangement of topics in the *Summae* was simply alphabetical.[30] Occasionally systematic practical works also existed such as the *Summa de casibus poenitentiae* written by St. Raymond of Peñafort between 1222 and 1229. This work contained three major divisions—sins against God, sins against neighbor, and questions such as irregularities, impediments, and dispensations.[31]

By the fifteenth century, however, a crisis existed with regard to auricular confession. Numerous circumstances contributed to the problem. The ignorance and lack of learning on the part of priests was a prime factor. In addition, the people of the time were not much given to introspection. The obligation of the Fourth Lateran Council to confess one's sins to one's own priest appeared especially burdensome. In Flanders, for example, most people were delaying the confession of their sins to their last moments or to very special occasions.[32]

The Council of Trent sought not only to deal with the problem of the practical lack of interest in the sacrament of penance but also with the positions of the reformers with regard to penance. The Catholic practice, in keeping with its emphasis on the human response, insisted on the confession of sins and personal works of satisfaction, whereas the reformers stressed the gift of justification as found in the absolution. Absolution represents God's unconditional gift of pardon to the sinner. For Luther, the power of the keys is given to the whole church but exercised through the ministers and preachers of the word. Luther himself retained a high regard for private confession and made it an important part of his own spiritual life. The other reformers did not give that much significance to penance. But even Luther understood confession to be free and not obligatory, thus going against the decree of the Fourth Lateran Council.[33]

In this context of the need for pastoral reform in the light of the positions taken by the reformers, the fourteenth session of the Council of Trent set forth nine *capita* (short, concise treatments) explaining the meaning and practice of penance and fifteen canons phrased negatively against those who deny some aspects of the teaching.[34] Trent understands the sacrament of penance in the context of a judgment and sees the priest acting primarily as a judge to determine if absolution is to be given or denied. In this context the penitent's act of confession takes on great importance. The integral confession of mortal sins according to number and species is required by divine law so that the minister of the sacrament by the power of the keys can pronounce the sentence of remission or retention of sins. The minister of the sacrament is not able to make this judgment or impose a fitting penance from only a general confession of sins without knowing the species and number of the sins that have been committed. Trent clearly notes that formal integrity and not material integrity is required—in other words, one must use ordinary diligence in examining one's conscience in preparation for confession. If without one's own fault a sin is forgotten, the absolution still retains its force.

The heavy insistence on the juridical character of the sacrament of penance and the need for the integral confession of mortal sins according to number and species had a great influence on the future direction of moral theology. In its theoretical response to the reformers and in its attempt to renew the celebration of the sacrament of penance Trent insisted on this juridical character of the sacrament. The very name given to the sacrament of penance after this time—confession—indicates the predominance of this aspect. A more balanced approach would highlight the centrality of contrition or change of heart with confession and satisfaction related to contrition and recognize that the primary judgment is the official proclamation and gift of God's forgiveness—the saving judgment. But Trent in response to the reformers and the needs of the time put the emphasis on the juridical character of penance and the integral confession of sins. This reform required that confessors and penitents be trained to administer and receive the sacrament of penance understood primarily in judicial terms.

A second important influence on the future development of moral theology came from the Council of Trent's legislation with regard to seminaries. The twenty-third session in 1563 called for these institutions to be erected in every diocese to prepare and educate the local clergy. The word seminary comes from the Latin *seminarium* used to describe a place where young seedlings are prepared so that as more mature trees they may be transplanted elsewhere. According to Trent the program of studies in the seminary should especially include what was necessary for hearing confessions.[35]

Trent was responding to a very important need at this time—an intellectually trained and spiritually grounded clergy. In an earlier period of history future clerics were trained in a cathedral school. However, with the breakdown of feudalism, this institution went out of existence. Some clerics pursued the long and rigorous university course where they studied the masters in theology and law. However most of the local clergy did not have such a university education. The ignorance of many local clergy was abysmal. Often they knew little beyond how to administer the sacraments of the church. Any real reform in the church required well-trained priests whose spiritual formation and theological knowledge provided what was necessary for their fruitful ministry among God's people.[36]

One can safely assume that the fathers of Trent never explicitly realized how their actions would help to create the new discipline of moral theology. In retrospect one clearly recognizes what happened. Trent emphasized the sacrament of penance as an integral part of the spiritual renewal of Catholicism. However, priests had to be trained to serve as ministers of the sacrament and to carry out their function as judge. Seminaries were instituted for the training of priests. The seminaries consequently had the mission of training priests so they could faithfully administer the sacraments especially hearing confessions.[37]

The *Institutiones theologiae moralis*, a new genre of moral theology which later became known as the manuals of moral theology, came into existence within the Society of Jesus at this time immediately after Trent. The Society of Jesus founded by Ignatius of Loyola received its canonical establishment in 1540. The Jesuits established the Roman College before the Council of Trent as a preparation for priesthood. The Jesuits made the administration of the sacrament of penance a primary ministry of the society and proposed a two year course to prepare future priests to hear confessions. In 1603 the Jesuit John Azor published his *Institutiones theologiae moralis* based on the two-year course that he had taught in accord with the *Ratio studiorum* of the Jesuits. In accordance with these directives the first year covered human acts, conscience, law, sins, and the Decalogue except for the seventh commandment. The second year treated the seventh commandment, sacraments, censures, the different conditions and duties of particular individuals.[38]

The spirit of the Jesuits also influenced their interest in the problems of the world and the casuistry required to arrive at answers to the pertinent issues of the day. The Jesuits were a new type of religious order with a more worldly mission than earlier religious communities. Jesuits retained the traditional religious vows but worked in the world and did not stress the community aspect of their religious life as did the older orders. They were more active and involved in the affairs

and concerns of the world. Their spirit helped commit them to the
ministry of the sacrament of penance and to offer direction and help
to people in their daily lives.[39]

Azor and his early followers set the course for moral theology
which perdured with some exceptions until the Second Vatican
Council. The content first prescribed by the *Ratio studiorum* of the Jesuits
and developed by Azor changed very little during the next 350 years.
Also the basic approach and method of Azor remained fundamentally
unchanged. The purpose of training confessors, especially for their role
as judges in the sacrament of penance, dictated the approach and
content of moral theology. The development marked by the *Institutiones*
obviously had continuities with the past. We have already seen how
the practice of the sacrament of penance influenced approaches to
moral theology. Casuistry, likewise, had often been employed in earlier
approaches. The Dominicans of the School of Salamanca in Spain in
the sixteenth century in their commentaries on the second part of the
Summa employed casuistry in a very creative way and discussed many
particular cases involving the new developments in political, social,
and economic life that they were facing at the time. Jesuit theologians
in the latter part of the sixteenth century, for example, Gabriel Vasquez
(d. 1604) and Francis Suarez (d. 1617), especially in their works on
justice considered important problems of daily life and discussed many
different cases.[40]

What is new with the *Institutiones* or manuals is the fact that they
became identified with all moral theology. The speculative considerations of moral theology and the roles of grace and the virtues disap-
peared as an integral part of the discipline. The *Institutiones*, unlike the
alphabetical Summas of an earlier time, did attempt to give some
minimal theoretical basis to their approach, but the theoretical was very
thin and totally subordinated to the pastoral and practical purposes of
the manuals.

The new type of moral theology with its important but narrow
focus became cut off from all other aspects of theology. Dogmatic
theology no longer interacted with moral theology. Separation at times
might be necessary to achieve particular purposes, but moral theology
now became totally isolated from the broader theological enterprise.
Moral theology also became separated from scripture with scripture
being used only as a proof text to show that certain actions were wrong.
Spiritual or ascetical theology had no place in this new genre that dealt
primarily with the minimum requirements of the Christian life. Nothing

was said about the fullness of the moral life or the call to perfection. The basic reality of conversion or change of heart was not developed at all. These pastoral manuals did not really dialogue with new or different philosophies because such dialogue was outside their very practical and limited scope.

Although moral theology was cut off from most other theological disciplines, it became closely associated with canon law. The discussion of the individual sacraments well illustrates how these new textbooks employed many canonical aspects. The treatment deals only with the conditions required for a valid and licit celebration of the sacraments on the part of the minister and the recipient. Validity refers to what is required so that there may truly be a sacrament. Liceity presupposes validity but spells out what is required to ensure a legally correct administration and reception of the sacrament. The teaching on the sacraments was primarily legal and not moral or spiritual at all. This approach fit the fundamental purpose of the *Institutiones*—to prepare priests to administer and the faithful to receive the sacraments in accord with the law. By their purpose and nature these manuals had a minimalistic approach dealing with what is sin and its gravity with regard to morality and what is valid and licit with regard to legalities such as the administration of the sacraments.

The basic concern of the *Institutiones* and later manuals centered on the morality of particular acts especially in terms of their sinfulness and the degree of their sinfulness. However, the consideration of human acts was wrenched out of its context in the Thomistic approach. For Aquinas the individual moral act was inserted in the overall context of teleology with a person striving toward the ultimate end and with acts coming from the powers or faculties that are modified by good or bad habits. Aquinas discussed law last in his treatment of general moral theology and even there law was understood as an ordering of reason pointing to the good and ultimate fulfillment of the individual. Thomistic morality was intrinsic—based on what is truly good and fulfilling for the person.

The *Institutiones* substituted a deontological model based on law for the Thomistic model of teleology. Thomas never had a distinct tract on conscience, but the *Institutiones* made this a very central consideration. Law became the objective norm of morality (with all the different levels of law—eternal, natural, positive) and conscience the subjective norm of morality. These two considerations constituted the heart of the manuals. In this context a tension or even opposition soon developed between law and conscience. Law was something imposed from the outside. Thomas Aquinas never understood law in opposition to freedom, but now the door was open to see morality only in the context of this tension between law, often understood as something extrinsic imposed from outside, and the freedom or conscience of the individual. Subsequent developments made this tension and even apparent opposition between law and conscience more prevalent.

CRISIS OF LAXISM AND RIGORISM

The seventeenth and eighteenth centuries saw a crisis developing in moral theology that would culminate in a long and bitter struggle over the extremes of laxism and rigorism.[41] One significant historical development involved the intervention of the papacy to help resolve this crisis and thus pave the way for a greater involvement of the papal magisterium in deciding specific moral issues and in the life and work of moral theology itself.

Casuistry and the theory of probabilism stand out as two prominent and distinctive aspects of the moral theology of the seventeenth century. Both of these constitute helpful approaches in moral theology, but their abuse can and did lead to problems especially in the acceptance of laxism by some authors of the time. Casuistry in the preceding centuries had been and still was especially helpful in dealing with new moral issues which frequently arose in the political, social, cultural, and economic changes of the times. By applying principles to cases and comparing cases with one another the moral theologian could see similarities and dissimilarities and then offer more adequate solutions to issues in the light of changing circumstances.[42] John T. Noonan, for example, has treated the development and change of the church's teaching on usury. Noonan has pointed out how the casuists in the late sixteenth century were able to bring about this change in practice despite strong papal teaching condemning interest on the basis of divine and natural law. Within thirty years these papal bulls and documents condemning interest-taking on a loan were deprived of any force in influencing practical decisions. This casuistry learned from the experience of people was able to bring about significant change when older teachings heavily supported by papal teaching were no longer adequate in the light of changed circumstances.[43]

However, the seventeenth century witnessed the abuse of casuistry in the form of laxism which was a tendency to downplay or deny

- OK, but fairly narrow topic
- inelegant writing

not been torn apart, one from
. Free market forces have not
thing unless they consume the latest
There is no doubt about that. They
cornmeal gruel called pozol. They do
can't afford to. They need the pesos
re basic items like cooking oil or
ow signs of repeated mending. No
and children go barefoot except on

erially, they do have spiritually.
a community. As a Tzetal
olic community they work, play and

de and self assuredness among
bered by over five hundred years of
meet all comers as equals. And

obligations in the moral life of the Christian.[44] The reduction of the judgment of the morality of human acts to the tension between law and conscience and the heavy emphasis on the legal aspects of moral theology opened the door to the legal penchant for finding loopholes and exceptions in the law to justify or defend the actions of a client. Lawyers by definition try to find ways to defend the actions of their client and find a way around the law. In addition a great value or benefit of casuistry was its ability to deal with newer questions arising in changed circumstances. People at this time were very conscious of living in a new age. But the danger existed of being too uncritical of so-called modern developments. One illustration of this too uncritical acceptance of contemporary realities concerned the consideration given to the acceptance of class differences and the roles of nobles and gentlemen. The question was raised: could a gentleman kill in response to a slap which was an attack on his honor? Did the gentleman have to turn away and not pursue the insulter? The question was debated by the casuists. John Azor agreed with the opinion that one is obliged by charity to prefer the life of a neighbor to one's honor but not when the choice is occasioned by an evil act of the neighbor. Azor concluded that the noble person or gentleman might morally kill the one who has beaten or slapped him because otherwise the honor of innocent people could easily and readily be defamed.[45] In 1679 Pope Innocent XI condemned the proposition that it is permitted for a gentleman to kill an aggressor who attempts to calumniate him if the shame cannot otherwise be avoided; similarly he may not kill one who slaps or beats him and then flees.[46]

Note how some casuists gradually expanded categories for the sake of the nobleman. Killing in defense of life and of temporal goods of great value was now extended to honor and even to a verbal insult. Scripture was invoked to justify this extension—the tongue is mightier than the sword. The classic case of killing in self-defense requires the killing to be done in the actual defense of one's own life. Now the gentleman was justified in killing the one who attacked his honor even after the attacker fled. This case illustrates how the factors already mentioned could abet the move to laxism.

Developments in the theory of probabilism also occasioned the abuse of casuistry known as laxism.[47] Here too probabilism in itself was something good that was open to abuse. The position of probabilism was first formulated by Bartholomew Medina, a Dominican professor at Salamanca, in 1577. One can follow a probable opinion even though the opposite opinion is more probable. Note that the English word probable does not do justice to what is involved here. The Latin word *probabile* means provable—it can be proved or arguments can be made on its behalf. The acceptance of probabilism brings about a somewhat subtle shift in moral understanding. The purpose of the moral judgment is not to attain the moral truth but to achieve the security of knowing that one is not acting wrongly. Probabilism gives one the practical certitude to act in a particular situation. Probabilism remained the acceptable position for a century and became the common teaching of both Jesuits and Dominicans as well as most others.

The Jesuits generally accepted probabilism and developed it.[48] Gabriel Vasquez developing a point implicit in Medina distinguished between intrinsic and extrinsic probabilism. Intrinsic probabilism rested on the authority or excellence of the arguments proposed for the position; extrinsic probabilism rested on the authority of the wise people or experts who held it. As time went on extrinsic probabilism became the most important form. The manuals would list the names of the experts who held a particular position. Soon the question became how many authors were necessary to have a truly probable opinion that one could safely follow in practice. From earliest times it was admitted that one outstanding author could constitute a probable opinion. Thus the situation arose in which casuistry perhaps with the good motive of not imposing unnecessary burdens on the Christian people strove to find extrinsic support for the fact that a position was probable.

Francis Suarez (d. 1617), a most significant Jesuit theologian, did much to introduce legal considerations into moral theology and developed the basic role of practical reflex principles in moral deliberation.[49] The question of probabilism was an attempt to answer the question of how can one move from speculative doubt to practical certitude. One needed certitude to act properly but how could such certitude be achieved in the light of theoretical doubt about what should be done. Practical or reflex principles drawn from law and jurisprudence supply the answer. Suarez appealed to two such principles—the principle of possession and the principle of promulgation. (Paul Laymann, a Jesuit, later called these principles reflex principles.) The principle of possession states that freedom is in possession (the individual starts with such freedom) and it can only be taken away by a certain obligation. As long as the position in favor of freedom from the law is probable, the obligation is not certain and an individual remains free to act in accord with a probable opinion. The second principle of promulgation recognizes that a law that is not promulgated does not oblige. But these moral laws are promulgated by our certain knowledge of them. As long as an opinion is probable there is no certain knowledge or promulgation of a more probable and thus safer position. The concept of extrinsic probabilism and practical or reflex principles drawn from law serve a good purpose, but laxism used them for its own purposes.

Laxism was not a school but rather a loose movement.[50] Some authors were not laxists in general but they did propose some laxist positions (e.g., Thomas Sanchez, S.J.). Blaise Pascal in his influential and devastating work *The Provincial Letters* accused the Jesuits as a whole of being laxists. This charge is false. Even some Jesuits most strongly attacked by Pascal such as Anthony Escobar cannot truly be called laxist even though some of his positions were such. Another Jesuit, Thomas Tamburini (d. 1675), was frequently condemned in his time as a laxist, but Alphonsus Liguori and others give a much more balanced judgment about Tamburini. Two acknowledged laxists were not Jesuits. Anthony Diana (d. 1663), a Theatine, resolved twenty thousand cases in his *Resolutionum moralium* and is generally recognized to be a laxist. John Caramuel y Lobkowitz (d. 1682), a Spanish Cistercian priest and later a bishop, according to Alphonsus Liguori earned the title "prince of laxists." Laxists were not evil persons but carried their approach too far in an effort to accommodate the weaknesses of people and not impose unnecessary burdens on them.

The laxist positions can best be seen in the list of condemned errors authoritatively proposed by the Holy Office under Pope Alexander VII in 1665–66 (forty-five propositions) and Pope Innocent XI in 1679 (sixty-five propositions).[51] However, as the editor of the authoritative collection of church documents notes, these propositions are condemned as they exist, but at times they have been taken out of their original context. The condemnations properly do not mention the names of the authors of these positions, but the editor does mention the authors holding such positions.[52]

Laxism came into existence as an abuse of both probabilism and casuistry which were two closely related realities. Laxists chipped away at the meaning of probabilism and tended to reduce it as much as possible. Thus, for example, one could follow a less probable opinion or a tenuously probable opinion. Both these positions were condemned by Innocent XI.[53] The individual condemned propositions illustrate the abuse of casuistry which ostensibly attempted to save the ordinary Christian from the imposition of too burdensome obligations. The abuse of casuistry arose by going from one acceptable case to others that exceeded the bounds of acceptability. As noted earlier, it was generally accepted that one could kill in actual self-defense or in the defense of temporal goods of great moment. Alexander VII condemned the proposition that one can kill a false accuser, a false witness, or even a judge who is about to give an unjust sentence if there is no other way for an innocent person to avoid harm.[54] Likewise the same pope condemned the proposition that a husband who kills his wife apprehended in adultery does not sin.[55] Innocent XI condemned the proposition that one can kill a thief who is stealing one gold piece or that one can kill in self-defense not only to protect what one actually possesses but also those things one hopes to possess.[56]

The condemned propositions show the danger that arises when cases are considered only in themselves without seeing them in the total context of living the Christian life. Alexander VII condemned the opinion that one is never obliged in one's lifetime to make an act of faith, hope, or charity on the basis of the divine commands pertaining to these virtues.[57] Later Innocent XI condemned the opinion that it is enough to make the act of faith once in a lifetime.[58] (In the 1950s in Rome I was taught that in the light of this condemnation and of other condemnations one was obliged to make an act of faith at least more than once in a lifetime!) Innocent XI condemned the proposition that one is not held to love the neighbor with an internal and formal act and similar propositions that one is able to satisfy the precept of loving the neighbor with only external actions.[59]

Many condemned opinions concerned matters of church law. For example, one satisfies the precept of hearing mass who hears at the same time two or even four parts of the mass from different celebrants.[60] (Note how the eucharistic participation is described as a passive hearing on the part of those who are present rather than as their active participation in celebration.) One who is unable to recite a major part of the divine office does not have to recite the remaining smaller part because the smaller part is governed by the larger part.[61] On a fast day one does not break the fast by often eating small amounts even though the total amount becomes quite large (the proposed reason being that one does not thus have a full meal which breaks the fast).[62] Laxism thus arose in the seventeenth century.

Laxism existed side by side with more rigorous approaches to moral theology. The struggle between the more benign and the more rigorous approaches to moral theology became very acrimonious in the life of the church in the latter half of the seventeenth century and lasted for more than a hundred years. The dispute ultimately focused on the positions of probabilism and antiprobabilism but a strong contributing factor to the debate, and especially to its rancor, came from Jansenism.

Jansenism arose as an attempt to reform the life of Christians and in reaction to the fact that many people in the world seemed to live only nominally Christian lives. Jansenism gets its name from Bishop Cornelius Jansen (d. 1638) whose posthumously published *Augustinus* contained his position. Closely associated with the movement was Jean Duvergier de Hauranne (d. 1643) called Abbé Saint Cyran who had as his disciple Mère Angélique Arnauld (d. 1661), the Abbess of the Convent of Port Royal, and her brother Antoine Arnauld (d. 1694).[63]

The theological position of Jansenism set the stage for its understanding of morality and of the disciplinary life of the church, particularly with regard to the sacraments. Theologically Jansenism espoused a pessimistic view of human nature, the absolute necessity of grace which no one could refuse, a form of predestination, an opposition to the use of reason in theology, and a heavy emphasis on the patristic tradition. In moral theology this position called for a rejection of reason and casuistry and a moral rigorism that opposed human concupiscence and called people to truly adhere to the will of God. For Jansenists the two contrasting moral realities were the divine law and human concupiscence. Pleasure by its very nature was suspect. Tutiorism (always following the safer course) and rigorism characterized their approach to morality. They strongly attacked probabilism. Their pessimism expressed itself in the understanding of the human as almost equivalent with concupiscence and especially as illustrated in their approach to marriage. The marital act by its very nature is disordered and can be excused only by the intention of procreation. All aspects of human life lack any true autonomy and must be seen only in relationship to God.[64]

The practical and disciplinary rigorism of Jansenism came to the fore in the understanding of the sacraments. Arnauld in his book on frequent communion put so many conditions on the reception of communion that communion became a very rare occurrence in Christian life. One had to be truly disposed to receive communion. The sacrament of penance was also understood in the light of this rigorism and in the perspective of the early church. In opposition to their charge that Jesuit confessors too easily absolved sinners who were not really going to change their life and their ways, the Jansenist confessors often refused or delayed absolution until they were absolutely certain that penitents were properly disposed and were going to live a truly Christian life.[65]

Already in 1643 Arnauld and another anonymous author published condemnations of Jesuit morality and casuistry under the title *The Moral Theology of the Jesuits Faithfully Extracted from Their Books*. However, the frontal assault on Jesuit moral theology came from Blaise Pascal whose contribution to mathematics and physics had already made him renowned. His most famous work in religious matters was his *Pensées*, but before that work and under the strong Jansenistic influence of Arnauld he wrote his *Provincial Letters*. These letters first appeared anonymously beginning on January 23, 1656, as *Letters Written to a Provincial Gentleman by One of his Friends on the Subject of the Present Debates in the Sorbonne*. Pascal was not a theologian but a literary genius who used satire to great advantage. The first three letters dealt with the central theme of Jansenism about sufficient and efficacious grace but then Pascal turned in the next eleven letters to the moral teaching of the Jesuit casuists. Since he was not a trained theologian he used the earlier attack on the Jesuits coauthored anonymously by Arnauld. The Jesuit Anthony Escobar helped Pascal immensely for his *The Book of Moral Theology Woven out of Twenty-Four Doctors of the Society of Jesus* presented in an abbreviated form without context and development the practical positions taken by Jesuit moralists. This book supplied Pascal with most of his ammunition. With rhetorical skill and great wit Pascal put his opinions in the mouth of a fictitious "good Jesuit father" who naively admires the great ingenuity of this casuistry which refrains from making Christians carry too heavy burdens. The cases and practical conclusions are similar to the condemned propositions mentioned above. For example, a judge may accept a bribe in an inconclusive case. Pascal used these solutions to ridicule all casuistry and the work of the Jesuits. So successful was Pascal that to this day the adjectives Jesuitical and casuistic are pejorative terms and often used synonymously.[66]

Jesuit authors attempted responses to Pascal, but they were not very successful at least in the court of public opinion. The more lax position deserved condemnation and even spoofing but the whole enterprise of casuistry and Jesuit moral theology came under a huge shadow because of Pascal's work.[67]

Just as Rome intervened to condemn the extreme of laxism so too Rome condemned the extreme moral rigorism of Jansenism. Recall, however, that Jansenism was much broader than just moral rigorism and involved a worked out theological system. The Bull *Cum occasione* of Innocent X in 1653 condemned the theological errors of Cornelius Jansen about grace.[68] The followers of Jansen distinguished between the question of fact and the question of right. The condemnations are proper but they do not express the real teaching of Jansen.[69] (Note that such a defense has often been used by those accused by Rome of errors. See, for example, the reaction of Cardinal James Gibbons to Leo XIII's condemnation of Americanism in 1899.[70]) Rome responded by trying to deny this Jansenist way of avoiding the problem.[71]

After much infighting, the Holy Office under Pope Alexander VIII in 1690 condemned thirty-one errors of the Jansenists dealing mostly with morality. Two of these condemnations touched on the moral tutiorism of Jansenist teaching. The first condemned proposition claimed that it is not permitted to follow a probable opinion or even the most probable opinion.[72] The second condemned proposition mentioned that although ignorance of the natural law exists such ignorance existing in the state of fallen nature does not excuse from formal sin.[73] This condemned proposition denying invincible ignorance of the natural law was a touchstone of Jansenist morality.

Thus as the seventeenth century progressed two extremes of laxism and tutiorism (one must always follow the safer course, and one can never follow even a most probable opinion against the law) were condemned. The main protagonists in this acrimonious debate involving much political intrigue and maneuvering were the Jansenists and the Jesuits who did have help from others.

However, Rome's condemnations of the extremes did not bring peace to moral theology. Even before the condemnations of the extremes a fierce struggle began between the probabilist camp and the antiprobabilist camp. The antiprobabilist camp generally accepted the position of probabiliorism—one could safely follow the opinion for freedom from the law if it were more probable than the position in favor of the law. Here too the struggle was between a more rigorous or a more benign approach to the moral life.

After 1656 the Dominicans became identified with probabiliorism although for the previous hundred years since Medina they had supported probabilism. J. B. Gonet (d. 1681) and his disciple Vincent Contenson (d. 1674) who developed the theory of probabiliorism were the two most significant Dominican theologians. In some ways the Jesuit-Dominican feud over probabilism was a continuation of the older sharp discussions about grace in the beginning of the century. The Jesuits were generally identified with the defense of moderate probabilism, but the leaders of the Society of Jesus definitely wanted to distance themselves from laxism. However, a few Jesuits did write against probabilism.[74]

The case of Tyrsus Gonzalez de Santalla well illustrates the intensity, intrigue, and collusions that were part and parcel of this acrimonious struggle. Tyrsus Gonzalez, a Jesuit, attacked probabilism and proposed probabiliorism. The Jesuit professor wrote a book defending his position and dedicated it to the general of the Jesuits, Father Oliva. Oliva denied permission to publish the work. Gonzalez's opinions were brought to the attention of Pope Innocent XI who was opposed to probabilism. The pope through the Holy Office issued a decree, the first part of which told Gonzalez to teach and defend intrepidly the more probable opinion. The second part of the decree ordered the general of the Jesuits to permit Jesuits to write in favor of probabiliorism and to inform all Jesuit universities that Jesuit theologians were free to write in such a manner. Apparently the message of this decree was never communicated to the members of the Society of Jesus. But the story and the intrigue do not end here. With the help of Pope Innocent XI Gonzalez was elected general of the Jesuits in 1687. But his own religious order would not allow him to publish his book favoring probabiliorism. In 1694 Gonzalez finally succeeded in publishing the book he had originally written in 1671.[75]

By the end of the seventeenth century in France and throughout Europe probabilism was in retreat and rigorism dominated pastoral practice. The generally accepted textbooks expounded this antiprobabilist rigorism. Francis Genet (d. 1705) published his *Manual of Moral Theology* in 1676. Genet's manual became very popular even outside France in both Italy and Germany and was later used by Alphonsus Liguori. Its rigorism is manifested in a number of ways. Genet relies heavily on scripture and the writers of the earlier church while downplaying reason because of its corruption by sin. Likewise, he does not cite many contemporary authors. Genet also denies the possibility of invincible ignorance of the natural law and proposes a form of probabiliorism. One cannot follow a probable opinion in the face of a more probable opinion. Genet's rigorism showed itself in practice in his often counseling the refusal or delay of absolution in the confessional. If a penitent does not show the signs of contrition, absolution should not be given. Signs of true contrition include penance already begun, the practice of the Christian life, and a hatred of sin. To fall on the first occasion into the same sin is a sign that true contrition is lacking. In many cases absolution should not be given. In doubt, absolution should be delayed.[76]

ALPHONSUS LIGUORI

The polemics of the seventeenth century continued into the eighteenth with the focus of the more rigorous-more benign controversy centering on probabilism. Our purpose is not to develop the total history of these times but to study briefly the important work of Alphonsus Liguori (1696–1787). Alphonsus became a doctor of the church and the patron of moral theology and confessors because of his work. To appreciate the work of Alphonsus some background is necessary.

Significant developments occurred in the world of the eighteenth century. Political changes abounded with the American and French revolutions coming at the end of the century. Economic development occurred and maritime commerce increased. In the intellectual world the Enlightenment began and spread its influence throughout much of Europe.

This was not, however, a very creative period for Catholic theology in general and moral theology in particular. The older controversies continued. Polemics were the order of the day and the controversies were multiple. Alphonsus Liguori was intimately involved in these discussions. In the specific field of moral theology rigorism, Jansenistic tendencies, and probabiliorism remained quite strong. Alphonsus disagreed with these positions and defended what can best be called a moderate probabilism. In the seminaries of the eighteenth century the rigorist and probabiliorist manual of Francis Genet, originally written in French and then translated into Latin, was most popular in Europe.

The eighteenth century controversies over moral theology centered in Italy. Two Dominican theologians, Daniel Concina (d. 1756) and John Vincent Patuzzi (d. 1769), strongly attacked probabilism and disagreed sharply with many Jesuit theologians and with Alphonsus Liguori. Concina wrote a two-volume history of probabilism and a twelve-volume Christian moral theology which resolutely defended probabiliorism and attacked probabilism. Concina claimed to be opposed to rigorism but some of his opinions veered toward the more rigorous.[77] Patuzzi and Alphonsus engaged in a heated controversy over probabiliorism. In 1762 Alphonsus published his brief dissertation on the moderate use of probabilism in which he disagreed with a certain modern author who in actuality was Patuzzi although Alphonsus did not mention his name. Patuzzi replied in the latter part of 1764 but used the pseudonym Adelfo Dositeo. The discussion continued during the next few years.[78]

One of the primary victims of the sharp polemics, intrigues, and controversies of the time was the Jesuit order. From the middle of the eighteenth century talk circulated about the suppression of the Jesuits. Starting in 1759 the Jesuits were expelled from some countries. In 1773 Pope Clement XIV completely suppressed the Jesuits. (The Jesuits were restored in 1814.)[79] With the Jesuits on the defensive and finally suppressed Alphonsus emerged as the principal opponent of probabiliorism and defender of moderate probabilism.

People without a sense of history fail to realize the extent and depth of the theological controversies in the past. Alphonsus's latest English biographer devotes a chapter to "The Theological Wars: 1749–1762."[80] Alphonsus also had trouble with censors—both royal and ecclesiastical. Alphonsus lived in what was then the kingdom of Naples under the Spanish monarch, Charles III, whose prime minister Bernard Tanucci was a lifelong opponent of Alphonsus and the religious congregation he founded. Royal censors were very alert to anything or anyone like Alphonsus favoring the papacy. On the other hand, the ecclesiastical censors were often of the rigorous or probabiliorist position. One of his writings on moderate probabilism published in Venice had to be smuggled into Naples to avoid the censors.[81]

Our concern is with Alphonsus's moral teaching but something must be said about the man, his work, and his writings. Born into an ancient Neapolitan family in 1696, Alphonsus started out as a lawyer but then became a priest. He had a special concern for poor rural people and engaged in preaching, giving missions, catechizing, and hearing confessions among them. In 1732 he founded a religious community of men which became known as the Congregation of the Most Holy Redeemer, often called the Redemptorists. His community of priests and brothers living in common had the special mission of caring for country people. His young religious congregation experienced problems from without, especially from the kingdom of Naples, and much intrigue and deception from within. Alphonsus did not lead a tranquil life. He was appointed Bishop of Sant'Agata dei Goti in 1763 and in this small rural diocese near Naples continued his work of reform. He suffered from a painful illness and finally in 1775 Pope Pius VI accepted his resignation as bishop. He continued to govern his congregation and worried about his future and that of his congregation after the suppression of the Jesuits. He suffered the indignity of seeing his own congregation divide into two branches (later healed) before his death in 1787.[82]

Alphonsus Liguori was a prodigious writer who published over one hundred works. However, he enjoyed the assistance of many of his confreres with his writing.[83] His spiritual writings based on the revelation of God's love for us often disagreed with Jansenist approaches. Perhaps his most influential spiritual book was the *Glories of Mary* which defended devotion to Mary against some Jansenist tendencies and supported the Immaculate Conception as well as Mary's role as the universal but not exclusive mediatrix of grace. His apologetic works attacked the ideas of the Enlightenment. His dogmatic works written mostly as a bishop included the *Refutation of Contemporary Errors, the Exposition and Defense of Catholic Teaching* with a special emphasis on the role of the pope.[84] His strong support of Marian causes such as the Immaculate Conception and of papal prerogatives greatly enhanced his standing and influence as the church became more ultramontanist in the nineteenth century.

Alphonsus also wrote many handbooks for confessors and dissertations on the subject of moral theology that were often of a polemical and controversial nature against more rigorous approaches, but *Theologia moralis* was his primary contribution. About one third of his publications dealt with moral theology. Without a doubt Alphonsus wrote *Theologia moralis* primarily for the church and not the academy. The outline of his life mentioned in the foregoing paragraphs provides the background for understanding his writing and moral theology. The first line of his preface to the *Theologia moralis* indicates the reason for the book. His congregation is dedicated to giving missions, guiding consciences, and hearing confessions especially among the rural poor. Alphonsus wanted to provide a moral theology textbook for the members of his congregation which would equip them with what they needed to fulfill their apostolate.[85] This objective explains the origins and determines the scope of his moral theology.

Alphonsus's *Theologia moralis* went through nine editions. The first edition appeared in 1748 and was basically his annotations on the manual of the Jesuit, Hermann Busenbaum. Alphonsus began teaching young Redemptorists moral theology in 1744 and thought the students would be better served if they had a manual to follow and not just the notes of the professor. The new professor read many manuals and decided to use Busenbaum especially because of its excellent methodology—a clear, precise, and orderly casuist approach to moral theology. Busenbaum, originally from Westphalia, published his *Medulla* in 1650 and the work met with great success. Alphonsus was not the only one to take over the text and add his own comments. In so doing Alphonsus showed his allegiance to the Jesuit approach. Later on Alphonsus was attacked for adhering to the Jesuit school. At times he thought about moving away from Busenbaum and writing his own moral theology from the beginning but he never did. As time went on he added more of his own material and made the text his own but still followed Busenbaum's plan and often quoted Busenbaum. In later editions, however, Alphonsus no longer referred to Busenbaum on the title page. No doubt the attitude against him by many anti-Jesuits had some influence here. Alphonsus himself considered the eighth edition (1779) to be the definitive edition. Leonard Gaudé published a critical edition of Alphonsus's *Theologia moralis* in 1905.[86]

Theologia moralis is divided into seven books which in the Gaudé edition comprise four volumes. Book One—"The Rule of Human Acts"—treats just two subjects, conscience and law. There is no separate treatise in the beginning on human acts probably because Busenbaum had no such chapter. This first book constitutes the total development of his fundamental or general moral theology and serves as the schematic basis for all that follows. This treatment not only shows the very practical orientation of the work but also locates morality in the tension between conscience and law. Book Two treats the precepts pertaining to the theological virtues of faith, hope, and charity. Notice that the virtues as such are not treated but only the precepts related to them. The long Book Three deals with the Ten Commandments and the precepts or commandments of the church. Book Four discusses the particular precepts related to different states of life. Book Five discusses sin and sins and does begin with a short section on human acts—the tract that Busenbaum had not included in the beginning of his work. Book Six, the largest of them all, treats the sacraments but primarily from the perspective of legal and moral obligations in their administration and reception. Book Seven deals with ecclesiastical censures and irregularities. This brief overview shows the pastoral and casuistic nature of Alphonsus's moral theology.

Alphonsus Liguori made a significant contribution to Catholic moral theology by charting a sane middle course between the extremes in the battle that had engulfed moral theology for well over a century. The two aspects of the struggle in his time focused especially on rigorism and probabiliorism, two distinct but related positions that Alphonsus effectively refuted thereby bringing peace and an end to the turbulent struggles of the past hundred years.

Alphonsus himself points out how he changed his position as a result of his pastoral experience from the rigorism of Genet in which he was originally trained.[87] In the preface to the later editions of his *Theologia moralis* (beginning with the second edition) Alphonsus points out a twofold problem of rigorism—the forming of an erroneous conscience and the desperation that comes when the faithful do not think they can live in accord with what is demanded. When many Catholics hear the more rigid approaches they often fall into mortal sin either because of an erroneous conscience that causes them to think something is a mortal sin when it is not or because they despair of salvation because it is presented as so difficult and almost impossible. The rigorist approach confuses counsels with precepts, weighs conscience down with new commandments, has no understanding of human weakness, forgets the human situation with all its differences of persons, places, and circumstances, and renders intolerable the burden that Jesus said was light. In the light of the circumstances of the time Alphonsus directed most of his work against the rigorists, but he also recognized the opposite danger of laxism which tended to justify the sins of human beings and find excuses for all types of human weakness.[88] One contemporary Redemptorist scholar, Marciano Vidal, describes the morality of Alphonsus as a movement from rigorism to benignity.[89] Alphonsus strongly opposed the theory of probabiliorism which was so prevalent in his day and which appeared to him as a form of the rigorism he also opposed. In its place he proposed a moderate probabilism which avoided the extreme of a tenuous probabilism.[90]

Alphonsus's middle way in these controversies and his ultimate acceptance in the church was based on his understanding of conscience, his innate good pastoral and practical judgments, his teaching with regard to the sacrament of penance, and his acceptance and endorsement by the popes and church authorities.

Alphonsus's most significant contribution to moral theory centered on the tract on conscience which he did over from the beginning after his first edition based solely on Busenbaum. Our consideration cannot develop the whole theory of conscience especially in the light of all that has been written about Alphonsus's treatment of conscience.

His very first words on the subject are most revealing, though as Domenico Capone points out, they have been forgotten by nearly all who claim to be writing moral theology in the tradition of Alphonsus.[91] The founder of the Redemptorists begins his discussion on conscience by asserting that divine law is the remote or material rule of human actions and conscience is the proximate or formal norm of human actions. Such distinctions ground his basic approach. Although conscience should be conformed to divine law in all things, the goodness or nature of human action becomes known to us insofar as it is apprehended by conscience. Alphonsus here appeals to the teaching of Thomas Aquinas.[92] This understanding of conscience and not law as ultimately determining the formal moral goodness or malice of the act (which is later nuanced and developed by Alphonsus) opposes a rigorism based on the objective divine law alone. It also grounds Alphonsus's acceptance against the Jansenists of the possibility of invincible ignorance of the natural law.

Although Alphonsus invokes Aquinas to support his position on this matter, in some ways Alphonsus goes beyond Aquinas. Actual conscience for Alphonsus is the judgment or dictate of reason about the morality of an act here and now to be done or omitted. Thomas Aquinas maintained that an involuntarily erroneous conscience renders the act involuntary and excuses from sin but it does not make the act good because it is necessary that the act be good according to both nature and reason. Alphonsus goes beyond Aquinas and proposes that a person acting with an invincibly erroneous conscience not only acts without sin but performs a good and meritorious act.[93] Such an understanding of conscience rejects the rigorism of those who insist unilaterally on the law of God and recognizes a greater role of the person and the subject.

Contemporary Redemptorist commentators have emphasized this basic understanding of conscience in Alphonsus and have studied its development in him and its implications for moral theology today. Domenico Capone has particularly emphasized the role of prudence in Alphonsus's understanding of conscience and the insertion of the judgment of conscience into the dynamism of the human person moving toward its end in the glory of God and the love of neighbor.[94] Vereecke highlights the importance that Alphonsus's treatment of conscience gives to truth, reason, and freedom.[95] Vidal interprets Alphonsus's whole development as a movement from rigorism to benignity and like Capone shows the moral life as the way of perfection with the moral judgment not based on science but on the prudential exercise of a person's conscience.[96]

What about these contemporary interpretations of Alphonsus on conscience? I believe they point to an important aspect in Alphonsus's understanding of conscience. As Capone points out previous students and commentators on Alphonsus have not recognized this personal, dynamic, and prudential understanding of conscience.[97] However, at the very least this understanding of conscience is somewhat buried within the more legalistic framework of Alphonsus's moral theology. Even though this personalist approach to conscience does not influence the structure of Alphonsus's moral theology or govern his whole approach, it does indicate how he differed from more rigorist approaches with their failure to give enough importance to the person.

In the past most of the attention given conscience in Alphonsus focused on his teaching about the moral systems. In the history of moral theology the term *moral system* refers to the solution of the problem created by theoretical doubt about what should be done. In the legalistic approach to morality in the manuals of moral theology the theoretical doubt focused on whether or not there existed a law requiring something. Probabiliorism maintained that one could follow the opinion in favor of freedom (no law existing) only if this position is more probable than the opinion in favor of the existence of the law. Alphonsus defended a different approach.

Alphonsus, deeply influenced by his pastoral experience, gradually developed his thinking in opposition to probabiliorism particularly in a sharp controversy with the Dominican John Vincent Patuzzi. In 1762 Alphonsus published his small volume on the moderate use of probabilism which was basically incorporated into the sixth edition of his *Theologia moralis* in 1767. Alphonsus wanted to avoid the extremes of rigorism and probabiliorism, on the one hand, and the opposite extreme of laxism and the tendency to extenuate the meaning of probability. His approach was called moderate probabilism or equiprobabilism. Substantially this remained Alphonsus's approach. However, in later years especially in the light of the strong attacks against the Jesuits and probabilism, Alphonsus sometimes changed his terminology but apparently not his basic positions.[98]

According to Alphonsus, one can follow an opinion in favor of freedom from the law, if the opinion is equally as probable as the opinion favoring the law. In this case, the law is not sufficiently promulgated. If a law is not promulgated, it does not oblige. An uncertain law is not able to enjoin a certain obligation. Note what Alphonsus does in this case. One is in theoretical doubt. The doubt has to be removed before one can act. Alphonsus appeals to two reflex principles to justify the movement from theoretical doubt to practical certitude— a law that is not promulgated does not oblige and an uncertain law does not oblige.[99] An acrimonious debate arose in the nineteenth century about what Alphonsus meant by equiprobabilism and how it related to probabilism.[100] One point is certain. With the Jesuits on the defensive and later even suppressed, Alphonsus opposed the probabiliorists and ultimately won acceptance within the church for a moderate probabilism.

Alphonsus's practical solution of particular cases and problems, in addition to his theoretical understanding of conscience and his moral system, helped to overcome the rigorism and Jansenism of the times. His approach to particular problems shows a great prudence for dealing with the actual reality and its many different circumstances and steering a middle course between laxism and rigorism. Alphonsus approached each particular question with an attempt to study it and discern the truth in the particular case or situation. His pastoral experience obviously had a great influence on his approach to particular cases. Recall that Alphonsus's primary approach to moral theology was pastoral and not academic. Moral theology served his work as missionary, preacher, catechist, bishop, and above all confessor. His commonsensical, prudential, and pastorally sensitive approach to particular cases won wide support.[101]

Theologians and academics generally, and especially if they are writing in a later period, tend to see the practical solution of cases as coming directly from the theory. In reality, however, this is not always the case. Many times the solution to individual issues comes first and then theory comes along to explain systematically, coherently, and consistently all the different positions that have been taken. I believe that such is true with regard to the natural law theory of Thomas Aquinas. The Christian tradition had developed its positions on many moral issues long before the rise of scholasticism. Thomas Aquinas developed his theory to explain and justify in a consistent way these various teachings. We know for a historical fact that Alphonsus proposed his solutions to most practical cases before he developed his theory of conscience and especially his moral system of equiprobabilism. His mature thinking about the moral system of equiprobabilism only appeared in the sixth edition of his *Theologia moralis*. Most of his practical solutions had been proposed before that time.

Here a surprising tension or contradiction arises. Alphonsus showed an exemplary prudence and pastoral sensitivity in deciding the issues and problems facing Christians in their daily life, but he himself had great problems and difficulties in directing his own spiritual and moral life. Alphonsus suffered from scrupulosity throughout his life although sometimes the problem was much more intense than at others. His scrupulosity followed the usual pattern often manifesting itself in three different areas—anxiety about past sins that have already been confessed; sexual sins, especially internal sins of thought and desire; and a morbid fear of committing sin at any particular moment. His scruples affected his personal life and his ministry especially at critical times such as before celebrating mass or at the consecration of the mass when the celebrant says the words of institution. His ministry in the confessional at times became excruciating and as a young priest he even contemplated abandoning this ministry. His rigoristic training influenced the problem but he underwent continued hesitations and doubts as he broke away from his earlier training. His spiritual directors insisted on blind obedience to their commands, an approach to scrupulosity that was generally accepted until the 1950s. This struggle with scrupulosity continued in greater or less intensity throughout his life.[102]

Alphonsus's most recent English biographer notes that the therapy for his scrupulosity inevitably left its mark on his personality and conduct. Alphonsus became absolutely dependent on others in regard to the smallest details of his spiritual life, such as his acts of self-denial, and in regard to major decisions concerning his missionary society, his bishopric, and his retirement. Especially in the light of the acrimonious disputes often involved in Alphonsus's life, his spiritual director, Thomas Pagano, forbade him to mention his doubts and scruples to others for fear of their being used against Alphonsus. As the years went by, however, his scrupulosity became known and was common knowledge at the time of his death.[103] Ironically, the man who was wracked with personal scruples became the exemplar of pastoral prudence in deciding particular moral cases and issues.

The approach of Alphonsus to the sacrament of penance constitutes a good illustration of his more benign approach to moral theology especially in the light of the Jansenistic and rigorist tendencies often associated with the sacrament of penance at that time. Marciano Vidal refers to the "Copernican revolution" in the practice of the sacrament of penance brought about by Alphonsus.[104]

In keeping with tradition Alphonsus gave great importance to the role of confessor as judge. Since the disposition of the penitent is absolutely necessary for the sacrament to have its effect, the minister of the sacrament is constituted as a judge who must be certain about these dispositions and the readiness of the penitent to receive the grace of absolution.[105] The whole of Alphonsus's moral theology as well as his teaching on penance strongly emphasizes the role of the confessor as judge, but the founder of the Redemptorists in the very beginning of his discussion on penance calls to mind the role of the confessor not only as judge but also as father and doctor. Here again Alphonsus insists on avoiding the extremes of laxism and rigorism. Laxism in this matter has probably been the greater problem in the history of the church precisely because the greater number of human beings are prone to sin and to take advantage of the possibilities that laxism offers. However, rigorism also does a great deal of harm because it makes the faithful hide their sins or drives them to despair and opens the way for more sinning.[106]

One of the characteristic opinions of the Jansenist and rigorist approaches concerned the denial or deferral of absolution. Here again Alphonsus tried to develop his approach as a middle way. The Jansenist position maintains that the confessor should never absolve the penitent unless one is certain that the penitent has the proper disposition and will not sin again.[107] Can a penitent who is in a proximate, necessary occasion of sin be absolved? Proximate occasion is distinguished from remote as an occasion in which human beings commonly and generally sin. A necessary occasion, as distinguished from a voluntary occasion, cannot be physically or morally removed. In such a situation the penitent must use all necessary means to make the proximate occasion into a remote occasion and thereby avoid the danger of formal sin. Alphonsus maintains that the penitent can be absolved in the proximate, physically necessary occasion of sin and even in the case of a proximate, morally necessary occasion of sin which cannot be removed without the sin of scandal.

The doubtful case concerns remaining in a proximate, morally necessary occasion of sin which cannot be removed without notable temporal harm to one's life, honor, or fortune. Alphonsus recognizes that the position asserting that one can absolve a penitent who promises to use the means to make the proximate occasion remote in this case is most probable. However, in practice Alphonsus counsels the deferral of absolution. Delaying absolution in this case is the best medicine that the confessor can give the penitent. Experience shows that often if absolution is given immediately the penitent in reality fails to use the means to make the occasion remote and falls again into formal sin. When absolution is deferred the penitent is more vigilant and ready to use the means to make the occasion remote and thus to avoid sin. Alphonsus admits that some might consider such an approach rigid, but it is truly benign because it provides the penitent with a way of overcoming sin and eternal punishment. For Alphonsus if it is a question of freeing one from formal sin while permitting the penitent to remain in material sin (without formal guilt or culpability), the prudent confessor should always use the more benign opinion. However, if the benign opinion moves the penitent closer to the danger of formal sin as occurs in these particular circumstances, the more rigid opinion truly helps safeguard the salvation of the penitent.[108] Note how the entire discussion is based on the spiritual welfare of the penitent. Alphonsus also shows himself to be realistic about the human condition and invokes the role of the confessor as a doctor to determine what is the most prudent approach to take.

Alphonsus takes a similar approach to the *consuetudinarius* (one confessing a bad habit for the first time) and a *recidivus* (one who relapses into the same sin which has been confessed before). The confessor should absolve the *consuetudinarius* because one freely coming to the sacrament of penance shows the proper disposition and sorrow unless there is a positive presumption that the penitent is not disposed. The recividist presents a different problem. As is his custom in all these matters Alphonsus reviews what the earlier authors have held. Some maintain the penitent should always be absolved as often as the penitent comes to confession. The opposite opinion maintains that such a penitent cannot be absolved until he has proved his conversion over the long term. Alphonsus embraces a middle and more common position— the recividist cannot be absolved unless he shows extraordinary signs of a proper disposition to do away with the bad habit. These extraordinary signs include tears, a lesser number of sins, using appropriate means to bring about a change, and the role of very strong motivation. In these matters the confessor has to have a moral certitude about the disposition of the penitent. But it suffices that the confessor has a prudent probability about the dispositions of the penitent and no prudent suspicion of indisposition. At best these external signs of the penitent can give only a probable judgment about the interior disposition of the person. Here again Alphonsus appeals to the confessor's role as doctor to determine whether absolution should be delayed for a particular penitent. The spiritual welfare of the penitent becomes the primary consideration.[109] Note again the criterion of the spiritual welfare of the penitent, the role of the confessor not only as judge but also as doctor, and the commonsense approach to the issues.

One illustration used by Alphonsus strikes the contemporary reader as most rigid. Constantine Roncaglia, according to Alphonsus, maintains that absolution is not to be denied to a young woman or man who see each other and get to know one another in preparation for marriage. After all, one has to know the person she is going to marry. From a speculative viewpoint Alphonsus agrees but not in practice. He would only allow the engaged couple to see each other once or twice. Rarely do people not sin in such meetings at least in words and thought. You cannot expect these young people not to be stimulated and feel sexual arousal about the sexual relations they will have in their marriage.[110] Yes, times have changed but more is at work here than just changing customs. Alphonsus like most other moral theologians, perhaps because of their celibacy, was fearful of sexuality and especially of the interior sins of thought, feeling, and desire.

On the whole, however, Alphonsus's approach to the role of the confessor in the sacrament of penance well illustrates his attempt to avoid both laxism and rigorism and his commonsense approach to practical issues. His primary concern is the spiritual welfare of the individual in the light of a trust in the favor of God's grace and a commonsensical and realistic appreciation of how human beings grow spiritually. He will defer absolution—but only if it is unavoidable.[111]

The intrinsic merits of Alphonsus's moral theology are evident but he was not the most acclaimed moral theologian of his age. It took time before Alphonsus became generally accepted as an exemplar for moral theologians. Recognition by the church authority of the works and ideas of Alphonsus constitutes a very important reason for the ultimate acceptance of his approach. Alphonsus was beatified in 1816, canonized as a saint in 1839, made a doctor of the church in 1871, and declared the patron of confessors and moral theologians in 1950.[112] This authoritative acceptance of Alphonsus made him the central figure in Catholic moral theology in the nineteenth and the first half of the twentieth century.

Alphonsus's moral teaching and pastoral prudence deserved widespread praise and acceptance, but other factors played a part in his acceptance by church authority. Alphonsus had long been a supporter of papal power, opposing the secular rulers in Naples, and favoring the papal states. Alphonsus strongly attacked the approach of Gallicanism which in the eighteenth and nineteenth centuries tended to downplay the papal role in the church and to give more significance to local bishops and councils. Recall that papal infallibility, which Alphonsus staunchly defended, was declared at the First Vatican Council in 1870. A year later, Alphonsus was made a doctor of the church. Likewise, Alphonsus had been a strong proponent of Marian devotion, especially stressing the Immaculate Conception which was defined in 1854. In the nineteenth century as will be explained later, Alphonsus became a symbolic embodiment of a strong pro-papal ultramontanism. One must recognize that these factors played a significant role in the official acceptance of Alphonsus's moral teachings in the nineteenth century.

How to evaluate the work of Alphonsus? Much of the secondary literature in praise of Alphonsus cited in this study comes from contemporary Redemptorist authors. A critical analysis must at least raise the suspicion about a possible lack of objectivity on the part of such spiritual sons of Alphonsus. Perhaps these contemporary Redemptorists are trying to put their founder in the best possible light. On the other hand, the newest biography of Alphonsus by the Irish Redemptorist Frederick M. Jones appears to be an honest and critical biography including all the warts.

All should agree that Alphonsus was not primarily an academician but a church person and minister of the gospel writing primarily for the needs of the church especially related to the evangelization of the rural poor. His pastoral prudence, realistic anthropology, and belief in the power of God's grace and the superabundance of redemption (the motto of the Redemptorists is *copiosa apud eum redemptio*) combined to make him a sure guide for casuists and confessors. On the negative side, Alphonsus's significance and importance tended to solidify the role of the manuals as the whole of moral theology. Alphonsus himself wrote much on spirituality that was not incorporated into his moral theology. Likewise, as Capone and others have pointed out, Alphonsus's approach has elements that move away from a legal model of moral theology. However, the founder of the Redemptorists supported the concept of moral theology as a separate discipline cut off from scripture, theology, spiritual theology, philosophy, and other contemporary disciplines, following predominantly a legal model (conscience versus law), and geared primarily to train confessors as judges in the sacrament of penance to determine what is sinful and the various degrees of sinfulness.

NOTES

1. There is no definitive history of moral theology. Louis Vereecke is the recognized authority in the field, but he has not published books as such or a general history. He has published four volumes of printed notes for his students at the Accademia Alfonsiana in Rome. Entitled *Storia della teologia morale moderna,* these volumes have been widely diffused and cited, and they are for public sale. They cover the period from 1300 to 1789—*Storia della teologia morale dal XIV° al XVI° secolo: da Guglielmo di Ockham a Martin Lutero (1300–1520); Storia della teologia morale in spagna nel XVI° secolo e origine delle "Institutiones Morales" (1520–1600); Storia della teologia morale nel XVII° secolo: la crisi della teologia morale (1600–1700); Storia della teologia morale nel XVIII° secolo: Concina e S. Alfonso de' Liguori, l'Aufklarung (1700–1789).* Summaries of his research on the history of moral theology have appeared—L. Vereecke, "Moral Theology, History of (700 to Vatican Council I)," *New Catholic Encyclopedia* (New York: McGraw-Hill, 1967), 9, pp. 1119–1122; L. Vereecke, "Storia della teologia morale," *Nuovo dizionario di teologia morale* (Milano: Paoline, 1990), pp. 1314–1338. A very helpful collection of his essays has been published—Louis Vereecke, *De Guillaume d'Ockham à Saint Alphonse de Liguori: Etudes d'histoire de la théologie morale moderne 1300–1787* (Rome: Collegium S. Alfonsi de Urbe, 1986). The best available one volume history of moral theology is Guiseppe Angelini and Ambrogio Valsecchi, *Disegno storico della teologia morale* (Bologna: Dehoniane, 1972). Although I have written summary histories of moral theology (e.g., *Encyclopedia of Religion, Encyclopedia of Bioethics, Westminster Dictionary of Christian Ethics*) and have had an interest in some historical issues, I do not claim expertise in this area. In what follows I am heavily dependent on Vereecke and other secondary sources.

2. Acts of the Apostles 9:2; 18:25–26; 19:9, 23; 22:4; 24:14, 22.

3. For a contemporary overview in English of the moral teaching of the early church, see Francis X. Murphy, *The Christian Way of Life,* Message of the Fathers of the Church, vol. 18 (Wilmington, Del.: Glazier, 1986). This series, Message of the Fathers of the Church, edited by Thomas Halton also contains other volumes dealing with particular moral issues; for example, Peter Phan, *Social Thought,* vol. 20 (Wilmington, Del.: Glazier, 1984); Louis J. Swift, *The Early Fathers on War and Military Service,* vol. 19 (Wilmington, Del.: Glazier, 1983). For a discussion of the same period that goes into more depth in considering individual authors, see George Wolfgang Forell, *History of Christian Ethics: From the New Testament to Augustine* (Minneapolis: Augsburg, 1979).

4. James A. Kleist, trans., *The Didache, The Epistle of Barnabas. . .,* Ancient Christian Writers, vol. 6 (Westminster, Md.: Newman, 1948), pp. 15–25; Murphy, *Christian Way of Life,* pp. 22–30.

5. Forell, *History of Christian Ethics,* pp. 61–74. For a more in-depth discussion, see Oliver Prunet, *La morale de Clement d'Alexandrie et le Nouveau Testament* (Paris: Presses Universitaires de France, 1966).

6. H. de Romestin, trans., *St. Ambrose: Select Works and Letters,* Nicene and Post-Nicene Fathers of the Christian Church, vol. 10 (Grand Rapids, Mich.:

William B. Eerdmans, 1989), pp. 1–89; Murphy, *Christian Way of Life*, pp. 182–188.

7. William Babcock, ed., *The Ethics of St. Augustine*, Studies in Religion, vol. 3 (Atlanta, Ga.: Scholars Press, 1991); Forell, *History of Christian Ethics*, pp. 154–180.

8. John K. Ryan, ed., *The Confessions of St. Augustine* (Garden City, N.Y.: Doubleday Image, 1960) Book 1, n. 1, p. 43.

9. Murphy, *Christian Way of Life*, pp. 217–221; G. R. Evans, *The Thought of Gregory the Great* (New York: Cambridge University Press, 1986).

10. Kenan B. Osborne, *Reconciliation and Justification: The Sacrament and Its Theology* (New York: Paulist, 1980), pp. 84–101; James Dallen, *The Reconciling Community: The Rite of Penance* (New York: Pueblo, 1986), pp. 102–118.

11. John Mahoney, *The Making of Moral Theology: a Study of the Roman Catholic Tradition* (Oxford: Clarendon, 1987), pp. 5–17.

12. Dennis Billy, "The Penitentials and 'The Making of Moral Theology,'" *Louvain Studies* 14 (1989): 143–151.

13. These excerpts from the *Penitential of Finnian* and the *Penitential of Columban* are cited in Paul F. Palmer, *Sacraments and Forgiveness: History and Doctrinal Development of Penance, Extreme Unction, and Indulgences* (Westminster, Md.: Newman, 1959), pp. 141–144.

14. Vereecke, *Dizionario di teologia morale*, pp. 1322–1323. The same basic reasons were earlier proposed by Thomas Bouquillon, *Theologia moralis fundamentalis*, 3rd ed. (Bruges: Car. Beyaert, 1903), p. 93. Bouquillon, who will be discussed at greater length, had a keen interest in and knowledge of history. It is fascinating that Vereecke, the most acclaimed contemporary historian of Catholic moral theology, here follows what Bouquillon had written many years before. See also Marie Dominique Chenu, *Nature, Man, and Society in the Twelfth Century: Essays on New Theological Perspectives in the Latin West* (Chicago: University of Chicago Press, 1968).

15. Thomas Bouquillon, "The University of Paris," *Catholic University Bulletin* 1 (1895): 349–364; 491–512; 2 (1896): 11–20.

16. Bouquillon, *Catholic University Bulletin* 1 (1895): 492–495.

17. Ibid., pp. 355–357.

18. The best English biography of Thomas Aquinas is James A. Weisheipl, *Friar Thomas d'Aquino: His Life, Thought, and Work* (Garden City, N.Y.: Doubleday, 1974). For an authoritative overview, see W. A. Wallace and J. A. Weisheipl, "Thomas Aquinas, St.," *New Catholic Encyclopedia*, 14, pp. 102–115.

19. For a recent English reprinting of a classic modern commentary, see Etienne Gilson, *The Christian Philosophy of St. Thomas Aquinas* (Notre Dame, Ind.: University of Notre Dame Press, 1995). For a brief overview of Aquinas's ethics, see Ralph McInerny, *Ethica Thomistica: The Moral Philosophy of Thomas Aquinas* (Washington, D.C.: Catholic University of America Press, 1982). The term "moral theology" was first used by Alan of Lille (d. 1203). See Angelini-Valsecchi, *Disegno storico*, p. 88.

20. Thomas Aquinas, *Summa theologiae*, 4 vols. (Rome: Marietti, 1952).

21. *Iª IIᵃᵉ, Prologus.*

22. $I^a II^{ae}$, q. 91, a. 3.

23. $I^a II^{ae}$.

24. $II^a II^{ae}$.

25. $I^a II^{ae}$, q. 90–96.

26. For my discussion of these aspects, see my *Directions in Fundamental Moral Theology* (Notre Dame, Ind.: University of Notre Dame Press, 1985), pp. 119–172.

27. Vereecke, *Ockham à Liguori*, pp. 149–203; 391–465. For a different interpretation of Ockham, see Marilyn McCord Adams, "The Structure of Ockham's Moral Theory," in *The Context of Casuistry*, ed. James F. Keenan and Thomas A. Shannon (Washington, D.C.: Georgetown University Press, 1995), pp. 25–52.

28. H. Denzinger et al., eds., *Enchiridion symbolorum definitionum et declarationum de rebus fidei et morum*, 32 ed. (Herder: Barcelona, 1963), nn. 1667–1693.

29. Ibid., n. 812.

30. For a summary description of these books, see E. Dublanchy, "Casuistique," *Dictionnaire de théologie catholique* (Paris, 1932), 2, cols. 1859ff; T. Deman, "Probabilisme," *Dictionnaire de théologie catholique*, 13, cols. 418ff; Albert R. Jonsen and Stephen Toulmin, *The Abuse of Casuistry: A History of Moral Reasoning* (Berkeley: University of California Press, 1988), pp. 138–142.

31. A. Teetaert, "Raymond De Penyafort," *Dictionnaire de théologie catholique*, 13, cols. 1806–1823.

32. Louis Vereecke, "La confession auriculaire au XVI ^{e} siècle: Crise et renouveau," *Ockham à Liguori*, pp. 467–472.

33. Ibid., pp. 472–474. See also Thomas N. Tentler, *Sin and Confession on the Eve of the Reformation* (Princeton, N.J.: Princeton University Press, 1977).

34. Denzinger, *Enchiridion*, nn. 1667–1693; 1701–1715.

35. Louis Vereecke, "Le Concile de Trent et l'enseignement de la théologie morale," *Ockham à Liguori*, pp. 496–497; 502–505.

36. Ibid., pp. 497–500.

37. Ibid., pp. 503–504.

38. Ibid., pp. 506–508. For a more in-depth discussion of Azor and the beginnings of the *Institutiones*, see Vereecke, *Storia*, 2, pp. 113–125. For the early Jesuit approach to confession, see John W. O'Malley, *The First Jesuits* (Cambridge: Harvard University Press, 1993), pp. 136–152.

39. Jonsen-Toulmin, *Abuse of Casuistry*, pp. 146–151.

40. Jonsen-Toulmin refer to this time as the period of high casuistry, *Abuse of Casuistry*, pp. 137–175.

41. The best available source for this period is Vereecke, *Storia*, vols. 3 and 4.

42. Jonsen-Toulmin, *Abuse of Casuistry*, pp. 139–227.

43. John T. Noonan, Jr., *The Scholastic Analysis of Usury* (Cambridge: Harvard University Press, 1957); John T. Noonan, Jr., "The Amendment of Papal Teaching by Theologians," in *Contraception, Authority, and Dissent*, ed. Charles E. Curran (New York: Herder and Herder, 1969), pp. 41–75.

44. See the classic history of I. von Döllinger and H. Reusch, *Geschichte der Moralstreitigkeiten in der römisch-katholischen Kirche*, 2 vols. (Nördlingen,

1889); also E. Amann, "Laxisme," in *Dictionnaire de théologie catholique*, 9, cols. 37–86; Th. Deman, "Probabilisme," in *Dictionnaire de théologie catholique*, 13, cols. 417–619. However, these sources tend to have an antiprobabilist bias. For the best overall contemporary study of this period see Vereecke, *Storia*, 3, pp. 44–69.

45. Jonsen-Toulmin, *Abuse of Casuistry*, p. 224.

46. Denzinger, *Enchiridion*, n. 2130.

47. In the next few paragraphs on probabilism, I am closely following Jonsen-Toulmin, *Abuse of Casuistry*, pp. 164–175.

48. For the role of Jesuits in moral theology in general and on this particular issue, see Eduardo Moore, "Los Jesuitas en la historia de la teologia moral," in *Historia: Memoria futuri: Mélanges Louis Vereecke*, ed. Real Tremblay and Dennis J. Billy (Rome: Editiones Academiae Alphonsianae, 1991). pp. 227–249. See for an earlier period, Moore, *La Moral en el siglo XVI y primera mitad del XVII* (Granada, 1956).

49. Vereecke, *Storia*, 2, pp. 105–109.

50. For an overview of laxist authors and those falsely charged with laxism, see Vereecke, *Storia*, 3, pp. 59–65.

51. Denzinger, *Enchiridion*, nn. 2021–2065; 2101–2167.

52. Ibid., before n. 2021.

53. Ibid., nn. 2102–2103.

54. Ibid., n. 2038.

55. Ibid., n. 2039.

56. Ibid., nn. 2131–2132.

57. Ibid., n. 2021.

58. Ibid., n. 2117.

59. Ibid., nn. 2110–2111.

60. Ibid., n. 2153.

61. Ibid., n. 2154.

62. Ibid., n. 2049.

63. Jonsen-Toulmin, *Abuse of Casuistry*, pp. 231–233.

64. Vereecke, *Storia*, 3, pp. 101–113.

65. Ibid., pp. 89–91.

66. Jonsen-Toulmin, *Abuse of Casuistry*, pp. 231–238; Vereecke, *Storia*, 3, pp. 87–101.

67. Jonsen-Toulmin, *Abuse of Casuistry*, p. 243; Vereecke, *Storia*, 3, pp. 135–140.

68. Denzinger, *Enchiridion*, nn. 2001–2007.

69. Ibid., note before n. 2010.

70. John Tracy Ellis, *The Life of James Cardinal Gibbons, Archbishop of Baltimore, 1834–1921*, 2 vols. (Milwaukee: Bruce, 1952), 2, p. 71.

71. Denzinger, *Enchiridion*, nn. 2010–2012. For a brief description of the infighting in the condemnation of Jansenism, see L. J. Cognet, "Jansenism," *New Catholic Encyclopedia*, 7, pp. 820–824. For an in-depth treatment, see J. Carreyre, "Jansénisime," *Dictionnaire de théologie catholique*, 8, cols. 318–529.

72. Denzinger, *Enchiridion*, n. 2303.

73. Ibid., n. 2302.

74. Vereecke, *Storia*, 3, pp. 135–146.
75. P. Bernard, "Gonzalez de Santalla, Thyrse," *Dictionnaire de théologie catholique*, 6, col. 1493–1496.
76. James R. Pollack, *François Genet: The Man and his Methodology*, Analecta Gregoriana, vol. 237 (Rome: Gregorian University Press, 1984). See also Vereecke, *Storia*, 3, pp. 122–127.
77. R. Coulon, "Concina, Daniel," *Dictionnaire de théologie catholique*, 3, pp. 676–707.
78. For a summary of the controversy between Patuzzi and Alphonsus, see Charles E. Curran, "Invincible Ignorance of the Natural Law According to Saint Alphonsus—An Historical-Analytic Study from 1748 to 1765," (S.T.D. diss., Accademia Alfonsiana, Rome, 1961), pp. 100–233.
79. J. F. Broderick, "Jesuits," *New Catholic Encyclopedia*, 7, especially pp. 906–907.
80. Frederick M. Jones, *Alphonsus de Liguori: The Saint of Bourbon Naples* (Westminster, Md.: Christian Classics, 1992), pp. 262–295.
81. Ibid., pp. 264–266.
82. For a concise overview of the life and work of Alphonsus, see L. Vereecke, "Alphonsus Liguori, St.," *New Catholic Encyclopedia*, 1, pp. 336–341.
83. Jones, *Alphonsus de Liguori*, p. 263.
84. Vereecke, *New Catholic Encyclopedia*, 1, pp. 338–340.
85. Alphonsus de Ligorio, *Theologia moralis*, 9th ed., ed. Leonardus Gaudé, 4 vols. (Rome: Typographia Vaticana, 1905), 1, p. lv. Future references will be to the Gaudé edition.
86. Marciano Vidal, *La morale di Sant'Alfonso: Dal rigorismo alla benignità* (Rome: Editiones Academiae Alphonsianae, 1992), pp. 69–114.
87. Alphonsus de Ligorio, *Dissertatio scholastico-moralis pro uso moderato opinionis probabilis* (Neapoli, 1749), p. 45; Alfonso de Liguori, *Confessore directo per le confessioni della gente di campagna* (Venezia, 1764), pp. 515–516.
88. Gaudé, ed., 1, p. lv.
89. Vidal, *La morale di Sant'Alfonso*.
90. Domenico Capone, "Dissertazioni e Note di San Alfonso sulla probabilità e la coscienza dal 1748 al 1763, " *Studia moralia* 1 (1963): 265–343; "Dissertazioni...dal 1764 al 1769," *Studia moralia* 2 (1964): 89–155; "Dissertazioni ...dal 1769 al 1777," *Studia moralia* 3 (1965): 82–149.
91. Domenico Capone, "Per la norma morale: Ragione, coscienza, legge," in *Historia: Memoria futuri*, ed. Tremblay and Billy, p. 221.
92. Gaudé, ed., 1., lib. 1, n. 1, p. 3.
93. Vereecke, *Ockham à Liguori*, pp. 553–560.
94. Capone, *Historia: Memoria futuri*, ed. Tremblay and Billy, pp. 199–225.
95. Louis Vereecke, "La conscience selon Saint Alphonse de Liguori," in *Ockham à Liguori*, pp. 553–566.
96. Vidal, *La morale di Sant'Alfonso*, p. 275.
97. Capone, *Historia: Memoria futuri*, ed. Tremblay and Billy, p. 221.
98. The authoritative exposition of the development of Alphonsus's teaching on probabilism is Capone, *Studia moralia* 1 (1963): 265–343; 2 (1964): 89–155; 3 (1965): 82–149.

99. This presentation is a brief summary of a somewhat complex and much discussed issue. See Gaudé, ed., 1, lib. 1, nn. 40–89, pp. 21–70. See also Vereecke, *Ockham à Liguori*, pp. 560–566.

100. Vidal, *La morale di Sant'Alfonso*, pp. 211–216.

101. Vereecke, *Ockham à Liguori*, pp. 579–585.

102. Jones, *Alphonsus de Liguori*, pp. 69–73.

103. Ibid., pp. 73–74.

104. Vidal, *La morale di Sant'Alfonso*, pp. 270–272.

105. Gaudé, ed., 3, lib. 6, n. 43, pp. 36–37.

106. Ibid., n. 426, p. 421.

107. For a further development of these aspects of deferring absolution, see Vereecke, *Storia*, 4, pp. 126–133; Raphael Gallagher, "The Fate of the Moral Manual since Saint Alphonsus," in *History and Conscience: Studies in Honor of Father Sean O'Riordan, CSSR*, ed. Raphael Gallagher and Brendan McConvery (Dublin: Gill and Macmillan, 1989), pp. 212–239.

108. Gaudé, ed., 3, lib. 6, nn. 455–456, pp. 463–465.

109. Ibid., nn. 459–464, pp. 467–477.

110. Ibid., n. 452, p. 459.

111. Gallagher, *History and Conscience*, pp. 215–216.

112. Vidal, *La morale di Sant'Alfonso*, p. 201.

2

The Nineteenth Century

To appraise Catholic moral theology in the nineteenth century in the United States of America requires some background of what was happening in the nineteenth century in general. Significant developments occurred in the intellectual, political, and economic orders.[1]

ROMAN CATHOLICISM IN THE NINETEENTH CENTURY

In the intellectual order the Enlightenment continued to grow and prosper in the nineteenth century with its emphasis on the power of human reason. Under the aegis of the scientific method great scientific and technological breakthroughs occurred. The physical sciences of chemistry and physics developed. Electricity came to the fore. In the more philosophical arenas the reason of the individual was exalted. The world became anthropocentric with the human being as the center and guide. A very optimistic anthropology and worldview followed from such an approach. The Enlightenment's exaltation of the human being often downplayed or denied faith and human dependence on God. The scientific method became for many the sole way of arriving at truth. This brief sketch illustrates the way in which most nineteenth century Catholics viewed the Enlightenment. Much debate continues today about the Enlightenment, but many Catholic thinkers find more positive aspects about the Enlightenment and seek to dialogue with the Enlightenment and incorporate its positive aspects into Catholic thinking.[2]

The Enlightenment also had significant political aspects. This new movement emphasized an unwillingness to accept the old order with its hereditary monarchical rule, its stratified class society, and the union between church and state. The political Enlightenment stressed the importance of human dignity and equality, democracy, and human rights. However, all recognize that abuses existed such as certain developments associated with the French Revolution and the rising secular anticlericalism in France which tried to privatize the role of religion and the church. Often the cry was made for a purely secular state in which religion, faith, and the church were reduced only to the private sphere. Note how the United States' understanding of the separation of church and state did not entail such a secularization.

France was not the only political problem for the Catholic church. Catholic Austria under the Emperor Joseph II tried to subordinate the church to the imperial throne at the end of the eighteenth century, and the Catholic church had to deal with this Josephinism in both Austria and Bavaria in the nineteenth century. In the late nineteenth century Otto von Bismarck's *Kulturkampf* in Prussia tried to shackle the Catholic church and its public role. In Italy the popes' refusal to give up their temporal power was seen as the primary obstacle to emergent nationalism and the unification of the country. Again, one can understand how easy it would be for some Catholics to see only the negative aspects of these political developments which overthrew the old order and the union between church and state. In the economic sphere the scientific and technological developments of the eighteenth and nineteenth centuries fostered the industrial revolution with its exploitation of the worker and the increasing number of poor workers migrating to the growing cities.

What was the reaction of Roman Catholicism to these developments which became so prevalent in the nineteenth century?[3] With the hindsight of time one can now have a better perspective on what was happening. Generalities at best can never give all the shades of meaning and development, but they are not necessarily false. Attempts were made earlier in the century for some type of accommodation with the intellectual and political currents of the Enlightenment, but as time went on the Catholic church became quite defensive and opposed most attempts at rapprochement. The French Traditionalists early on emphasized divine revelation and tradition as the source of moral and religious truths that are communicated by tradition and not by reason. Especially in Germany George Hermes, John Sebastian von Drey, and Anton Günther tried to make accommodations with Enlightenment thought and its emphasis on the subjective and the historical. Ontologism, which was a general orientation rather than a coherent system, was strong in Italy (Vincent Gioberti and Anthony Rosmini), in France, and with the Louvain School in Belgium. Because ontologism tried to wed an Augustinian approach to a post-Kantian conception of philosophy as an ideal system of necessary knowledge, it was perceived as subjectivism.[4]

At this time neoscholasticism came to the forefront with the work of two Jesuits—the Italian Matthew Liberatore and especially the German Joseph Kleutgen, both of whom were teaching in Rome. For Kleutgen only Thomas Aquinas's theology of grace and nature could correctly deal with the proper relationship of faith and reason. Scholasticism had declined precipitously by the beginning of the nineteenth century but now a powerful renewal took place. The Jesuits who generally supported scholasticism were suppressed in 1773 but reestablished in 1814 and gained control of the Roman College (now the Gregorian University) in 1824. The Jesuits under Liberatore and Kleutgen were the spearhead of the revival of Thomism in the form of neoscholasticism.[5]

Neoscholasticism, advocated by Joseph Kleutgen and others, called for an epistemological realism and essentialism in which concepts are extracted from sense experience as opposed to subjectivistic and idealistic epistemologies present in the post-Kantian environment. A Thomistic anthropology based on matter and form presented a unified understanding of the human being and avoided a Cartesian dualism. A metaphysics of substance and accidents together with faculty, habit, and acts provided an apt way for understanding the human being and her acts. This whole approach opposed more historically conscious approaches and those that accepted in some way a turn to the subject.

Particularly distinctive of neoscholasticism was its understanding of the relationship between grace and nature, between the supernatural and the natural orders, and between faith and reason. This approach was used by the papacy to condemn two opposite approaches in nineteenth century Catholic thought. On the one hand, the traditionalism of Félicité Lamennais, Louis Bautain, and the Catholic Tübingen school deprived human reason of its proper role and autonomy by positing a primitive divine revelation as the basis for the human knowledge of the first principles of metaphysics and ethics. Human reason itself could know the natural end of human beings and the way to it according to the neoscholastics. However, certain knowledge of the mysteries of faith (e.g., the Trinity) comes only from the free assent of faith arising from the operative supernatural habit of faith in the intellect of the individual who is elevated to the supernatural order by the entative habit of grace.[6] On the other hand Rosmini, Gioberti, and the ontologists were wrong in conceding to natural reason an intuition of God's own being which only grace can give.[7] Likewise the German theologians Günther and Hermes were semirationalists who claimed reason could make true judgments about Christian mysteries.[8] The distinction between the natural order and the supernatural order served to protect the gratuitousness of the supernatural and was the basis for understanding the proper role of grace and nature on the one hand, and faith and reason on the other. Such an approach served as the basis for the nineteenth century papal magisterium and the First Vatican Council to condemn the extremes of fideism and rationalism.[9] Fideism claimed that some sort of revelation was necessary for the human mind to know God or to justify the demands of the moral life. Neoscholasticism insisted on the ability of reason to prove the existence of God and to know the natural law. Rationalism, on the other hand, claimed that human reason could have some knowledge of the mysteries of Christian revelation, but neoscholasticism insisted that only faith can obtain such knowledge.

Cardinal Gioacchino Pecci, archbishop of Perugia, who had been trained in scholasticism and was a stalwart defender of Thomas Aquinas, became Pope Leo XIII in 1878. In 1879 he issued the encyclical *Aeterni Patris* calling for the restoration of Christian philosophy according to the mind and method of Thomas Aquinas in Catholic schools.[10] Leo and subsequent popes used this neoscholastic approach and authoritatively imposed it to explain Catholic faith, to develop a coherent philosophy and a strong apologetic, and to address the problems in the modern world. For example, a collection of Leo's encyclicals on social issues was edited in the United States by Etienne Gilson in 1954 under the title: *The Church Speaks to the Modern World: The Social Teachings of Leo XIII.*[11]

However, a darker side existed in the papal imposition of neoscholasticism as the method and approach to philosophy and theology within Catholicism. First, neoscholasticism did not give enough importance to historicity and subjectivity; in fact, these two emphases came to the fore only during and after the renewal of Catholicism at the Second Vatican Council. Second, the popes imposed this one approach for the whole church, refusing to recognize any legitimate pluralism of philosophies and theologies. Third, Catholic thinkers in the twentieth century have pointed out that neoscholasticism's objective, ahistorical approach and its insistence on the supernatural-natural distinction do not actually reflect the true positions of Aquinas. At the very minimum a pluralism of Thomisms emerged in the twentieth century.[12] Fourth, the authoritative mandating of neoscholasticism was a defensive move. The hierarchical church was fearful of the new intellectual developments, condemned those who attempted to incorporate some of these newer approaches, and went back to the safe and time tested teaching of the past. For many Catholics the Middle Ages became the golden period of history as well illustrated in the famous book written by James Joseph Walsh, a Catholic physician and writer, in 1907—*The Thirteenth, Greatest of Centuries.*[13]

Fifth, the imposition of neoscholasticism as *the* Catholic philosophy and theology involves a great irony. In his own day Thomas Aquinas was not satisfied with merely repeating what had been said in the past but used the newly translated works of Aristotle to better understand and explain Catholic theology and life. The nineteenth- and twentieth-century popes used Aquinas for exactly the opposite purpose—to prevent any dialogue with modern intellectual developments. At the end of the nineteenth century and in the beginning of the twentieth century some Catholic scholars and intellectuals gave more importance to history and subjectivity in a movement that the neoscholastic advisers of the papacy labeled *Modernism.* The papacy strongly opposed Modernism and any attempt to dialogue with modern intellectual thought and insisted ever more strongly on Thomistic philosophy and theology as the Catholic approach.[14]

The Catholic and papal (the two were becoming more closely linked) approach to nineteenth-century political developments was also very defensive. Official papal statements strongly supported the union of church and state, rejected democracy as the best form of government, and condemned the modern liberties.[15] The "Syllabus of Errors" issued by Pius IX in 1864 contained eighty condemned propositions reflecting modern philosophical and political developments to which the church was unalterably opposed.[16] Only in the twentieth century did the hierarchical church change its teaching in these areas. Pius XII in the 1940s first spoke positively about democratic governments and as time went on papal teaching gave a greater significance to democracy. The Declaration on Religious Freedom of the Second Vatican Council in 1965 finally accepted religious freedom and the proper separation of church and state. Papal teaching remained skittish about rights language because of the danger of individualism and abuses that occurred in practice, but finally in 1963 Pope John XXIII in the encyclical *Pacem in terris* developed for the first time in hierarchical teaching a systematic Catholic approach to human rights.[17]

On the economic scene the church had to face the problems created by the industrial revolution and the plight of the worker. The consciousness of these problems grew as the nineteenth century progressed and in different countries different approaches came to the fore. In 1891 Pope Leo XIII published his encyclical *Rerum novarum*, which defended the right of workers to a just wage, affirmed their right to organize, and called for some state intervention to protect workers. Leo here applied his Thomistic approach to the economic problems facing society.[18]

Many Catholics saw a common thread running through all these issues, namely, liberalism with its emphasis on the individual and the rights of the individual cut off from God and from other communities. These Catholics were opposed to religious, intellectual, political, and economic liberalism. Religious liberalism began with Luther who broke away from the authority of the church. Intellectual liberalism made the reason of the individual supreme and cut people off from God and God's law. Political liberalism accepted democracy and with it the notion that majority vote makes something right or wrong. Economic liberalism supported the right of the individual to do whatever one wants to make money and opposed any restraints put on entrepreneurs.[19]

As the nineteenth century progressed the hierarchical church became more and more defensive in regard to other Christian religions especially Protestantism and in regard to what was happening in the modern world. I do not want to blithely accept all that was occurring in the nineteenth century. Problems and aberrations existed. However, an honest attempt to dialogue with the world, to learn from it what was true and to correct what was false, would have been better than a purely defensive approach. The Catholic understanding of the divine mediated in and through the human justifies such a dialogue. The Second Vatican Council proposed such an approach, but in the nineteenth century, in reaction to the impact of the Enlightenment and the French Revolution, the hierarchical church followed a defensive and fearful harkening back to a known and seemingly safer path especially in intellectual, cultural, and political areas. As one might expect this defensive posture went hand in hand with a more centralized and authoritarian approach inside the Catholic church, often called ultramontanism, which grew as the century progressed.

Struggles about the role of the papacy in the church and the relationship of the church to the state had been ongoing for a long time before the nineteenth century began. Gallicanism, for example, is based on complex theological and political understandings together with their practical applications which had especially characterized the life of the church in France perhaps even from the end of the Middle Ages. Political Gallicanism gave the French king independence from Rome in temporal affairs and a special place in church affairs. Theological Gallicanism emphasized the role of the Gallican church and downplayed the papacy. The tension surrounding Gallicanism in its ecclesial form continued well into the nineteenth century [20] Eighteenth-century Febronianism (from the pseudonymous author, actually the auxiliary bishop of Trier, whose book appeared in 1763) again limited the role of the papacy claiming it was only a primacy of honor. Like Gallicanism, Febronianism dealt with the role of the pope in both secular and church matters.[21]

These tensions in the nineteenth century often surfaced around the concept of "ultramontanism." This term refers to "beyond the mountains" and is taken from the perspective of Northern Europe looking south to Rome. Ultramontanism defended the freedom of the pope against the liberal rulers of the time and strongly supported the centralization and authority of the church under the pope. Those who supported papal infallibility in the nineteenth century were often called ultramontanes. The ultramontanists triumphed in the nineteenth century.[22]

As the papacy lost its temporal significance and its own papal states in the nineteenth century, the spiritual authority and primatial power of the papacy grew. The papacy took on an expanded role with regard to teaching in the church. The political changes in the eighteenth and nineteenth centuries did away with the university schools of theology which had been quite vigorous before and somewhat of an independent source of theological and doctrinal guidance for the church. Recall that already in the seventeenth century Alexander VII, Innocent XI, and Alexander VIII intervened forcibly and effectively in the condemnation of laxism, tutiorism, and many positions taken on practical issues. Now, in the nineteenth century, we can already see the growing number of papal condemnations in the disputes of the day. The Roman congregations often intervened in many different areas including moral issues.[23]

A comment made in the article "Encyclical" in the *New Catholic Encyclopedia* published in 1967 illustrates and at the same time partially conceals this development. "It is only in recent times, from the reign of Pius IX to the present, that encyclicals have become frequent expressions of the pope's ordinary teaching authority."[24] All would agree that the frequent use of encyclicals began in the nineteenth century. More significant is the reference to "the pope's ordinary teaching authority" with the implied understanding that this ordinary teaching authority was a well accepted theological term long before the nineteenth century. Such, however, was not the case.

The first use of the term ordinary magisterium or ordinary teaching authority of the pope occurred in the letter *Tuas libenter* of Pope Pius IX addressed to the archbishop of Munich in 1863. This letter was occasioned by a congress of German Catholic intellectuals held in Munich. In this letter the pope condemns the many false positions existing at that time, the tendency to ignore the teaching of the older scholastic scholars and teachers in the church, and the opinion that the pope and the Roman congregations by their interventions impede the free progress of science. Theologians and scholars should not limit their subjection to church teaching to only those things that have been defined by a decree of ecumenical councils or by the popes; rather their submission should extend to those things taught by the ordinary magisterium of the church with regard to faith.[25]

Thus the term ordinary magisterium to describe the pope's teaching in a noninfallible way came into existence only in the nineteenth century with the increased use of such a papal role. In his study of the papal document *Tuas libenter* and the ordinary magisterium, John P. Boyle shows how the proponents of neoscholasticism (especially Kleutgen) also supported and strengthened this understanding of the ordinary magisterium of the pope.[26] Thus the nineteenth century witnessed not only the solemn proclamation of papal infallibility (with its many conditions) but also the theoretical importance and practical role given to the ordinary, as distinguished from the extraordinary or infallible, teaching authority of the pope.

What happened to Catholic moral theology in the nineteenth century? Perhaps the most significant development lies outside the scope of this book but deserves a quick mention. John Michael Sailer (d. 1832) and John Baptist Hirscher (d. 1865) in Germany were dissatisfied with the genre of the manuals of moral theology. Moral theology should not only deal with the minimum requirements of the moral life in the light of the needs of the sacrament of penance. The discipline should discuss the whole of the moral life of the Christian. These pioneers appealed to scripture and dogmatic theology, and in no way embraced neoscholasticism. The Tübingen school in Germany took over and developed such an approach. But the new approach had no real influence on moral theology outside Germany and even within Germany its influence was limited.[27]

The manuals of moral theology remained the general approach to the discipline. A number of manuals which served as textbooks were published at this time.[28] Secular priests (e.g., Thomas Gousset in Belgium and Peter Scavini in Italy) and religious order priests wrote such textbooks for seminarians.[29] Among the Jesuits the work of the Frenchman, John Peter Gury (d. 1866), stands out. Gury's compendium of moral theology was the most important text published after the reestablishment of the Jesuits in 1814. He closely followed the approach of Busenbaum and Alphonsus Liguori. His work went through many editions (forty-three editions between 1850 and 1890) and was later augmented and brought up to date by others.[30] The most important of Gury's editors and developers was the Italian Jesuit, Anthony Ballerini (d. 1881). The Gury-Ballerini manual with subsequent developers and editors made its way into most European countries and the United States.[31] Redemptorists such as Joseph Aertnys (d. 1915) and Clement Marc (d. 1887) wrote manuals based on the work of St. Alphonsus.[32]

What effect did all these developments in the nineteenth century church have on the manuals of moral theology? It seems that the more theoretical intellectual issues coming from the Enlightenment and post-Kantian philosophy did not have all that much direct influence on the moral theology of the manuals. Louis Vereecke indicates that in the preceding century the manuals were little affected by the more theoretical and philosophical debates of the time.[33] The same judgment should be made about the nineteenth century in general. The manuals by definition did not treat theoretical philosophical positions. Their approach was totally practical. The whole method as illustrated by Alphonsus was to cite the opinions of previous authors and select what appeared to be the best solution to the cases. The footnotes of these manuals make no references to the broader philosophical and theological literature. Footnotes invariably refer to the older manualists. The very narrow and practical scope of the manuals, which is rightly criticized for impoverishing what should be the total discipline of moral theology, kept these books and their authors somewhat isolated from the more theoretical and philosophical discussions of the day.

However, developments within the church and its relationship to the contemporary world especially its growing centralization and authoritarianism definitely influenced the manuals of moral theology and their authors. The seventeenth century saw the strong intervention of the papal teaching office in settling disputed questions. Recall that many of the propositions condemned at that time were originally submitted to Rome for condemnation by theological faculties such as Louvain. From that time on papal interventions began to play an ever greater role in the manuals. Thomas Bouquillon lists nineteen different authors who wrote commentaries on these various papal condemnations.[34] The Gury-Ballerini manual begins with almost one hundred pages containing a chronological series of condemned propositions from the condemnation of John Wyclif in 1418 to the condemnations by Pius IX.[35] Note the increase of interventions by the papacy and the Roman congregations as the nineteenth century progressed. The critical Gaudé edition of Alphonsus (1905), unlike Alphonsus' own editions, places the condemned propositions of Alexander VII, Innocent XI, and Alexander VIII at the very beginning of the four volumes after Alphonsus's preface and before the first tract on conscience.[36] The later nineteenth-century manuals faithfully report the decisions of the Roman congregations and look on these interventions as decisive for moral theology.

What about the role of Thomas Aquinas and Alphonsus Liguori in moral theology in the nineteenth century? Both of these theologians received strong papal approval and were proposed as guides in theology and moral theology. Even before the nineteenth century, Alphonsus, for example, testified to the important role of Thomas Aquinas. In the preface to his moral theology, which stayed basically the same from the second edition, Alphonsus indicates the primary importance he allotted to Aquinas. Aquinas alone is mentioned in this context.[37] In his tract on conscience Alphonsus refers to Aquinas as "the most distinguished (*princeps*) of theologians."[38]

Alphonsus thus illustrates that even before the nineteenth century Catholic moral theologians gave special attention to Thomas Aquinas. The manuals came into existence when scholasticism was still strong and by their very genre they continued to cite these scholastics. However, this great acclaim for Aquinas existed side by side with an approach to moral theology which did not follow the method and approach of Aquinas in the *Summa*. Even after the rise of neoscholasticism and the authoritative imposition of this form of Thomism, the basic approach of the manuals remained the same. Neoscholasticism heavily influenced late nineteenth-century dogmatic theology but not moral theology. The long tradition of the manuals and the authoritative approbation of Alphonsus insulated the manuals from basic changes. At best somewhat perfunctory treatises on the ultimate end and human acts were regularly incorporated into the manuals, but their limited purpose, legal model, emphasis on canon law, and casuistic concerns remained intact.

What about the role of Alphonsus himself in the moral theology of the nineteenth century? In this century a remarkable change took place—moral theology became Liguourian or Alphonsian. At the beginning of the century especially in France the older rigoristic approaches to moral theology dominated. Jean Guerber refers to the apparently unique phenomenon in the history of theology that the teaching of one author could become in a few decades the common teaching of the church. In France Guerber singles out two books that were most influential in this rapid development.[39] Bruno Lanteri, a priest from Piedmont and the founder of the Oblates of the Virgin Mary, published in Lyon in 1823 some reflections on the holiness and teaching of Alphonsus.[40] Much more significant was the work of Thomas Gousset.[41] Gousset, born in 1792, taught moral theology in the seminary at Besançon and later became archbishop and cardinal of Rheims. Trained in the older French rigorism Bousset discovered Alphonsus by chance in 1829 and vowed to devote himself to promoting the teaching of Alphonsus. His influence in bringing French moral theology into the Liguorian sphere was enormous.[42] In describing the same period, Ph. Lécrivain points out the important role that Alphonsus's missionary and preaching work had in the spread of his moral theology in France during this time.[43]

In Italy the influential Peter Scavini (d. 1869) published a three-volume moral theology covering fundamental moral theology, special moral theology, and the sacraments. In a short preface Scavini indicates that his purpose is to propose a moral theology based on Alphonsus who developed a middle way between laxism and rigorism. The preface gives great praise to Alphonsus. Scavini's whole purpose is to introduce Alphonsus's work to the seminary student who is learning moral theology for the first time.[44]

However, in the latter half of the nineteenth century Alphonsus's own teaching and understanding of moral theology became distorted through what Ph. Lécrivain calls the twofold dangers of rigorism and Liguorianism.[45] As the nineteenth century progressed Alphonsus became very closely identified with the ultramontanist position with its emphasis on the central authority of the papacy, Marian devotion, and strong opposition to the intellectual and historical developments of the nineteenth century. In Germany Alphonsus became associated with conservative and ultramontantist groups who strongly opposed much of what was taking place in the German university world of theology.[46]

England furnishes an excellent example of the identification of Alphonsus with the ultramontanist position. His attacks on the Enlightenment, his spirituality, and the enormous influence of the *Glories of Mary* on Marian piety all helped this identification. Above all, the insistence on the prerogatives of the papacy made Alphonsus a leading figure in the nineteenth century. His moral theology came to be seen and understood in the same restorationist perspective of the time. Nicholas Wiseman, who became the first archbishop in England with the restoration of the hierarchy in the mid-nineteenth century and a cardinal, wrote a life of Alphonsus. The community of the Redemptorists became identified with the restorationist and ultramontanist cause. Alphonsus's moral theology was severely attacked by Protestants in England. These attacks only tended to identify Alphonsus all the more with the ultramontane tendencies of nineteenth century English Catholicism. Protestants singled out Liguori's position on equivocation.[47] John Henry Newman, later a cardinal but no ultramontanist, entered into the discussion of Alphonsus's moral theology in his debate with Charles Kingsley. Although Newman did not agree with Liguori's position, he defended it as not unreasonable and as one held by many Protestants as well.[48]

As pointed out before, approbation by church authority and the papacy played a great role in the prominence given to the moral teaching of Alphonsus. Such papal support readily identified his theology with ultramontanism. The support began with the first step toward canonization in 1803, the declaration that there was nothing deserving censure in his works. The last and most significant step was the proclamation of Liguori as a doctor of the church in 1871. As one would expect the Redemptorist order tried very hard to win this honor for their founder. In this attempt some Redemptorists tried to show that Alphonsus in the eighteenth century had already condemned the doctrinal errors which Pius IX and the Catholic restorationists were fighting in the nineteenth century. Thus by the end of the nineteenth century Liguori's teaching and influence owed much to its acceptance by the papacy but also became identified with ultramontanism and with many of the defensive and restorationist tendencies of the day. In such historical circumstances commentators interpreted Alphonsus's moral theology in a more rigoristic and authoritarian way.[49]

The second danger and risk facing the interpretation of Alphonsus in the nineteenth century was "Liguorianism." This means that Alphonsus's thought was used by his disciples to create a new school of orthodoxy which distinguished itself from all other approaches. This risk became a reality in the latter part of the nineteenth century. The occasion came from the writings of the Jesuit Anthony Ballerini and the subsequent development of an Alphonsian-Redemptorist system of moral theology known as equiprobabilism as distinguished from the probabilism school of the Jesuits. Both sides strenuously tried to support their different positions and appealed to Alphonsus. The attempt to build up and defend an Alphonsian moral system and school in the midst of a polemical atmosphere could only distort the real thinking of Alphonsus.[50] The publication in 1873 of the *Vindiciae Alphonsianae* and the *Vindiciae Ballerinianae* illustrates the high point, or in truth, the low point of this debate. Raphael Gallagher refers to these polemics as "an arid debate."[51]

By the end of the nineteenth century Alphonsus's moral teaching was interpreted much differently from the understanding in his lifetime. Gallagher refers to the transformation and fossilization of Liguori's moral theology. A major irony of the nineteenth-century development of moral theology was the changed understanding of the work and role of Alphonsus. The seeker of the pastorally viable middle way based on intrinsically convincing arguments became an establishment theologian used as an extrinsic authority to head off any possible changes and developments. A defensive, ahistorical reading of Alphonsus lost sight of his theological insistence on God's mercy and his own prudential approach to moral issues.[52]

Marciano Vidal refers to the ideological reading of Alphonsus in the nineteenth century which thoroughly distorted Alphonsus's own positions. Vidal points out three ironies in the way Alphonsus was used in the nineteenth century and even into the twentieth. Alphonsus, who struggled against the moral rigorism of his own day, was used to combat the presumed moral laxism of the times. Alphonsus, who went about building a moral theology with doubts and tentativeness and never his own system apart from Busenbaum, was used as a guarantee of doctrinal certitude. Alphonsus, who loved, admired, and defended the Jesuits, was now used in a virulent dispute against the Jesuits.[53] There can be no doubt that by the end of the nineteenth century

Catholic moral theology regularly cited the words of Alphonsus but often lacked and even distorted his true spirit. Ironically the papacy in the nineteenth century gave the highest approval to Thomas Aquinas and Alphonsus Liguori as models and examples of Catholic theology, but these nineteenth century interpretations did not always faithfully represent the approach of these two important figures.

But there is a further and greater irony in the nineteenth-century papal support of the theology of Thomas Aquinas and Alphonsus Liguori. If both enjoyed such approbation, they obviously had to be in agreement with one another. But in reality such was not the case. They differed profoundly in their approach to moral theology despite significant similarities.

What about the casuistry found in these nineteenth-century manuals? Although Pascal's attacks in the seventeenth century had given casuistry a bad name in many quarters, the manuals continued to employ their casuistic approach. However, as a general rule the casuistry in these manuals after this time was pedestrian and repetitive, lacking the creativity and imagination that had characterized an earlier casuistry.[54] The poorer quality of this casuistry continued and became even more pronounced in the nineteenth century.[55] A number of factors contributed to this development.

First, the very genre of the *Institutiones* or manuals worked against a creative casuistry. Recall that the more creative casuistry of the sixteenth and seventeenth centuries (e.g., the Spanish theologians at Salamanca) came from the genre of commentaries on Aquinas not from the manuals. As a result of seventeenth- and eighteenth-century controversies moral theology adopted a more inward focus so that moral theology was not involved in a dynamic dialogue with the new developments in the world. The nineteenth century with its defensive attitude toward contemporary developments significantly added to this approach so that theologians were not really addressing many of the newer issues that were arising. Instead of pursuing and developing new questions the manualists tended merely to repeat the solutions to cases given by past authors (often involving internal church law questions) and choosing the most appropriate. The ecclesial atmosphere was also not conducive to a creative interplay or dialogue with contemporary developments in the world. Again, the footnotes in the manuals are most revealing about this lack of dialogue with all new developments except in relationship to new church decrees and laws and to developments in the civil law.

The more authoritative interventions by the hierarchical magisterium made the moral theologians somewhat fearful of stepping over the line and also brought about the expectation that vexing questions would be solved by authoritative intervention, not by discussion among the moral theologians. For all these reasons, the casuistry of the nineteenth-century manualists was rather perfunctory, repetitive, and not all that interesting or stimulating.

UNITED STATES CATHOLICISM IN THE NINETEENTH CENTURY

In the beginning the Catholic church in the United States was centered in the colony of Maryland. Colonial Catholicism in the 1780s showed a strong movement in the direction of a national church influenced by a republican spirit and the Catholic Enlightenment. But by the time of the death of the first archbishop of Baltimore, John Carroll (d. 1815), the American church was definitely headed toward a more traditional and European Catholicism with all the same tendencies as the developments in Europe at that time. Most of the nineteenth and the early part of the twentieth century saw the Catholic church grow dramatically in numbers as it tried to cope with the huge immigration from Ireland, Germany, Italy, and the Eastern European countries. Most of the energy of the American Catholic church went to caring for the spiritual and to some extent the temporal needs of the immigrants. The parish became the center not only of the spiritual life of the immigrants and their descendants but also of their temporal and cultural life.[56]

Jay Dolan describes four central traits or characteristics of the American Catholicism that grew up in the nineteenth century—authority, sin, ritual, and the miraculous. Whereas the previous section indicated how the church as a whole became more authoritarian and centralized as the nineteenth century progressed, Dolan documents the same development in American Catholicism. To be Catholic in the late nineteenth-century United States meant to submit to the authority of God as mediated through the church with its pope, bishops, and pastors.[57]

The same factors fostering the growth of ultramontanism in Europe were present in the United States, but distinctive American conditions also facilitated the development of ultramontanism with its emphasis on a centralized and authoritarian papacy. The long papacy of Pope Pius IX contributed to the rise of ultramontanism. As the papal temporal authority was attacked and basically lost, a greater emphasis was given to the spiritual power of the papacy. In 1866 the American bishops authorized an annual collection to be taken up in every parish for the pope. The North American College, founded in Rome in 1859, trained American priests with a special devotion to the papacy and to ultramontane theology. Unlike many of the older European countries, bishops in the United States were directly appointed by the pope. The definition of papal infallibility in 1870 and the authoritative interventions by Roman congregations in doctrinal, moral, and disciplinary matters symbolized the increased centralization and authoritarianism of the papacy. The American church held seven provincial councils of Baltimore (Baltimore at that time being the only American archdiocese for the whole country) and two plenary councils (1852 and 1866) to help govern the church in the United States. The Third Plenary Council of Baltimore (1884) was summoned by the Vatican with the intention of bringing the American church more under the sway of Rome. No further national councils were ever held in the United States, which is most indicative of the increased centralization of the Catholic church. For the vast majority of American Catholics as an immigrant minority this devotion to the papacy gave them a sense of their own identity and unity.[58]

Catholic life in the nineteenth-century United States emphasized sin and forgiveness in the sacrament of penance. The two distinctive aspects of Catholicism were the sacraments of the Eucharist (the mass) and penance (confession), and these aspects set Catholics apart from most other Christians. In the frontier experience priests often spent much of their time hearing the confessions of the people they occasionally visited in their pastoral journeys. The experience of the confessional was perhaps the most intimate religious ritual experience for these Catholics. Stephen Badin, an early missionary in Kentucky, spent most of his days during these pastoral visits in the confessional and even issued tickets for admission to the sacrament because of the number of people coming.[59]

The emphasis on sin and confession became a central characteristic of regular Catholic parish life as the nineteenth century developed. Works, both good and bad, have always been important in the Catholic tradition so that the emphasis was on both faith and works. Prayerbooks at this time emphasized sin and the need for confession. Devotional practices stressed the sins that human beings commit and the need for reparation. The parish mission, a very important part of the spiritual life of every parish, underscored the reality of sin, the fear of hell, and the need to confess one's sins and live a better life. However, sin in the Catholic understanding was not the last or the strongest word. God's mercy and forgiveness could be found in the sacrament of penance through the absolution of the priest.

At the beginning of the nineteenth century most of the faithful probably confessed their sins the minimum of once a year, but by the 1860s priests complained about the long hours spent in the confessional. The very fact that other churches did not generally accept confession made this aspect of Roman Catholicism all the more distinctive and important especially in the light of an overdefensive attitude of Catholics vis-à-vis Protestants. Sin and confession formed a very significant part of the life and ethos of Catholics in the nineteenth century in the United States and even grew in the first half of the twentieth century.[60] Such an important aspect of American Catholic life emphasized the importance of moral theology preparing confessors for the sacrament of penance.

As might be expected in the context of a greatly expanding church of immigrants trying to find its own identity in a new and pluralistic country the intellectual life of the church was not stressed.[61] To supply priests for the ever growing number of faithful was a top priority for the bishops of the United States. Despite some sharp divisions among the bishops on a number of different issues, most agreed that it was preferable to have native born priests. However, in the first part of the nineteenth century most priests were foreign-born missionaries who came to this country from afar. Many priests in the early part of the century came from France and the French became early leaders in the American hierarchy and church. To prepare students for the priesthood seminaries had to be built and staffed. Seminaries thus became a major concern of the American Catholic church at this time.

It became increasingly evident in the light of existing circumstances that the Catholic church in the United States could not and should not strive to have a seminary connected with the cathedral church in every diocese as had been decreed by the Council of Trent. Freestanding seminaries usually serving archdioceses or larger dioceses and some other freestanding seminaries run by religious orders for their own members and others for the secular clergy from a number of different dioceses ultimately became the rule. The First Plenary Council of Baltimore in 1852 called for the existence of at least one major seminary in each ecclesiastical province—a group of dioceses under their archdiocese. The Second Plenary Council of Baltimore in 1866 reiterated the legislation. The Third Plenary Council of Baltimore in 1884 in dialogue with Rome came up with more specific legislation on major seminaries.[62]

Seminary teaching was often the responsibility of a very small faculty in the first part of the century because seminaries with small enrollments needed at most a faculty of one or two. Since the manuals served as textbooks the professor simply read from and commented on these textbooks. Thus one person could teach a number of different courses quite easily. Obviously not much preparation was needed. The Sulpicians, founded in France as the Society of Saint Sulpice in 1641 to train seminarians, staffed a number of seminaries (beginning with St. Mary's in Baltimore, the first seminary founded in this country in 1791), but did not ordinarily give their members any training after their ordination until well after the late 1870s. The Vincentians, who likewise staffed a number of seminaries in the United States, forbade their members to earn degrees until the 1880s because of St. Vincent's insistence on the vanity of learning. Some diocesan priests were sent to Rome to earn doctorates so they could teach in diocesan seminaries, but even in Rome the course of study was no longer than some American seminaries required simply for ordination without a degree. In general there was little or no interest in academic degrees for these priests to be. The whole purpose of their education was to prepare them for the ministry of the church and the administration of the sacraments.[63]

The Third Plenary Council of Baltimore (1884) established a committee to propose a model curriculum for the major seminary which would include two years of philosophy and four years of theology. The resulting committee report placed heavy and equal emphasis on moral theology and dogmatic theology requiring six hours of each in the first three years of theology and three hours in the fourth year.[64] The equal weight given to moral theology and dogmatic theology continued in the United States until the Second Vatican Council and contrasted with the usual European approach of giving more importance to dogmatic theology.

In the light of the American Catholic ethos with its emphasis on sin and confession one can understand the emphasis on moral theology. In reality and in practice moral theology became the most important subject. Bishops needed priests and were even willing to cut short their study if they were trained in moral theology. In 1813 John Carroll, the archbishop of Baltimore, writing to a Jesuit superior called for the early ordination of priests even if they had not studied all the treatises on divinity provided they knew the obvious and general principles of moral theology.[65] Archbishop Samuel Eccleston of Baltimore in writing about a particular seminarian in 1845 told the seminary president that he could not ordain the seminarian until he had a good course in moral theology. Give preference to moral theology and postpone dogmatic theology if necessary.[66] Not only was the practical ministry of the priest the primary criterion of seminary training but the needs of the ministry could shorten that training provided the preparation in moral theology was adequate.

Father Ferdinand Coosemans, the provincial of the Missouri province of the Society of Jesus in the United States, described his own course of study. "My study in moral was confined to Gury which I studied for a year and a half without having time to consult other authors; I was at the same time Prefect of the students and professors. For one year only did I study dogma, but I failed in my examination partly for lack of talent, partly because of the distractions occasioned by my prefecting and teaching. I was ordained priest that same year."[67] If this was happening in a religious community with a strong intellectual apostolate one can imagine what was happening elsewhere. As time went on, as illustrated in the directions from the Third Plenary Council of Baltimore, a regular course of study with four years of theology was required of all students for the priesthood.

What was the general tenor of the moral theology taught in the United States in the nineteenth century? The Sulpicians and Vincentians were early founders of seminaries in this country and brought with them a background of French theology and spirituality. In general the French at this time were often somewhat Gallican in their dogmatic theology and ecclesiology and tended to be more rigorous in moral theology.

Stephen Badin, one of the first students at St. Mary's Seminary in Baltimore and the first priest ordained in the United States by Bishop John Carroll (1793), was a tireless missionary in Kentucky and the Midwest. However, Badin was very strict with his Catholic flock, rigorous in his morality, and definitely tinged by Jansenism. In Kentucky his moral rigorism brought him into conflict with the English Dominicans ministering in the same area.[68] Badin illustrates the presence of French rigorism and morality in the United States in the first part of the nineteenth century.

In theory, Louis R. Deloul (1787–1858), the superior of the Sulpicians in the United States, shared both Gallican and somewhat rigorist tendencies. Deloul advocated a transformational synthesis between Catholicism and American culture,[69] but in moral theology he considered Liguori "too sweet."[70] However, as in Europe the more benign moral theology of Alphonsus gradually became accepted in the new country. Jean Baptiste Bouvier, a moderate Gallicanist, adopted the Liguorian approach in moral theology which had a great influence in France at that time and in places under French influence in the United States. After the middle of the nineteenth century, the Jesuit John Peter Gury, who claimed to be following the teaching of Alphonsus, became most influential in Europe and in the United States.[71]

What about the intellectual life and intellectual concerns of the Catholic church in the United States in the nineteenth century? The heavy emphasis on the immediate pastoral needs of the church definitely overshadowed all else but the intellectual aspect was not totally absent. One strong component of the intellectual life of the American Catholic church came from the noted adult converts to Catholicism. Orestes Brownson (1803–1876), who edited his *Brownson Quarterly Review*, was an early supporter of bringing Catholicism and Americanism closer together before moving to more conservative positions near the end of his life.[72] Isaac Thomas Hecker (1819–1888), who founded the Paulist Fathers, started a monthly publication of the Paulists called *The Catholic World*, and later became associated with Americanism.[73]

The more intellectual aspect of American Catholicism at this time expressed itself in some criticism of the seminary system, support for a national Catholic university, and near the end of the century in the questions of Americanism and moderate Modernism.

Criticism of the seminary formation for its lack of intellectual depth and rigor increased as the nineteenth century progressed. A Vatican document prepared for the 1884 Third Plenary Council of Baltimore pointed out that few American bishops appointed during the 1870s were highly regarded for either learning or piety. Administrative ability seemed to be the major qualification of many United States bishops.[74] John Lancaster Spalding, the bishop of Peoria and the leading intellectual among the United States bishops, gave a very important address at the Third Plenary Council of Baltimore calling for a Catholic university because of the intellectual needs and challenges of the times. Spalding bluntly made the point that the seminary is not a school of intellectual culture and never will be either in this country or abroad.[75] Efforts to improve the intellectual aspect of seminary education continued but critics continued to call for more improvement.

Near the end of the century two critical books appeared on the subject of seminary education including the intellectual formation of the priest. John B. Hogan (1829–1901), an Irish-born but French educated and trained Sulpician, had been sent to the United States and became the first president of St. John's Seminary in Boston. Between 1891 and 1895 he wrote a series of articles in the *American Ecclesiastical Review* which were published as a book under the title *Clerical Studies* in 1898.[76] Hogan emphasized the great development in the natural sciences, stressed the more historical approach to human knowing, and gave a rather minimalistic interpretation of Leo XIII's *Aeterni Patris* thus showing his own distance from neoscholasticism. Hogan was very knowledgeable in most theological areas and the depth and breadth of his learning comes through in his book.[77]

John Talbot Smith (1855–1923), a priest of Ogdensburg, was released by his bishop in 1889 and devoted himself to literary and historical study and writing in New York City for twenty years. He published *Our Seminaries* in 1896, a scathing criticism of the entire system of clerical training in America. Smith pointedly rejected the first place given to moral theology both in the curriculum and in the minds of the students. His order of importance for the disciplines was scripture, philosophy, dogmatic theology, literature, and moral theology.[78] Thomas Bouquillon, the first holder of the chair of moral theology at the new Catholic University of America, used Smith's judgment about moral theology to show why Catholic moral theology needed to be renewed at the end of the nineteenth century and how it should have a much greater intellectual foundation and basis.[79]

Catholic intellectual life in the United States in the nineteenth century also rallied support for a Catholic university as an intellectual center for the life of the church. Both Brownson and Hecker had proposed the idea. The Second Plenary Council of Baltimore discussed it but took no action. Mention has already been made of Bishop John Lancaster Spalding's speech in its favor at the Third Plenary Council of Baltimore in 1884. Spalding is looked on as the founder of the Catholic University of America. As the leading intellectual among the American bishops he was the strongest and most convincing voice in favor of such an institution. He reminded his hearers in various addresses about the growth of universities in the United States in the nineteenth century and the need for the Catholic church to have such an intellectual center. Not only did Spalding give intellectual leadership for the existence of a Catholic university, he also arranged for a gift of $300,000 from the young heiress Mary Gwendoline Caldwell to support the institution. Between his intellectual leadership and his source of funding Spalding was able to convince the Third Plenary Council of

Baltimore to approve such an enterprise and to set up a committee to work out all the details. Spalding himself turned down the proffered rectorship of the new university which was called the Catholic University of America. There had been much opposition and infighting among the bishops with many opposed to the institution. However, the Catholic University of America formally opened on November 13, 1889, with ten faculty members and forty-six students. Catholic University really began only as a graduate school of theology for clerics and not as a seminary, but in October 1895 the schools of philosophy and science opened for all qualified male students.[80]

The two intellectual movements that have received the most attention in late nineteenth-century American Catholicism are Americanism and Modernism with the latter coming to the fore only in the twentieth century. The exact meaning of Americanism is hard to determine.[81] Americanists should be distinguished from Americanizers. The latter focused on the relationship of American Catholics to the American environment; the former urged a different American understanding of spirituality and somewhat of ecclesiology. However, the positions often overlapped. In general the American Catholic church in the nineteenth century faced in a practical and pastoral way the relationship between Catholicism and the American culture and ethos. The practical problem arose in terms of the pastoral care of the ever-growing immigrant population. Should they be helped to become good Americans or should they retain their language, customs, and traditions? Proponents of the first position saw no basic incompatibility between being American and being Catholic. The second position feared that the nineteenth-century United States was a Protestant society and too close an accommodation would result in Catholics losing their faith. The opposition to immigrants and Catholics on the part of some other Americans only intensified the problem. In general the liberal or Americanizing tendencies won out and the immigrants were helped to enter into the mainstream of American life.

At this time the American bishops were divided between the more liberal group calling for more accommodation with the political and cultural ethos and the more conservative bishops (e.g., Michael A. Corrigan, archbishop of New York; Bernard J. McQuaid of Rochester, and many German bishops) who feared too great an accommodation. The leaders of the liberal or Americanizing group were John Ireland, archbishop of St. Paul, Minnesota; John Keane, the bishop of Richmond and later the first rector of the Catholic University; Denis O'Connell, the rector of the North American College in Rome; and John Lancaster Spalding of Peoria who in his own way also favored such an approach. Cardinal James Gibbons, the leader of the hierarchy as the archbishop of Baltimore, sided with the Americanizers.

The different approaches also surfaced in the debate about education. Catholic schools were begun in the middle of the century to protect and strengthen the faith of immigrant children. John Ireland, however, tried to work out a plan in cooperation with public schools to include religious education for the students in accord with their own religious beliefs which would eliminate the need for the Catholic school. Conservatives bitterly attacked Ireland's approach which also did not succeed in practice.

Part of the struggle over the founding of Catholic University came from this conflict between the more liberal and conservative bishops with the liberals in favor of the university which began with a liberal rector (Keane), although some conservatives (especially Germans) served on the faculty.[82] Thomas Bouquillon, the Belgian-born professor of moral theology at Catholic University infuriated many conservatives by publishing a pamphlet in support of Ireland's plan which included a recognition for a proper role of the state in education and did not see education as belonging only to the family and the church.[83]

The more theoretical proponents of the liberal American agenda also saw the need to bring about some changes in spirituality and in the church in the light of the American experience. This was Americanism in the proper sense. Isaac Hecker, probably the leading Catholic intellectual in the Americanist camp, advocated a spirituality based on the presence of the Holy Spirit and greater individual freedom for life in the church but did not see these as giving in to an alien spirit.[84] Progressive Catholics in France admired the liberal Americans and Ireland often spoke in France. Abbé Felix Klein translated and adapted Walter Elliott's biography of Hecker while contributing his own enthusiastic preface. The book was an immediate success but Americanism became a source of great debate in France.

In his 1899 apostolic letter *Testem benevolentiae* Pope Leo XIII condemned Americanism with its basic claim that the church should modify its doctrines in accord with the contemporary spirit in order to attract others to Catholicism. Specifically Leo condemned rejecting external spiritual direction; extolling the natural virtues and the active ones over the supernatural and passive virtues; dismissing religious vows as not compatible with Christian liberty. Cardinal Gibbons and the leading Americanizers accepted the document and denied they had ever held such positions. Klein himself later talked of a phantom heresy.[85] Scholars have continued to discuss the exact relationship between the condemned Americanism and the teachings of some of the Americanists especially Hecker. William L. Portier points out the two different viewpoints or worldviews at work between Hecker and the papal document. *Testem benevolentiae* with its neoscholastic approach gave no importance to history and the subjective whereas Hecker's moderately traditionalist theology of history called for newer concrete responses to the needs of new times and places.[86]

Modernism is also difficult to define or describe precisely because the most concise definition and understanding is found in the condemnation of Pius X in his encyclical *Pascendi dominici gregis* of 1907.[87] All can agree that Modernism gave greater importance to historicity, subjectivity, and development in biblical studies, philosophy, and theology while rejecting the official neoscholasticism of the times. Within this general perspective some approaches were more radical than others. The Americans involved in the discussion were basically subordinate and derivative figures. The name most associated with Catholic Modernism is the French biblical scholar Alfred Loisy.[88] Chapter seven will analyze the influence of moderate Modernism in John B. Hogan's approach to moral theology.

Some scholars see a definite connection between Americanism and Modernism based on the common interest in history and the subject.[89] In general, both approaches were reactions against the neoscholasticism that was then the official Catholic approach. The condemnation of Americanism and especially the condemnation of Modernism with the practical implementation of that condemnation brought about a very defensive posture for the Catholic church and a repressive atmosphere for any creative theological thought that lasted until the middle of the twentieth century and really until the Second Vatican Council (1962–1965). Ultramontanism reigned supreme in United States' Catholicism in the first half of the twentieth century.

A word of caution is in order. This study focuses on three approaches to Catholic moral theology written in the United States near the end of the nineteenth century. The condemnations of Americanism and Modernism as such came after most of the theology considered here was written. There were tensions and obvious differences in the earlier attempts to deal with moral theology, but one has to be cautious about reading in labels and categories that only became more distinct and clear at a later period. Further, moral theology with its primary aim of preparing confessors for the sacrament of penance was not the primary battleground in the discussions of both Americanism and Modernism.

This historical context is necessary to evaluate properly the three different approaches to moral theology in the United States in the late nineteenth century. The first approach, as exemplified in the manual of Aloysius Sabetti, is the classical approach of the manuals of moral theology written for seminarians. Sabetti's manual was the most popular such manual ever published in the United States. Thomas J. Bouquillon's manual of fundamental moral theology claims to offer another approach coming from the perspective of a university professor, as distinguished from a seminary professor, and heavily influenced by his neoscholastic leanings. The third approach of John B. Hogan, who never published a manual or monograph on moral theology, differs from both of the first two by proposing a more historically conscious approach to moral theology and casuistry. The primary purpose of this book is to examine and analyze these three approaches in some detail.

NOTES

1. For the best overview of the Catholic church in the midst of the nineteenth century which is closely followed here, see Roger Aubert et al., *The Church in the Age of Liberalism*, History of the Church, vol. 8, ed. Herbert Jedin and John Dolan (New York: Crossroad, 1981).

2. R. Bruce Douglass and David Hollenbach, eds., *Catholicism and Liberalism: Contributions to American Public Philosophy* (Cambridge: Cambridge University Press, 1994).

3. The best study in English of intellectual developments in nineteenth century Catholicism and the basis for the following paragraphs is Gerald A. McCool, *Catholic Theology in the Nineteenth Century: The Quest for a Unitary Method* (New York: Seabury, 1977).

4. Ibid., pp. 37–128.

5. Ibid., pp. 145–215.

6. Denzinger, *Enchiridion*, nn. 2811–2814.

7. Ibid., nn. 3201–3241; 2841–2847.

8. Ibid., nn. 2828–2831; 2738–2740.

9. Ibid., nn. 3000–3045. For an explanation and commentary on the influence of neoscholasticism on the First Vatican Council, see McCool, *Catholic Theology in the Nineteenth Century*, pp. 216–226.

10. Leo XIII, "*Aeterni Patris*," in *The Papal Encyclicals 1878–1903*, ed. Claudia Carlen (Wilmington, N.C.: McGrath, 1981), pp. 17–27.

11. Etienne Gilson, ed., *The Church Speaks to the Modern World: The Social Teachings of Leo XIII* (Garden City, N.Y.: Doubleday Image, 1954).

12. McCool, *Catholic Theology in the Nineteenth Century*, pp. 241–267.

13. James Joseph Walsh, *The Thirteenth, Greatest of Centuries* (New York, 1907).

14. Gabriel Daly, *Transcendence and Immanence: A Study in Catholic Modernism and Integralism* (Oxford: Clarendon, 1980); R. Scott Appleby, *"Church and Age Unite!": The Modernist Impulse in American Catholicism* (Notre Dame, Ind.: University of Notre Dame Press, 1992).

15. Peter Steinfels, "The Failed Encounter: The Catholic Church and Liberalism in the Nineteenth Century," in *Catholicism and Liberalism*, ed. Douglass and Hollenbach, pp. 19–44.

16. Denzinger, *Enchiridion*, nn. 2901–2980.

17. Paul E. Sigmund, "Catholicism and Liberal Democracy," in *Catholicism and Liberalism*, ed. Douglass and Hollenbach, pp. 217–241.

18. Leo XIII, *"Rerum novarum,"* in *Papal Encyclicals 1878–1903*, ed. Carlen, pp. 241–261. See also Paul Misner, *Social Catholicism in Europe: From the Onset of Industrialization to the First World War* (New York: Crossroad, 1991).

19. See, for example, William J. Engelen, "Social Observations IV: A Lesson in Social History," *Central-Blatt and Social Justice* 14 (January 1922): 321–323.

20. M. Dubruel, "Gallicanisme," *Dictionnaire de théologie catholique*, 6, cols. 1095–1137.

21. T. Ortolan, "Febronius," *Dictionnaire de théologie catholique*, 5, cols. 2115–2124.

22. Aubert, *Church in the Age of Liberalism*, pp. 304–330.

23. Thomas Bouquillon, "Moral Theology at the End of the Nineteenth Century," *Catholic University Bulletin* 5 (1899): 267.

24. G. K. Malone, "Encyclical," *New Catholic Encyclopedia*, 5, p. 332.

25. Denzinger, *Enchiridion*, nn. 2875–2880.

26. John P. Boyle, *Church Teaching Authority: Historical and Theological Studies* (Notre Dame, Ind.: University of Notre Dame Press, 1995), pp. 10–42.

27. Angelini-Valsecchi, *Disegno storico*, pp. 128–130.

28. For greater detail about the manuals of the nineteenth century, see Bouquillon, *Theologia moralis fundamentalis*, pp. 157–158; J. Guerber, *Le ralliement du clergé français à la morale liguorienne* (Rome: Gregorian University Press, 1973); Ph. Lécrivain, "Saint Alphonse aux risques du rigorisme et du liguorisme," *Studia moralia* 25 (1987): 359–395; Gallagher, *History and Conscience*, pp. 212–239.

29. Thomas Gousset, *Théologie morale à l'usage des curés et des confesseurs*, 2 vols. (Brussels, 1849); P. Scavini, *Theologia moralis universa*, 3 vols. (Lucani, 1851).

30. Ioannes P. Gury, *Compendium theologiae moralis* (Lyon, 1850); Gallagher, *History and Conscience*, p. 227.

31. J. C. Willke, "Ballerini, Antonio," *New Catholic Encyclopedia*, 2, p. 31.

32. Iosephus Aertnys, *Theologia moralis juxta doctrinam S. Alphonsi* (Tournai, 1886–87); Clemens Marc, *Institutiones morales Alphosianae* (Rome, 1872).

33. Vereecke, *Ockham à Liguori*, pp. 49–50.

34. Bouquillon, *Theologia moralis fundamentalis*, pp. 141–142.

35. Ioannes P. Gury and Antonius Ballerini, *Compendium theologiae moralis*, 10th ed., 2 vols. (Rome: Propaganda Fide, 1889) 1, pp. xxxv–cxxxii.

36. Gaudé, ed., pp. lvii–lxiii.

37. Ibid., p. lvi.

38. Ibid., 1, lib. 1, n. 57, p. 26.

39. Guerber, *Le railliement*, pp. 4–5 and throughout.

40. P. B. Lanteri, *Réflexions sur la sainteté et la doctrine du bienheureux Liguori* (Lyon, 1823).

41. Thomas Gousset, *Justification de la théologie morale du B.A.-M. de Ligorio* (Besançon, 1832).

42. Gallagher, *History and Conscience*, pp. 222–223.

43. Lécrivain, *Studia moralia* 25 (1987): 364–375.

44. Petrus Scavini, *Theologia moralis universa*, 4th ed., 3 vols., (Innsbruck, 1851), 1, pp. 9–12.

45. Lécrivain, *Studia moralia* 25 (1987): 359–395.

46. Otto Weiss, "Alfonso de Liguori und die Deutsche Moraltheologie im 19 Jahrhundert," *Studia moralia* 25 (1987): 123–161.

47. John Sharp, "The Influence of Saint Alphonsus Liguori in Nineteenth Century Britain," *Downside Review* 101 (1983): 60–76.

48. Joseph L. Altholz, "Truth and Equivocation: Liguori's Moral Theology and Newman's *Apologia*," *Church History* 44 (1975): 73–84.

49. Vidal, *La morale di Sant'Alfonso*, pp. 209–211.

50. Ibid., pp. 211–216.

51. Gallagher, *History and Conscience*, p. 235.

52. Ibid., pp. 236–237.

53. Vidal, *La morale di Sant'Alfonso*, pp. 201–202.

54. Jonsen-Toulmin, *Abuse of Casuistry*, pp. 269–278.

55. Arthur Vermeersch, "Soixante ans de théologie morale, 1870–1930," *Nouvelle revue théologique* 56 (1929): especially 875–876.

56. This paragraph summarizes the analysis of Jay P. Dolan, *The American Catholic Experience: A History from Colonial Times to the Present* (Notre Dame, Ind.: University of Notre Dame Press, 1992), pp. 101–346.

57. Ibid., pp. 221–240.

58. Patricia Byrne, "American Ultramontanism," *Theological Studies* 56 (1995): 306–314.

59. Clyde F. Crews, *An American Holy Land: A History of the Archdiocese of Louisville* (Wilmington, Del.: Glazier, 1987), pp. 50–51.

60. Dolan, *American Catholic Experience*, pp. 225–229.

61. For an overview of American Catholics and the intellectual life, see Margaret Mary Reher, *Catholic Intellectual Life in America: A Historical Study of Persons and Movements* (New York: Macmillan, 1989).

62. Joseph M. White, *The Diocesan Seminary in the United States: a History from the 1780s to the Present* (Notre Dame, Ind.: University of Notre Dame Press, 1989), pp. 145–164.

63. Ibid., pp. 131–133.

64. Ibid., pp. 237–239.

65. Ibid., p. 124.

66. Ibid., p. 139.

67. Cited in John Tracy Ellis, "The Formation of the American Priest: An Historical Perspective," in *The Catholic Priest in the United States: Historical*

Investigations, ed. John Tracy Ellis (Collegeville, Minn.: Saint John's University Press, 1971), p. 8.

68. Crews, *An American Holy Land*, pp. 48–49; 67–69.

69. Kauffman, *Tradition and Transformation*, pp. 110–111; 312.

70. White, *Diocesan Seminary*, p. 139.

71. Ibid., p. 140.

72. Thomas R. Ryan, *Orestes A. Brownson: A Definitive Biography* (Huntington, Ind.: Our Sunday Visitor, 1976).

73. David J. O'Brien, *Isaac Hecker: An American Catholic* (New York: Paulist, 1992).

74. White, *Diocesan Seminary*, p. 151.

75. Ibid., pp. 158–159. See David Sweeney, *The Life of John Lancaster Spalding, First Bishop of Peoria, 1840–1916* (New York: Herder and Herder, 1965).

76. John B. Hogan, *Clerical Studies* (Boston: Marlier, Callanan, 1898).

77. Chapter seven will analyze Hogan's approach to moral theology in great detail.

78. John Talbot Smith, *Our Seminaries: An Essay on Clerical Training* (New York: W. H. Young, 1896), p. 270.

79. Bouquillon, *Catholic University Bulletin* 5 (1899): pp. 244–268.

80. C. Joseph Nuesse, *The Catholic University of America: A Centennial History* (Washington, D.C.: Catholic University of America Press, 1990), pp. 3–64.

81. For what has become the classical study, see Thomas T. McAvoy, *The Americanist Heresy in Roman Catholicism, 1895–1900* (Notre Dame, Ind.: University of Notre Dame Press, 1963); for a summary treatment of this period, see James Hennesey, *American Catholics: A History of the Roman Catholic Community in the United States* (New York: Oxford, 1981), pp. 184–203.

82. Nuesse, *Catholic University*, pp. 38–48.

83. Daniel F. Reilly, *The School Controversy, 1891–1893* (Washington, D.C.: Catholic University of America Press, 1943).

84. William L. Portier, "Isaac Hecker and *Testem benevolentiae*: A Study in Theological Pluralism," in *Hecker Studies: Essays on the Thought of Isaac Hecker*, ed. John Farina (New York: Paulist, 1983), p. 32.

85. McAvoy, *Americanist Heresy*, pp. 217–322.

86. Portier, *Hecker Studies*, pp. 38–39.

87. Pope Pius X, "*Pascendi dominici gregis*," in *The Papal Encyclicals 1903–1939*, ed. Claudia Carlen (Wilmington, N.C.: McGrath, 1981), pp. 71–98.

88. For the best recent discussion of Modernism, see Gabriel Daly, *Transcendence and Immanence: A Study in Catholic Modernism and Integralism* (New York: Oxford, 1980).

89. R. Scott Appleby, "*Christ and Age Unite!*": *The Modernist Impulse in American Catholicism* (Notre Dame, Ind.: University of Notre Dame Press, 1992), pp. 169–206; Kauffman, *Tradition and Transformation*, p. 168. For the opposite opinion, see Michael Gannon, "Before and After Modernism: The Intellectual Isolation of the American Priest," in *Catholic Priests in the United States*, ed. Ellis, p. 337.

PART TWO

Aloysius Sabetti: Manualist

3

Sabetti's Context and Method

One would expect the American Catholic church in the nineteenth century to produce manuals of moral theology to serve as textbooks for seminarians studying for the priesthood. These manuals prepared the future priests to serve as confessors in the sacrament of penance with special emphasis on their role as judge to determine what is sinful and the degree of sinfulness.

This section will focus on the manual originally written by the Jesuit Aloysius Sabetti in 1884, *Compendium theologiae moralis*, which continued to go through subsequent updatings with newer editions put out by Sabetti's successors in teaching moral theology at Woodstock College, the Jesuit scholasticate in Maryland.[1] Sabetti's Latin manual was the most influential and long lasting of the nineteenth-century moral manuals written in the United States. Over thirty editions were published.[2] In a 1935 doctoral dissertation Theodore Heck, a Benedictine monk, examined the course of study in thirty-two seminaries training diocesan priests at that time. Ten of the seminaries reported using Sabetti as the textbook in moral theology. Jerome Noldin, an Austrian Jesuit, wrote the most popular textbook which was used in twelve seminaries preparing diocesan priests.[3]

OTHER MANUALS

Before analyzing and criticizing Sabetti's work, other nineteenth-century manuals written in the United States deserve mention. Francis Patrick Kenrick, then the coadjutor bishop of Philadelphia, wrote the first manual of moral theology in this country—a three-volume textbook published in 1841–1843 primarily for the students in St. Charles Seminary in Philadelphia which he had founded.[4]

Kenrick, who later became the archbishop of Baltimore (1851–1863), the primatial see in this country, was the most learned of the American bishops of his time. Born in Ireland, he studied for the priesthood in Rome at the College of Propaganda where he made a brilliant record. Kenrick volunteered for the American mission in Kentucky where he taught at St. Joseph's Seminary. He quickly built his reputation and was later recognized as the foremost theological scholar in the American church of his time. In 1829 he was chosen secretary of the First Council of Baltimore and the following year he was appointed coadjutor bishop of Philadelphia with full jurisdiction. At that time he had been ordained only nine years.

From 1834 to 1840 Kenrick published four volumes of dogmatic theology primarily for his seminarians and then immediately published his three volumes of moral theology. He translated both the Old and New Testaments into English. His apologetic writings included defenses of transubstantiation, the primacy of the apostolic see, the Catholic doctrine on justification, and the Catholic approach to baptism and confirmation.

Kenrick did not originally intend to write a manual of moral theology for his students after he finished his dogmatic theology. However, the need for such a work became evident. Although the norms and rules of conduct as derived from scripture do not change, they must be applied in different times and places so the student must know the local conditions.[5]

Kenrick's knowledge of American sources appears especially in his development of the virtue of justice. In keeping with the custom of the manuals the tract on justice is the longest, encompassing about 200 pages.[6] Like the older manuals his discussion basically considers only two subjects—ownership and contracts. Naturally much of the material depends heavily on local law and customs. He frequently cites Sir William Blackstone, Kent's *Commentaries*, Purdon's *Digest* as well as the laws of the individual states especially those of Pennsylvania, Delaware, and New Jersey. His knowledge of American legislation appears throughout the book. Kenrick points out, for example, that priests who officiate at marriages for minors who have not consulted with their parents are subject to fines. He then lists the fines in Pennsylvania, New Jersey, and Delaware.[7]

Kenrick's work definitely belongs to the genre of manuals of moral theology written in a church context and primarily in the service of the church, more specifically for ministers preparing for the sacrament of penance. In his preface he mentions only two sources by name—St. Thomas of the older school and St. Alphonsus of the more recent.[8] His short introduction expands a bit on his sources. Thomas Aquinas stands out among all the students of Christian ethics of his

age, and because of his intelligence and clarity he has earned the title
of "Angel of the Schools." Recall that at this time the papacy had not
yet mandated the work of Aquinas. Perhaps Kenrick picked up his
love for Aquinas while a student at the Propaganda College in Rome.
Kenrick claims to have always had the work of St. Alphonsus before
him as he was preparing his own textbook. Raphael Gallagher points
out that Kenrick, unlike many others, had a true and sophisticated
understanding of Alphonsus's approach.[9] Kenrick also mentions other
sources such as Suarez, Lessius, de Lugo, and Sanchez.[10]

Perhaps the most distinctive characteristic of Kenrick's moral theology, and something which sets it apart from the manualist tradition
in Europe, involves the citation of non-Catholic authors. The then
bishop of Philadelphia calls attention to this approach in his preface.
Often he cites non-Catholic sources, especially Anglican, since it is
helpful to know that they often agree with us and there is much common ground among us.[11] Kenrick here recognizes the realities of his
adopted country where Catholics are a minority and live side by side
with a majority of non-Catholics. In his short three page introduction,
Kenrick gives three footnotes, but two of them are to *Ductor dubitantium*,
the 1660 work of Jeremy Taylor, the Anglican bishop. The first reference
uses a quotation from Taylor to support Kenrick's position that moral
theology cannot have the same certitude as dogmatic theology. Since
moral theology deals with the application of principles to cases, often-
times one has to be satisfied with a high probability. In the second
reference Kenrick criticizes Taylor for describing Thomas Sanchez and
other Catholic writers on marriage as guilty of a filthy curiosity (*turpis
curiositatis*). Kenrick, in response, refers to Sanchez as most pure. Kenrick also points out that Taylor himself has criticized the failure of
Protestants to write books on cases of conscience because they do not
accept private confession.[12]

One aspect of Kenrick's moral theology has been studied at length
and is often mentioned—his teaching on slavery.[13] Kenrick himself
mentions his treatment of slavery in the introduction to his moral
theology. Most European manuals no longer discuss the subject but
he will consider whether slavery is licit and what are the obligations
of masters and slaves.[14] Kenrick's position on slavery is somewhat
complex. He understands slavery as the state of perpetual subjection
by which one is held to give one's labor to another in return for
maintenance. Kenrick, in accord with the tradition, defends such slavery as not repugnant to the natural law but stoutly disagrees with those
who say that slaves are not persons. The then bishop of Philadelphia

proposes four titles that theologians gave to justify slavery—capture in war, sale, punishment for crime, and nativity. Kenrick admits that the ancestors of slaves in the United States had been brought here unjustly. How then could he continue to justify slavery? Kenrick appeals to prescription. The defect of title was validated by the lapse of a very long time. In addition to appealing to prescription to justify the status quo, Kenrick also hints that resulting problems for the common good could justify limiting the freedom of slaves. However, Kenrick insists that masters should treat their slaves kindly.[15]

Joseph Brokhage, writing a doctoral dissertation during a time when apologetics and defense of church leaders were quite strong, concludes his thesis by criticizing Kenrick on two major points. First, the slavery he defended as not being opposed to natural law was not the slavery practiced in the United States. Second, he failed to point out the obligations of the state to work toward emancipation since he admitted the slaves were unjustly brought to these shores in the first place.[16]

This major problem does not nullify the many contributions which Kenrick made. His manual was the first and for some time perhaps the best attempt to produce a Catholic moral theology for United States' seminarians. His own experience of more than twenty years in priestly ministry in this country definitely gave him a good feel for what was needed by Catholic priests. Subsequent manuals composed in the United States followed his approach and often cited his positions on specifically American issues and problems such as the relationship with non-Catholics. However, none of them did it in the same depth as Kenrick. Kenrick has been praised for relating marital sex to love more than any other Catholic moralist.[17] His book was also well-received in Europe. His biographer cites a very favorable review from the eminent German theologian Matthias Scheeben.[18]

In 1860–1861 a somewhat revised second edition of Kenrick's moral theology was published in Belgium, but no future editions ever saw the light of day.[19] The question of why no further editions were published calls for some discussion. Although Kenrick's work was the first American work of moral theology and although he served as archbishop of the primatial see of Baltimore and was looked upon as the leading theologian in the country, his textbook on moral theology did not have much direct influence beyond his own times. Three reasons might explain this fact.

Kenrick's book was used in the seminaries at Louisville, St. Louis, New York, Cincinnati, Charleston, Baltimore, Emmitsburg, and Philadelphia. The Fifth Provincial Council of Baltimore in 1843 agreed that the archbishop of Baltimore should commend Kenrick's works to all American seminaries. Kenrick wrote to his brother that such a commendation had not appeared because of fear of hurting the majesty of the city of Rome by introducing the work of a stranger.[20] Although John Tracy Ellis, the leading American Catholic historian of his day, attributes the popularity of the manual of Gury to the fact that he had taught in Rome, John Boyle rightly points out that Gury taught in Rome for only one year and wrote his moral theology at Vals in France.[21] Almost all the textbooks in moral theology used in this country in the twentieth century were not written by authors teaching in Rome. Thus the fact that Kenrick was not a Roman author does not seem to explain why his book was not republished in the United States.

Joseph M. White in his history of diocesan seminaries in the United States notes the lack of influence of Kenrick's moral manual in the United States and suggests in passing that it might possibly result from his teaching on slavery.[22] However, a subsequent editor could have changed this teaching on slavery and thus solved the problem.

A third proposed reason for the fact that Kenrick's moral manual was not used in the United States after his death comes from the difficulty of reading his Latin prose. Kenrick's priest brother, who later became archbishop of St. Louis, criticized Francis Patrick for the classical style of his Latin, but Kenrick's biographer claims that the style of the moral theology is more popular than that of the dogmatic theology.[23] I think, however, that the moral manual also has a somewhat difficult Latin style. Anthony Konings in the beginning of his moral theology published in the United States in 1874 maintains that in matters pertaining to the United States he has been guided by the acts of the Second Plenary Council of Baltimore and the "moral theology which Kenrick of bright and happy memory, wrote, simplifying somewhat his more difficult and obscure style."[24] Kenrick's classical and more obscure Latin style probably did turn some people away from using his textbook.

I believe another important reason contributed substantially to the lack of influence of Kenrick's manual after his death. Quite simply no one bothered to come out with further editions and updatings. Later manuals in the United States as best illustrated by Sabetti went through many revisions and updatings. These revisions and updatings were necessary to keep the manual abreast of recent developments especially in terms of legal developments and responses from the Holy See concerning specific questions. Anthony Konings' book apparently went through several editions even after his death but was not reedited in the twentieth century.[25] The successors of Sabetti, especially Timothy Barrett and later Daniel F. Creeden, came out with later editions and revisions. Why did no one revise Kenrick's work which was heavily used by both Konings and Sabetti? What happened in the case of Sabetti and Konings is paradigmatic of all the manuals that went through subsequent revisions after the author's death. These moral theologians belonged to a religious community teaching seminarians from their own order. Their successors belonged to the same religious community with its unique esprit de corps. The prestige of the religious community and of the particular seminary was enhanced by keeping the volumes in print. Because of new developments especially in the form of recent documents from Rome some updating was always necessary. If a particular textbook became popular, the teaching successors of the original author felt obliged to continue the work. This was true in Europe and in the United States.

Francis Patrick Kenrick was a diocesan priest. Diocesan priests do not live in community and do not have the same camaraderie and esprit de corps as religious. In addition, Kenrick left Philadelphia and became the archbishop of Baltimore. His successors in Philadelphia, in both dogmatic and moral theology, apparently felt no great urgency to update and revise Kenrick's manuals. As a result, the first manual of moral theology written in this country which had been used early on in many seminaries was discarded and its influence on the future was primarily indirect through the work of the subsequent manualists who willingly recognized their dependence on Kenrick both for his method of adaptation to the American scene and for his analysis of particular American subjects.

Mention has already been made of the manual by Anthony Konings, first published in this country in 1874, which continued the Redemptorist interest in moral theology. Konings had taught moral theology and canon law at the Redemptorist house of studies in Holland, became the provincial of the Holland province of the Redemptorists (1865–1868) and came to the United States in 1870 to teach moral theology and canon law at the Redemptorist seminary in Ilchester, Maryland. Four years later he published his manual which depended especially on Alphonsus Liguori, John Peter Gury, and Kenrick. Konings became well known as a responder to moral queries and wrote two other noteworthy works—*A Commentary on Faculties for Confessors in the United States* and a piece on absolving parents who sent their children to public schools which became the basis for the practice later adopted for the United States by the Council of Baltimore. His manual was reedited by his successor, Joseph P. Putzer but was not reedited in the twentieth century and thus lost its influence.[26] Raphael Gallagher, himself a Redemptorist, criticizes Konings for following the external forms of Alphonsus's teaching but not the inner vitality.[27] Thus in the United States as in Europe the late nineteenth-century followers of Alphonsus failed to appreciate his spiritual discernment, his insistence on prudence, and his pastoral benignity.

One other manual that appeared at the beginning of the twentieth century deserves mention. Adolphe Tanquerey (1854–1932) was born in France, received his doctorate in theology in Rome in 1878, and was a member of the Society of St. Sulpice (Sulpicians). He taught dogmatic theology in France until 1887 when he was assigned to St. Mary's Seminary in Baltimore where he taught dogmatic theology (1887–1895), canon law (1889–1893), and moral theology (1896–1902). Tanquerey was a prolific author. In 1894 he published his two-volume synopsis of dogmatic theology. In 1902 Tanquerey published the first two volumes of his synopsis of moral theology but he returned that year to France to teach at St. Sulpice and his third volume of moral theology was published there. Tanquerey's work did not give great importance to the American setting, but his work was widely used in the United States especially in seminaries run by the Sulpicians until the Second Vatican Council. Later editions edited by F. Cimetier included a supplement for Great Britain and America with regard to legal and moral issues.[28] Tanquerey's manual was not published until the early twentieth century so it lies beyond the nineteenth-century focus of this study. However, it is mentioned here because of its proximity to our time frame and also because its use in the United States in the first part of the twentieth century was substantial but not as great as Sabetti.[29]

All these manuals mentioned were primarily in the service of the church written by professors of moral theology training seminarians in preparation for their ministry especially in the sacrament of penance. This section will focus on the manual of Aloysius Sabetti which had the greatest influence in the Catholic church in the United States because of its subsequent editions and widespread use.

OVERVIEW OF THE WORK AND THE AUTHOR

In accord with our contemporary understanding Aloysius Sabetti is really not the author of probably ninety percent of the book which bears his name. Sabetti himself never tried to deceive anyone in this regard. The title page identifies the compendium as first written by John Peter Gury, updated by Anthony Ballerini, and now shortened and accommodated to the use of seminarians of this region by Aloysius Sabetti. This transplanted Neopolitan Jesuit, who was teaching moral theology to Jesuit seminarians in Woodstock, introduces the book to his readers as definitely not totally new but with the hope that it will be useful. He has merely taken the Gury manual, edited by Ballerini, and redacted it for American use. The excellent quality of this older manual influenced him to adapt this book to the American context rather than try to write a new volume of his own.

His redaction of Gury-Ballerini involved a number of steps. First, he eliminated from the volume those aspects dealing specifically with the French situation. Second, he updated some of the material especially on the matters of censures in the light of more recent Roman documents. Third, he included the pertinent realities such as local church regulations or civic laws from the American scene. Since moral theology deals with practical applications one must know the diverse local conditions. Fourth, Sabetti worked to improve the practical usefulness of the Gury-Ballerini manual. Subsequent updatings had increased the notes at the bottom of the page and added to the growing size of the manual. In fact, the footnotes often took up more space on the page than the text. Our author did away with all the footnotes and put everything into the text in the same type of print. He also shortened the book and tried to make his points as clearly and concisely as possible.[30] Sabetti indicated that he was using the third edition of the Gury-Ballerini manual, so one can readily compare the original with the adaptation.[31] However, the modern reader who reads the brief preface is still unprepared for the extent to which Sabetti depended on and used Gury-Ballerini.

The contemporary American reader and scholar come from a very different perspective. The author presents one's own thought. Any material taken from another must be carefully cited and noted. The American academy today is very conscious of plagiarism and looks upon intellectual work as the private property of the individual scholar. Sabetti and the manualists came out of a different tradition. Their writing was done in and for the church. Sabetti was merely trying to hand on to his own students the best possible textbook in moral theology. He makes no claim to originality but only wants to help students from the common patrimony of the Catholic tradition. Sabetti closely follows the Gury-Ballerini manual not only in its general outline and development of particular issues but even in its ideas and very words.

Take the consideration of the third commandment as an illustration. Sabetti adopts the precise outline and divisions of Gury-Ballerini. After an eleven line introduction that is almost word for word from Gury-Ballerini, Sabetti incorporates the specific divisions of the treatise as found in his source but sometimes combines what Gury-Ballerini treats separately. Chapter one in both texts deals with those things that are prescribed on Sundays and feast days. The first article in Sabetti combines the first two articles in Gury-Ballerini and deals with the obligation of hearing mass (note the term "hearing" which indicates the passive role of the faithful and contrasts with the contemporary emphasis on the active participation of all). This article treats the same three points as Gury-Ballerini: bodily presence, the attention of the mind, and the proper place for the mass with a subdivision discussing private oratories and then the parochial mass. The second article treats the causes excusing one from hearing mass. Chapter two deals with the works that are prohibited on feast days. In this chapter Gury-Ballerini has a second article dealing with the causes that can justify such work on feast days. Sabetti does not break the chapter into two articles but incorporates in a briefer way at the end of the one chapter the three reasons—charity, piety, and necessity—which justify the doing of servile work. Sabetti, as mentioned, does away with the various copious footnotes of his guide and incorporates the more important part of this material into the text. In keeping with his pedagogical interests Sabetti strives for a very clear presentation and definitely condenses the material of the original. Gury-Ballerini uses twenty-three pages to discuss what Sabetti condenses to eleven pages.[32] In this particular section on the third commandment and throughout the book Gury-Ballerini uses further subdivisions of principles, resolutions, and questions. Sabetti employs the heading *"Dico"* (I say) instead of principles and likewise uses resolutions and questions although he sometimes included under the heading of questions what Gury-Ballerini treats under resolutions. Sabetti not only follows the outline, basic divisions, ideas, and words of Gury-Ballerini but even uses the same citations. For example, on the obligation to hear mass, Sabetti uses practically the same words and mentions the same citations as found in Gury-Ballerini.[33]

Generally speaking Sabetti very closely follows the ideas and very words of his guide when discussing concepts and principles but leaves out some of the material treated in the further developments of questions and resolutions and especially the footnotes. For example, in discussing the obligation to hear mass on Sundays and feast days the American Jesuit leaves out Gury-Ballerini's question about the obligation on feast days to attend Sunday afternoon vespers.[34] Under the moral and continual bodily presence required for hearing mass, Sabetti raises four questions: Whether one must see the priest or hear his words? What constitutes a grave or light omission of a part of the mass? Does one satisfy the obligation who hears two half-masses from different priests? Does one who comes into mass after the consecration have an obligation to stay for the remainder?[35] All these four questions are treated in the same substantial manner by Gury-Ballerini but in greater detail after citing the opinions of other authors.[36] Sabetti leaves out from his source only a short question about the obligation to supply for missing a smaller part of the mass.[37] Concerning the obligation to attend the parochial mass (i.e., in the parish church) Gury-Ballerini discusses the older legislation and then points out that this older law is no longer binding in France.[38] Sabetti follows his guide, including the references, until the last part where he maintains there is no obligation to attend the parochial mass because in the United States parishes in the strict sense of the word do not exist. He quotes Kenrick as saying that in the United States one fulfills the obligation by hearing mass reverently in any place.[39]

This discussion well illustrates the important point that Sabetti makes no claim to be an original thinker and is quite content to follow the outline, the substance, the sources, and at times the very words of Gury-Ballerini after first reducing the original and making it more orderly while occasionally bringing in those aspects that are distinctive and proper to the American scene. A fellow professor at the Jesuit theologate at Woodstock has confirmed this judgment. "He never claimed any originality for his volume; I do not mean originality of principles for that would be a very dangerous claim for any theologian to make; but not even an originality of treatment. He simply took up Gury and applied his principles to changed circumstances of time and place."[40] Another commentator points out that especially in his first fourteen years at Woodstock Sabetti was very wary of giving his own opinions and even more so in defending them. However, after an encounter with a particularly articulate but unbalanced interlocutor Sabetti gained confidence and began to speak more in his own voice.[41]

Sabetti's compendium fits squarely into the tradition of the manuals of moral theology. In his introduction to the work our Jesuit author makes no specific mention of the sacrament of penance but it is evident that his whole purpose is to prepare seminarians and priests for their role as confessors in deciding about the morality and gravity of particular actions. According to the Council of Trent the faithful have to confess their sins according to number and species.[42] The manuals primarily focused on what was sinful and the gravity of the sin. For example, in the discussion of the obligation to hear mass on Sundays and feast days, Sabetti's very first sentence asserts that all the faithful who have the use of reason are held *sub gravi* (under grave obligation) to be present at mass as is evident from various places in canon law and from all the catechisms in which the certain precept of hearing mass on these days is declared.[43]

Although the introductory note to the reader does not mention the sacrament of penance, Sabetti clearly states the nature of his work— a brief and practical manual with the intended audience of young students in our seminaries preparing themselves for priesthood and missionaries laboring in the Lord's vineyard. The students do not need dense dissertations, controversies, doubts, or new and strange approaches but brief and solid solutions provided by their professors. Missionaries (recall that for Sabetti pastoral work in the United States was missionary work) will find a short treatment in which solutions that have perhaps been forgotten will at a moment's notice be perceived.[44]

From what we know of Sabetti as written by himself and by colleagues and students at the time of his death, he was ideally suited to write this type of manual.[45] Sabetti was born in southern Italy in 1839, into a pious family as the last of fifteen children. He fulfilled his boyhood dream by entering the Society of Jesus in Naples in 1855. These were difficult days in Italy especially for ultramontanist supporters of the papacy such as the Neapolitan Jesuits. The forces of change and revolution wanted a unified secular Italy, but the pope fought this approach before finally losing out in 1870. Sabetti had to finish his philosophy studies in Vals in France and then serve as a prefect in a French boarding school for four years. He started his theological training at the Jesuit College in Rome in the fall of 1865 but because of fear of the fall of Rome was almost immediately sent back to Vals for his theology. (One of the reminiscences at the time of his death called him a pupil of the illustrious Gury who taught at Vals, [46] but I am not sure of this. Sabetti himself does not mention this relationship. Gury went to Rome in 1864 and died in 1866.[47] Thus it does not seem that Sabetti studied under Gury in Vals or in Rome.) Sabetti was ordained a priest in 1868, came to America, and began teaching at Woodstock College in 1871 where he stayed teaching until his death in November 1898. Although his health failed near the end, he did travel to Rome in 1896 as an elected representative of his province and also visited his birthplace at that time.[48]

Aloysius Sabetti was not an intellectual and really did not claim to be a scholar. He received the same education as other Jesuit priests and had no special graduate training in moral theology. The Italian-born Jesuit did not originally come to the United States to teach at Woodstock College, but to work among the Indians in New Mexico. However, after six months of preparing to go to New Mexico Sabetti was told that he was to teach at Woodstock College. He later affectionately referred to his Woodstock students on many occasions as "his Indians." At first he taught dogmatic theology. When Father Francini the professor of moral theology died in 1873, Sabetti began teaching moral theology and continued until September of 1898. For a very short time he also continued to teach some dogmatic theology. In addition to teaching moral theology he also gave a case of conscience once a week proposing the solutions that should be followed in confessional practice and in pastoral guidance. Sabetti also taught the class on rites which was a practical course on how to administer the sacraments. For example, he used a doll for the seminarians to practice the proper way to baptize a child.[49]

In addition to his compendium Sabetti wrote cases of conscience and a few articles on moral theology for *The American Ecclesiastical Review* which began in 1889.[50] In the first volume the editor, Father Herman J. Heuser (1852–1933), happily informed his readers that Father Aloysius Sabetti, "the highest authority on moral theology in this country," has agreed in the future to furnish the moral cases for this journal.[51] *The American Ecclesiastical Review* like many similar journals for priests in other countries and in the United States (e.g., what later became known as *The Homiletic and Pastoral Review* began in the United States in 1900) regularly included cases of conscience to keep priests updated and informed about particular cases and questions that might arise in the confessional. The first case, published in Latin in 1889, dealt with a young Catholic woman (Sabetti calls her a girl—*puella*) working as a domestic for a non-Catholic family who had secretly baptized the newly born infant in the family, obviously against the parents' wishes, using the formula, "I christen thee in the name of the Father, and of the Son, and of the Holy Ghost." She then explained all this to her confessor. Sabetti raises three questions in the light of the case: (1) Can the children of nonbelievers not yet having the use of reason be licitly baptized if their parents are unwilling? (2) Was the form (the words used by the young woman) valid? (3) What practically should the confessor say and do? [52]

Further, many priests and bishops wrote him asking his advice on particular questions and issues.[53] Cardinal Gibbons consulted him often and followed his opinions on the proposed condemnations of the Knights of Labor and the Odd Fellows.[54] Sabetti was planning to publish a book of cases of conscience using the materials he had written and taught about but his health gave way before he could do this work.[55] He also wrote a few articles in *The American Ecclesiastical Review* dealing with the interpretation of certain documents. Thus all his writings were of the same genre, written not for scholars but for priestly ministers.

The testimony of his colleagues and students confirms the impression from his writings that Father Sabetti was not really an intellectual or original scholar. Patrick Dooley in his discussion of the early Woodstock mentions the scholarly work of Fathers Meyer, Mazzella, and De Augustinis. "It does not detract in the least from his (Sabetti's) merit to say that in point of talent he could not equal any one of the three just mentioned, yet in point of achievement he surpassed them all in winning credit for the house."[56]

His personality seemed perfectly suited for the work he did in preparing ministers for the sacrament of penance. Almost all the published material we have about Sabetti the person comes from reminiscences from colleagues and students published in *Woodstock Letters* shortly after his death. One must approach these comments written on the occasion of his death with the proper hermeneutic, for such reminiscences usually filter out the negative and accentuate the positive. However, the various commentators paint a very similar picture of Aloysius Sabetti. Above all he was a sympathetic person. Dooley describes him as a "loving and sympathetic personality."[57] A fellow professor maintained that Sabetti had in an eminent degree the quality of sympathy.[58] In one paragraph Father Ennis used the noun sympathy or its adjective five times to describe Sabetti.[59] Italians have the habit of calling a person "simpatico" which is a term of great respect and endearment which would seem to be a most appropriate description of this transported Southern Italian.

Sympathy is a very important virtue for one who is a moralist. One must be able to appreciate and feel for people in their predicaments. Too often a cold detached personality cannot appreciate the reality that is being lived through and described. The confessor and the moral theologian should be sympathetic. The Jesuit students at Woodstock recognized the sympathy of their moral professor for in times of doubt and problems they would go to him for help. The great majority of students chose him for their confessor rather than another member of the faculty.[60]

Sabetti was apparently an easy-going, lovable, roly-poly man who was interested in helping other people and well liked by all. He was if anything somewhat naive and was often teased by fellow faculty members and students alike. However, he enjoyed being teased and would think something awry or that he had offended someone if he were not teased.[61] Sabetti did not take himself too seriously but could often laugh at himself and others according to these reminiscences. Recall that for the first fourteen years he seldom ventured to give his own opinions on a particular subject.[62] His humility, self-effacement, and ability not to take himself too seriously all helped him to be a good moral theologian in terms of preparing confessors for the sacrament of penance.

Another important characteristic for a good moralist is clarity. Anyone reading Sabetti's textbook can appreciate this virtue in the author. The clarity, order, and conciseness of his written exposition indicate the same characteristics in his thinking. The testimony of his colleagues and friends underscores the clarity of his writing and of his thinking. Clarity and sympathy are the two words most used about Sabetti in the reminiscences about him. He was perfectly clear in his explanations. When a difficulty arose he was never satisfied until his questioners understood and accepted the answer.[63] Father Ennis acknowledges that there are probably works wherein questions are treated more extensively and with greater erudition but none are clearer or of easier application than Sabetti.[64]

Precision is closely allied to clarity. Sabetti was precise in his thinking and his writing. In his writing he adapted the material of Gury-Ballerini to his students by reducing its length and sharpening its force. In the introduction to his compendium, Sabetti claims that the students do not need long disquisitions but brief and solid solutions.[65] Also our author is almost boastful (a quality not usually associated with him) in claiming to have verified all the citations in his compendium with his own eyes. But then Sabetti adds, with his characteristic modesty, insofar as human frailty allows, there will be no errors in these citations.[66] Anyone who has worked with the older manuals of moral theology knows how difficult and frustrating it can be to look up the citations which are given since they are often inaccurate. It seems that authors just cited citations given by previous authors and did not verify them. Sabetti had obviously experienced the same problem and now he wanted to make sure that his citations were accurate. Precision in analyzing the situation, in describing the heart of the problem, and in proposing solutions is a most important characteristic for the manualist. Sabetti's precision is evident throughout his work.

The moral theologian needs a good pastoral sense as well as common sense. Beware of the zealot or the one who acts too hastily. A fellow professor lauded Sabetti for his "mental stability and equipoise."[67] This clearheaded common sense comes through in his writing and helps give him his reputation. Sabetti knew that he had to be familiar with the problems and issues of people. He often spent his vacations hearing confessions and working in a parish so that he would be in touch with what was happening and never become one who taught but never practiced what he taught.[68]

The personal traits mentioned here certainly dispose a person to be a good teacher—clear, precise, knowledgeable, accurate, sympathetic, friendly, vivacious, and with a good sense of humor. From all the available evidence Sabetti was an outstanding teacher. Remember too that he taught in Latin. However, he had an excellent command of Latin and could speak the language fluently and easily. Students loved to hear him roll out his characteristic Italian *c*'s and he would make sure often to incorporate the *c* sound in his speaking, e.g., *caecus caecum ducit*—the blind leads the blind.[69] Sabetti was a very enthusiastic teacher.[70] A student describes his class as recreative and rejuvenating especially after the strain of the class in dogmatic theology.[71]

Once his compendium was published Sabetti did not want his students to take notes in class. He frequently reminded them, in Latin of course, that it is all in the textbook. No problem, just read the text. He would often propose cases and then seek their help in solving them. He encouraged their responses by saying they had started out right but now they had to develop their answers. If the students should start down the wrong path, he quickly tried to bring them back. He bantered easily in Latin and often sprinkled his remarks with humor. He enjoyed it immensely when the students responded to this humor. His enthusiasm and lively classes endeared him even more to his students. His approach contrasted sharply with the lecture format apparently used by most of his colleagues in this Jesuit seminary.[72] Students were even disappointed when occasionally for some reason or another the moral class was canceled on a particular day.[73]

On the other hand Sabetti's characteristic clarity, precision, and order together with his practical concerns and lack of deeper scholarly interests contributed to the negative qualities often associated with the manuals of moral theology. The Woodstock Jesuit was not interested in the theological and philosophical grounding of the principles of moral theology. His forte was to reduce and condense what others wrote to deal more adequately with the practical realities of moral theology. As a result the more speculative and theoretical aspects of moral theology received little or no discussion. In addition, the penchant for clarity and precision tends to reduce the role of human prudence. Everything is spelled out down to the most minute detail. Cases are looked upon as objective dilemmas but the whole subjective attitude of the person is neglected. The moral theologian provides clear and precise answers that the confessor can then give to the penitent. Recall that Sabetti often described his role as giving solutions to his students.

His own writings and the writings of others tell us about his theology and something about him as a person and a teacher. What about his broader understanding of the church and the world and his approach to the significant issues of his times? Unfortunately no published sources are available here. However, indirectly one can get some idea about his own approach to the vexing questions of late nineteenth-century American Catholicism.

Sabetti joined the faculty of Woodstock College in 1871 and taught there for twenty-eight years.[74] Woodstock had been founded in 1869 and the first faculty involved a good number of Neapolitan Jesuits. Mention has already been made of Camillo Mazella and De Augustinis. The Neapolitan Jesuits, of which Sabetti was one, were staunch ultramontanists in their support for both the temporal and the spiritual power of the papacy. They opposed the *risorgimento* forces in Italy that tried to take away the temporal power of the papacy. Recall that much of Sabetti's training was interrupted and changed because of the difficult conditions in Italy leading to the pope's loss of temporal power even in Rome in 1870.

In the United States Woodstock became identified with the ultramontanist pro-papal position. Mazella, the professor of dogma, was a strong proponent of neoscholasticism and opposed any attempt to dialogue with modern philosophical approaches. Mazella was chosen to succeed John Baptist Franzelin as the professor of dogma at the

Gregorian University in Rome after the pope made Franzelin a cardinal. Mazella himself later became a cardinal. Thus in thinking and ecclesiology Woodstock was squarely in the neoscholastic camp.[75] In sacred scripture Anthony Maas and his colleague James Conroy strongly opposed the new historical criticism and higher criticism. Woodstock in the late nineteenth century was a bastion of reaction and stood in contrast to the more liberally oriented Catholic University of America in the 1890s.[76] Woodstock faculty generally opposed the liberal Americanizing of John Ireland. For example, Father René Holaind, S.J., wrote a refutation of Thomas J. Bouquillon's defense of the principles supporting Archbishop John Ireland's position on working out a cooperative venture with public education.[77]

One can surmise without too much fear of error that Sabetti with his Neapolitan Jesuit background and his long association with Woodstock shared such sentiments. He too would be an ultramontanist, opposed to the separation of church and state, fearful of the modern liberties and new developments in the intellectual and scientific world. In the light of the overview of Sabetti, his work and his times, this study will now analyze and criticize his moral theology.

THE MORAL MODEL

Contemporary theologians talk about three different models for moral theology—the deontological, the teleological, and the relationality-responsibility model.[78] Obviously if all approaches to moral theology are reduced to just these three models each model must embrace many different approaches which in some ways are even mutually contradictory. Not all moral theologians even on the contemporary scene deal explicitly with the question of the ethical model they are using, but in reality all approaches will use one or another of these models as the primary way of understanding the moral life.

Sabetti does not explicitly consider the question of models but he obviously follows the deontological model. The deontological model sees the moral life primarily in terms of duty and obligation. Sabetti structures his development of moral theology on the basis of a law model. This legal model is common to all the manuals and coheres very well with their purpose which is to point out sinful acts and their degree of sinfulness.

The first three short treatises in the compendium clearly show forth the legal model at work in this manual as in all manuals. The first treatise discusses human acts, the second, conscience, and the third, laws. The very nature of the matters discussed here, as well as the fact they are the first three matters considered, shows the legal model at work. However, Sabetti could have been even more explicit about the model he is using if he had not chosen to eliminate the very first introductory paragraphs found in Gury-Ballerini's discussion of human acts and laws. Sabetti apparently left them out in his attempt to shorten the discussion, but they are very important short paragraphs because they explain the basic framework of the approach taken. The first paragraph introducing human acts maintains that since moral theology concerns the proper evaluation of human acts, the nature of things and common custom calls for the book to begin with a discussion of human acts.[79] The introductory paragraph on law succinctly states that law is the external and remote rule of human acts just as conscience as the dictate of reason is the internal and proximate rule of human acts.[80] Sabetti, with his penchant for clarity might have done better to retain these two short introductions which explicitly give the reason for treating these three topics at the very beginning of the manual and explain the legal model employed. Sabetti himself, near the beginning of his discussion of conscience, points out that conscience is the proximate rule of the will.[81] The fourth tract treats sins, and in keeping with the legal model, Sabetti defines sin as the free transgression of any law binding in conscience.[82]

This legal model dictates the basic approach taken not only in the short discussion of the fundamentals of morality but also in the consideration of particular moral acts. The major discussion of the morality of human acts, for example, follows common practice. It employs the schema of the ten commandments with each commandment developed on the basis of the sins opposed to the commandment. In discussing the first commandment, for example, Sabetti begins by pointing out that this commandment, insofar as it is affirmative, prescribes the acts of the virtue of religion, specifically the obligations of adoration and prayer. The purpose and model of the manual dictate how these realities are treated. Prayer must constitute an important part of the life of the Christian person. One would expect to see both adoration and prayer as the response of the Christian to the gift of God's loving self in Jesus through the Spirit. But the one page consideration is interested only in the legal and minimal aspects. Sabetti makes two statements about prayer. The first treats the necessity of prayer. Prayer is certainly necessary for all adults by a necessity of precept as is evident from many texts in the scriptures. In addition, according to most authorities, prayer is also necessary by a necessity of means because it is the ordinary way instituted by God for attaining graces.[83]

The above first statement made by Sabetti about prayer deserves some comment. Something is necessary by a necessity of means if it is required by the nature of things to achieve a necessary goal. Something is required by a necessity of precept if one is commanded to do it by a competent authority. In this case the first reason for the necessity of prayer is the precept found in the bible. A legal model tends to make the will of the legislator the primary source of obligation. Sabetti does mention that most authorities hold to the obligation of prayer as a necessity of means, but the emphasis here is not on the internal reasons why prayer is necessary as a means to the end but simply that most authorities hold it to be so. The one and only reason that prayer is considered by most to be required by a necessity of means concerns the need to obtain the necessary graces. But even at this time Catholic theology did not reduce prayer to supplication for the necessary graces to live a Christian life. Prayer involves adoration, contrition, and thanksgiving as well as supplication. In the light of the narrow purpose of the manuals these other aspects of prayer are not mentioned. Prayer becomes merely a means to obtain the necessary grace to obey the law.

Today one rightly rejects such an approach and understanding. The Christian life involves our loving union with a gracious God who comes to us. Prayer is an absolutely necessary means to perceive, receive, and grow in that union with God. The very nature of the Christian life calls for prayer. Prayer is not something established primarily by a precept or command coming from the outside but arises from the very nature of the Christian life itself. A legalistic approach easily becomes extrinsic and sees something to be good because it is commanded. However, prayer is commanded because it is good intrinsically and necessary for the Christian life. The Christian life is distorted if its obligations are seen primarily as coming from an external power not based on the intrinsic meaning and unfolding of the reality itself. Sabetti and the manualists in general put heavy emphasis on morality as obedience to an external authority who in this case is God who commands us to do certain things.

The legal model in moral theology tends to emphasize the role of human acts in salvation and forgets that salvation is primarily God's gracious gift. Historically such an approach has been identified with the heresies of pelagianism and semipelagianism. We save ourselves by our own works. According to the brief treatment in this text we should do the act of human praying in order to obtain the divine grace to avoid sins and be saved. Note that the human act of prayer comes before divine graces! Thus one sees in this discussion of prayer the dangers of legalism, extrinsicism, and a tendency to downplay and subordinate the divine gift and God's grace.

Sabetti's second statement about prayer records the need to pray frequently but that does not mean without interruption, for that is impossible given human weakness. The biblical words from Luke 18 about praying always mean to pray frequently and at the opportune time. The two questions raised in this one page discussion of prayer have to do with when the precept to pray obliges. Per accidens, the obligation to pray arises whenever prayer is necessary to attain a certain end. Clearly the precept to pray obliges per se often and frequently in our life. However, the experts are greatly divided over when this obligation arises. In practice one can hold the opinion maintaining that one who prays at least once a year does not commit a grave sin. Notice here the tendency to become minimalistic because of a hesitancy to convict a certain act of being a mortal sin. To his credit, Sabetti, following Gury-Ballerini, points out that the confessor should be more solicitous about inculcating in the penitent the necessity of praying frequently than in determining a grave fault when prayer is omitted. Sabetti, following his guide, also raises a question that was still common among Catholic children (and even adults) in the pre-Vatican II American church—does one sin at least venially by not saying morning and night prayers? The short, precise and clear response is this: per se one does not sin because there is no law which prescribes determined prayers at particular times or days. Here again, the primacy is on the law as the force of obligation and law understood as something external to the lived reality.[84]

The first commandment in addition to prescribing certain acts also forbids certain acts which are then discussed under the two headings of superstition and irreligiosity. In keeping with the precision of the manuals these terms are first defined and the various types of superstition and irreligiosity are discussed. Superstition is, according to Aquinas, the vice opposed to the virtue of religion by excess either because it gives divine worship to someone or thing to which it is not due (the more common form) or gives divine worship in an inappropriate way or manner. Four species of superstition are succinctly defined and discussed. Idolatry is the action by which the worship due to God alone is given to a creature. Vain observance is a superstition that uses means that are neither proportionate nor instituted by God to achieve a certain effect. The three types of vain observance are seeking knowledge without labor, seeking health by inappropriate means, or seeking assurance from the observance of fortuitous events that one will have good or bad luck in the future. The above is a paraphrase of Sabetti but shows the clear mind at work and the concise and precise way in which the material is discussed.

These same attributes are present in the discussion of the nature and gravity of vain observance. Vain observance is a grave sin because it gives divine honor to a creature while expecting from the creature what one should expect from God alone and because it is based on an implicit pact with the devil. However, it will often be only a venial sin because of its imperfection, simplicity, or because a certain ignorance or timidity accompanies it as often happens among uneducated people.[85] Here the author clearly recognizes the many factors that in practice make this only a light or venial sin. In a similar way Sabetti discusses divination and magic.[86] The contemporary reader is struck by the frequency with which these considerations involve the work of the devil. Belief in good and evil spirits still retains an important role in Sabetti's manual in the late nineteenth-century United States.

The entire elaboration of the ten commandments, consuming almost one hundred pages, follows the legal model and clearly illustrates this method at work. After the ten commandments Sabetti treats in the customary way of the manuals the commandments or precepts of the church. Sabetti mentions in the beginning that different enumerations of these binding commands are found in different sources but there is not much difference with regard to substance. Sabetti here follows the number and wording of these commandments that had been formally adopted by the Third Plenary Council of Baltimore in 1884. The six precepts of the church are (1) to hear mass on Sundays and feast days, (2) to observe fasting and abstinence on certain days, (3) to confess sacramentally at least once a year, (4) to receive the eucharist (communion) in paschal time, (5) to contribute to the fitting support of the pastor, and (6) to abstain from the celebration of marriage in those circumstances forbidden by the church.[87] This discussion takes up almost twenty pages, but the material about marriage is discussed in the later section on the sacraments and not here.[88]

The legal model certainly encouraged the development of such a list of church commandments to go along with the ten commandments of God. These commandments then become the means that the faithful use to examine their consciences before going to the sacrament of penance.[89] Note that here Sabetti, following the ordering of the Third Council of Baltimore, differs from that proposed by Gury-Ballerini. Gury-Ballerini treats commandments of the church but makes distinct commandments of hearing mass on feast days and Sundays and also of observing fasting and abstinence and leaves out the commandments of supporting the pastor and obeying the marriage laws of the church.[90]

The tenth and last tract before the long discussion of the sacraments continues to flesh out and illustrate the legal model by discussing particular obligations. The first part, comprising eight pages, deals with the particular obligations of lay people.[91] Sabetti notes that he will treat primarily those obligations relating to the public good and especially to legal matters. Other roles of the laity such as workers, merchants, and teachers are discussed elsewhere in the book. Thus he discusses the obligations of judges, lawyers, defendants, and witnesses. A final short section discusses the obligations of doctors. Here again, for example, he states the general obligations of doctors clearly and concisely and then develops further ramifications. Doctors are responsible under grave obligation to have sufficient knowledge and skill and to use diligence proportionate to the gravity of the matter. If doctors are deficient in these things, they are accountable for all the damage that follows from their acts. In addition, doctors should gratuitously help the poor who are in need.[92] Much of the discussion focuses on the obligations of clerics and religious.[93] The short discussion given to the particular obligations of the laity in comparison to clerics and religious indicates the greater importance and emphasis given to the clerical and religious life as well as the tendency of the manuals to emphasize church laws which are more numerous with regard to religious and clerics.

There are two tracts in the entire book apart from the treatment of the sacraments that do not seem at first sight to follow from and be structured by the legal model. The fifth tract deals with the virtues. Virtue is defined as the habit of acting according to right order. Theological virtues, (faith, hope, and charity) have God as their immediate formal object, whereas the moral virtues have the correctness of the action as their immediate formal object. The moral virtues can be reduced to the four cardinal virtues of prudence, justice, fortitude, and temperance. This section, however, discusses only the theological virtues because the moral virtues are discussed throughout the other parts of the compendium.[94] In the beginning of the discussion of faith, Sabetti mentions that he will not consider faith as it is treated in dogmatic theology but will discuss only the necessity of faith, the formal logic of faith, and the vices opposed to faith. Thus the treatise is not about the virtue of faith but about the acts of faith. The necessity of faith discusses both the internal and external acts of faith that are required. The material object again deals with the act of faith. The vices opposed to faith are the two acts of infidelity and heresy.[95] Thus the discussion of the virtue of faith is really a discussion of the acts of faith precisely under the legal rubric of what is required and when and also the acts opposed to faith. Sabetti discusses hope and charity in the same way.[96] So despite its title the tract deals with acts in the light of what is prescribed or prohibited. The legal model has totally influenced the way that Sabetti treats the theological virtues.

Tract VIII on justice and rights constitutes the longest discussion on strictly ethical matters, prescinding from the sacraments.[97] The discussion begins with the definition of justice and a description of the four kinds of justice. Legal justice inclines one to render to society what is required for the common good. Distributive justice regulates how the honor, offices, and common burdens are to be distributed among the members of society according to a due proportion of merits and abilities. Vindictive justice inclines the ruler to inflict appropriate punishments on the guilty for the good of society. (Sabetti here has not made the transition to the American scene but merely repeats the word *princeps,* used by Gury-Ballerini,[98] which is not accurate in the American scene) Commutative justice inclines the will to render a strict right to a private individual, that is, to observe the equality of thing to thing. By that is meant that commutative justice deals with the inherent arithmetical equality which is the same for all no matter who the persons are. After this discussion of the four kinds of justice Sabetti concludes that his book will treat only commutative justice because in the strict sense commutative justice alone merits to be called justice.[99]

The reason proposed by Sabetti for treating only commutative justice has been traditionally proposed in the Catholic tradition. Commutative justice involves a strict mathematical equality of what is due and what is given. The other types of justice aim at a proportional equality and therefore in theory are not strict justice. However, the real reason for not treating the other aspects of justice comes from the very nature of the manuals. They are geared to the confessor and the penitent and hence deal primarily with individual morality. The entire aspect of social ethics as distinguished from individual ethics is missing in these textbooks. Thus in Sabetti there is no discussion of the state, the political order, the economic order or cultural realities. All these aspects lie outside the parameters of the manuals of moral theology.

This individualistic orientation coheres very well with a legal model. The law determines what the individual should and should not do. Thus the discussion on justice does not consider all the ramifications of justice especially in terms of the relationship of society to the individual but considers just the relationship of one individual (note this could be a moral individual such as a corporation as well as a physical individual) to another individual. For all practical purposes the discussion on the virtue of justice really amounts to a discussion of the seventh and tenth commandments. Sabetti signaled this reality earlier in his treatment of the ten commandments. He skips the seventh and tenth commandments because the tract on justice and rights will discuss the "various sins of injustice" concerning property and possessions.[100]

Why did Gury-Ballerini, whom Sabetti followed, originally develop a separate treatise on justice when the matter more logically fits under the seventh and tenth commandments? The puzzlement grows in the light of the fact that Busenbaum and Alphonsus Liguori treated the material under the seventh and tenth commandments and did not have a separate consideration of justice.[101] We will probably never know why Gury-Ballerini did this. Perhaps the size of the treatise itself was a reason. This section is larger than the section on all the other commandments put together. But perhaps Gury-Ballerini was influenced by the sixteenth-century books on rights and justice which were significant commentaries on the work of Aquinas and the source for quite a bit of what is found in the manuals.

Sabetti devotes over three hundred pages to his discussion of the sacraments. The opening tract on the sacraments in general introduces separate tracts on each of the seven sacraments—baptism, confirmation, eucharist, penance, extreme unction, orders, and matrimony. The fundamental definitions are developed on the basis of a legal model. A sacrament is a sign permanently instituted by Christ to sanctify and confer grace.[102] The very definition is geared to examine the validity of the sacrament from a legal perspective. The primary question concerns what is required to truly constitute the sacrament. Contemporary theologians often speak of sacraments as encounters with God and the community but such understandings are difficult to analyze from a legal perspective.

The legal perspective is primary and focuses the entire discussion on sacraments. The basic questions concern validity (what is required so that the church acknowledges this reality as a true sacrament) and liceity (what is in keeping with the laws of the church but not affecting the basic validity of the sacrament). For example, the wearing of certain vestments might be required for liceity or the lawfulness of the sacrament but not for its validity. The discussions of the sacraments in general and of each of the individual sacraments follow the same general outline. The role of the sacraments in the life of the community and of the individual Christian is not mentioned. The whole spirituality of the sacramental life is missing. The legal perspective by definition deals with the minimum and with the minimum understood primarily in the light of visible external criteria.

Sabetti and the manualists first discuss the matter and form of the sacraments. The matter is the sensible reality determined by its form to become a sacrament. The form that determines the significance of the matter regularly consists in the words of the minister.[103] Thus, for example, in baptism the matter is the ablution with water and the form involves the words spoken by the minister, "I baptize you in the name of the Father and of the Son and of the Holy Ghost." The questions raised in this section concern what words are required for validity (e.g., is "I christen" a valid form?) and what material is truly water (e.g., what about snow?).[104]

The discussion of the sacraments in general next considers the minister of the sacrament who must have the proper attention (the attention required for a truly human act which is compatible with some distractions) and intention (a virtual intention but not a habitual or interpretive intention suffices for validity). Under this heading Sabetti repeats the general teaching that neither faith, nor probity of life, nor the state of grace is required on the part of the minister for a valid sacrament although they are required for a licit administration at least if the minister is consecrated to confer the sacrament and confers it solemnly in accord with the prescribed ritual.[105] Sabetti earlier mentioned the famous reason why the sacrament is valid without faith or the state of grace in the minister—the sacraments are said to work *ex opere operato*—by the very fact that the work or the sacrament has been done.[106] Thus if the matter and the form are present with the necessary attention and intention there is a valid sacrament. The discussion of each sacrament goes more specifically into the question of the minister of that particular sacrament. For example, the ordinary minister of confirmation is the bishop while a simple priest is the extraordinary minister.[107]

Sacraments in general then treats the subject in terms of both validity and lawfulness. In penance, for example, the discussion of the subject treats the three acts of the penitent—contrition, confession (with the requirement of the integral confession of sins according to number and species), and satisfaction.[108] The last part of the sacraments in general discusses the ceremonies in the administration of the sacraments.[109] Thus the discussion of the sacraments in general and of each individual sacrament follows the same basic approach about the requirements of validity and lawfulness with regard to matter and form, the minister, the subject of the sacrament, and the ceremonies.

The legal influence on the understanding of sacraments is even more pronounced with regard to marriage. Marriage is both a contract and a sacrament. As a contract marriage is an agreement by which a man and a woman legitimately give to each other dominion over their bodies for acts that are per se apt for the generation of offspring and obligate themselves to an indivisible partnership of life. As a sacrament marriage is a sacrament of the new law conferring grace for sanctifying the legitimate union of husband and wife and for faithfully undertaking progeny and educating them piously and virtuously.[110] However, the sacrament is understood primarily as a contract and the concept of contract pervades the whole treatise.

The Catholic church has developed an elaborate legal system to deal with marriage, and the centrality of the concept of contract underscores this legal approach. What is required for a valid contract? Church law developed a long list of impediments. Prohibitive impediments render the marriage contract unlawful but not invalid. Diriment impediments render the marriage null and void and include, for example, substantial error and consanguinity. Note that one can attain a dispensation from some impediments.[111] The church court system has been developed to deal with marriage annulments. The official Catholic position then and now holds to the indissolubility of marriage thus forbidding divorce and remarriage but marriage can be declared null and void if there is no true contract from the very beginning.

After the long treatment on the sacraments, Sabetti has two tracts (XIX and XX) on censures and irregularities. By definition these are legal realities discussed in canon law and developed accordingly by Sabetti and all the manualists.[112]

Thus Sabetti in keeping with all the manualists emphasizes a legal model and consistently and coherently develops the entire book on that basis. From the ethical perspective some of the negative aspects of such an approach have been mentioned—the emphasis on the individual, the minimal, the extrinsic, and human effort as distinguished from divine grace. The legal model also distorts the understanding of God and of the church. God is seen primarily as the lawgiver. The love, mercy, and forgiveness of God are mentioned, but they are subordinated to the role of God as lawgiver. God the lawgiver also provides the reward and sanction for the law. Often the fear of the sanction becomes more important than our love for God. The justice of God assumes a greater significance than the mercy of God. God's grace constitutes the primary reality in the Christian life but is here reduced to a means to obey the law. The legal model coheres well with the ultramontanist ecclesiology which stresses the church as a hierarchical society with the pope enjoying fullness of power. Such a model downplays the church as the people of God or even the body of Christ.

Positive features of the legal model also deserve mention. The legal mind at work in Sabetti and other manualists results in a very precise and concise approach. Definitions and concepts are clearly given. Important distinctions are delineated so that one can classify the different types of actions. Principles are enumerated in a very accurate and concise manner. The manuals stand out for their clear and orderly presentation. Such an approach has much to recommend it especially to the beginning student who is trying to learn a discipline for the first time.

A good illustration of both the ethical strengths and weaknesses of this approach comes from the object of the marital contract in the definition of marriage. Marriage is a contract in which the persons give to each other the mutual dominion over their bodies with regard to acts that are per se apt for generation and oblige themselves to a community of life.[113] This approach obviously coheres with the heavy emphasis on procreation and the downplaying of the love union of the couple. Love is a very difficult concept to explain or prove in legal terms. Acts per se apt for generation describe the external acts that tradition understands to be reserved for marriage alone, but it does not do justice to the full object of what is involved in marriage.

The phrase per se apt for generation serves as a model of brevity and precision. The act per se apt for generation describes the penetration of the penis in the vagina and the depositing of male seed there. (Note here the male perspective and the active role of the male vis-à-vis the passive role of the female.) The Catholic understanding of marriage had to deal with the important distinction between sterility and impotency. Antecedent and permanent impotency constitutes a diriment impediment. Such impotent people cannot marry. But the church has always allowed sterile people to marry. Think, for example, of older people. Sterile people can copulate, that is they can perform the act which is per se apt for generation by depositing male semen in the vagina of the female. In fact, all humans can do no more than that. Whether or not generation follows is another question.[114] This understanding recognizes the difference between the human act and the act of nature. Human beings must be able to copulate; that is, to place the human act. Nature takes over from there and ultimately determines whether or not there will be offspring. The phrase, acts per se apt for generation, thus shows a clear and a precise understanding which attempts to explain coherently and consistently some very complex aspects of the teaching on marriage. But the object of marriage involves much more than such acts.

SOURCES

As already indicated Sabetti's immediate and primary source is the third edition of Gury-Ballerini's manual. In fact, primary source is much too weak a term to describe Sabetti's dependence on Gury-Ballerini. However, Gury-Ballerini is not original either especially with regard to its basic purpose, structure, and content since it belongs to the literary genre of the manuals of moral theology. This genre developed from the Jesuit manuals at the beginning of the seventeenth century. All other sources in Sabetti must be seen in their subordination to the literary genre of the manuals of moral theology. One cannot understand the use of these other sources except insofar as they fit into the genre of the moral manual.

Sabetti himself never explicitly talks about his sources except for the few names he mentions in his short preface to the reader.[115] Sabetti is so absorbed with the practical work that he is doing that he never steps back to tell the reader about either his method or his sources. Many later manuals inserted a short introduction dealing with the nature of the discipline and its sources.[116] Since Sabetti does not reflect on his sources, our analysis of them is based on how he actually uses them in his manual.

SCRIPTURE. Sacred scripture constitutes a very significant source for the theological enterprise in general. However, for Sabetti in particular and the manualists in general, scripture does not play an important role. Scripture does give us the ten commandments which are used as the primary outline for dealing with the morality of particular acts, but their use fits into the legal model based on the eternal law, divine positive law, and natural law. In discussing the morality of acts and their sinfulness the manual, in keeping with the Catholic tradition, places heavy emphasis on the use of reason and the natural law. Natural law principles generally govern the discussion. The scriptures do talk about certain acts as being right or wrong and these passages are often quoted. However, the scriptures do not shape the overall structure of the manual and are not the primary source used in the discussion of particular issues. The scriptures are often used as proof texts to support a point that is made on other grounds. There is no critical understanding of the scriptures themselves and usually no recognition of diverse historical and cultural circumstances between scriptural times and nineteenth-century realities. These approaches to and uses of scripture are illustrated throughout the compendium.

The very first treatise in the compendium discusses human acts. By definition such a discussion will be based primarily on reason. As expected, scripture plays a very marginal and insignificant role in this discussion. The first scripture quote from Romans 3:8 appears on page six.[117] The author is here discussing what later becomes known as the principle of the double effect. The third condition states that the good effect should follow at least equally immediately as the evil effect. The reason is that if the cause directly and immediately has a bad effect and the good effect occurs only by means of the bad effect, then good comes from evil. But it is never right to do evil no matter how small in order to procure some good. The well known axiom taken from the apostle (Rom 3:8) maintains that evil is not to be done in order that good may come from it.

In this entire discussion on human acts the scriptural quotations are almost nonexistent, have no real import on the discussion, and appear in a haphazard way without any systematic justification. Sabetti employs a scriptural citation in the discussion about the morality of acting for pleasure alone. To eat and drink to satiety for pleasure is not per se a grave deordination and does not exceed a venial sin. Two reasons are given. First, the person in eating and drinking seeks a good not an evil, but does this in an improper way. Second, such a person ordinarily does not make the improper way of seeking the good the ultimate end of one's life as is the case with those the apostle mentioned in Philippians 3:19 "whose god is their belly."[118]

Near the end of the treatise on human acts Sabetti raises the question whether all actions are commanded to be referred to God in accord with the command of the apostle in 1 Corinthians 10:31: all things should be done for the glory of God. There is no obligation to actually and explicitly refer all our actions to the glory of God. These words of scripture are to be understood as a counsel and not a command or in a negative sense as meaning you should do nothing against God.[119] Very frequently the Catholic tradition has used that distinction between command and counsel to deal with scriptural injunctions, but Sabetti has no separate discussion about counsels as such.

One would naturally expect to find a greater use of scripture in certain treatises such as the treatise on the theological virtues. This is the case, but again scripture is not used in a systematic and consistent way. The proof text approach again stands out. The discussion of faith begins with the necessity of faith. The basic principle states that the internal act of faith is necessary for justification for all adults with a necessity of means and is also required by a necessity of precept sometimes in one's life. The first part is evident from the teaching of the apostle in Hebrews 11:6, that without faith it is impossible to please God; and from the Council of Trent, session six, chapter six, where the way of preparation for justification is described and faith is listed among other necessary requirements. The second part rests on the first proposition condemned by Alexander VII which maintains that the human person at no time in one's life is held to make an act of faith, hope, or charity by force of the divine precepts pertaining to these virtues. This precept is both negative, prohibiting one to deny the true faith, and affirmative in obliging one sometimes to profess faith even with fear of the danger of losing one's life. The reason for the negative obligation is because denying faith is denying God's very self. The reason for the positive obligation is that the honor due Christ sometimes demands that the faithful profess their faith in Christ even if they might lose their lives. Christ himself says in Luke 9:26 that if a person is ashamed of me, the Son of Man will be ashamed of that person when he comes in majesty. Especially in dealing with questions and cases about when the act of faith is required no scripture citations are employed. Instead Sabetti appeals to reasoning about the precept, to the condemnations of Innocent XI, and to the position of older theologians.[120] One would not expect to find much use of scripture here for the scriptures seldom deal explicitly with the minimum requirements of the Christian life. Scripture is used to support the basic obligation of faith but the development and expansion of that obligation especially in terms of its minimal requirements do not depend on scriptural support.

One finds the same general approach in Sabetti's discussion of charity. The first article establishes the special obligation of loving God above all from the words of Christ in Matthew 22:37: "you shall love the Lord your God with your whole heart . . . this is the greatest and the first commandment"; and from the first proposition condemned by Alexander VII.[121] The juxtaposition of the great love command of Jesus with the papal condemnation is rather jarring, since the condemned proposition states that one never has to make an act of charity by reason of the divine precept pertaining to this virtue.

The treatment of loving one's neighbor is most surprising. Sabetti states that there is an obligation of loving the neighbor truly and with an internal affect. This obligation is proved from the natural law because in the neighbor the same formal motive of love exists—namely, the participative goodness of God, for all people are created in God's image and capable of receiving the friendship of God and divine beatitude. The obligation is also proved from proposition ten, condemned by Innocent XI, which maintains that one is not held to love the neighbor with an internal and formal act.[122] The second part of the love command of Jesus found in the scriptures and probably the best known of all the commands of Jesus is not used to support the obligation to love the neighbor!

Scripture is invoked in the condemnation of contraception which even goes by the name of onanism. Sabetti points out that the name comes from Onan who was under obligation to his dead brother to raise up a child for his brother with the brother's wife. Onan spilled his seed on the ground, however, and did not fulfill what was required, and therefore God struck him because he had done a detestable deed. Sabetti assumes that the text forbids all contraceptive intercourse.[123]

REASON. Human reason is a very important source of moral wisdom and knowledge for Sabetti and the manualists in general. Reason is at work in developing the structure of the manual, and it is reason that makes this textbook very coherent and consistent in its approach. The proper object of moral theology is the morality of human acts and the analysis of the component parts and aspects of human acts is the work of human reason (as will be analyzed later). The compendium constantly tries to clarify its position by making important distinctions.

No concept is mentioned without various distinctions to make clear and precise what is involved. The important distinction between positive and negative precepts with their different types of obligations has been frequently mentioned in these pages. Whenever the author states a principle or a norm (under the heading "I say") reasons are given to support the principle or norm. These reasons can include citations from sacred scripture or church documents and an explicit reference to natural law, or they may give only human reason to justify the principle or norm. The method of discussing particular cases and deciding on their morality involves a sensitive practical reasoning process. A later section will analyze the method of casuistry used by Sabetti and others.

Very often Sabetti asserts that a particular principle or norm is based on the natural law. Often he will succinctly give the reasons why this is so. The natural law constitutes a distinctive Catholic approach to morality and no one should be surprised to find its frequent use in Sabetti. However, in keeping with the very pragmatic and ministerial purpose of the manual the theoretical discussion of natural is short indeed. Contemporary readers are not prepared to see the natural law discussed in just one page![124]

Sabetti defines the natural law in accord with Thomas Aquinas as the participation of the eternal law in the rational creature. He expands that definition to say that the natural law is the necessary divine command manifested by the natural light of reason commanding the right order to be observed and forbidding it to be disturbed. Here again Sabetti moves away from Aquinas's emphasis on law as an ordering of reason to law as a command of God's will obligating the rational creature to observe the essential relations of the human being to God, to oneself, and to the neighbor because otherwise God would contradict God's self.[125] The object of the natural law insofar as it is a prohibiting law are intrinsically evil actions or actions that directly go against those relations; insofar as it is a prescriptive law, it commands intrinsically good acts. The negative acts fall under the precept at all times; the positive acts only fall under the precept when the essential order would be violated if they were not done.[126]

Note how Sabetti reduces the object of natural law to commands prohibiting or prescribing intrinsically evil or good acts. However, this is not the position of Aquinas who sees the natural law as based on God ordering all things. In fact, in the very next paragraph Sabetti contradicts himself. Here he raises the question whether one can not know the object of the law of nature. The primary precepts of the natural law, for example, good is to be done, evil is to be avoided, do not do to another what you would not wish to be done to you, are known to all. Likewise the proximate conclusions of the natural law such as most principles of the decalogue cannot be unknown except rarely or for a brief time in youngsters and the uneducated. However, one cannot know and often does not know the remote conclusions of the natural law as is evident from the many controversies that exist among theologians.[127] Here the natural law includes remote conclusions about which people can disagree and not just intrinsically evil or good acts. By reducing the natural law at times to dealing with just intrinsically evil or good acts one sees again the force of the legal model at work.

Thus Sabetti's discussion on natural law is minimal, superficial, confused, and basically not in conformity with Thomas Aquinas notwithstanding that he cites Aquinas three times during this less than one full page discussion.

Sabetti's approach to particular questions shows how often he invokes natural law in terms of principles or norms that are intrinsically evil or good, (thus showing again how his practical concerns have colored his more theoretical positions and even led him to distort the teaching of Aquinas) and how he assigns reason to support these precepts or norms. His discussion of the fifth commandment furnishes a good example. The first chapter under the fifth commandment discusses suicide. No one can directly kill oneself but sometimes one can indirectly concur in one's own death. The reason for the first principle is that according to the natural law the human being does not have direct dominion or power over one's own body but only that useful dominion and administration that he or she has received from God. The human being is essentially a servant related to God and the condition of being a servant means that it is not in the power of the servant to determine one's time of service. The second principle permitting indirect killing is based on the principle of an act having two effects which has already been explained.[128]

The first resolution maintains that no one can mutilate oneself except if it is necessary for the conservation of the whole body because a human being does not have dominion over her members but is only the custodian. Sabetti briefly describes here what later became known as the principle of totality which plays an important role in Catholic medical ethics. According to this principle a part may be sacrificed for the good of the whole because the part by its very nature exists for the good of the whole. In this context Sabetti gives a concise discussion about ordinary means. The affirmative obligation to care for one's life does not demand that one do everything possible but rather that one use ordinary means to care for life. Ordinary means are those that do not involve great burdens, an enormous expense related to the financial condition of the person, or cause quite severe suffering.[129] Later Catholic theologians developed at great length this notion of ordinary means but Sabetti here succinctly states the core reality. Sabetti justifies capital punishment with a syllogism and claims that this reasoning is supported by the practice of legislation and by the universal consent of all. God, the author of society, has given to society all the means necessary to conserve itself and to procure the common good. But among these means the death of certain criminals is often mentioned. *Ergo....* *Ergo* is followed by an ellipsis because the reader can readily supply the conclusion of this syllogism.[130]

The killing of an unjust aggressor, provided the proper limits are observed, is justified by canon law—*Si vero* 8, *de sent. excomm.* which states that all laws and rights permit one to repel force with force— and by natural law. Again, a syllogism is provided as a natural law proof. Everyone who has the right to preserve one's life also has the right to use those means that are necessary to achieve this end unless they are otherwise forbidden. But to kill an unjust aggressor when it is the only way of saving one's own life does not violate the certain rights of the other, for if the aggressor freely and willingly calls into danger the life of another that aggressor cannot retain the right to his own life over against the certain rights of the innocent victim.[131] The principles and norms proposed by Sabetti are often justified by explicit appeal to the natural law with a brief explanation of the reason in the form of a syllogism. Note that other reasons are given in the form of authorities—scripture, canon law, or church documents. Great importance is given to the role of reasoning in determining these principles and norms.

EXPERIENCE. What about experience as a source of moral wisdom? Sabetti does not often appeal to experience although at times he will mention the common consent of people.[132] He also recognizes that custom and the common estimation of human beings constitute an excellent way for determining the servile work prohibited on Sunday.[133] The reader should not be surprised by the scarcity of appeals to human experience as a source of ethical wisdom. Human experience is often invoked in dealing with changing realities. In the new circumstances the older norms and approved ways of acting no longer seem adequate. At heart, however, Sabetti and the manualists do not accept that kind of change. In his preface, Sabetti willingly recognized the different customs and needs in this country, but the whole book indicates that basic principles and norms do not change. They are based on natural law and human reason. Such an understanding stresses the eternal, the immutable, and the unchanging and gives little place to the particular, the contingent, and the changing.

One obvious place to look for a change in principle based on American experience would be the understanding of the separation of church and state and the American insistence on political freedoms. Here the American experience was quite different from the continental and especially the ultramontanist experience in Italy and Rome. However, in its long tract on justice Sabetti's compendium leaves out any consideration of legal or distributive justice and does not discuss the political order at all. In fact, at that time at Woodstock the question of church and state was treated in the courses taught by Camillo Mazella, the professor of dogmatic theology. Mazella with the same Neapolitan Jesuit and ultramontanist background as Sabetti strongly maintained the need for the union of church and state. Students publicly defended this position at Woodstock in disputations. In fact, Cardinal Gibbons at one of these public events gently prodded the student about whether or not this theory was applicable in the United States. In this whole area the Jesuit faculty at Woodstock often opposed the Americanizing tendencies of the liberal wing of the American church as represented by Archbishop Ireland, Bishop Keane, to some extent Cardinal Gibbons, and by the administration and many faculty of the newly founded Catholic University of America.[134] Sabetti never dealt with such issues in his published writings, but it is safe to say he probably agreed with the position of his colleague with whom he shared so much. At least in his moral theology he gave no consideration to experience as a source of moral wisdom calling for a change in existing principles, concepts, or norms; for him, these moral realities are timeless and eternal and therefore experience is apparently irrelevant. At best experience in some cases helps to interpret the law.

CHURCH TEACHING. A fourth source of moral wisdom comes from church teaching as found in official documents of the hierarchical church. One type of church teaching involves church law. In the light of the legal model followed in the compendium one expects to find a heavy emphasis on church law; and such is the case especially in those treatises such as the sacraments that directly involve church law. For example, the long segment on the impediments of marriage naturally depends heavily on such law. The last treatise in Sabetti's manual which deals with censures has an appendix on indulgences and runs over ninety pages. Censures by definition are spiritual and material penalties by which a delinquent and contumacious baptized person is deprived of some spiritual goods by the power of the church. The entire treatise is thus based on the explanation and interpretation of church law.[135]

Recall that Sabetti wrote before the code of canon law was drawn up and made effective in 1918. Sabetti cites the older *Corpus Juris Canonici* which embraced six different parts. He also recognized that the constitutions of councils such as Trent and the constitutions of popes are included in church law.[136] Trent is mentioned especially in the discussion of the sacraments since that council dealt with so many of these issues.

One of the functions of moral theologians was to explain and interpret new documents that came from Rome. Sabetti, for example, wrote a commentary in the *American Ecclesiastical Review* on the decree *Quemadmodum* which was promulgated on December 17, 1890. This decree dealt with abuses in religious life centering on the manifestation of conscience, the recourse to extraordinary confessors, and the frequency of holy communion. The purpose of Sabetti's commentary is to make a few notes on its bearing and meaning and to solve some difficulties of interpretation that may arise.[137]

What is surprising is to find appeal to church legal sources as reasons justifying positions with regard to morality, as distinguished from legality. Recall, for example, that the legitimacy of killing in self-defense is justified in the first instance by canon law and then by the natural law.[138] This order indicates the great influence of church law over all aspects of morality.

With regard to the specifically moral aspects as distinguished from legal aspects Sabetti frequently appeals to the official teaching of the church. Although the Gury-Ballerini manual begins with a chronological list of all condemned propositions from 1418 to the *Syllabus of Errors* in 1864, [139] Sabetti does not begin his book with such a long listing since it would be against his attempt to shorten Gury-Ballerini. However, the American seminary professor clearly gives great import to these authoritative interventions and to the increasing role of the Roman congregations.

Sabetti's discussion of abortion shows the significant role of the Roman congregations. Three different historical issues arose—craniotomy, the acceleration of birth, and ectopic pregnancy. Sabetti was personally involved in these three controversies and very familiar with their historical development. He very clearly distinguished these three issues.[140] A much more thorough and recent history of these debates is told by John Connery, [141] but Sabetti gives a very detailed analysis of them.

Craniotomy as a way to save the mother's life in dire situations was beginning to be used by some doctors in the nineteenth century. At this time Caesarean section was not considered safe so the operation generally was not performed. Two influential Italian theologians, Peter Avanzini in 1872 and Joseph Pennacchi in 1884, both editors of the Vatican journal, *Acta Sanctae Sedis*, argued in favor of craniotomy if it were necessary to save the life of the mother. Sabetti reports four Roman interventions on this question. On November 28, 1872, the Sacred Penitentiary (which receives internal forum cases of conscience) responded to the question whether craniotomy could ever be accepted by saying that the approved authors should be followed. Sabetti admits that this response could reasonably be interpreted to mean that craniotomy was not condemned. On December 10, 1883, the Congregation for the Inquisition or the Holy Office (now called the Congregation for the Doctrine of the Faith) responded that it was still considering the issue of craniotomy. The same congregation responded to another query on May 31, 1884, saying it cannot be safely taught that craniotomy is lawful when both the mother and child will die without it. In 1889 the same congregation again repeated that the lawfulness of craniotomy cannot be safely taught and the same is true of whatever surgical operation that aims directly at the killing of the fetus or the pregnant mother.[142]

A second issue involved the acceleration of birth. To save the life of the mother can the doctor accelerate the birth of a nonviable fetus which will die outside the womb in a very short time? The German Jesuit, August Lehmkuhl, argued that such an action was not directly killing since it did not kill the fetus but only put it outside the womb where it could not live for long. However, the mother would be saved and the fetus could be baptized and guaranteed eternal salvation.[143] Sabetti disagreed with Lehmkuhl and argued that the action in this case is direct killing.[144]

In the light of the circumstances of the time and the tendency to ask Rome to give solutions to these complex questions, one would expect a question about this acceleration of birth to be sent to Rome. Archbishop Sonnois of Cambrai submitted precisely this case. The Congregation of the Holy Office responded in 1895, in accord with the decrees of 1884 and 1889, that the procedure could not be safely used.[145] This response came after Sabetti's 1894 and 1896 discussions had been written.

The third issue regarded the case of ectopic pregnancies—the fetus was outside the natural site of the uterus and was threatening the life of the mother. The *American Ecclesiastical Review* carried on a long discussion about this case beginning in 1893 including comments from many medical doctors and solutions proposed by three moral theologians—Joseph Aertnys, a Dutch Redemptorist; August Lehmkuhl; and Aloysius Sabetti.[146] Aertnys judged that the removal of the nonviable ectopic pregnancy was wrong. Lehmkuhl justified it on the basis of his theory of accelerated birth (this debate was before the 1895 condemnation). Sabetti strongly disagreed with Lehmkuhl's reasoning but came to somewhat the same conclusion on the basis that the ectopic pregnancy, precisely because it was where it should not be, was a materially unjust aggressor against the mother's life and could therefore be directly removed or killed. Sabetti was adamant that in no way was he justifying craniotomy and if his opinion in the ectopic pregnancy case caused others to favor craniotomy in other cases he would willingly repudiate his position.[147] The Holy Office intervened in 1898 in a somewhat guarded manner and then more clearly in 1902: it is not licit to remove a nonviable ectopic fetus from the mother to save her life.[148] By that time Sabetti had died.

This history as lived out and participated in by Sabetti illustrates a very significant role in moral theology for the hierarchical magisterium and especially the pope and the Roman congregations. Theologians had been discussing all three issues. The congregations were somewhat hesitant and uncertain in the beginning. But within a comparatively short time the congregations, especially the Holy Office, solved the problems.

One could and should distinguish different levels even within the hierarchical teaching office. Many of these interventions on specific moral matters came from Roman congregations and not directly from the pope although often approved by the pope. However, there is a difference in authority between the two. Likewise one can speak about private responses that are directed to one person or area and public responses that are addressed to the whole church, and an important distinction exists between disciplinary and doctrinal interventions.[149]

The very legal model of morality used in the compendium brings morality under the category and aegis of law. In solving problems related to church law Sabetti and the other manualists of the time cited appropriate decrees and responses from the Roman congregations. It was quite natural to treat moral problems in the same way. The accepted term of teaching authority indicates how the judicial perspective colored the concept of teaching.

Aloysius Sabetti firmly believed that responses from Roman congregations settled the issues once and for all. In his commentary on the decree *Quemadmodum* of the Congregation of Bishops and Regulars (religious) of December 17, 1890, our author indicates his judgment about the authority of these documents. The Holy See makes its mind known through the various congregations.[150] Since the Roman congregations do not have legislative power by their own right, it follows that when they formulate a true law, as in this case, it is not the congregation that acts "but the Holy Father himself, who, in the exercise of his supreme power, makes use of the same congregation as a means to promulgate it. The binding power of this decree is thus the greatest; to disobey it would be a sin."[151] Note the use of superlatives—"supreme" and "greatest"—and the consequent erroneous understanding of papal teaching authority. Sabetti would readily admit that infallible teaching has a greater binding power.

In the question about abortion and craniotomy, Sabetti clearly recognizes the interventions of the congregation as solving the matter. Recall that on craniotomy the congregation replied that it cannot safely be taught that craniotomy to save the life of the mother is morally acceptable. Sabetti asserts "that an opinion which cannot safely be taught will never be held as probable by Catholic theologians."[152] He goes on to say that Rome "could not have spoken more clearly"—an obvious exaggeration in the light of the very wording of the document. Before these statements some Catholic theologians such as Lehmkuhl had proposed tentative solutions accepting craniotomy, but in his later edition Sabetti points out that Lehmkuhl, taking his inspiration from Rome, as every true theologian does, clearly condemns craniotomy.[153] In his compendium Sabetti briefly states that at one time authority was doubtful and tenuous about craniotomy but now it is certain.[154]

How would Sabetti have reacted to the response of the Holy Office that the ectopic pregnancy could not be removed as a material unjust aggressor—a position he held before his death and before the decree that condemned it? Without any doubt Sabetti would have accepted this and changed his opinion. He would do exactly what

Lehmkuhl did with regard to craniotomy. Not only did Lehmkuhl change his position on craniotomy but also on the issue of the acceleration of the birth of a nonviable fetus. Lehmkuhl in later editions admits he did not think it appropriate in a somewhat doubtful and controverted matter to insist on an obligation against accelerating birth in these cases threatening the life of the mother until such an obligation would become clear or the church would judge on the matter. Now he accepts the decision of the congregation that this cannot be safely taught.[155] Sabetti, with his understanding of the teaching authority of Roman congregations and his praise for Lehmkuhl's change of position, would have done the same thing in his case.

Sabetti's ultramontanism comes to the fore in his recognition of the role played by the Roman congregations in determining the morality of particular acts. His discussion of the authoritative papal teaching function is unnuanced and even distorted. Responses from the Holy Office solve disputed issues. Debate or doubt can no longer exist.

THEOLOGIANS. What about the theologians on whom Sabetti depends? In addition to Gury-Ballerini, the two other authors most cited by Sabetti are Thomas Aquinas and Alphonsus with the latter being cited more frequently.

One would expect Sabetti to follow Aquinas quite closely. The Jesuits, the Italian Jesuits, and the Woodstock faculty were strong supporters of the return to Thomas Aquinas in the nineteenth century and the neoscholasticism of Pope Leo XIII.

John A. Gallagher refers to the theology of the neo-Thomist manuals of moral theology and devotes two chapters to studying them. Gallagher here is heavily dependent on McCool's analysis of nineteenth-century neo-Thomism and scholasticism. Neo-Thomistic moral theology was brought from Europe into the burgeoning American Catholic seminaries. These manuals, according to Gallagher, were composed from shortly before 1879 until Vatican II.[156] In his discussion of the neo-Thomistic manuals of moral theology, Gallagher mentions Sabetti on six different occasions.[157]

A reading of Sabetti confirms his heavy dependence on Thomas Aquinas. Sabetti cites only Alphonsus Liguori more than Aquinas. One can compare this with both Gury-Ballerini and Alphonsus. Alphonsus, for example, also gives a special emphasis to Aquinas but he cites many different authors even from medieval times and frequently lists the various authors who hold pro and con positions on a particular issue.

Sabetti leaves out many of these citations but frequently quotes Thomas Aquinas.

I am sure that neoscholasticism had some impact on Sabetti and on specific considerations in his compendium. In reality, however, neoscholasticism never had much substantial influence on the manuals of moral theology in general and on Sabetti in particular. Neoscholasticism did not affect the basic purpose, orientation, structure, and method of these manuals which remained fundamentally the same as they were before the rise of neoscholasticism. Previous chapters have shown how these manuals differed from the approach taken by Thomas Aquinas.

Thomas's whole approach to moral theology differs from the professional and ministerial purpose of Sabetti in preparing confessors for their work in the sacrament of penance with specific emphasis on the existence of sin and its gravity.

Extrinsic arguments make the same point that neoscholasticism did not really affect the manuals of moral theology with regard to their basic substance. Thomas J. Bouquillon of the Catholic University of America, a contemporary of Sabetti's, strongly criticized the manual tradition and implicitly Sabetti on the basis of a Thomistic understanding.[158] Many Thomists also criticized the manuals for not truly following the method and spirit of Aquinas.[159] Thus neoscholasticism did not have great effect on the basic substance, method, and approach of the manuals of moral theology.

It is true that many Thomistic notions are found in the manuals in general and in Sabetti in particular but their appearance antedates the rise of neoscholasticism in the nineteenth century. Gallagher, for example, points out the Thomistic approach to human acts, conscience, law, and the determinants of morality.[160] But all of these are found in Alphonsus Liguori and the earlier manuals. For example, Alphonsus's discussion of the human act and of the determinants of morality (object, end, and circumstances) depends very heavily on Aquinas. No one is cited more in these pages than Aquinas, and the treatment is basically the same, with some developments, as that found later in Sabetti.[161] As noted, the discussions on conscience and law actually do not follow the spirit and method of Aquinas. What Gallagher interprets as the effects of neo-Thomism actually come from the earlier genre of the manuals of moral theology which often cited Aquinas.

Neo-Thomism and the scholastic renewal under Kleutgen and Leo XIII had a significant impact on Catholic dogmatic theology but not that much on the manuals of moral theology. However, both dogmatic and moral theology were heavily influenced by the growing role of the ordinary magisterium in theology as already pointed out. Why did the rise of neoscholasticism not affect the manuals of moral theology?

The manuals of moral theology had been in existence for a very long time. They were the received literary genre. As long as moral theology was conceived as a preparation for the ministry of the sacrament of penance, this genre fit very well. The manuals of moral theology were quite insulated from many of the broader theological and philosophical discussions of the day. Moral theology became cut off from every other theological discipline and tended to have an existence of its own. This isolated and insulated existence meant that the manuals tended to keep going in their own way without any great change and with little influence from other disciplines and factors.

The philosophical basis of the manuals was sketchy and very shallow at best. Their concern was not with philosophy but with practical matters. In addition, recall that Alphonsus and other manualists frequently cited Aquinas more than any other theologian. They thought they were following Aquinas but they were dealing not with speculative theology but with practical considerations of human acts. The rise of neoscholasticism did not change the fundamental approaches which had been in place for some time and claimed to be in the tradition of Aquinas and Alphonsus.

The papacy in the nineteenth century authoritatively intervened to champion and endorse the approach of Thomas Aquinas in philosophy and dogmatic theology and of Alphonsus in moral theology. This papal action gave great prominence to both theologians and obviously supported the position that the two approved theologians followed the same basic method and approach. Extrinsic authority tended to combine and identify the two. But in reality very significant differences remained between the two approaches. Nor could one retain the unity by appealing to Thomas Aquinas in the scientific and theoretical area and Alphonsus in the pastoral and pragmatic area. As pointed out earlier the papal approbation tended to distort somewhat the positions of both Thomas and Alphonsus. Papal approbation also distorted the relationship between these two approaches and encouraged the erroneous position that the late nineteenth-century manuals of moral theology were neoscholastic.

In the preface to his compendium Sabetti refers to Alphonsus as the most wise doctor of the church in moral matters and professes and prides himself on being a disciple of Alphonsus.[162] However, a complication arises. Sabetti notes that he uses as a basis for his own compendium the third edition of Ballerini in which the Italian Jesuit responds to the difficulties of the *Vindiciae Alphonsianae*.[163] Sabetti is here referring to the controversy between Ballerini and some Redemptorists over the proper interpretation of Alphonsus. Ballerini, in his inaugural lecture at the Roman College (the Jesuit college later called the Gregorian University) in the 1863–1864 school year and in the notes to his earlier edition of Gury, had claimed that Alphonsus was a probabilist, not an equiprobabilist, and had criticized some aspects of Alphonsus's approach. Some Redemptorists thought that Ballerini wanted to deprive Alphonsus of his prestige as the most outstanding moral theologian and also feared that Ballerini's positions might be used to prevent Alphonsus being declared a doctor of the church. These Redemptorists responded to Ballerini in the *Vindiciae Alphonsianae*. A Belgian Jesuit, V. de Buck, in response published *Vindiciae Ballerinianae*. This defense of Alphonsus led to "Liguorianism" which distorted Alphonsus's own approach by making it more rigid and inflexible than it was.[164]

Sabetti was very much aware of the controversy and personally followed the interpretation of Ballerini. But he had to justify his position in the light of the official recognition given to Alphonsus so he added his own six page appendix to the treatment on conscience in which he dealt with the question of the authority of Alphonsus.[165]

Sabetti first argues that equiprobabilism is not the only reasonable and correct approach to follow. Then the American Jesuit raises the question whether it was historically true that Alphonsus was an equiprobabilist. Sabetti following Ballerini maintains that the founder of the Redemptorists was a simple probabilist. Alphonsus did not claim to create something new in this matter; he accepted the basic principles of probabilism; namely, an uncertain law cannot induce a certain obligation and a doubtful law does not oblige. Alphonsus explicitly said he was following probabilism on a number of occasions. In his later years Alphonsus did speak of equiprobabilism but this was to oppose laxism and to insist on a truly probable opinion.

Although at the very minimum Sabetti is not certain that Alphonsus was an equiprobabilist, it is still necessary to deal with the question whether one can depart from a position taken by Alphonsus. All agree that Alphonsus is the greatest authority in moral matters and his opinion can regularly be followed in determining when there is no obligation to follow a law. Regularly, but not always. Alphonsus himself held that it was more probable that there was no obligation to denounce a confessor who consents to a woman soliciting him in the confessional. But Alphonsus apparently did not know about the constitution of Pope Benedict XIV requiring a denunciation in this case. Thus, one can disagree with Alphonsus provided there is solid reason or the grave authority of other doctors and due moderation is observed. By its phrase "nothing worthy of censure" in Alphonsus and similar phrases the Holy See was not saying every position and opinion of Alphonsus was true for that would be to canonize his thought. The Holy See has not done this with either Thomas Aquinas or Alphonsus. In addition, Alphonsus was willing to disagree with some of the positions taken by Thomas Aquinas. Throughout the book Sabetti does occasionally disagree with a position taken by Alphonsus.

Nevertheless, Sabetti follows the approach of the manuals and of Alphonsus with regard to the model, method, and structure of moral theology. The legal model aims at determining which acts are sinful based on the commandments of God and the church. It is true to say that all manualists after Alphonsus followed this same approach, perhaps at times without the nuances and subtleties that brought Alphonsus closer to Aquinas—the role of the moral subject in the approach to conscience and the promulgation of law, the prudential nature of morality, and, in the light of his spiritual writings, the teleological drive of charity to God as the ultimate end.[166]

Other subtle differences exist between Alphonsus and Sabetti. The last chapter mentioned the thesis of Raphael Gallagher that manualists in the last half of the nineteenth century often failed to appreciate the nuances in Alphonsus's treatment of the small but very significant question of how confessors should treat the *consuetudinarius* (the person with a bad habit) and the *recidivus* (the person who keeps falling back into the same sin after each confession). This question had been a bone of contention between rigorists and laxists with Alphonsus proposing his middle way of benignity. The question is this: Should the confessor deny, give, or defer absolution in these cases?[167] The position of Sabetti in this matter, following Ballerini, is basically the same as that proposed by Alphonsus and favors the benign approach. The person with a bad habit who sincerely confesses a sin can be absolved immediately without any further proof of having changed his habit. A habit is only an inclination and not a sin. Ordinarily a recidivist who keeps falling into the same sin after each confession should not be absolved merely because he or she comes to confession. The mere fact of coming to confession does not give an efficacious hope of changing and avoiding the sin. In order to absolve the penitent the confessor must have the hope that the penitent will avoid the sin. However, the individual who gives extraordinary (but also understood as new and special) signs of sorrow can be absolved. These extraordinary, new, or special signs are then listed. Sabetti concludes that the confessor who acts with the spirit of God and love will hardly ever have to deny absolution because by persuasion and exhortation he can elicit these signs of sorrow even in the most obdurate of penitents.[168]

The words and formulas are basically the same as those Alphonsus used, but there are subtle differences of two types. First, Alphonsus refers on occasion to the deeper theological aspects of the question. Yes, the problem concerns the judgment made by the confessor about the disposition of the penitent to avoid sin, but in his much longer discussion Alphonsus recognizes the role of grace and its effect in the whole process. Sabetti never once mentions grace in his more compact discussion. Alphonsus's optimism and benignity with regard to the penitent were primarily rooted in his optimism about the grace of God. Although Alphonsus does not make that optimism of grace central in his discussion, his references to grace are most instructive. Some maintain that the recidivist is truly disposed only after a time of proof that sin can be avoided. Alphonsus retorts that the necessary reality is not the proof of time but the change of the will. Since this change of the will depends on divine grace, it can occur instantaneously.[169] If the penitent falls again because of an intrinsic weakness (e.g., of the will) absolution should rarely be deferred because in such a penitent one can hope for more change from the grace of the sacrament than from deferring of absolution.[170] In responding to objections Alphonsus repeats that there is a greater hope of emendation through the hope of grace received in the sacrament than through putting off absolution.[171] Without the grace of the sacrament many people become dejected and desperate.[172]

Second, in his longer discussion Alphonsus not only recognizes rules to guide the confessor but also the need for the prudence and good Christian sense of the confessor. In responding to the question whether the deferral of absolution to a properly disposed penitent is the proper remedy, Alphonsus reviews the opinions of others and then concludes that one cannot give a certain rule but the confessor should be guided by the circumstances and commend oneself to God to seek inspiration about granting or delaying absolution.[173] On the question of giving or deferring absolution to a disposed penitent the confessor should be guided by the light given by God.[174]

Sabetti makes no explicit reference to grace or to prudence and prayer on the part of the confessor in deciding what to do. These differences seem to point to a fundamental difference. Sabetti deliberately aims to give a short, clear, concise guide for confessors in his compendium. The American author puts in one volume what the Gaudé edition of Alphonsus developed in four large volumes. But in such an attempt Sabetti tends to leave out references to grace as unnecessary and to supply clear rules and solutions that do not call for much prudent interpretation. The advantages of a clear, brief, and sure presentation have the flip side of so stressing the human role that it forgets to mention the divine and in so formulating norms that the role of prudence is reduced. Something of the spirit, feel, and theology of Alphonsus is missing despite the use of his general method and at times his words and formulas.

In the light of the context and method of Sabetti's approach developed here, the next chapter will discuss the content of his moral theology.

NOTES

1. Aloysius Sabetti, *Compendium theologiae moralis* (Woodstock, Md.: Woodstock College Press, 1884). In 1882 Sabetti published 100 copies of a trial edition which he used with his students at Woodstock and submitted to others for their evaluation and responses. See Edmund G. Ryan, S.J., "An Academic History of Woodstock College in Maryland (1869–1944): The First Jesuit Seminary in North America" (Ph.D. diss., Catholic University of America, 1964), p. 64. Thirteen editions were published in his lifetime. This book uses the seventh edition published by Fr. Pustet in Germany and New York in 1892. References will be given to the paragraph numbers (n.) which are basically the same in the earlier editions as well as to the page numbers of the particular edition used here.

2. Francis J. Connell, "The Theological School in America," in *Essays on Catholic Education in the United States*, ed. Roy J. Deferrari (Washington, D.C.: Catholic University of America Press, 1942), p. 224. Paul E. McKeever, "Seventy-Five Years of Moral Theology in America," *American Ecclesiastical Review* 152 (1965): 19–20; John P. Boyle, "The American Experience in Moral Theology," *Proceedings of the Catholic Theological Society of America* 41 (1986): 26.

3. Theodore H. Heck, *The Curriculum of the Major Seminary in Relation to Contemporary Conditions* (Washington: National Catholic Welfare Conference, 1935), pp. 46–47.

4. Francis Patrick Kenrick, *Theologia moralis*, 3 vols. (Philadelphia: Eugene Cummiskey, 1841–1843). For biographical details of Kenrick, see Hugh J. Nolan, *The Most Reverend Francis Patrick Kenrick Third Bishop of Philadelphia 1830–1851* (Washington, D.C.: Catholic University of America Press, 1948); also Nolan, *New Catholic Encyclopedia*, 8, pp. 155–156.

5. Kenrick, *Theologia moralis*, 1, p. iii.

6. Ibid., 2, pp. 2–212.

7. Ibid., 1, p. 100.

8. Ibid., p. iv.

9. Gallagher, *History and Conscience*, pp. 220–222.

10. Kenrick, *Theologia moralis*, 1, pp. 2–3.

11. Ibid., p. iv.

12. Ibid., pp. 2–3.

13. Joseph D. Brokhage, *Francis Patrick Kenrick's Opinion on Slavery* (Washington: Catholic University of America Press, 1955).

14. Kenrick, *Theologia moralis*, 1, p. iv.

15. Ibid., pp. 255–258.

16. Brokhage, *Kenrick on Slavery*, pp. 242–243.

17. Peter Gardella, *Innocent Ecstasy: How Christianity Gave America an Ethic of Sexual Pleasure* (New York: Oxford, 1985), p. 23.

18. Nolan, *Francis Patrick Kenrick*, pp. 242–243. See also Connell, *Essays on Catholic Education in the United States*, ed. Deferrari, pp. 221, 222.

19. Kenrick, *Theologia moralis*, 2 vols., (Mechlin and Baltimore: H. Dessain, 1860–1861).

20. Nolan, *Francis Patrick Kenrick*, p. 244.

21. Boyle, *Proceedings of the Catholic Theological Society of America* 41 (1986): 26.

22. White, *Diocesan Seminary*.

23. Nolan, *Francis Patrick Kenrick*, p. 244.

24. Anthony Konings, *Theologiae moralis Sancti Alphonsi compendium*, 7th ed. (Cincinnati, Ohio: Benziger, 1888), p. 7.

25. A. Sampers, "Konings, Anthony," *New Catholic Encyclopedia*, 8, p. 249.

26. Ibid.; also Connell, *Essays on Catholic Education in the United States*, ed. Deferrari, p. 223; McKeever, *American Ecclesiastical Review* 152 (1965): 18–19.

27. Gallagher, *History and Conscience*, pp. 229–230.

28. J. A. Laubacher, "Tanquery, Adolphe Alfred," *New Catholic Encyclopedia*, 13, p. 934; McKeever, *American Ecclesiastical Review* 152 (1965): 21; Kauffman, *Tradition and Transformation*, pp. 183–184.

29. Heck, *Curriculum of the Major Seminary*, pp. 46–47.

30. Sabetti, *Compendium*, pp. v–vii.

31. Ibid., "Notandum," facing p. 1.

32. Ibid., nn. 240–255, pp. 179–189; Ioannes Petrus Gury et Antonius Ballerini, *Compendium theologiae moralis*, 10th ed., 2 vols., (Rome: Typographia Polyglatta, 1879), 1, nn. 337–362, pp. 332–354.

33. Sabetti, *Compendium*, n. 240, pp. 179–180; Gury-Ballerini, *Compendium*, 1, nn. 338–339, pp. 332–333.

34. Gury-Ballerini, *Compendium*, 1, n. 340, p. 333.

35. Sabetti, *Compendium*, n. 242, pp. 180–182.

36. Gury-Ballerini, *Compendium*, 1, nn. 341–343, pp. 334–336.

37. Ibid., n. 343, p. 337.

38. Ibid., nn. 349–350, pp. 345–346.

39. Sabetti, *Compendium*, n. 248, pp. 184–185.

40. "Father Aloysius Sabetti: A Fellow Professor's Reminiscences," *Woodstock Letters* 29 (1900): 216.

41. Patrick J. Dooley, *Woodstock and Its Makers* (Woodstock, Md.: The College Press, 1927), p. 87.

42. Sabetti, *Compendium*, nn. 741–743, pp. 535–538.

43. Ibid., n. 240, p. 179.

44. Ibid., p. vii.

45. The editor of *Woodstock Letters* had asked the priests of the house to prepare their own autobiographies. At Sabetti's death his autobiography was published—"Father Aloysius Sabetti," *Woodstock Letters* 29 (1900): 208–213. At the same time the editors also published reminiscences about Sabetti from fellow Jesuits at Woodstock.

46. "Father Aloysius Sabetti: A Fellow Professor's Reminiscences," *Woodstock Letters* 29 (1900): 216.

47. J. H. Campana, "Gury, Jean Pierre," *New Catholic Encyclopedia*, 6, p. 866.

48. "Sabetti," *Woodstock Letters* 29 (1900): 229.

49. Ibid., 215–217; Dooley, *Woodstock and Its Makers*, pp. 86–89.

50. *American Ecclesiastical Review*: Index vol. 1–50, p. 283. Note the original name *American Ecclesiastical Review* was changed for a time to *Ecclesiastical Review*, and then changed back to the original.

51. "Note," *American Ecclesiastical Review* 1 (1889): 70.

52. A. Sabetti, "Casus moralis," *American Ecclesiastical Review* 1 (1889): 137–143.

53. "Sabetti," *Woodstock Letters* 29 (1900): 227.

54. John Tracy Ellis, *The Life of James Cardinal Gibbons*, 1, pp. 462, 497–498.

55. "Sabetti," *Woodstock Letters* 29 (1900): 228.

56. Patrick J. Dooley, *Woodstock and Its Makers*, p. 86.

57. Ibid.

58. "Sabetti," *Woodstock Letters* 29 (1900): 216.

59. "Father Aloysius Sabetti: Reminiscences of Father Ennis," *Woodstock Letters* 29 (1900): 221

60. "Father Aloysius Sabetti: A Pen Picture of Father Finn," *Woodstock Letters* 29 (1900): 223; "Sabetti," Ibid., p. 217.

61. "Sabetti," *Woodstock Letters* 29 (1900): 221; 213. Dooley, *Woodstock and Its Makers*, p. 86.

62. Dooley, *Woodstock and Its Makers*, p. 87.

63. "Sabetti," *Woodstock Letters* 29 (1900): 217.

64. Ennis, *Woodstock Letters* 29 (1900): 219.

65. Sabetti, *Compendium*, p. vii.

66. Ibid.

67. "Sabetti," *Woodstock Letters* 29 (1900): 218.

68. Dooley, *Woodstock and Its Makers,* pp. 87–88.

69. "Sabetti," *Woodstock Letters* 29 (1900): 226.

70. Ibid., p. 216.

71. Ibid., p. 219.

72. Ibid., pp. 223–226.

73. Ibid., p. 216.

74. For the early history of Woodstock College and the theological orientation of its faculty, see John L. Ciani, "Metal Statue, Granite Base: The Jesuits' Woodstock College, Maryland, 1869–1891," a paper delivered at the Cushwa Center of Notre Dame University in 1993.

75. Ibid., pp. 29–34.

76. Gerald P. Fogarty, *American Catholic Biblical Scholarship: A History from the Early Republic to Vatican II* (San Francisco: Harper and Row, 1989), pp. 40–48.

77. René I. Holaind, *The Parent First* (New York: Benziger, 1891). Salvatore Brandi, a former Jesuit professor at Woodstock and then editor of *Civiltà Cattolica,* the semiauthoritative Vatican publication, also attacked Bouquillon. A translation appears in English as a pamphlet—S. M. Brandi, *Education: To Whom Does It Belong? A Review* (New York: Benziger, 1892).

78. For my approach see my *Directions in Fundamental Moral Theology* (Notre Dame, Ind.: University of Notre Dame Press, 1985), pp. 11–14; 188–190.

79. Gury-Ballerini, *Compendium,* 1, above n. 1., p. 1.

80. Ibid., above n. 81, p. 77.

81. Sabetti, *Compendium,* n. 30, p. 21.

82. Ibid., n. 124, p. 85.

83. Ibid., n. 202, p. 143.

84. Ibid., nn. 202–203, p. 143.

85. Ibid., nn. 204–206, pp. 144–145.

86. Ibid., nn. 207–211, pp. 146–150.

87. Ibid., n. 326, p. 233.

88. Ibid., nn. 326–344, pp. 233–251.

89. Ibid., n. 757, p. 552.

90. Gury-Ballerini, *Compendium,* 1, n. 473, p. 516.

91. Sabetti, *Compendium,* nn. 558–566, pp. 365–373.

92. Ibid., nn. 565–566, pp. 372–373.

93. Ibid., nn. 567–627, pp. 374–417.

94. Ibid., n. 151, p. 107.

95. Ibid., nn. 152–161, pp. 107–115.

96. Ibid., nn. 162–199, pp. 115–139.

97. Ibid., nn. 345–557, pp. 252–364.

98. Gury-Ballerini, *Compendium,* 1, n. 518, p. 475.

99. Sabetti, *Compendium,* nn. 345–346, pp. 252–254.

100. Ibid., n. 309, p. 220.

101. Gaudé, ed., 2, lib. 3, tract 5, nn. 486–961, pp.3–354.

102. Sabetti, *Compendium,* n. 628, p. 418.

103. Ibid., n. 631, p. 420.

104. Ibid., nn. 654–657, pp. 438–441.

105. Ibid., nn. 634–636, pp. 421–423.
106. Ibid., n. 628, p. 418.
107. Ibid., n. 672, p. 454.
108. Ibid., nn. 729–767, pp. 523–562.
109. Ibid., nn. 649–650, pp. 432–433.
110. Ibid., n. 852, p. 653.
111. Ibid., nn. 867–928, pp. 668–722.
112. Ibid., nn. 944–1061, pp. 738–840.
113. Ibid., n. 852, p. 653.
114. Ibid., nn. 914–916, pp. 704–705.
115. Ibid., pp. v–vii.
116. For example, E. F. Regatillo and M. Zalba, *Theologiae moralis summa*, 3 vols., (Madrid: Biblioteca de Autores Cristianos, 1952), 1, pp. 3–31.
117. Sabetti, *Compendium*, n. 8, p. 6.
118. Ibid., n. 27, p. 18.
119. Ibid., n. 28, p. 19–20.
120. Ibid., nn. 151–154, pp. 107–111.
121. Ibid., n. 166, p. 118.
122. Ibid., n. 168, p. 129.
123. Ibid., n. 940, p. 735.
124. Ibid., nn. 107–108, p. 75.
125. $I^a II^{ae}$, q. 94; see also Mahoney, *Making of Moral Theology*, pp. 224–258.
126. Sabetti, *Compendium*, n. 107, p. 75.
127. Ibid., n. 108, p. 75; for the position of Aquinas, see $I^a II^{ae}$, q. 94.
128. Sabetti, *Compendium*, n. 262, p. 197.
129. Ibid., nn. 263–264, pp. 197–198.
130. Ibid., n. 265, p. 199.
131. Ibid., n. 268, p. 200.
132. Ibid., n. 265, p. 199.
133. Ibid., n. 252, pp. 186–187.
134. Ciani, "Metal Statue, Granite Base," pp. 37–45.
135. Sabetti, *Compendium*, nn. 994–1061, pp. 738–840.
136. Ibid., n. 110, pp. 77–78.
137. Aloysius Sabetti, "Commentary on the Decree 'Quemadmodum,'" *American Ecclesiastical Review* 6 (1892): 161–170.
138. Sabetti, *Compendium*, n. 268, p. 200.
139. Gury-Ballerini, *Compendium*, 1, pp. xxxv–cxxxii.
140. Aloysius Sabetti, "*Animadversiones in controversia de ectopicis conceptibus*," *American Ecclesiastical Review* 11 (1894): 129–134.
141. John Connery, *Abortion: The Development of the Roman Catholic Perspective* (Chicago: Loyola University Press, 1977), especially pp. 225–303.
142. Aloysius Sabetti, "The Catholic Church and Obstetrical Science," *American Ecclesiastical Review* 13 (1895): 129–130.
143. Augustinus Lehmkuhl, *Theologia moralis*, 7th ed., 2 vols. (Freiburg: Herder, 1893), 1, nn. 841 ff., pp. 500 ff.
144. Sabetti, *American Ecclesiastical Review* 11 (1894): 132.
145. Connery, *Abortion*, pp. 291–292.

146. Joseph Aertnys et al., *"Casus de conceptibus ectopicis, seu extra-uteri-nis,"* *American Ecclesiastical Review* 9 (1893): 343–360.

147. Sabetti, *American Ecclesiastical Review* 11 (1894): 134.

148. Connery, *Abortion*, p. 302.

149. Much has been written about the papal magisterium or teaching office in theology in the last years. For a representative sampling of the literature, see Charles E. Curran and Richard A. McCormick, eds., *Readings in Moral Theology No. 3: The Magisterium and Morality* (New York: Paulist, 1982); *Readings in Moral Theology No. 6: Dissent in the Church* (New York: Paulist, 1988).

150. Sabetti, *American Ecclesiastical Review* 6 (1892): 165.

151. Ibid., p. 166.

152. Sabetti, *American Ecclesiastical Review* 13 (1895): 130.

153. Ibid., pp. 130–131.

154. Sabetti, *Compendium*, n. 273, p. 204.

155. Augustinus Lehmkuhl, *Theologia moralis*, 9th ed., 2 vols. (Freiburg: Herder, 1898) 1, nn. 842–844, pp. 501–502.

156. John A. Gallagher, *Time Past, Time Future: An Historical Study of Catholic Moral Theology* (New York: Paulist, 1990), p. 48.

157. Ibid., pp. 41, 51, 59, 76, 93, 94.

158. Bouquillon, *Catholic University Bulletin* 5 (1899): 256–268.

159. See, for example from a later period, J. M. Ramìrez, "Moral Theology," *New Catholic Encyclopedia*, 9, pp. 109–117.

160. Gallagher, *Time Past, Time Future*, pp. 79–94.

161. Gaudé, ed., 2, lib. 5, *"Tractatus praeambulus, de actibus humanis in genere,"* pp. 689–703. It is true that Alphonsus did not have a separate discussion of human acts at the beginning before treating conscience and law. In this he was following Busenbaum.

162. Sabetti, *Compendium*, p. vi.

163. Ibid., p. viii.

164. For a summary of the debate, see Vidal, *La morale di Sant'Alfonso*, pp. 211–216.

165. Sabetti, *Compendium*, *"Appendix de systemate equiprobalismi,"* pp. 46–51.

166. Capone, *Historia: Memoria futuri*, pp. 199–225.

167. Gallagher, *History and Conscience*, pp. 212–239.

168. Sabetti, *Compendium*, nn. 803–805, pp. 608–610

169. Gaudé, ed., 3, n. 459, p. 470.

170. Ibid., n. 464, p. 476.

171. Ibid.

172. Ibid, n. 464, p. 477.

173. Ibid, n. 463, p. 475.

174. Ibid, n. 464, p. 477.

4

The Content of Sabetti's Moral Theology

This chapter will focus on four important aspects of the content of Sabetti's moral theology—fundamental moral theology, sexuality, casuistry, and some distinctively American issues.

FUNDAMENTAL MORAL THEOLOGY

Although the discussion of general or fundamental moral theology in Sabetti and the manuals is skimpy and schematic, it still serves as the basis for what is found in special moral theology. This section will briefly analyze Sabetti's understanding of the four treatises on human acts, conscience, laws, and sin.

HUMAN ACTS. Sabetti defines the human act as that which proceeds from the deliberate will of a human being. Cognition, volition, and freedom are the three realities that constitute a human act, but the tract on conscience discusses the cognitional aspect while freedom and the volitional are combined under the rubric of the voluntary act.[1] The discussion later considers how ignorance, concupiscence, fear, and force or violence affect the voluntary nature of the human act.[2]

The most significant consideration involves the morality of human acts. The essence of morality consists in the relation of the human act to the eternal law which is the divine reason or the will of God commanding the natural order to be conserved and forbidding it to be disturbed. Secondarily, morality consists in the relationship of the human act to right reason, for human reason participates in and hence makes known divine reason. The essence of morality does not consist in freedom alone, for the person must freely conform to God's reason and law.

More specifically, there are three founts or principles of morality—the object, the end, and the circumstances. The object is that about which the moral act is immediately concerned and in which the will of the agent proximately and per se terminates. The object can be good, bad, or indifferent. The first and essential morality of the act comes from the object which can be changed by the circumstances and the end. Some acts such as hatred of God and blasphemy are intrinsically wrong by reason of their object, for they are repugnant to the absolutely necessary right order. Circumstances are accidental determinants of the morality of an act. The end considered here is the end of the agent—that is, the end to which the agent directs her intention. Since the intention orders the act to the particular end it affects morality. Two important points are mentioned in this brief and schematic presentation which is quite faithful to Gury-Ballerini. The first and essential morality of the act is determined by the object. The end or circumstances cannot make good an action which is absolutely intrinsically evil. The axiom "good from the whole cause and evil from any defect" also governs. The action must be good from all three sources or principles. If the object, the end, or the circumstances are evil, the act itself is evil.[3]

Intimately connected with the consideration of the object but treated earlier in Sabetti is the indirect voluntary or the voluntary in cause.[4] The direct voluntary is intended in itself and per se, that is, in the order of intention it is the immediate object of the will. The indirect voluntary is not willed in itself but in another or rather is seen as following from something else which is directly willed and follows either as an effect from a cause or as something connected with it, for example, killing a person by carelessly throwing a stone. Some refer to the two as the voluntary in itself and the voluntary in its cause.

Sabetti then considers the morality of the indirect voluntary or the voluntary in cause. Here the American Jesuit proposes what became known as the famous principle of the double effect which plays so great a role in Catholic moral theology. One can place a cause which is good or indifferent from which immediately follows a double effect—one good and one bad—if four conditions are fulfilled: (1) the good effect and not the evil effect is intended; (2) the cause or the act must be good or indifferent; (3) the good effect must follow equally immediately from the cause; and (4) there must be a proportionate reason for placing the cause.

Sabetti, closely following Gury-Ballerini as usual, thus shows that the principle of double effect that is so prominent in Catholic theology in the twentieth century was substantially present in the late nineteenth century. The conditions for the indirect voluntary make more specific the definition of direct. A direct killing, for example, is an act which by its very nature or the intention of its agent aims at killing either as a means or as an end. This definition remains implicit in Sabetti. However, a primary problem involves determining whether the morality of the act or the cause is either good or indifferent. Sabetti never really develops the question here or in his discussion of the object, but he does give the classical example of a general in war firing on and attacking an enemy tower in which some civilians are present together with the enemy troops. In this case attacking an enemy stronghold in war is not wrong, and the harm done to innocent civilians follows only indirectly and per accidens and thus is only permitted and not intended. Today many Catholic moral theologians disagree with the concept of direct and the principle of the double effect, but the hierarchical magisterium strongly supports these understandings.[5]

CONSCIENCE. Conscience is the judgment about the goodness or badness of an act to be placed. The treatise does not mention consequent conscience; that is, the judgment made after an act has already been placed as illustrated by the pangs of conscience after committing an evil act. A correct or true conscience, which represents the object as it is, must always be followed. A vincibly (one's fault) erroneous conscience (which does not represent the object as it is) cannot be followed without fault. However, an invincibly erroneous conscience can be followed without fault.[6]

   Much of the treatise deals with the certain and doubtful conscience. One needs a certain conscience in the sense of being morally certain to act.[7] A doubtful conscience involves the suspension of assent between two opposites. A probable opinion involves an act of the intellect adhering to a position, and thus differing from a doubtful conscience, but with fear of the opposite. Thus this conscience is not certain. Sabetti rejects the extreme positions of tutiorism and laxism, then opts for probabilism as opposed to both probabiliorism and equiprobabilism. Probabilism, with the other systems in general, maintains that one must follow the safer course when it is a question of an absolute obligation of achieving a certain end as in the case of something necessary by necessity of means or something required for the validity of a sacrament. Note the limitations on probabilism that followed some of the earlier debates. However, when it is simply a question of something being licit or illicit (that is, according to or against the natural or positive law) one can follow even a less probable opinion in favor of freedom from the law provided that it is solidly probable. A fundamental reason is that a law that is not certain involves no obligation. The will is bound by knowledge of the precept; where there is solid probability on the side of freedom, there is no certain law and hence no certain obligation. In this manner the agent can move from theoretical doubt to practical certitude and then act properly. Intrinsic probabilism is based on the reasons adduced for the position; extrinsic probabilism rests primarily on the authorities holding a position. Sabetti in an elitist way limits intrinsic probability to only the learned in moral matters. Elsewhere he states that the authority of Alphonsus regularly suffices for freeing from the law.[8] Precisely because of the nature of extrinsic authority the manualists often cite other authors to prove extrinsic probability. Sabetti, in the light of his pedagogical purpose, does not usually give a long list of authors and their opinions but makes a summary judgment about probability.

Notice how this entire discussion is based on and confirms a legal model. The individual is in possession of freedom and the law must be certain to take away the freedom. Such an extrinsic approach emphasizes the opposition between law and freedom on the one hand, and obligation and conscience on the other. Here too the conscience of the individual person in the determination of obligation is often supplanted by outside authority.

The second longest discussion under conscience deals with scrupulosity.[9] A scrupulous conscience, because of an insufficient or vain reason, doubts the morality of an act and fears sin where sin is not. The length of the discussion testifies to the existing problem of scrupulosity within the Catholic church at that time. In the tributes to Father Sabetti on his death students mentioned how helpful he was when scrupulous students went to him for confession or direction.[10] In this context, Sabetti discusses the signs, the causes, the harms, and the remedies of scrupulosity. Scrupulosity occurs frequently about daily actions, bad thoughts, and previous confessions. The primary solution for the penitent involves absolute and blind obedience to the confessor who should be patient, benign but firm, responding without hesitation and with authority.

The solution for scrupulosity employs the legal model to its ultimate extent. Blind obedience to the confessor is demanded. This approach was common among Catholic moralists until near the middle of the twentieth century when insights from psychology began to suggest a different approach.[11] Experience seems to suggest that scrupulosity flourishes in the context of a legal and extrinsic understanding of morality, with emphasis on sin and avoiding sin. Since Vatican II there has been much less scrupulosity among Catholics.

The particular considerations under conscience show the strength and all pervasive influence of the extrinsic legal model. However, this treatise also properly shows that conscience must relate to moral reality and cannot be based on an unlimited personal freedom to act in accord with one's own wishes as so often occurs in our contemporary society.

LAW. The treatise on law is divided into various sections—law in general and the principal species of law. Law in general discusses the nature and properties of law, the legislator, the object of law, the subject, its promulgation, acceptance, obligation, causes freeing from the law, the interpretation of the law and epikeia, dispensation, and cessation of the law.[12] In reality, however, this section deals not with law in general but for the most part with human law. The opening definition of human law is from Aquinas. The treatise on the author of the law discusses only the church and civil society.[13] Thus the whole treatise on law is heavily skewed to human and positive law either ecclesiastical or civil.

The original definition of law as an ordering of reason for the common good promulgated by the one who has the care of the community comes from Thomas Aquinas.[14] However, in most of the consideration law appears to be more an act of the will of the legislator than an act of practical reason. For example, in response to the question can the legislator prescribe under a light obligation what is in reality a grave obligation, the answer is more probably yes because the quality of the obligation depends on the will of the legislator just as the law itself depends on the will of the legislator.[15] In the same vein epikeia is described in relationship to the will of the legislator. Epikeia means that the case does not fall under the law because of the circumstances from which one can certainly or at least probably judge that the legislator would not want that case to fall under the law.[16] This approach is Suarezian and not Thomistic.[17] Such an understanding of law with its obliging force coming from the will of the legislator coheres with the basic approach of the whole volume. Morality does not arise intrinsically from within the person but is imposed on the person by an external will. The entire context both of the manuals themselves and of the times can explain why there is no direct discussion of civil disobedience or the fact that the law might not be just. Sabetti's consideration is limited to the moral or physical impossibility of fulfilling the law, but he later discusses purely penal laws.

The second part of this treatise discusses very succinctly the principal types of law—the natural law (notice there is no distinct discussion of the eternal law which is the ultimate basis of all law), divine positive law, ecclesiastical law, civil law, penal law, irritating law, custom, and privileges.[18] One point deserves further comment.

Penal laws are those that do not oblige one in conscience to do or omit something but do oblige one to accept the penalty for violating the law when the penalty is imposed. Are today's civil laws only penal laws? De jure, they can be; de facto laws concerning taxes are generally thought to be penal. A few contend, and not improbably, that today's civil laws are only penal. Whatever may be the case, it is altogether preferable not to speak about this distinction to the people, especially the more simple ones, but to gently lead them to obey all laws.[19] Sabetti gives no reason for his prudential remark. Was he fearful of what other Americans might say if word spread that Catholics did not have to obey civil laws but only accept the penalty?

Sin. The treatise on sin is based on and fully consistent with the purpose of the compendium in preparing judges for the sacrament of penance and with the legal model adopted throughout the volume. The first part treats sin in general under the headings of the nature of sin, the gravity of sin, and the specific and numerical distinction of sins. Sin is commonly defined as the free transgression of any law obliging in conscience. A sin is formal if the person knowingly and freely violates a law obliging in conscience; otherwise it is a material sin. The gravity of sin is the quality or measure of malice by which the sin is a greater or less offense against God. But how is this gravity measured? A sin is mortal if because of the violation of a gravely obliging law one loses divine friendship and is subject to eternal damnation. Otherwise the sin is venial. Three conditions are necessary for mortal sin—grave matter or a law obliging gravely, full attention of the mind, and full consent of the will.[20]

We are dealing here with free and voluntary acts that are supposed to be primarily internal and not external characteristics of the act, but now all the emphasis has swung to the external act. The cognitional and voluntary aspects of the act are presumed and may lessen the subjective guilt but do not affect the quantity and measure of mortal sin which is based on the matter alone—the violation of a gravely obliging law. Of course the gravity of sin based on such a criterion is much easier to judge. Mortal sin, however, as the turning away from God is primarily an internal act. At the very minimum the gravity of the obligation grounds a presumption that the will is gravely involved, but at most this condition should only be a presumption which cedes to the truth. But in Sabetti and in the moral manuals mortal sin is primarily reduced to the objective gravity and that in turn is reduced to the grave legal obligation. The definition of mortal sin still included the concept of breaking friendship with God but the concept was reduced to violating a gravely obliging law.

Grave matter is of two types. Some matter is always grave (blasphemy, heresy, sins against sexuality) and never admits of light matter. Other realities like theft or detraction are grave but can admit of light matter, as, for example, stealing a small amount of money.[21] Sins of sexuality always involve grave matter. To state the same reality in another way: there is no parvity of matter in the sixth commandment. Why? The reason is that venereal pleasure even without full sexual actuation is a certain, inchoate ejaculation of the seed or a natural and necessary movement toward it, but the ejaculation of semen outside the legitimate use of marriage is a grave disturbance of an essential order since by its nature it tends to the destruction of the human race.[22] One readily detects many weaknesses in this argument—it applies only to males; it assumes that imperfect acts are always going to lead to full sexual actuation; it assumes that these will lead to the destruction of the human race. Such an understanding gave a gravity and importance to the sixth commandment that was not true of any other commandment. Sabetti here fails to mention that the Superior General of the Society of Jesus, Claudius Aquaviva, in 1612 forbade Jesuits to teach the possibility of parvity of matter in sexual sins.[23]

Since grave matter was the primary determinant of mortal sin, it was only natural that Sabetti and others would ordinarily speak of mortal sin *ex toto genere suo* and not the more accurate way even in accord with their own understanding, of grave matter *ex toto genere suo*.[24] Sabetti thus understands mortal sin primarily and at times exclusively in terms of the matter as is evident from such language.

The Council of Trent calls for the material integrity of sacramental confession as the general rule. This insistence requires the confession of sins according to number and species.[25] Species of sins are determined by the opposition to different virtues or to different aspects of the same virtues. Here the language of virtue is used, but the reality deals with sinful acts. Thus a person with a vow of chastity committing a sexual sin with a married relative commits four different sins against chastity, religion, piety, and justice. The numerical distinction of sins within the same species comes from the diversity of the total object (e.g., hurting the person is included under the sin of murder) or from the multiplication of acts which have been morally interrupted.[26] With this heavy overemphasis on mortal sin as a particular individual act one quickly loses sight of the original definition that mortal sin involves the breaking of our friendship with God. In the context of breaking friendship with God it does not make sense to speak of three, four, five, or fifty mortal sins as discrete individual acts apart from that basic relationship. Such an approach thus tends to distort the very meaning of mortal sin as the breaking of one's relationship with God.

The discussion of specific sins first treats internal sins, which follows from the understanding of the human act as coming from the will. The Catholic tradition has insisted that not only external acts are sins. The internal sins are morose delectation, sinful joy, and evil desire. A short section very briefly mentions and defines the seven capital sins—pride, avarice, lust, envy, wrath, sloth, and covetousness.[27] The appendix on drunkenness, since it seems to be out of place in a discussion of sin in general, makes the reader think it is an addition made here by Sabetti in accommodation to a specific situation on the American scene. References to American practices in the discussion such as making a pledge not to drink seem to reinforce such a judgment.[28] However, in reality Gury-Ballerini has the same basic discussion without the American characteristics and in the very same place.[29]

TREATMENT OF SEXUALITY

The discussion of the sixth and ninth commandments in Sabetti presents the traditional manualistic teaching. The first chapter discusses the nonconsummated sins of impurity (impure kisses, touches, looks, books, and words) and the consummated sins of impurity on the basis of the traditional types of sins according to nature, that is, where the "natural" aspect of depositing male semen in the vagina of the female takes place (e.g., fornication, adultery), and sins against nature where that physical process does not occur (e.g., masturbation, sodomy).[30] The very last section in the separate chapter on marriage treats the conjugal debt and discusses onanism.[31] The basic positions are well known.

Sabetti's treatment of sexuality like his entire compendium merely repeats the traditional teaching of the manuals. Some comments about his method and conclusions are in order. His schema on consummated external sins against sexuality follows the traditional distinction between sins against nature and sins according to nature. But note the understanding of nature here. Nature refers to the physical act of depositing male semen in the vagina of the female. This physical act must always be present and can never be interfered with. This explains why masturbation, contraception, and sodomy are always wrong. The sins according to nature are those in which the physical and biological process is present, but the human, rational aspect (namely the bond of marriage) is missing—fornication, adultery, incest, rape. Such an understanding makes the physical act normative and forbids any interference in it.

The distinction between sins against nature and sins according to nature shows a significant ambiguity in the understanding of the word natural which has special importance for one claiming to follow a natural law approach. Here we have sins according to nature! The "natural" and the "human" are not the same. I maintain that artificial contraception for spouses can be justified on the basis of human reason interfering in the physical, biological processes for the good of the marriage and the spouses. The human is more than just the biological or physical aspects. Sabetti's whole approach to human sexuality gives too much importance to the physical and the biological at the expense of other aspects of the human.

One is surprised not to find in the discussion of marriage a separate consideration of the famous question of the ends of marriage. Apparently the practical and succinct nature of the manual precludes such a consideration. However, Sabetti accepts procreation as the primary end of marriage. Onanism is wrong because it goes against the primary end of marriage.[32] Polyandry is wrong because it goes against the primary end of marriage which is the procreation and education of offspring.[33] The very definition of marriage accepts procreation as the primary end of marriage since the object of the contract involves acts per se apt for the generation of offspring.[34] Such an approach also serves as a strong support for the condemnation of artificial contraception.[35]

The recognition of procreation as the primary end of sexuality and marriage also underscores the problem of identifying the human with the physical and the biological. The human being is a rational animal. Humanity adds rational nature to the animal nature which is primary and basic. Animal sexuality has procreation as its end. Human sexuality adds to the primary end the secondary ends of mutual help and fostering conjugal love. But the animal nature of sexuality remains sacrosanct and one cannot interfere in the procreative aspect of the sexual act to achieve other human goods.

Sabetti's discussion of artificial contraception or onanism in his manual deserves mention for two positions taken by him that are not found as such in Gury-Ballerini. The very last question in the whole text on marriage in general and the conjugal debt in particular asks if spouses who abstain from sexual intercourse certain days during the month to avoid having children commit sin. From the moral perspective if spouses can abstain totally, why can they not abstain for fifteen days per month? But is not the intention or end of avoiding children wrong? To wish to avoid children is not evil in itself or per se but only when this is achieved through a positive means of preventing conception or of destroying the conceptus. Thus from an ethical perspective Sabetti defends what was later called the rhythm method or natural family planning. However, from today's understanding of biology a huge problem exists. Our author admits that there is an opinion, which is not absolutely certain, that conception occurs immediately before or after menstruation. Consequently a child will not be conceived if the spouses have relations only during those fourteen or fifteen days most distant from the time of menstruation.[36] Today we know this is absolutely the wrong time to have relations if one wants to avoid conception.

Second, this section ends with a *monitum* (a warning). Sabetti follows Gury-Ballerini in saying that the confessor should avoid the two extremes of always or never asking married penitents about the sin of onanism. If there is a basis in the light of circumstances that the person has been practicing onanism and has not confessed it, the confessor should inquire about it but altogether prudently and cautiously. However, since among us this plague does not have such deep and universal roots as elsewhere, it would be better to have too few rather than too many questions about onanism.[37] Sabetti here appeals to his own experience of Catholic spouses in the United States for a more benign approach.

The manuals and the Catholic tradition have often been accused of overemphasizing sexuality at the expense of other more important aspects of the Christian life. Yet all would have to admit the importance of sexuality and its ramifications, for good or evil, in human life. Does

Sabetti give an overemphasis to sexuality in relation to other aspects of the moral life? A number of factors indicate that sexuality is not given undue importance in Sabetti.

The discussion of the sixth and ninth commandments is quite short consisting of only thirteen pages. The treatment is precise and concise; for example, fornication and adultery together take up less than one page.[38] The conjugal debt takes up eight pages in the discussion on marriage.[39] Many people would be surprised how little space is dedicated to sexuality.

The priest as judge in the sacrament of penance has to know the number and species of sin and hence must question the penitent about these matters. However, this questioning should be moderate and discreet. The confessor must avoid scandal and especially teaching people some new way to sin. Gravity, modesty, and paternal charity must be shown in questioning the penitent. Sabetti proposes an axiom accepted by all—in sexual matters with regard to the integrity of the sacrament, it is better to be deficient in many cases than to go too far in one case. In doubt whether one should ask a certain question, the answer will be no. It is a lesser evil for material integrity to be lacking than to incur the danger of losing a soul.[40] This caution is based on good pastoral and common sense that recognizes the danger of an overemphasis on sexuality and the harm that it might do to the penitent.

Gury-Ballerini in the beginning of their consideration of the sixth and ninth commandments cite and make their own the words that Alphonsus used in the beginning of his treatise on sexuality. Alphonsus strongly contended against the Jansenists, but his attitude toward sexuality is most negative and fearful. Alphonsus maintains at the beginning of his discussion that we are painfully about to begin the treatise whose very name can poison the minds of human beings. Would that he could explain himself quite briefly and obscurely. Since, however, this subject is the more frequent and more abundant matter of confession, because of which the greater number of souls will go to hell, Alphonsus hopes to instruct clearly, but most chastely, future priests and discuss many particulars. He beseeches his students that they read this tract on sexuality only for this purpose, turning totally away from any curiosity, and often at the same time raise their minds to God and commend themselves to the immaculate Virgin Mary lest while seeking to acquire souls for God they themselves should suffer the loss of their own souls.[41]

Sabetti does not begin his treatment of the sixth commandment by repeating these words of Alphonsus. Rather his discussion of the sixth and ninth commandments is in the same detached manner as all the other commandments. Leaving out the words of Alphonsus fits in with Sabetti's efforts to be more brief and concise, but it might also indicate some disagreement with the sentiments expressed there.

However, many indications point in an opposite direction. Sexuality is different from all the other commandments because here alone there is no parvity of matter. Internal sins and imperfect sexual acts such as impure kisses and readings always involve grave matter.[42] Thus sexuality stands out from all the others and the fear of sexual sin is ever present in this treatise.

Sabetti also shares the traditional language of the manuals and of Alphonsus in referring to the parts of the body. He does not seem to use the words genitals or private parts with regard to the human body. Sabetti refers to the genitals as the *verenda*, from the verb to fear, and the *pudenda* from the verb to be ashamed. He also refers to these as the *partes turpes*—the unsightly or filthy parts. Other parts of the female body such as the arms, the legs, and the breasts are referred as the *partes minus honestae* (less respectable parts).[43]

In the light of these distinctions various moral conclusions are drawn. Here again concrete norms seem to usurp any role for prudence. Likewise the talk is not about whether the matter is grave but whether or not the sin is grave or light. It is a mortal sin to look at the *verenda* of a person of the opposite sex. It is per se venial to look at the *pudenda* of a person of the same sex. It is per se a mortal sin to look at the *partes minus honestae* of a woman (the presumption is that a man is looking). One who (again obviously a male) looks at the bare breasts of a beautiful woman with notable delay and without cause will ordinarily not be excused from a mortal sin.[44] The terminology, the language of sin, and the precise norms dealing with nonconsummated sins of impurity all indicate a fearful and negative approach to human sexuality.

In addition to these external sins against chastity, both consummated and nonconsummated, internal sins also exist. Sabetti does not treat these internal sins here under the sixth commandment because they have been discussed under the consideration of sin in general in fundamental moral theology. The three types of internal sins are morose delectation, or freely taking pleasure in a bad thing presented through the imagination as present without any desire for it; simple joy, or the deliberate approbation of a bad action done by oneself or another by which the will accepts and takes pleasure in the evil that was done; sinful desire, or the act of the will seeking an evil act as something to be attained and therefore to be accomplished by one's own act. Sabetti gives different examples of these internal sins with a good number of illustrations coming from sexuality.[45] In discussing scrupulosity Sabetti states that scrupulosity most often occurs with regard to daily actions, bad thoughts, and past confessions. The compendium then lists the types of bad thoughts in the following order—chastity, faith, charity.[46]

Our Jesuit theologian often uses examples from sexuality as well as from many other areas to illustrate the principles and concepts found in that part of the book which deals with fundamental moral theology. But the references to sexuality often predominate, as in the discussion of scandal. Scandal is a word or deed less right (either evil or having the appearance of evil) which leads another into sin. After discussing the general teaching with appropriate distinctions and norms Sabetti notes that what has been presented up to now furnishes what is necessary to solve all the cases involving scandal, but because of special difficulties it will be helpful to say something in particular about impurity, obscene books, and dances—all dealing with sexuality. The most grave scandal (*gravissimum*) is to make, represent, or present something that notably provokes sexual libido because no more subtle poison of the soul can be drunk. Note that the word *turpis*, which means bad or dirty is used for sexual sins with no other noun.[47] Of all the types of scandal none is more detestable than what comes from bad and obscene books.[48]

What about dancing? Per se dances are not illicit if they are done in responsible ways; that is, without any immodest touching, acts, or gestures. Per se dances are acts of joy and are not prohibited by law. However, they can become gravely illicit. Some claim that the recent round dances popular in this country are gravely illicit. But provided there is no case of special prohibition, the possible malice of these dances consists in the danger of provoking sexual libido which is essentially relative and therefore different for different persons.[49] In a later solution to a case in the *American Ecclesiastical Review* Sabetti further explains that special case of prohibition. Some bishops have prohibited round dances. Perhaps the dances in that particular diocese are quite bad and so offensive that the avoidance of sin is morally impossible. Perhaps the bishop has reserved the sin to himself because of the dangers involved in such dances, but then the reserved sin is of disobedience to the bishop and a serious matter and not the sin of impurity connected with the dances.[50]

Sabetti as a Jesuit priest was a male celibate as were all the authors of these manuals. These authors had to look at the issues of sexuality from that perspective whether they were conscious of it or not. As celibates they would be very fearful of sexual arousal because of the threat to their own vow or promise. One would expect them to be overly sensitive and perhaps to some degree even hyper about the allurements of sexuality and the danger of sexual arousal, and the facts bear out this supposition. The celibate fear of sexual arousal and pollution is exemplified in a seemingly farfetched case of the person who eats meat on Friday foreseeing that it will result in pollution. The question was raised to determine what is the sin of the person.[51]

The perspective in the discussion of sexuality is almost entirely from the part of the male. Pollution or masturbation is defined as the ejaculation of the semen without intercourse with another. The subsequent discussion of eight paragraphs develops the whole position on pollution in these terms but at the end one question is raised: can women have the sin of pollution? Sabetti recognizes that doctors in his day agree that women do not have true semen. The malice of pollution for women is in the carnal pleasure they experience outside marriage.[52] The later manualists like Sabetti knew more about female biology, but they did not redo the discussion to take that into account. The male perspective also comes through in the discussion of sins of cooperation, since it is usually the case of cooperating in the sin of the male who is going to the prostitute or writing amorous letters to a woman not his wife.[53]

In addition to this predominately male perspective, Sabetti and the other manualists tend to see the female as the source of the problem for the male's sexual arousal. With regard to scandal the question focuses on the dress, ornamentation, and cosmetics of women. If the woman purposefully dresses to provoke the sexual libido of men she sins mortally.[54]

The same tendency to blame the woman comes through elsewhere. Does the scandal of the weak, which comes from the infirmity or ignorance of the person, justify not obeying a precept? With regard to positive human precepts controversy exists but the more probable opinion holds that the natural law precept of avoiding scandal of the weak ordinarily prevails over a positive human law. Thus a woman may miss mass occasionally on a Sunday if she knows her presence is the occasion of sexual arousal for a certain man.[55]

The fear of the alluring and enticing power of sexual pleasure comes through often in this book. In the treatise on force and fear in the first tract on human acts Sabetti discusses rape. In the course of the discussion he agrees with Alphonsus that it hardly seems possible for the woman being raped not to consent to sexual pleasure.[56] The holder of such a position does not seem to recognize that rape involves a traumatic and devastating violation of the person which dominates over all else. The oppressed woman would ordinarily not consent to any "sexual pleasure" that might occur.

In keeping with the tradition and the times, Sabetti refers to sodomy as a "horrendous crime." The horror comes from the union of two persons of the same sex and from the terrible penalties inflicted by God on Sodom.[57] Some revisionist Catholic moral theologians today not only disagree with such a description of homosexual acts but also accept the moral goodness of such actions within the context of a permanent commitment between two homosexual persons.[58]

Even marriage itself, apparently because of its connection with sexuality, has something shameful about it. Sabetti recognizes that people, especially women, are excused from the obligation of hearing mass on Sundays and feast days because of a notable shame (*verecundia*). Thus women are excused from attending mass the day on which the banns of their marriage are to be announced in church.[59]

In the light of all this evidence one can conclude that Sabetti shared the attitudes of Alphonsus and Gury-Ballerini toward sexuality even if he did not cite Alphonsus's words at the beginning of his discussion. Sabetti is merely reflecting the Catholic tradition of the times with its negative and fearful view of sexuality.

CASUISTRY

Human reason occupies a central place in the approach of Sabetti and the manualists to evaluate the morality of particular acts. Sometimes this reason will employ arguments from scripture and church authority but these fit within the larger framework of human reason enlightened from other sources going about its work. This section will discuss Sabetti's casuistry.

THE METHOD IN THE COMPENDIUM. Every consideration begins with a definition characterized by a very precise and concise formulation. For example, scandal is defined as a word or deed less upright giving to another the occasion of a spiritual fall. These terms are then briefly explained. "Word or deed" also includes omissions. "Less upright" refers to something that is evil in itself or has the appearance of evil. "Giving the occasion" recognizes that the proper cause of sin is the will of the primary agent. "Spiritual fall" includes either mortal or venial sin.[60] Dominion, for example, is defined as the right of disposing of a certain thing as one's own in every use that is not prohibited by law or agreement.[61] Another example: drunkenness is voluntary excess in drinking to the point of losing reason.[62] Such succinct definitions clearly delineate what is being talked about.

After the definition Sabetti ordinarily strives for precision and further classification by presenting the important distinctions or types of what is being considered. Such classification enables the student to discern precisely what a particular case involves. Sabetti, for example, accepts the classical definition of lying as speech against what is in one's mind. There are three types of lies: a malicious lie inflicts unjust harm on another; an officious lie is told for the advantage of oneself or another; a jocose lie is told for the sake of a joke or amusement. This threefold distinction obviously paves the way for the judgment about the morality and the gravity of lying. A lie differs from a mental reservation, which is an act of the mind distorting or restricting the words of a certain proposition to a meaning different from the natural and obvious meaning. There are two types of mental reservations. A pure mental reservation means that the true meaning of what is spoken can in no way be perceived by the hearer. A broad or improper mental reservation occurs when the true sense of the speaker can be perceived from the circumstances. One can morally use a broad mental reservation, but not a strict one, when there is a just cause. Sabetti illustrates a broad mental reservation with the classical case of the servant who tells a caller that the master is not home when in reality the master is home. People generally understand such speech to mean that the master is not home for the purpose of visiting or talking.[63]

Such careful distinctions help the student and the priest in the confessional to sort out and classify the matter under discussion. These distinctions supply one with a grid of classifications so that one can exactly determine the object of an act. Is this a lie, a pure mental reservation, or a broad mental reservation? If it is a lie, what kind of lie is it? The legal approach tends to classify, compare, contrast, and differentiate. All this abets an orderly and clear process. The first step in ethical analysis is to determine what is occurring. What is the reality that must be morally analyzed? In my judgment the legal model is not the most adequate model for the moral life, but it does furnish one with the ability to distinguish, compare, and contrast, thus enabling the confessor to identify more readily and accurately the moral reality in question. Such legal training prepares one to hone in on and exactly discern the reality under discussion and how it can be related to similar or dissimilar issues. At times such a legal perspective can become a straightjacket or claim a greater certitude than the moral reality is able to bear but its clarity and precision are obvious.

The example of almsgiving illustrates Sabetti's method of casuistry.[64] A true precept of giving alms to the needy exists as is proved from the general law of charity obliging us to love our neighbor and from scripture which is supported by two proof texts—Ecclesiasticus 4:1 and Matthew 25:42. The precept of giving alms includes two presuppositions—indigence or necessity on the part of one receiving the alms and a superfluity on the part of the giver. Necessity can be of three different types: extreme necessity means that the danger of death or of another evil almost equal to death is so proximate that it cannot be avoided except with the help of another. Grave necessity renders one's temporal existence very burdensome. Ordinary and common necessity is that state in which one is able to provide for oneself without grave difficulty. Poor beggars on the street generally fall into this category, for their life, according to their condition, is not too burdensome or miserable. Superfluous goods are of two types. Superfluous for life are those goods that one is able to live without. Superfluous to one's state in life are those goods that are not necessary for honest and decent living according to one's state in life; for example, having servants, entertaining guests. (This whole discussion well illustrates the class differences found throughout Sabetti.)

Three practical and succinct rules follow: (1) I am obliged to come to the assistance of my neighbor in extreme necessity certainly and only with goods necessary for my own state in life. Certainly, because the right order of charity demands that the life of my neighbor take precedence over my own far inferior good; only, however, because my life is nearer to me than the life of my neighbor and therefore I do not have to sacrifice what is necessary for my life. (2) In grave necessity which comes close to extreme necessity I should help the neighbor with goods that are somewhat necessary for my state in life or with a slight harm to my state in life. Notice the attempt to find another category between the categories of extreme and grave. In a grave necessity which is not bordering on the extreme it is enough to assist the neighbor from those goods which are superfluous for my state in life. (3) In common necessity, although there is no obligation of giving alms to this or that person in particular, the common opinion of the theologians maintains that the person having goods superfluous to one's state and never giving any alms cannot be excused from sin.

What about the gravity of this precept to give alms? Almsgiving, like the precept of charity, per se constitutes a grave obligation, but it does not oblige gravely in every necessity. In extreme and grave necessity touching on the extreme the obligation is grave. The theologians are divided not only about whether there is a grave obligation to give alms to a particular poor person who labors under a simply grave necessity but whether there is a grave obligation for helping poor people in general who are in common need.

How much should be given to the poor? In extreme need or grave need touching on extreme one must give what suffices to take away the need here and now unless there are others willing to help. No one is required, however, to give a large sum of money for freeing a poor person from the danger of death or for obtaining extraordinary and very expensive remedies. In common need, a determined quantity cannot be assigned but more probably it suffices to give fifty percent of the goods that are superfluous to one's state.

The discussion of killing an unjust aggressor moves in the same direction. After justifying, as a last resort, the principle of killing an unjust aggressor to save one's own life, Sabetti elucidates this principle by justifying killing an unjust aggressor in the following cases: if the aggressor is out of her mind or drunk, for such a person is a materially unjust aggressor; in defense of material goods of great value; a woman in defense of her chastity; and killing the unjust aggressor to save the life of a neighbor. Sabetti gives a negative response to the case of killing an unjust aggressor of one's honor. Such a position is in keeping with the condemnation of Innocent XI. If the injury is already done, then the act is not defense. If the injury is in the process of being done, it can be repelled by means less than the death of the attacker. In this example of killing in self-defense one sees how the case of defense of honor differs from the other cases and therefore is not permitted.[65]

In the context of the compendium Sabetti approaches particular cases by proposing definitions and distinctions and then going from principles to rules to cases. However, this method is obviously dictated by the very purpose, method, and approach of the manuals themselves. The compendium does not pretend to be solving cases for the first time. The compendium's format comes from its pedagogical purpose of preparing seminarians and priests for the ministry of the confessional. Logically, the cases are seen as applications of principles and rules to the particular issue, but is this how Sabetti would deal with the morality of a case when it is first presented to him?

THE LOGIC OF SABETTI'S CASUISTRY.   We know that bishops, priests, and others frequently consulted Sabetti about moral cases. He discussed a case of conscience each week at Woodstock. Before he fell ill near the end of his life he apparently was planning on putting together a book on cases of conscience based on his previous work.[66] Sabetti published a number of solutions to cases of conscience in the *American Ecclesiastical Review*. However, the vast majority of these cases do not deal with moral issues as such but with canonical issues such as baptismal cases, marriage and its invalidity, confession, nuptial blessing, generic confession, matrimonial impediments, and the validation of marriages.[67] A few moral issues are discussed but the most in-depth discussion concerns ectopic pregnancy. An examination of this discussion should shed some light on his casuistry.

The *American Ecclesiastical Review*, as previously mentioned, presented a discussion among many doctors and some theologians on the question of ectopic pregnancy beginning in 1893. Three theologians took part in the discussion—August Lehmkuhl, a German Jesuit; Joseph Aertnys, a Dutch Redemptorist; and Sabetti. The original case had a number of parts dealing with different ways of removing the ectopic pregnancy which was threatening the life of the mother. Sabetti and Lehmkuhl both agreed that the ectopic pregnancy (i.e., the immature fetus outside the womb) which is threatening the life of the mother could be removed but they gave very different justifications for it.[68]

Sabetti himself begins his discussion with a reference to his own methodology in solving cases. It is easier and more intelligible to proceed from the certain to the uncertain.[69] The discussion also illustrates how his case method involved trying to find parallels with other aspects and why parallels did not exist in certain cases. One might speak here of what some contemporary authors call paradigm cases.[70] The crux of the method was to show that the case is permitted or not by comparing it with principles and with other cases.

Parameters of the discussion must be kept in mind. Sabetti had always opposed craniotomy to save the life of the mother and after the Congregation of the Holy Office's condemnation, he maintained that all Catholic theologians would agree. Direct abortion, including craniotomy, was always wrong even if it was done to save the life of the mother. Sabetti strongly insisted on the principle that the end does not justify the means and cited this axiom at the end of his discussions of abortion and craniotomy.[71]

Sabetti clearly recognizes he has to prove two points to make his argument that the ectopic fetus threatening the life of the mother can be killed to save the mother.[72] First, it is licit to kill even directly a materially unjust aggressor against one's life. In its own way this constitutes an exception to the principle that one can never directly kill another human being and somewhat modifies the principle that the end does not justify the means. But Sabetti does not go into these aspects. Sabetti understands direct as that which is a means to obtain the end. Killing the fetus is the means by which the mother is saved. The right to life implies that the individual has all the means necessary for protecting that right provided the means do not in some way contradict nature or the natural law. Since the aggressor is acting unjustly, he cannot claim any rights. Since the aggressor has lost the right to life by what he does unjustly, the one who kills him in self-defense does nothing wrong. But is this also true of the materially unjust aggressor; that is, the one who does not knowingly and willingly do the injustice against another's life? The ultimate reason why it is permitted to kill an unjust aggressor, observing the proper limits, does not come from the actual malice of the aggression but from the right to defend oneself which is the same whether the aggression is formal or material. The classical example here concerns the aggressor who is drunk or insane.

Second, is the ectopic fetus threatening the life of the mother a materially unjust aggressor? The presupposition of its threatening the life of the mother proves it is an aggressor. But is it unjust? Yes, the fetus is disturbing the order of nature by being present where it should not be. The ectopic fetus, by being where it should not be, is disturbing the course of nature and severely endangering the certain and persisting right of an innocent party.

Sabetti accepts as a general principle that whenever we find something unnatural and strange, one cannot say that removing it goes against the law of nature because nature does not contradict itself. Thus if a person is born with two noses or six fingers one can legitimately cut off the extra members. The person in this case does not commit a forbidden mutilation against the fifth commandment because the body is not deprived of its natural integrity. Since the fetus is acting against nature by being where it should not be, it is unjust in its aggression and, therefore, can be directly removed. But Sabetti recognizes an objection that can be raised against him. Logically, if the head of the fetus is too large and cannot be removed from the mother whose life is being threatened, one then can do a craniotomy to save the life of the mother. But the size of the head is not the same unnaturality as two noses, six fingers, or a fetus outside its natural place in the womb. The greater size of the head is an accidental and not a substantial unnaturality. Sabetti recognizes that his approach would justify a craniotomy in this one case if necessary to save the life of the mother threatened by an ectopic pregnancy. But such is his fear and horror of craniotomy that he would repudiate his position in the case of ectopic pregnancy if the proponents of craniotomy in other cases were to use it to justify themselves.[73] Precisely because Sabetti justifies direct killing of the unjust aggressor it makes no moral difference to him if the fetus is killed in the womb or outside the womb. In fact, he maintains the decision of what means to use belongs in this case to the doctor and not to the theologian.[74]

While defending his own position, Sabetti strongly rejects the justifying position proposed by Lehmkuhl. Lehmkuhl rightly points out that the primary difference between them is whether the removal of the fetus is a direct or indirect killing and secondarily whether or not the ectopic fetus is an unjust aggressor. Lehmkuhl argues that the removal of the fetus in this case is indirect and not a direct killing. Unlike Sabetti, Lehmkuhl does not allow the fetus to be killed in the womb. Lehmkuhl maintains that the removal of the fetus comes first and with it comes the saving of the mother. The death of the fetus only comes later. Hence the killing is indirect. The death of the fetus is not the means by which the mother is saved. This differs from craniotomy, since the death of the fetus is the means by which the mother is saved. Lehmkuhl appeals to other similar cases to show that the killing here is indirect. His main analogy comes from two shipwrecked people holding onto a plank to save themselves. Knowing that the plank cannot hold both, one person willingly gives up the plank even though she can't swim and will soon drown. Many prominent theologians agree with this approach. Lehmkuhl also appeals to the famous cases of Eleazar and Samson in the Hebrew Bible. Eleazar (1 Machabees 6:43ff.) walked under the elephant carrying the enemy king, slew the elephant which fell on him and killed him, but the king died too. Many theologians see that as an indirect killing. His action killed the elephant and equally immediately Eleazar and the king died. The death of Eleazar was not the means by which the king was killed.[75]

Sabetti admits the three other examples given by Lehmkuhl. In the case of the shipwreck, Eleazar, and Samson the killing is indirect. The action is good or indifferent, and from this action there follows equally immediately the good effect and bad effect. But the removal of the fetus is not a good or indifferent act. You are depriving the fetus of what is absolutely necessary for its life. This is directly killing. Sabetti appeals to the analogy of taking a fish out of water or cutting off a human being's supply of air. The removal of the fetus is a death-bearing means which brings about the good effect. The killing act is the means by which the good is accomplished. In Sabetti's mind there is an even more important factor at work in this analysis. Sabetti correctly recognizes that the theory proposed by Lehmkuhl would permit the acceleration of birth of an immature fetus which is not ectopic, in order to save the life of the mother. The American Jesuit steadfastly opposes such an action.[76]

Who is correct on this point? In accord with the understanding of the meaning of direct and of the condition of the double effect that the good effect must occur equally as immediately as the evil effect and the evil cannot be the means by which the good effect occurs, I think the case could be made for Lehmkuhl. If there were an artificial womb available, the fetus would not have to die. This shows that the good effect of saving the mother is not achieved by means of the bad effect of the death of the fetus. However, this position would definitely have resulted in a different approach to conflict situations involving abortion. The problem revolves around how you define the object of the act. Here the object of the act is the removal of the fetus. The act itself does not kill the fetus. Sabetti adds a circumstance to the object of the act—after the fetus is removed it will die. Lehmkuhl's argument, however, has weaknesses of its own. For example, he maintains that one can think of certain actions which in ordinary circumstances are a direct killing or the equivalent of it but in extraordinary circumstances there is no malice and the death is only permitted.[77] Logically, Lehmkuhl should not say that circumstances change the object. The act would be the same, that is indirect killing in all circumstances but in the normal circumstances no proportionate reason justifies the indirect killing.

At the end of the nineteenth century, both authors agreed on what was meant by direct and the conditions of the principle of the double effect. Direct refers to both the intention of the agent and to the nature of the act especially the causality of the act. You may not directly intend and directly do the evil deed. Sabetti saw the act as directly killing because the act takes away what is absolutely essential for the life of the fetus. Lehmkuhl understood the causality and the object of the act to be the removal of the fetus and not the death that would follow later.

Although Sabetti recognizes that the removal or killing of an ectopic pregnancy in the womb is a direct killing, he still wants to justify such an action when the life of the mother is threatened. He appeals to the principle that one can directly kill a materially unjust aggressor. His argument here is somewhat weak. The ectopic pregnancy is not where nature wants it to be. Therefore, it is an unjust aggressor because it is disturbing the course of nature and threatening the life of the mother. The fetus should not be doing what it is doing just like the drunk or mentally deranged attacker.[78] One could argue, as Lehmkuhl does, that the ectopic fetus is really not an unjust aggressor because, unlike the drunk or deranged person, the fetus is doing nothing. The fetus's own condition is not caused by itself but by its parents and natural causes.[79]

The hierarchical magisterium soon condemned both Lehmkuhl's defense of indirect abortion and Sabetti's defense of direct abortion in the case of the ectopic pregnancy threatening the mother's life.[80] Later Catholic theologians developed the understanding that the tube or organ containing the fetus becomes infected and hence one could remove the infected tube or organ which happens to contain the fetus. The action does not constitute a direct killing because the act is directed at the diseased or infected organ even though the fetus is contained in it and will die.[81]

The extended debate on the ectopic pregnancy sheds some light on the nature of Sabetti's casuistry. Sabetti's approach to solving moral cases was more complex than the compendium's approach of seeing it as the application of principles and norms to particular cases. This case history shows a comparative and contrasting analysis with other cases to determine the morality of the case under discussion. Lehmkuhl and Sabetti make different claims in this area even though they come to somewhat the same conclusion.

Another important factor is also at work in Sabetti's casuistry. Sabetti seems to have a basic intuitive moral judgment that the action is good or bad. This intuitive or nondiscursive judgment is part of the whole process. A positive judgment about a particular act looks for a way, if possible, to justify such a conclusion. In this case Sabetti used the principle of repelling a materially unjust aggressor to justify aborting the ectopic pregnancy. One of his students indicated the very significant role of intuitive and nondiscursive judgments in Sabetti's approach which cannot be found or discovered in the manual itself or in his solution of cases of conscience. When asked a question in class he would often give an answer without seeing clearly the intermediate steps. On several occasions he replied, "Here is the answer, I'll give the reasons tomorrow; I don't see them clearly now." The student reporting this noted that such a jump to a solution with the frank recognition that Sabetti could not now give his reasons increased rather than decreased one's confidence in him.[82] Such testimony sheds light on how Sabetti's mind worked but even the genre of cases of conscience does not reveal this factor at work. Sabetti's casuistry certainly recognizes a great role for principles and norms and their applications; but a comparative and contrasting analysis with other cases takes place and also the intuitive judgment about the morality of the act plays a significant role. It is important to remember that Sabetti never in his writings about cases explicitly mentions this nondiscursive, intuitive judgment, but it obviously played a significant role for him.

The question arises: can the judgment about a particular case ever cause the theologian to modify or change a specific principle or norm? Sabetti never recognizes this possibility in any of his cases because he never explicitly adverts to this intuitive judgment. For him the insistence on eternal immutable principles and norms also appears to argue against such a modification. This more inductive approach to principles also goes against the heavy emphasis on deduction throughout his work. His classicist approach with little or no historical consciousness would not in general be open to such changes or modifications in principles and norms. In reality, however, such changes have occurred in the history of Catholic moral theology and John B. Hogan, an Irish-born American contemporary of Sabetti who will be studied in chapter seven, recognized the possibility of such modifications.[83]

Another important factor in casuistry for Sabetti was the intervention of the hierarchical teaching office. As pointed out before, Sabetti believed that once Rome had spoken even through a curial congregation, the debate was finished. Sabetti not only did not resent this Roman involvement but greatly respected it and was appreciative of it. Here again one notices an extrinsicism at work. The practical cases deal with what Sabetti in theory called the somewhat distant and remote conclusions from the first principles of the natural law where different positions exist and theologians often hold different sides. But Roman authority could intervene and decide the case once and for all despite this apparent lack of certitude. Where does that certitude come from?

OTHER CHARACTERISTICS OF SABETTI'S CASUISTRY.   A scientific and thematic approach strives for consistency and coherency. Sabetti's casuistry exhibits these characteristics. His casuistry clearly illustrates the fitting together of principles, norms, applications, and solutions to other cases. A case is never treated in isolation but is always related to other factors and other cases. In addition, all these aspects cohere with the definitions and distinctions made in the short treatise on fundamental moral theology. One expects that the discursive reasoning process would strive for such consistency. Sabetti well illustrates such a process at work.

A rather distinctive characteristic of Catholic moral theology as illustrated in Sabetti and the whole tradition concerns the emphasis on the internal aspect of human acts and not just the external. The very first page of the compendium defines the human act as that which precedes from the deliberate will of a human being. Acts can be either internal, which are acts done by the internal powers of the soul such as acts of thinking or loving, or they can be external or mixed acts that the will accomplishes through the organs of the body.[84] Our Jesuit author consistently recognizes the importance of the internal aspect in his discussion of particular issues. The discussion of specific sins, for example, logically includes two sections—internal sins of morose delectation, sinful joy, and sinful desires and the second section treating the seven capital sins which are really mixed sins and the bases of all other sins.[85] Recall the role of intention in the concept of direct killing and in the principle of double effect. One cannot either directly intend or directly do the killing in ordinary circumstances.

In his casuistry Sabetti consistently recognizes the internal aspects of the act by focusing on attention and intention. Attention refers to the mind and intention refers to the will, the two basic and distinctive human powers of the soul. The obligation to be present at mass on Sundays and feast days requires both physical bodily presence and attention. One naturally has to deal with how much attention is necessary to fulfill the obligation. Here too the emphasis is on the minimum necessary to avoid sin. Attention requires that one turn the mind to what the priest is doing. This can be done in three ways: turning the mind to the material words and actions of the priest, to the sense of the words and mysteries involved, or to God's self through prayer and meditation. Someone preparing for confession during mass or reading a spiritual book (but not for the sake of studying its style) fulfills the obligation. Someone who is involuntarily distracted throughout the whole time of the mass, unless one is so taken away by extraneous thoughts that she in no way attends to what is going on, fulfills the obligation. One involuntarily sleeping during a notable part of the mass does not fulfill the obligation but might be excused from sin. The person who occasionally nods during mass satisfies the obligation precisely because she adverts in some way to what is being done.[86]

Intention deals with the will but here again significant distinctions are in order. An actual intention comes from the will here and now acting. A virtual intention is an act of the will already made which continues to exist so that it exercises its force on what is done now. A habitual intention is an act of the will that was made in the past and never revoked, but does not influence the present action. The habitual intention is merely concomitant and not causal with regard to the act now being done. An interpretive intention is one that was never made but predictably can be presumed and would have been made if the person were able to think about it.[87]

Intention becomes quite important in the discussion of the sacraments both with regard to the minister and the subject of the sacraments. For the minister of the sacrament actual intention is best and most desirable but a virtual intention is sufficient. The habitual or interpretive intention does not constitute a human voluntary act.[88] For adults some intention is needed in receiving the sacraments. For many of the sacraments a habitual intention, even somewhat implicit and confused, suffices. Since the sacrament confers a gift and a benefit on the subject, a habitual intention is enough to receive it.[89] For adults who are unconscious an interpretive intention suffices for the sacrament of extreme unction because the unconscious person who lived a Christian life is thought to want to receive extreme unction in danger of death.[90] Sabetti consistently deals with the role of attention and intention in human acts, but from the manualistic perspective of the minimum necessary to fulfill the obligation and avoid sin.

A point of clarification is in order. While Sabetti in accord with the Catholic tradition recognizes the role of attention and intention, the subjective aspects of the act can never change the intrinsically evil objective aspect of the act. The good intention or end cannot justify the means. In the notion of direct, direct refers both to the intention of the agent and to the nature of the act. But if the nature of the objective act is direct no subjective aspect or intention can change it.

Sabetti's casuistry is both realistic and commonsensical. These characteristics contribute to avoiding the extreme dangers of both rigorism and laxism. Realism comes through in the materials covered in the compendium and in the cases about which he wrote. These are real cases faced by real people and actual situations. Some ethicists are more concerned with imaginary cases which can better illustrate the principles; for example, promises made on a desert island or unreal analogies, but Sabetti was interested only in the practical issues that people face in their daily lives. Some years ago an American doctor complained that bioethicists were not dealing with the real issues he faced in his everyday life as a physician.[91] No one could accuse Sabetti of not dealing with the real cases that people face. Recall that he used to spend his vacation time in parochial work and hearing confessions so that he might have a feel for the practice of the sacrament of penance.

Common sense is closely allied with realism and shows itself in a proper response to the total situation at hand trying to give due weight to all aspects involved. Such common sense especially avoids the danger of a rigorism which looks only to the law and not to the situation of people. For Sabetti, the experience of people will never change the law, but it will mitigate or modify the law's applications and help to determine the reality under consideration.

Sabetti, for example, raises the question if those who accuse themselves of hating their neighbor should be considered to have sinned gravely. The answer is no. Often people confuse enmity or hatred properly so called with the detestation or hatred of a quality or defect of the person. Often the uneducated and the more fervent (an interesting combination!) labor under an invincible and natural aversion of the soul or experience only a certain indignation.[92]

In the discussion about drunkenness, Sabetti raises the question of the pledge not to drink that was often made by some Catholics to a priest. Although this promise is good in itself and can have a good effect for many, there are practical difficulties and problems in a priest's receiving such a promise. If the priest openly says what is theologically true; namely, that breaking the promise is no sin or at most a venial sin, the whole efficaciousness of the remedy might be lost. Sabetti here sees the fear of sin and hell as a very strong motivating factor for the person making the pledge and approves such an approach. On the other hand if the priest says nothing, grave sin will be committed because of the poorly formed consciences of those who break the pledge. Many think that the breaking of the pledge is a more grievous sin than full drunkenness.

The priest must use prudence and discretion in talking to people about taking the pledge. Therefore if someone has doubts about the obligation of the pledge and inquires about it, provided that such a person can easily understand the explanation and is not attracted to liquor by an altogether insane and immoderate love, it will be useful and even necessary to explain the nature of this pledge. It is not a vow but only an intention manifested to the priest and cannot be gravely obliging. In the other hypothesis it is better to say nothing and permit the grave sins that might follow. The hope of reducing drunkenness constitutes a sufficient reason to tolerate such sins coming from a poorly formed conscience.[93] Today many would disagree with such an approach because it is paternalistic and uses the fear of sin and hell as the primary motivating factor, but, given the premises, the prudence and common sense of Sabetti come through.

In discussing blasphemy which is speech against God in an insulting and contemptuous way, Sabetti asks if the American expression "God damn your soul" constitutes blasphemy. Per se it is blasphemous and also against charity. But our author perceptively recognizes that often in practice both malices are lacking, since there is no real desire of harming the other person.[94]

Sabetti's common sense as well as his precise and concise approach stands out in his consideration of a question that has very contemporary overtones. What about the custom among us of revealing the private life of magistrates or legislators? From the viewpoint of both justice and charity it is licit to reveal those crimes, even if they are hidden, which render a candidate or office holder less fit for exercising the office. The common good prevails over the private good. In accord with the Constitution and custom the candidate is understood to cede her private rights here by the very fact of running for office. However, there are limits; those who act out of prurient interest or just for the sake of revealing what is not related to the common good are to be condemned.[95]

Sabetti's practical moral reasoning has much to commend it in terms of its analysis, its striving for consistency and coherency, its realism, and its common sense. However, all these occurred in a context of immutable and unchangeable principles and norms, with belief in the existence of intrinsically evil specific actions, and in the expectation that Roman congregations would often intervene to solve these cases and stop the discussions.

SOME SPECIFIC AMERICAN CONSIDERATIONS

As a moral theologian Sabetti is writing for American seminarians and priests and indirectly for American Catholic people. His method involves applying the principles of the Catholic moral tradition to particular cases and issues. These particular applications must take into consideration the diversity and local character of each country.[96] Sabetti recognizes the role of cultural diversity in that the same act may have a different significance among us than it has elsewhere.[97] The cultural diversity can affect the meaning of acts but apparently not the principles or norms which are assumed by reason to be the same for all.

Sabetti was a comparatively recent immigrant to the United States. Where did he find his information about this country? In addition to being an immigrant, Sabetti apparently did not mix that much with the general populace. He lived in an isolated Jesuit theologate in Woodstock, Maryland, which by design and definition wanted to be a place apart from the hustle and bustle of daily life. The North American Jesuit obviously recognized the problem and spent his vacation times working in parishes in larger cities and hearing confessions. This experience gave him some feel for the American people and scene, but his compendium indicates that most of his knowledge of the American scene came from written sources.

Francis Patrick Kenrick, who wrote the first edition of his *Theologia moralis* in the 1840s and a second edition about twenty years later, was the primary source used by Sabetti. Kenrick too was an immigrant, having come to this country from Ireland after his ordination in Rome in 1821. As a diocesan priest and bishop he had much greater contact with the American scene than Sabetti and had more intellectual concerns.[98] Sabetti invariably cited and agreed with Kenrick on issues pertaining to the American scene. Kenrick thus served as Sabetti's primary guide for all matters dealing with aspects of Catholic life in the United States. Sabetti also quoted where appropriate the decrees of the Plenary Councils of Baltimore with regard to directions for Catholics in this country.[99]

The two major areas peculiar to the American experience were contacts with non-Catholics and the more general relationship to the legal, political, and cultural ethos of the United States.

RELATIONSHIP WITH NON-CATHOLICS. In his preface the Jesuit author mentioned that Gury-Ballerini contained little or nothing about the relationship of Catholics to non-Catholics.[100] Sabetti on these matters relies on the Councils of Baltimore and Kenrick. Some relations with non-Catholics are treated under the act of faith, as affirming the obligation to act in accord with the true faith and condemning the denial of the true faith.[101] In his compendium Sabetti never bothers to discuss the true faith. He assumes that the Roman Catholic church is the one true church and that all others including Protestants do not have the true faith. Protestants are generally referred to as heretics and schismatics or sects but never as churches.

Sabetti in his discussion about Catholic parents who give their child over to a Protestant orphanage might indicate some positive value in Protestantism. If parents do it only to avoid the danger of a bad name, they sin gravely. They could surely protect their good name in other ways and also provide for the eternal salvation of their child. But then he goes on and cites "the most outstanding Kenrick." If the parents are oppressed by very great poverty the most outstanding Kenrick does not dare to condemn those parents who so treat their own children with the intention and hope that, baptism having already been conferred, these parents will in the future work in the best way possible to obtain the eternal salvation of their children. One might expect the argument that spiritual goods are more important than any temporal goods so that the eternal salvation of the children must come first. Perhaps the citing of Kenrick and calling him outstanding indicates that Sabetti thinks the position needs some extrinsic support.[102] However, the possibility of eternal salvation depends on what the parents will do in the future and not what the Protestant orphanage does in the meantime.

In accord with Catholic teaching and the Council of Trent baptism conferred by heretics is valid if all the required elements are present. However, Sabetti agrees with Kenrick that in practice those who have been baptized as Protestants should almost always be rebaptized under condition since they may not have been truly baptized. Sabetti goes through a list of the sects and concludes that only the "heretical Orientals" and the Old Catholics can be presumed to have baptized validly. Problems and doubts are raised against baptism conferred in all the other sects including the Episcopalian.[103] The polemic against Protestantism at the time obviously influenced such a judgment which in these warmer ecumenical days is no longer held.

Sabetti deals with many separate questions and issues about Catholics' relationship with non-Catholics but no principles or norms are stated in the beginning for determining what the relationship should be. However, the responses given to the individual questions indicate the primary principle, namely, that *communicatio in sacris* or participation in worship with Protestants and others can never be allowed. The assumption is that such participation would deny the true faith. However, Catholic presence at some Protestant functions might not involve participation in their false worship. One can go to Protestant churches merely out of curiosity. Going to such a church is in itself an indifferent act. However, if there is a danger of perversion or scandal or if one's going is interpreted as a sign of one and the same religion existing between Protestants and Catholics one cannot go. Catholics regularly should not be present at sermons, baptisms, and marriages of heretics. However, if there is no participation in the worship and one's presence is only material and a sign of civic respect as is often the case among us, there is no sin. But Catholics cannot be godparents in a Protestant baptism. Likewise Catholics are not permitted to give money to support the building of Protestant churches even through bazaars and church suppers. But it can be permitted if this support appears from the circumstances not to be support of the sect but a sign of gratitude or benevolence. Here Sabetti points out that as a result of particular local circumstances actions might have an altogether different meaning among us in the United States than elsewhere.[104]

Catholic and Protestant polemics and differences created sharp divisions on many matters including the bible. Sabetti raised the question whether taking an oath on a Protestant bible is morally acceptable. The answer is no because such an action appears to be an approbation of the book in question and would give scandal. However, in practice there should be no problem. A Catholic version of the bible is usually given to one who asks or the person is allowed to bring one's own bible.[105] Sabetti thus illustrates the implacable opposition of Catholics to Protestants on the strictly religious level, but the need for social peace and harmony.

AMERICAN LAW, POLITICS, AND CULTURE. The section on justice and rights is the largest section of the book dealing with strictly moral matters as distinguished from the sacraments. The major sections include ownership (who, how, and when is it acquired), restitution, and all types of contracts. The civil law affects many of these cases. Sabetti in this part accepts such laws as binding and bases his discussion on them. Here too he depends heavily on Kenrick. Like Kenrick he frequently cites *Commentaries on American Law* by James Kent which went through many subsequent editions after the death of the original author.[106] To a lesser extent he used two sources not mentioned by

Kenrick—*A Law Dictionary Adapted to the Constitution and Laws of the United States of America and of the Several States of the American Union* . . . edited by John Bouvier and also *Wells' Every Man His Own Lawyer*.[107] However, Sabetti's discussion is not as extensive as Kenrick's and cites many fewer sources. He does not appear to have the same depth and breadth of knowledge of the American legal scene as Kenrick. However, Sabetti's whole purpose was to present a short, concise, one volume treatment of moral theology for seminarians and priests.

Sabetti has very little to say about American political and cultural realities. The compendium with its individualistic focus does not discuss the political order and the nature, function, and role of government. The long discussion of justice and rights deals only with justice between individuals. Sabetti considers purely penal laws in general and with regard to taxation. While not denying the probability of some purely penal laws, the Woodstock Jesuit urged people to obey such laws.[108] Perhaps he was fearful here of the image of Catholics and the church in the American society and did not want to give any ammunition to the strong anti-Catholicism that prevailed. But one can only surmise. His compendium makes no explicit reference to any anti-Catholicism in this country. Sabetti deals with the practical aspects of Catholic life in the United States as if it existed in a vacuum. The social setting with the exceptions of the legal discussions of justice and relations with Protestants and non-Catholics never really appears in his work.

A few indications show his opposition to some of the characteristic and distinctive aspects of the political and cultural ethos in the United States. Sabetti raised the question about the morality of Catholic American citizens taking the oath to uphold the Constitution. He quotes Kenrick and makes it his own. The oath is to be understood in its popular and accepted sense. One pledges allegiance to the magistrates and the laws according to the tenor of the Constitution. One does not necessarily assent to what the Constitution says about the freedom of thought, speech, religion, and the right of divorce.[109] The brief statement about Sabetti's opposition to the freedom of thought, speech, and religion fits in with Sabetti's whole background as an Italian-reared Jesuit and a member of the Woodstock faculty with their opposition to the intellectual and political developments of the nineteenth century. In the preface to his treatise on justice and rights Gury-Ballerini maintains that a sound discussion of justice and rights is necessary to heal the most dangerous evils of republicanism—to squander one's own things, to assault those of others, and to overturn all rights to satisfy one's hunger for pleasure.[110] Sabetti does not explicitly cite this strong condemnation of republican ideas and the Enlightenment, but he obviously would agree with them.

Sabetti does not recognize the American emphasis on equality and especially the equality of all citizens. He often refers to the authorities even in the United States as the rulers and princes. His view of society is totally hierarchical. His discussion of almsgiving indicated his acceptance of the traditional hierarchical nature of the different states in life and one's right to live in accord with one's state in life. Sabetti's emphasis on states in life is apparently gender blind for it also arises in his discussion of breast feeding. There is an obligation but not a serious one to nurse one's own baby. However, necessity, notable utility, or custom among noble families excuses from any guilt.[111] This indicates once again that Sabetti is repeating what is found in the European manuals.

Sabetti understands the role of the priest in the same hierarchical context. The role is authoritarian based on the power and authority of Jesus especially with regard to the sacraments and to teaching. Recall his emphasis in the sacrament of penance on the paternal love and concern of the confessor thus showing the paternalistic nature of such a role.

Our Jesuit author addresses one aspect of United States culture directly—the public school. In one sense the evaluation of the public school is not simply a cultural issue for Sabetti comes out of the tradition that sees the family and religion—not the state—as having a primary role with regard to schooling. Sabetti poses the issue in terms of parents sending their children to public schools that prescind from any religious education. Per se speaking and based on the principle of natural and positive law, these schools are evil and full of dangers. The text quotes the *Syllabus of Errors* and the Second and Third Plenary Councils of Baltimore in support of this position. The further question is then raised: despite what has been said is it ever possible for Catholic parents to send their children to public school? Yes, provided the conditions set down by the Council of Baltimore are met. The malice of the public school consists in the system of excluding religious education and in the dangers to faith and morals. Parents who are faced by a grave necessity to send their children to such schools do not approve the system itself and must use the necessary means to take away or greatly diminish the dangers. But the judgment about reasons justifying such attendance in public schools is to be made by the local bishop and not the parents.[112]

What about the role of women in American society? Again Sabetti does not address the question directly. One would expect him very much to mirror the understanding of his time especially seen from a European perspective. Such is the case. In his hierarchical view of society women are subordinated to men. The section on sexuality has pointed out some of Sabetti's attitudes toward women. With regard to the minister of the sacrament of baptism in case of necessity, a man is preferred to a woman as is made clear in the *Roman Ritual*.[113] Our author accepts the regulation in many states that women cannot validly make a will.[114] Only the mother's instinct (the father is not mentioned) can properly satisfy the natural needs of a child especially at a very tender age.[115]

Much more fascinating is what Sabetti has left out from Gury-Ballerini with regard to the relationship of husband and wife. Under the fourth commandment Sabetti has only two chapters—the obligation of children toward their parents and the obligation of parents toward their children.[116] Gury-Ballerini has two other chapters—the obligation of spouses and the obligation of other superiors and inferiors. Gury-Ballerini's discussion about spouses is quite succinct. Spouses have four mutual obligations—mutual love, conjugal life and cohabitation, giving each other what is necessary for the sustenance of their life, and rendering the conjugal debt when reasonably asked. The husband is held to provide and administer the goods for the family, to see to it that the wife fulfills her duties as a Christian, and to correct the delinquent wife. As a part of the explanation, Gury-Ballerini maintains that the husband is the head of the wife and the rector of the whole family. However, the husband is to correct her in a mild way because she is his companion and not his slave. The wife has three duties: to revere the husband, to obey him, and to take care of the house and the domestic chores.[117]

Although Sabetti had not included this material, Barrett, his subsequent editor, included almost word for word what Gury-Ballerini said about the relationship of husband and wife and also adds a long quotation from Pope Leo XIII's encyclical, *Arcanum*.[118] In the earlier section on the duties of parents toward their children, Barrett also added his own material to what Sabetti had. The domestic duties of the wife— care of the family, reverence to her husband, and education of the children—are sacrosanct and whatever takes wives away from these obligations is forbidden. All feminism (note the word *feminismus*) which tries to free a wife from her matrimonial obligations and to liberate a single woman from the natural and divine law is to be avoided as opposed to the nature of civil society, of the family, and of religion. Socialistic, atheistic, irreligious feminism is to be fought with all our strength.[119] Sabetti apparently left out Gury-Ballerini's chapter on the obligation of spouses in the light of his purpose to shorten and condense his basic source. Barrett has probably added the discussion from Gury-Ballerini and his own very strong attack on feminism in response to some of the feminist movements of his time although he does not mention them by name. Note the appeal to nature and to divine and natural law to justify the roles of the wife. This appeal illustrates the danger of the manuals with their lack of historical consciousness to give immutability and divine sanction to what may be a culturally conditioned phenomenon. Sabetti undoubtedly would have agreed with these ideas even though he did not write them.

In conclusion Sabetti does not pretend to be an original thinker but carries on the manualist tradition while trying to improve it from a pedagogical perspective. The differences with the Thomistic approach to moral theology are illustrated by their different understandings of the role of prudence. Sabetti as a manualist gives no great importance to prudence. At best prudence is mentioned in the context of the proper application of principles to cases.

In Thomistic ethics prudence is an intellectual virtue as well as a cardinal virtue which commands the acts of all the other virtues. Prudence is practical wisdom which directs the person to choosing the right means to the end. This virtue deals with the contingent and the individual as distinguished from the universal. The proper working of prudence, however, requires the presence of the other moral virtues directing the will to the right ends.[120]

Many reasons explain why Sabetti as a manualist practically ignores prudence and thus differs from the Thomistic approach. Sabetti does not give any major role to the virtues at all. Since prudence functions as a virtue in relationship with all the other virtues, Sabetti can easily bypass it. Prudence presupposes the teleological model for it deals with the means to achieve the end, but the Woodstock Jesuit in keeping with the manualist tradition employs a legal model which understands morality in terms of obedience to law as the remote norm of morality. Prudence as an intellectual virtue directing all the other virtues presupposes the primacy of reason in moral matters and not the primacy of the will. The legal model of the manuals is voluntaristic and hence downplays the role of practical reasoning. The manuals deal with the minimum or the outer circumference of the moral life—what is wrong and sinful. Law well marks out the area of the forbidden. Common sense reminds us that at the very minimum law is not all that helpful in dealing with matters above the minimal requirements. Prudence plays a very significant role in decisions about vocation, marriage partner, how best to use one's time, the proper observance of Lent, how to grow in human relationships, and how best to contribute to the common good. Prudence deals with the contingent, the particular, and the individual. The manual plays down these aspects and sees the particular only in the light of the universal norms or principles.

Sabetti develops his whole moral theology on the basis of the application of principles and norms to particular cases. Implicit in the approach of the manuals is a desire for certitude which the proper application of law can give. Prudence is not able to claim that same degree of certitude. Thus Sabetti and the manualists have reduced decision making to the application of principles and norms to cases and have left no room for prudence. Casuistry operating only in the direction of going from a certain norm to a certain conclusion about what is to be done or not done here and now has no real room for prudence. As such a casuistry became the primary and practically the sole model of decision making, the classical doctrine of prudence fell into oblivion.[121]

In summary Aloysius Sabetti successfully accomplished his purpose in writing a short and practical manual of moral theology primarily for seminarians in the United States. Sabetti was not an intellectual but an intelligent, dedicated, and loyal person of the church writing for the church and its needs. His temperament, personality, and clarity of thought and expression make him the ideal author of such a manual. However, the genre of the manual of moral theology has many shortcomings and negative aspects. In addition, Sabetti like all of us is a creature of his own time and circumstances. From a contemporary perspective one can and should be quite critical of Sabetti's work, but one should also appreciate how well his manual served the needs of the church and its many students in this country for more than fifty years.

N O T E S

1. Sabetti, *Compendium*, nn. 1–3, pp. 1–2.
2. Ibid, nn. 10–21, pp. 7–13.
3. Ibid, nn. 24–28, pp. 16–20.

4. Ibid, nn. 4–9, pp. 3–7.

5. For a sampling of the contemporary discourse about the description of human acts in Catholic moral theology, see Charles E. Curran and Richard A. McCormick, eds., *Readings in Moral Theology No. 1: Moral Norms and Catholic Tradition* (New York: Paulist, 1979).

6. Sabetti, *Compendium*, nn. 29–32, pp. 21–22.

7. Ibid., nn. 44–67, pp. 29–45.

8. Ibid., n. 71, p. 50.

9. Ibid., nn. 37–43, pp. 24–28.

10. "Sabetti," *Woodstock Letters* 29 (1900): 221.

11. C. Harney, "Scrupulosity," *New Catholic Encyclopedia*, 12, pp. 1253–1255.

12. Sabetti, *Compendium*, nn. 72–106, pp. 52–74.

13. Ibid., nn. 74–75, pp. 53–56.

14. Ibid., n. 72, p. 52.

15. Ibid., n. 87, p. 63.

16. Ibid., n. 95, p. 68.

17. Mahoney, *Making of Moral Theology*, pp. 231–241.

18. Sabetti, *Compendium*, nn. 107–123, pp. 75–84.

19. Ibid., n. 114, p. 80.

20. Ibid., nn. 125–128, pp. 85–90.

21. Ibid., n. 127, p. 88.

22. Ibid., nn. 279–280, pp. 208–209.

23. José M. Diaz Moreno, "La doctrina moral sobre la parvedad de materia 'in re venerea' desde Cayetano hasta S. Alfonso," *Archivio Teológico Granadino* 23 (1960): 42–47.

24. Sabetti, *Compendium*, n. 127, p. 88.

25. Ibid., n. 742, p. 536.

26. Ibid., nn. 129–134, pp. 91–97.

27. Ibid., nn. 135–146, pp. 98–103.

28. Ibid., nn. 147–150, pp. 104–106.

29. Gury-Ballerini, *Compendium*, 1, nn. 181–184, pp. 156–159.

30. Ibid., nn. 279–309, pp. 208–220. Many contemporary Catholic theologians point out the danger here of identifying the human with merely the physical structure of the act. For a contemporary discussion about Catholic sexual teaching, see Charles E. Curran and Richard A. McCormick, eds., *Readings in Moral Theology No. 8: Dialogue about Catholic Sexual Teaching* (New York: Paulist, 1993).

31. Sabetti, *Compendium*, nn. 933–943, pp. 729–737.

32. Ibid., n. 940, p. 735.

33. Ibid., n. 856, p. 657.

34. Ibid., n. 852, p. 653.

35. For developments within magisterial teaching on marriage, see Joseph A. Selling, "Magisterial Teaching on Marriage 1880–1968: Historical Constancy or Radical Development?" in *Historia: Memoria futuri*, ed. Tremblay and Billy, pp. 351–402.

36. Sabetti, *Compendium*, n. 943, pp. 736–737.

37. Ibid., n. 943, p. 737.

38. Ibid., nn. 289–292, pp. 214–215.

39. Ibid., nn. 933–943, pp. 729–737.

40. Ibid., n. 797, p. 603.

41. Gury-Ballerini, *Compendium*, 1, n. 410, p. 393.

42. Sabetti, *Compendium*, n. 280, pp. 208–209.

43. Ibid., nn. 283–286, pp. 211–213.

44. Ibid.

45. Ibid., nn. 135–138, pp. 98–101.

46. Ibid., n. 41, p. 27.

47. Ibid., "*Nota*" and n. 186, p. 131.

48. Ibid., n. 188, p. 132.

49. Ibid., nn. 186–193, pp. 131–135.

50. Aloysius Sabetti, "The Question of Round Dances," *American Ecclesiastical Review* 18 (1898): 207.

51. Sabetti, *Compendium*, n. 7, p. 5.

52. Ibid., nn. 301–304, pp. 216–219.

53. Ibid., n. 196, pp. 136–138.

54. Ibid., n. 187, pp. 131–132.

55. Ibid., n. 185, p. 130.

56. Ibid., n. 21, p. 13.

57. Ibid., nn. 305–306, p. 219.

58. For example, Robert Nugent, ed. *A Challenge to Love: Gay and Lesbian Catholics in the Church* (New York: Crossroad, 1983).

59. Sabetti, *Compendium*, n. 250, p. 186.

60. Ibid., n. 182, p. 128.

61. Ibid., n. 350, p. 256.

62. Ibid., n. 147, p. 104.

63. Ibid., nn. 310–313, pp. 221–223.

64. Ibid., nn. 175–177, pp. 124–125.

65. Ibid., nn. 268–269, pp. 200–202.

66. "Sabetti," *Woodstock Letters* 29 (1900): 228.

67. "Sabetti, S. J., The Rev. Aloysius," *American Ecclesiastical Review Index, Vol. 1–50*, p. 283.

68. Augustinus Lehmkuhl, Josephus Aertnys, Aloysius Sabetti, "*Solutiones theologorum*," *American Ecclesiastical Review* 9 (1893): 347–360.

69. Sabetti, *American Ecclesiastical Review* 9 (1893): 354.

70. Jonsen-Toulmin, *The Abuse of Casuistry*, pp. 253, 321–325.

71. Aloysius Sabetti, "*Animadversiones in casum*," *American Ecclesiastical Review* 9 (1893): 433; Aloysius Sabetti, "The Catholic Church and Obstetrical Science," *American Ecclesiastical Review* 13 (1895): 132.

72. Sabetti, *American Ecclesiastical Review* 9 (1893): 354–357.

73. Aloysius Sabetti, "*Animadversiones in controversia de ectopicis conceptibus*," *American Ecclesiastical Review* 11 (1894): 134.

74. Sabetti, *American Ecclesiastical Review* 9 (1893): 358.

75. Augustinus Lehmkuhl, "*Excisio foetus atque eius directa occisio*," *American Ecclesiastical Review* 10 (1894): 64–67.

76. Sabetti, *American Ecclesiastical Review* 11 (1894): 131–134.
77. Lehmkuhl, *American Ecclesiastical Review* 10 (1894): 65.
78. Sabetti, *American Ecclesiastical Review* 9 (1893): 356.
79. Lehmkuhl, *American Ecclesiastical Review* 10 (1894): 67.
80. Decree of the Holy Office, May 5, 1902, in T. Lincoln Bouscaren, *Ethics of Ectopic Operations*, 2nd ed. (Milwaukee: Bruce, 1943), p. 22.
81. Bouscaren, *Ectopic Operations*, pp. 147–171. Lehmkuhl even after the responses of the Holy Office maintained that removing the growth or tumor resulting from an ectopic pregnancy is only indirect killing and therefore permitted. See Bouscaren, *Ectopic Operations*, p. 62.
82. "Sabetti," *Woodstock Letters* 29 (1900): 218–219.
83. John Hogan, "Clerical Studies: Moral Theology III, Casuistry," *American Ecclesiastical Review* 10 (1894): 1–12. This article and others in the series published in the *American Ecclesiastical Review* appeared later as a book—John B. Hogan, *Clerical Studies* (Boston: Marlier, Callanan, 1898), pp. 223–235.
84. Sabetti, *Compendium*, n. 2, p. 2.
85. Ibid., nn. 135–146, pp. 98–103.
86. Ibid., nn. 242–245, pp. 182–183.
87. Ibid., n. 5, p. 4.
88. Ibid., n. 635, p. 422.
89. Ibid., n. 646, p. 429.
90. Ibid., n. 5. p. 4.
91. Charles B. Moore, "*This* is Medical Ethics?" *Hastings Center Report* 4, n. 5 (1979): 1–3.
92. Sabetti, *Compendium*, n. 147, p. 123.
93. Ibid., n. 150, p. 105.
94. Ibid., n. 221, p. 164.
95. Ibid., n. 316, p. 226.
96. Ibid., p. vii.
97. Ibid., n. 154, p. 111.
98. For biographical information, see Nolan, *Francis Patrick Kenrick*.
99. Sabetti, *Compendium*, p. vi.
100. Ibid.
101. Ibid., n. 154, pp. 109–111.
102. Ibid., n. 261, p. 194.
103. Ibid., n. 662, pp. 446–447.
104. Ibid., n. 154., pp. 109–111.
105. Ibid., n. 224, p. 167.
106. James Kent, *Commentaries on American Law*, ed. O. W. Holmes, Jr., 12th ed., 4 vols. (Boston: Little, Brown, 1873).
107. John Bouvier, ed., *A Law Dictionary Adapted to the Constitution and Laws of the United States of America and of the Several States of the American Union*, 10th ed., 2 vols. (Philadelphia: Childs and Peterson, 1860); John G. Wells, *Wells' Every Man His Own Lawyer and Business Form Book*, new ed. (New York: B. W. Hitchcock, 1867).
108. Sabetti, *Compendium*, nn. 113–114, pp. 79–80.
109. Ibid., n. 224, p. 167.

110. Gury-Ballerini, *Compendium*, 1, above n. 517, p. 472.

111. Sabetti, *Compendium*, n. 261, p. 193.

112. Ibid., n. 261, pp. 195–196.

113. Ibid., n. 659, p. 443.

114. Ibid., n. 512, p. 340.

115. Ibid., n. 261, p. 194.

116. Ibid., nn. 256–261, pp. 190–197.

117. Gury-Ballerini, *Compendium*, 1, nn. 378–381, pp. 363–365.

118. Aloysius Sabetti, *Compendium theologiae moralis*, ed. Timothy Barrett, 22nd ed. (New York: Frederick Pustet, 1915), n. 258, pp. 241–242.

119. Ibid., n. 257, pp. 239–240.

120. For Aquinas's discussion of prudence in the context of his approach to virtue in general, see $I^a II^{ae}$, q. 49–67; for prudence in particular, see $I^a II^{ae}$, q. 47–56. For a well-known discussion of prudence in the Thomistic tradition, see Josef Pieper, *The Four Cardinal Virtues* (Notre Dame, Ind.: University of Notre Dame Press, 1966), pp. 3–40.

121. Pieper, *The Four Cardinal Virtues*, p. 27.

PART THREE

Thomas J. Bouquillon: Neoscholastic

5

Bouquillon's Scholarly Interests and Concerns

Thomas Joseph Bouquillon like Sabetti was a moral theologian who came to the United States from Europe. However, great differences existed between them. Whereas Sabetti's *Compendium theologiae moralis* became a significant textbook for succeeding generations of students and went through multiple editions with two subsequent editors, Bouquillon's major work, *Theologia moralis fundamentalis*, went through three editions with the last one published shortly after the author's death.[1] No further editions ever appeared, and so Bouquillon had little or no influence as a textbook in moral theology. On the other hand, Bouquillon unlike Sabetti is comparatively well-known to students of American Catholic church history but for aspects other than his fundamental moral theology.

Sabetti's world was the seminary and his approach to moral theology was primarily pastoral. Bouquillon did his work primarily in universities and his approach was academic and intellectual as well as pastoral. At Catholic University he did not teach seminarians. In fact, Bouquillon strongly opposed the manual or compendium genre of moral theology. Bouquillon's work in moral theology thus stands in some contrast to that of Sabetti's.

Thomas Joseph Bouquillon was born near Lille in Belgium in 1840, the second of five children of a family of small landowners. He felt a call to the priesthood and had a brilliant record as a student at the minor seminary at Roulers and the major seminary at Bruges. In 1863 the bishop of Bruges sent this young student to Rome to continue his studies and he obtained a doctorate in theology at the Gregorian University in Rome in 1867. While in Rome, he lived at the Capranaca College where he became friends with Mariano Rampolla, the future cardinal and Secretary of State of Pope Leo XIII.[2]

With his Roman doctorate Bouquillon began to teach fundamental moral theology at the major seminary in Bruges in 1867 but two years later moved to the class of special moral theology which deals with specific actions. In August 1877 his bishop authorized him to accept the chair of moral theology in the faculty of theology of the newly established Catholic Faculties or Catholic University of Lille. However, in 1885 he left this chair at Lille for reasons that are not altogether clear and retired to the Benedictine monastery of Maredsous to work on a thorough revision of his book on fundamental moral theology which had first been published in 1873.[3] He had found it difficult to do such work while teaching, preparing courses, and directing students at Lille.[4] The second edition, eventually published in 1890, was entirely transformed and included a long history of moral theology which showed both his knowledge of the sources and his ability to synthesize and analyze their contributions.[5]

Meanwhile the bishops of the United States announced their intention to open, with papal authorization, the pontifical Catholic University of America in Washington, D.C. Bishop John J. Keane resigned from his diocese of Richmond, Virginia, to accept the rectorship of the new university. One of his most important tasks was to assemble a respected faculty, and he looked to Europe especially to the faculty of the University of Louvain in Belgium. Bernard Jungmann of the Louvain faculty called Keane's attention to Bouquillon who was now in "retirement" at Maredsous doing his writing. Keane deputed Edward Pace, an American priest already appointed to the faculty of the new university, to sound out Bouquillon to see if he would be a suitable candidate and if he would be interested in coming to the new institution. Pace reported favorably on Bouquillon but pointed out that he would need some wooing to induce him to go to Washington.[6] Bouquillon received contradictory advice from the friends he consulted. He would not be able now to work on his complete course in moral theology, but he found it hard to refuse so flattering an offer to be a part of the new enterprise of the Catholic church in the United States.[7] Canon H. Rommel, who on the occasion of Bouquillon's death wrote the best available biographical piece on him, describes Bouquillon as leaving for the United States in the fall of 1889 to take up his new professorship without enthusiasm and seeing it primarily as a duty to be fulfilled.[8]

Bouquillon joined the first faculty of the Catholic University of America and until his death in 1902 played a very significant role

—

within the university and the Catholic church in the United States. His health had always been somewhat frail although he was a tireless worker. At the turn of the century the Belgian-born professor had been in poor health for a few years but managed to finish his courses in May 1902. He departed for Europe in late June hoping to recover his health, but it was not to be. He died in Brussels on November 5, 1902.[9]

BOUQUILLON AS AMERICAN CATHOLIC LIBERAL

American church history remembers Bouquillon but not primarily for his work in fundamental moral theology. Bouquillon is best known for his involvement in the famous school controversy case, which together with other somewhat related incidents identified him with the cause of the liberals in the American Catholic church.[10] As mentioned in chapter two in the later part of the nineteenth century the American Catholic bishops themselves were divided into what has since been called liberal and conservative camps. The two camps disagreed sharply on the rapid Americanization of immigrants, the establishment of the Catholic University of America, the notion of the American state, cooperation with the state in the realm of education, Catholic participation in the Knights of Labor, and the condemnation of Henry George for his single-tax theory and the excommunication of his strong supporter, Father Edward McGlynn of New York. The leading liberal among the bishops was John Ireland, the archbishop of St. Paul, with Denis O'Connell (made a bishop only in 1907), John Keane, and others associated with them. The leaders of the conservative bishops were Michael Corrigan of New York and his suffragan Bernard McQuaid of Rochester with help from a number of German-American bishops who thought the Irish-dominated hierarchy did not appreciate their concerns.[11]

The school controversy had both theoretical and practical aspects. Theoretically the question centered on the role of the state in education. Bishop McQuaid of Rochester and others had strongly insisted that the state had no direct role to play in education. McQuaid had urged government help for Catholic schools. He argued that it is wrong for Catholics, as well as for Jews and infidels, to pay taxes for schools, in which the bible is read and religious exercises are held. In addition, the state has no right to educate being an incompetent agent to fulfill parental responsibilities. The topic stirred up great debate among American Catholics. Catholic schools were beginning to be built at this time. The Third Plenary Council of Baltimore in 1884 discouraged Catholics from sending their children to public schools. The question of schooling and the proper role of the state in education became an important issue for the American Catholic church in the latter part of the nineteenth century—and ever since.[12]

Archbishop Ireland, the champion of the American Catholic liberals, in the early 1890s proposed a plan for schools in Faribault, Minnesota, which was later accepted in Stillwater, Minnesota. The schools would become public schools paid for by the local community but before school hours the children would go to mass and then have catechism taught after the teaching of the secular subjects in the afternoon. Ambiguity surrounded the question of whether the boards of education would continue to hire the Catholic sisters as teachers, but the teachers had to be competent. Ireland pleaded that finances did not permit the establishment of Catholic schools for all and this was the best arrangement under the circumstances. Similar plans had been proposed in Poughkeepsie, New York, and elsewhere, but Ireland's plan drew strong opposition from both Protestants and Catholics. Many Protestants objected that such a plan was a capitulation to Catholicism. On the other hand, Catholic opponents saw it as a sellout of Catholic education and a capitulation to the state.[13]

The American Catholic archbishops were to meet in St. Louis on November 25, 1891, to discuss the issue. In this context Bouquillon's pamphlet, "Education: To Whom Does It Belong?" appeared.[14] Some accused Ireland of conspiring to have Bouquillon publish this pamphlet at this time since Bouquillon strongly defended some role for the state in education, but such a charge is not true.[15] Bishop Keane, the rector of Catholic University, has explained the origin of the Bouquillon pamphlet.[16] In the light of the discussion in the United States among Catholics about the role of the state in education, Bouquillon began to consider this matter in his courses. The students were interested and begged him to prepare two special lectures on the subject. These lectures were discussed at St. Mary's Seminary in Baltimore which was under the care of the Sulpician Fathers. Alphonse Magnien, the superior of the Sulpicians in the United States from 1878 to 1902, a staunch supporter of liberal Catholicism in the United States, and a friend and confidant of Cardinal Gibbons, the archbishop of Baltimore, asked for a copy of the manuscript.[17] Magnien read it with great approval, and recommended the manuscript to Cardinal Gibbons. Gibbons, apparently hoping that the scholarly and rather abstract treatise on the various roles of the individual, the family, the church, and the state in education would help the discussion in the United States, urged its publication in the *American Catholic Quarterly Review* published in Philadelphia. The article was then too late for the April 1891 issue but was returned to Bouquillon before the July issue with a curt note from the assistant editor refusing to publish it. The cardinal advised that it should be published as a pamphlet by Murphy and Company of Baltimore and so the pamphlet saw the light of day in November 1891 just before the meeting of the archbishops to discuss Ireland's school proposals.

In Bouquillon's own words the pamphlet deals only with theoretical principles, makes no practical applications, does not pretend to originality but follows in the footsteps of the great theologians especially Thomas Aquinas, and is guided by the teachings of the encyclicals of Pope Leo XIII on civil power, the constitution of the state, liberty, and the condition of the laboring classes. The pamphlet expresses his position on certain delicate issues and gives his reasons for the positions he adopts in this disputed area.[18] The pamphlet of less than thirty pages deals with four questions—the right to educate, mission to educate, authority over education, liberty of education from the point of view of the individual, the family, the state, and the church. The tone of the pamphlet is objective, scholarly, abstract, and rational. The presentation is eminently clear, logical, and nuanced.

The state has the special and proper right to teach human knowledge (not religion), for the diffusion of human knowledge is necessary for the temporal common welfare. The right of the state is neither unlimited nor exclusive for it supplements the rights of individuals and families. The state has the mission to educate in human knowledge, but this is not an essential duty such as maintaining peace and order but an accidental function supplying the defects of individuals. Authority over education belongs to the family, the state, and the church. The state with regard to education in the human sciences has the right to demand evidence of capability on the part of teachers, to insist on a minimum of education, and to prescribe the teaching of this or that branch of human knowledge considered necessary for the majority of its citizens. But note that the state cannot compel parents to send the child to a particular school. Under the liberty of education Bouquillon points out that teaching is subject to the divine law so no one is free to teach error or evil. The state has the mission to hinder this evil, but it cannot prevent all evil and at times can tolerate a teaching that is erroneous or evil.[19]

This scholarly, abstract, and heavily nuanced pamphlet set off quite a storm because of the circumstances and timing of its appearance. The *New Catholic Encyclopedia* includes all the practical aspects and discussion about the Faribault plan under the entry of "Bouquillon Controversy."[20] The controversy was sharp and at times became quite personal. The first response came from René I. Holaind, a Jesuit, former professor of ethics at Woodstock, and confidant of Archbishop Corrigan of New York, who published *The Parent First* within two weeks of Bouquillon's publication because of his fear that Bouquillon's pamphlet would have great effect on the meeting of the archbishops in St. Louis on November 28, 1891.[21] Holaind's pamphlet was polemical especially in contrast to Bouquillon's original. Father E. A. Higgins, S.J., a former provincial of the Jesuits, severely criticized Bouquillon in a December article in *Catholic News* of New York.[22] Within a month Bouquillon published a forty-two page pamphlet in response to Holaind with references to Higgins.[23] American Catholic journals entered the fray. The *Catholic World*, published by the Paulists, strongly supported Bouquillon, but the *American Ecclesiastical Review* published a number of articles critical of the Catholic University professor.[24] Salvatore M. Brandi, S.J., formerly a professor at Woodstock, published a strong attack on Bouquillon in *Civiltà Cattolica*, a semiauthoritative Vatican journal, and this article was subsequently published as a pamphlet in the United States.[25] Realizing the influential nature and importance of *Civiltà Cattolica*, Bouquillon responded in a forty-one page pamphlet.[26] Bouquillon was so worried about the reaction in Europe that he personally translated his three pamphlets into French so that Europeans would have access to his own words.[27] In his rejoinder to the *Civiltà Cattolica* article Bouquillon noted that many of those who disagreed with him were Jesuits.[28] The whole story of this controversy lies beyond the scope of this study. However, brief mention will be made of Bouquillon's methodology in this debate and his understanding of the state which is an important concept in moral theology and was at the heart of this dispute.

As for his method, this controversy showed Bouquillon's broad knowledge of classical theologians and contemporary writers in many different languages. His scholarly intent and bent are quite apparent. He was obviously hurt by the impassioned opposition, insinuations, suspicions, and even calumnies. He appeals to the words of Leo XIII to govern the debate—charity should govern and accusations should not be rashly made against those who loyally support the teaching of the church.[29] Despite his personal hurt Bouquillon showed himself to be a good controversialist. He did not back down. He calls upon his readers, for example, to decide whether Higgins or Bouquillon does not know how to read or is lying to the public.[30]

Bouquillon develops a Thomistic theory of the state standing in the middle between two opposite errors: the first sees the state as only a policeman; the second sees it as a parent. He claims his teaching is in perfect accord with Thomas Aquinas and with Leo XIII. In fact, in his response to Holaind he appeals to Pope Leo XIII's recently published encyclical, *Rerum novarum*, on the role of the state since the encyclical itself had not been available when he wrote his first pamphlet.[31] Those who accept the philosophically liberal notion of the state as policeman with no other function than to protect the material goods of the citizens readily disagree with his understanding of the role of the state in education. Today the importance of knowledge on the part of citizens is greater than ever before. The state consequently has an even greater need to decree compulsory education insofar as it is necessary. The Catholic University professor makes this point in contrast to Brandi who maintains that if the times are changed they now demand less interference of the state in the social realities of life. Bouquillon again uses *Rerum novarum* to bolster his argument. Leo XIII believes that the state should enter more actively than in former times into questions of labor and wages.[32]

On the other hand, the state is not the same as a parent. The state may tolerate evil and does not always have to oppose it. Teaching is subject to the divine law and no one is free to teach evil, error, or inopportune truth. The state must hinder as far as it prudently can an evil coming from mere physical liberty, but the state in education cannot prevent and hinder all evil. The law may tolerate evil in order that greater evils may be avoided or greater goods procured. However, the right to be legally undisturbed in doing evil is by no means the same as a moral right to do evil. One must only apply to education those general principles that solve questions of religious liberty, liberty of association, and the larger questions of the toleration of social evil.[33]

In this context Bouquillon both praises and justifies religious freedom in the United States. In the United States, although freedom of worship is recognized by law, the Catholic church is freer, more justly and fully protected in her rights and prerogatives; the pope is more pope, as Pius IX is reported to have said, and the papacy is less restrained in its inner and outward actions than in any land under the sun.[34] However, in accord with Bouquillon's basic theory the American system itself is an evil that is tolerated. Bouquillon, like Leo XIII, still accepted an authoritarian understanding of the state and could not justify democratic freedoms as good in themselves.

Our author strenuously insisted that in his understanding of the state he was following Aquinas, Suarez, and Leo XIII. Especially the *Civiltà Cattolica* attack made him and others worried about a Roman condemnation of his position.[35] Bishop Faict, his bishop in Belgium, every year happily received the professor on his return from the United States. But in 1893 the bishop was upset by what he heard about Bouquillon's role in the school controversy in the United States. However, he accepted the strong defense of Bouquillon by the rector of the seminary who pointed out that the Catholic University professor merely employed the principles found in his fundamental moral theology (a book carrying the bishop's imprimatur). The old bishop thanked the seminary rector and charged him to tell Dr. Bouquillon that he would receive him once again with open arms.[36] In the end Bouquillon was never condemned and in 1893 was warmly received in audience by Leo XIII.[37] This whole experience had been "a cruel ordeal" for the scholarly Bouquillon.[38] His significant and public involvement in the school controversy identified Bouquillon with the liberal wing of the Catholic church in opposition to the conservative faction represented by Archbishop Corrigan, Bishop McQuaid, and the Jesuits.

Other incidents of Bouquillon's life remembered in American Catholic history also firmly identify him with the so-called liberal wing of United States Catholicism at the end of the nineteenth century. Edward McGlynn, a well-known New York priest, publicly supported the candidacy of Henry George, the advocate of the single tax theory, for mayor of New York in 1886. McGlynn was suspended by Archbishop Corrigan of New York and later (July 1887) excommunicated. Corrigan and McQuaid also tried to get George's book put on the Index of Forbidden Books. Rome eventually put the book on the Index, but did not make the matter public. The American Catholic liberals opposed both actions. The excommunication of McGlynn seemed to imply that there was no room for freedom on political and social questions within Catholicism. The Catholic liberals with the help of Archbishop Francesco Satolli, the papal delegate in the United States, wanted to lift the excommunication. Satolli arranged this after receiving assurances from four professors at Catholic University that McGlynn's teachings were not in opposition to Catholic teaching.[39] Bouquillon was one of the four professors to make this judgment about McGlynn. In fact, he and his colleagues made their report about McGlynn on the letterhead of the "Academy of Moral Sciences" which was the seminar organized by Bouquillon.[40]

Catholic University in general, from the time of its conception and founding, had been identified with the liberal wing of American Catholicism. Again, Corrigan, McQuaid, and many Jesuits were opposed to it. John Keane, the first rector, was very much a part of the liberal camp.[41] After the school controversy Bouquillon was firmly in the liberal camp. Within the faculty itself, however, there were divisions. Joseph Schroeder, Joseph Pohle, and Sebastian Messmer were identified with the more conservative wing of the American church (note their German or German-Swiss origin), and were opposed to Bouquillon on the school controversy.[42] However, Bouquillon and his colleagues in the conservative camp did not engage in polemical and personal attacks. Bouquillon referred to Messmer's article in the *American Ecclesiastical Review* as the "most serious and equitable contribution" in the series of articles published in that journal.[43] Joseph Schroeder, who strongly opposed Bouquillon on the school controversy, nevertheless in the midst of that controversy referred to him as "truly already a statesman" in moral theology.[44]

The liberal wing of the faculty at Catholic University proposed and started the publication of the *Catholic University Bulletin* which was to be a bridge between the academy and the intellectually interested public. Thomas O'Gorman reported in a letter to Archbishop Ireland that Bouquillon, Shahan, Pace, and himself, had decided to start this journal as a private venture of their own. They feared that there might be some opposition from archbishops on the board if it were proposed as an official university publication. Likewise they did not want Archbishop Corrigan to get wind of it and try to persuade the Jesuits to start a review of their own. Cardinal Gibbons and Bishop Keane, according to O'Gorman, were in favor of the idea and they hoped to obtain funding from Father James McMahon, a New York priest who had already made a very sizeable gift to Catholic University.[45] This letter underscores once again how Bouquillon is identified with the liberal wing in the American Catholic church.

Students of American Catholic church history also know Bouquillon as a strong advocate of the role and importance of the social sciences. He had a great impact on John A. Ryan, the leading figure in Catholic social thought in the first half of the twentieth century in the United

States. Ryan in his memoirs described Bouquillon as the most erudite man he had ever known and working with the Belgian-born professor as the most fortunate experience of his student life. Ryan praised his scrupulousness in the preparation of lectures and his passion for exactness, accuracy, and thoroughness. Bouquillon gave comprehensive attention to social problems with emphasis on sociological and economic factors as well as the ethical.[46] Ryan himself went on to wed economics and moral theology as the leading exponent of liberal Catholic social thought in his day.[47]

Father William J. Kerby, who later became the founding head of the department of sociology at Catholic University and a moving spirit behind the founding of the National Conference of Catholic Charities, was likewise a student who learned much from Bouquillon.[48] In his eulogy at the memorial service for Bouquillon in Washington in 1902, Kerby praised his critical historical mind. Like Ryan, Kerby pointed out that his teacher possessed a knowledge of the sciences closely related to moral theology which was almost extensive enough to give his opinion authority in those areas while his acquaintance with more remote fields was exceptionally wide.[49] Ryan's leading role in economics and Kerby's in professional Catholic social work owe much to the training and inspiration given by Bouquillon.

In the only contemporary scholarly article on Bouquillon, C. Joseph Nuesse mentions this influence on Ryan and Kerby in developing the thesis that Thomas Bouquillon was the precursor of the social sciences at the Catholic University of America. The Belgian professor even before beginning his teaching at Catholic University expressed his disappointment with the state of Catholic moral theology and insisted that a highly scientific and living moral theology must be constantly in dialogue with the appropriate practical sciences.[50] Bouquillon was most interested in the theory of society and social issues. Nuesse discovered in the Bouquillon papers at Catholic University a document prepared for the rector probably in 1891 that provided a survey of Catholic social movements in continental Europe.[51] Bouquillon's report in the *Catholic University Bulletin* shows his interest in many scientific congresses that were taking place in 1897. In addition to congresses dealing with more specifically theological matters he also mentioned various congresses under the category of congresses for public morality, social and economic congresses, and professional congresses.[52] Nuesse concludes that Bouquillon was a precursor of the social sciences at Catholic University because he also insisted on the social facts bearing on moral issues and because of his manifest interest in and awareness of disciplinary developments that were then in their early stages.[53] Bouquillon's intense interest in the social sciences and his influence on Kerby and Ryan further underscore his sympathies for American Catholic liberalism.

Thus, Thomas Bouquillon is not an unknown figure in American Catholic history but ironically he is not remembered for his moral theology as such. His involvements in a number of areas somewhat related to his moral theology have stamped him as an advocate of the liberal Catholicism that was clearly evident in the United States in the last decade of the nineteenth century.

BOUQUILLON AS UNIVERSITY PROFESSOR AND SCHOLAR

In contrast to Sabetti whose home was the theologate or seminary and whose concerns were primarily pastoral, Bouquillon's setting was the university and his primary concerns and interests were scholarly and not immediately pastoral. After teaching for ten years in the seminary at Bruges, Bouquillon moved to the chair of moral theology at the new Catholic University of Lille. The Belgian priest left his university post to do scholarly writing at a Benedictine abbey before spending the last thirteen years of his life at the Catholic University of America in Washington, D.C.[54]

His life at Catholic University shows that he not only taught at a university but was also a person interested in the institution as such and its welfare. He fully participated in the life of the new university. In describing the early days of Catholic University, Bishop Keane, the rector, singled out the role of Bouquillon. "We were guided by the experience of the able men composing our faculty, especially the wonderful erudition and sagacity of Dr. Bouquillon."[55] Bouquillon served as vice dean and dean of the School of Theology.[56] Nuesse has shown how Bouquillon in his knowledge and interests was the precursor of the social sciences at Catholic University. The Belgian-born professor also served as one of three members of a committee on new schools and in 1895 the school of philosophy and the school of social sciences came into existence. The committee recommended that if both a school of law and a school of social sciences could not be started at the same time it would be better to begin with the school of social sciences.[57]

Mention has already been made of the founding of the *Catholic University Bulletin*. After Bouquillon's death it was reported: "His pen and his counsel were always at the disposition of the Editor-in-Chief; indeed, he was one of the original five who pledged themselves to execute the work."[58] Bouquillon's support for the *Catholic University Bulletin* carried on the tradition of his support for and participation in the *Revue des sciences ecclésiastiques*, the publication started in his time by the new Catholic University of Lille. Bouquillon obviously recognized the need for a theological faculty in a university to have a serious journal to develop their own scholarship and to share it with interested communities. The bulk of his articles appear in the journals of the institutions with which he was associated. The third of these journals was the *Messager des Fidèles de Maredsous*, later called the *Revue Bénédictine*, which was published at the Benedictine abbey where he was living.[59]

At Catholic University the Belgian professor taught students who were involved in further study in theology beyond the regular seminary course. He did not teach seminarians. In his first year of teaching he covered matters generally associated with fundamental moral theology—the ultimate end of human beings; society in general and domestic, civil, and religious societies in particular; and the supreme principles of law and moral obligation. But in subsequent years the topics were more specialized. In his second year he taught law, rights and obligations, natural law, international law, civil law including taxation and penalties, the rights of property and its vindication against communism. In the third year Dr. Bouquillon taught justice and charity with a commentary on *Rerum novarum* that he developed using political science, law, and economics. The fourth year he treated public and private charities and justice with regard to contracts especially discussing the business transactions then in vogue—speculation, monopolies, partnerships, and corporations. Bouquillon's discussion included the political and economic aspects as part of the ethical consideration.[60]

In teaching graduate students Bouquillon introduced the seminar to Catholic University. The Belgian professor was familiar with the German origins of the seminar which he described as a course to prepare students to do research on their own and to meet with other students for discussion and criticism of their research. Bouquillon proposed the inauguration of the seminar at a faculty meeting in June 1890. The following year he proudly reported that his seminar on suicide was the first seminar in moral theology in any Catholic university anywhere. During the academic year 1894–1895 the seminar was devoted to the ethics of workingmen's associations, strikes, and arbitration. The next year the seminar critically examined the Dudley lecture at Harvard University given by Reverend Brooke Herford in 1895.[61] In pioneering the use of the seminar Bouquillon found a very appropriate way and method to help graduate students in their research.

His own personality and bent made him more effective in the seminar format than in the lecture format. His lectures were always clear and logically ordered but his delivery was colorless.[62] He had a slight hesitation in speech that one supporter attributed to his searching for finding the proper term.[63]

Bouquillon was not only an active participant in the life of the university but he was a student of universities and an apologist for Catholic universities. In the first two volumes of the *Catholic University Bulletin* he wrote a three part series on the University of Paris, the mother and the model of all the universities of Europe.[64] Although these articles depend heavily on the research of Père Denifle, Bouquillon wanted to call attention to the important role of universities as seen in this most illustrious institution and at the same time give support and direction for the newly formed Catholic University of America.

In the very first issue of the *Catholic University Bulletin* Bouquillon wrote an apology for theology in universities. The article makes two points. First, the American church needs and can use an institution for teaching and learning theology on a graduate level. With the growth of the church in this country it is now possible to give some priests a training beyond the seminary level. Yes, there is need to train the teachers in our growing number of seminaries. But even beyond this the American church can profit from a body of men devoted to theological science and rooted in the spirit of Catholicism. The scientific world will listen to scientific teaching in theology as in other disciplines. If the church in America had such a collective group of scholars, the church would greatly benefit. Think of what the famous schools in the past have done for the good of the church.

Second, theology itself should have a primary place in a Catholic university. This setting is an important reality not only for the university but also for the discipline of theology. Theology must avoid becoming sterile or stagnant through a dialogue with all the other sciences. Such a vigorous theology will make its unchanging truths more clear and forceful for the modern mind. Unfortunately our age is one of secularization. But we are not without blame because the priest is shut up in the sacristy or cloister, theology is confined to the pulpit, and moral precepts are reserved to the confessional. Theology as part of the university will be in dialogue and contact with the other important aspects of human existence. The lecture halls of divinity schools should adjoin the laboratories in empirical sciences. In addition, theological methods can learn much from the sciences. He does not here refer explicitly to the seminar but it must have been in his thoughts.[65]

His contemporaries recognized Bouquillon's university interests and commitments. William Kerby described him as learned in the history of universities and consecrated to the welfare of his own, namely the Catholic University of America. He was a very constructive force at Catholic University by his university involvement and the inspiration of his own scholarly achievements.[66] Thomas Shahan, one of his faculty colleagues and a later rector of Catholic University, maintained in his necrology for Bouquillon that his commonwealth was the *Universitas studiorum* and he wanted no better citizenship, no sweeter companionship, no horizons or victories that it could not approve. As long as it endures Catholic University will owe his memory a debt of gratitude for it was he who really laid its academic foundations.[67]

Bouquillon's natural home was the university because he was primarily a scholar. The Catholic University professor undoubtedly saw his scholarship in relation to his priesthood and the service of the church. The best evidence of his scholarship comes from his love for books and his own magnificent library. He had a personal library of about 10,000 volumes which he assembled over his lifetime. This library was housed in his rooms at Caldwell Hall and in the seminar room for his students. Canon H. Rommel devotes five pages of his fifty-one page biography of Bouquillon to his library, its contents, and its arrangements.[68] He was a major influence on the then developing library of Catholic University as he had been at the Catholic University of Lille.[69]

His article on the Ambrosiana Library at Milan in the *Catholic University Bulletin* again showed his interest in and concern for libraries. Like the article on the University of Paris this essay does not pretend to break new ground but only to summarize the work done by other scholars. Bibliophile that he was, Bouquillon appreciated and honored people who shared his love for books. He lovingly referred to the Ambrosiana Library as "that monument more durable than solid brass which even yet seeks its equal among the great book treasuries of the world, an imperishable witness to the far-reaching vision as well as the good taste and the fine culture of the great archbishop of Milan."[70]

His contemporaries recognized his vast erudition and his love for books. According to William Kerby he delighted in the retirement and silence of his own library. No one ever heard him boast of what he had done or could do; his personality seemed lost in his learning. Nothing tempted him away from the pursuit of learning. By disposition he was introspective and retiring.[71] Thomas J. Shahan, who later became rector of Catholic University, put it very succinctly: "The faculty of theology always cherished him as its most learned member."[72]

The depth and breadth of his scholarship are exemplary. His main work, *Theologia moralis fundamentalis*, the third edition of which was published in 1903 shortly after his death, testifies to his scholarship. He also wrote moral treatises on the theological virtues and the virtue of religion. His many journal essays and articles also point to the depth and breadth of his interests. For example, his three part article on invincible ignorance of the natural law treats its subject in great depth.[73] His articles not only dealt with many aspects of moral theology but treated a very wide array of subjects. Throughout his writing one sees his great interest in history. Many articles deal specifically with historical topics while others give the historical background to the issue he is considering.

His interest in and knowledge of the social sciences has already been pointed out. His scholarly propensities are very evident in his *Catholic University Bulletin* article on "The Science of Bibliography and Some Recent Bibliographies."[74] Bouquillon insists that an education cannot be considered complete without some knowledge of bibliography. Were knowledge of bibliography insisted upon we would not have books that merely repeat what has already been said elsewhere or tiresomely rehearse old errors. Likewise students could do their research much better. He then discusses some different bibliographical works which themselves deal with a variety of subject matters—historical sciences, historical sciences in the Middle Ages, theology, social politics, education, the catalogues of the British Museum and the Paris Library, and some collective bibliographical works. The article is not a mere listing and description of these sources but also a critical analysis which shows the extent of his knowledge in all these fields.

His biographer pointed out how unfortunate it was that his health and somewhat early death prevented his finishing a whole treatise on moral theology. Rommel lists a number of reasons why Bouquillon was not able to publish an entire moral theology—his preoccupation to be complete and exact, his willingness to help younger scholars, his wanting to treat certain questions in the light of his American experience.[75] I am sure these are all true. His breadth also constitutes a major part of the problem. Over half the articles he contributed to the *Catholic University Bulletin* in the last years of his life do not explicitly deal with moral theology as such. His own scientific desire for both depth and breadth probably would have prevented him from ever publishing an entire moral theology.

Another indication of his scientific bent comes from his familiarity with the literature in all the modern European languages. In addition, he wrote in Latin, French, and English. The curiosity of a live intellect joined forces with the depth of the scholar in this moral theologian who was familiar with the literature in his field in all its dimensions and ramifications. He was personally deeply involved in the institutions of universities and libraries which are so essential for the work of scholarship. Thomas Joseph Bouquillon was a scholar par excellence.

BOUQUILLON'S INTEREST IN HISTORY

Bouquillon had a great interest in and love for history. Recall his interest in the history of universities and libraries. His contemporaries recognized his emphasis on history and praised his historical approach as a most distinctive characteristic of his work. Thomas J. Shahan pointed out his special interest in the Catholic theologians of the sixteenth and seventeenth centuries especially those of Spain and the low countries.[76] The most important characteristic of his mind according to William J. Kerby was his historical sense. Bouquillon's keen understanding of movements of both thought and life gave him the power to see and measure the converging complex processes which produce institutions, discern beginnings, trace relations, see developments, and analyze the intangible yet powerful forces that coalesce to make movements in human society. "Reading history as a moral theologian and reading theology as a critical historian, his appreciation of the supernatural as an historical fact as well as a theological truth, was remarkably accurate and profound."[77] His general interest in history did not make him an antiquarian. His historical sense always made him appreciate the particularities and distinctive characteristic of the period as shown by his interest in the newly developing social sciences. But as we will see the Belgian-born professor had a historical interest but not a historical consciousness.

Bouquillon's knowledge of and interest in history can be seen in many of his articles as well as in his major work on fundamental moral theology. Of special note here is the ambitious project he began in 1883 and never finished. In an article in the *Revue des sciences ecclésiastiques* he proposed his plan to sketch an outline of the history of theology, but his description of what he intended to do indicates that he was interested in much more than just a summary of the history of theology. He planned to expose the origin, developments, and different phases of theology; to examine for each epoch its spirit and method; to point out its merits and shortcomings, and finally to indicate its principal representatives. He proposed to divide the history of theology into three epochs—the first from the twelfth century to the reformers or the Council of Trent, the second from the Council of Trent to the end of the seventeenth century, and the third from the end of the seventeenth century to the First Vatican Council. In each epoch he would treat separately theoretical theology, polemical theology, and practical theology.[78]

Only one more article appeared in the *Revue des sciences ecclésiastiques* on this subject. He basically dealt with only the first epoch and ended with John Mair who wrote in the early sixteenth century. In this period he dealt only with the theoretical part of the proposed outline.[79] The work was never completed; in fact it was hardly begun. One had to have a great interest in history, a broad concern for all aspects of theology, and a reasonable command of the vast literature to even attempt such an undertaking.

In 1885 Bouquillon left his university position to "retire" to the Benedictine monastery at Maredsous to devote himself fully to his writing. Whether he had already abandoned the somewhat ambitious plan for his "outline" of the history of theology we do not know. Apparently he used his time at Maredsous to work on a thorough revision of his book on fundamental moral theology.[80] The first edition of 392 pages had been published in 1873.[81] This very thorough revision of the original was about twice as long as the first edition. The most distinctive aspect of the second edition was its section of almost one hundred pages on the history of moral theology.[82] This long history is found again in the third edition that was published just after his death in 1903.[83]

Bouquillon did not intend his history of moral theology to be a separate monograph but rather part of the introduction to fundamental moral theology. Thus severe space limits existed. Like any history it tells us as much about the author as it does about the subject matter. The Belgian-born professor's interest in and concern for bibliography is quite evident. His history in fact consists of two major aspects—very short synthetic and analytic descriptions of the different epochs in moral theology and a very long listing of the works that were published during that particular period. Bouquillon lists the various authors with a footnote reference to the works under the appropriate heading. Thus, for example, in the second period of the fathers of the church from the Council of Nicea to Gregory the Great (d. 604), Bouquillon devotes one paragraph to the characteristics of the period and then lists the principal writers under the following headings—moral letters, commentaries on scripture and homilies, sermons, catechesis, tracts, apologies or defenses, collections of canons, spiritual writings, liturgical writings, and legal codes.[84] What is most surprising is what is left out of the history. The history does not develop the positions of the major figures in the tradition—for example, Augustine, Thomas Aquinas, Suarez, Alphonsus Liguori. These authors and their works are listed alongside the lesser writers. However, their names do appear in the systematic and analytical descriptions usually found at the beginning of each epoch.

The major division in the history, as might be expected, separates the age of the fathers of the church from the age of the theologians beginning in the twelfth century. In the age of the fathers the approach to morality is scriptural, positive, polemical, and practical rather than speculative; exhortatory rather than didactic and methodological; particular and not systematic.[85] Moral science in the age of the theologians is scholastic since it takes place in schools where masters teach students; universal because it embraces the whole ambit of revelation; systematic because the parts are distributed harmoniously into an organic whole; didactic since it follows the form and necessities of the lecture system; speculative, for it seeks a deeper explanation of truths.[86]

Bouquillon's division of the age of the theologians into three epochs indicates very clearly where he is coming from. The first epoch from the end of the twelfth century, to the pseudo-reformation (note his term); the second epoch from the pseudo-reformation to 1830; and the most recent epoch from 1830 to the present.[87] As will become evident in the subsequent description, the high points are the development and later acceptance of Thomas or scholasticism and the low points come from failure to follow the scholastic approach.

The first epoch of the theologians itself contains two periods—that which is truly the scholastic period and the golden period which began in the twelfth century and ended in the early fourteenth century, reaching its highest point between 1230 and 1280. Many factors contributed to the progress and perfection of this golden age of theology. The church had emerged victorious in the long struggle for its freedom and then celebrated the great Lateran Council with its copious fruits of doctrine and holiness. The new religious orders produced a flowering of holiness and learning. The erection and extension of universities stimulated the theological enterprise. A better translation of Aristotelian texts and their general acceptance by the popes contributed to a new theology. The necessity of mounting an efficacious defense of revealed truths against the Muslims facilitated the development of theology. This age was a period of renewal and renaissance perhaps more profound in general than that of the fifteenth century.[88] One only wonders if this idyllic portrait really corresponded to the realities.

Theology at this time was full, ample, and one; all the truths were discussed under every aspect and in response to all errors. This theology was informed by a truly Christian philosophy, namely, the wisdom of the ancients perfected and corrected by Christian principles to serve the explanation of revealed truths so that the happy marriage between faith and reason was attained without which true theology cannot exist. Theology in this period was perfectly analytical—the matter was logically divided and subdivided into its parts until one arrived at a well determined proposition. Its form was didactic and technical—simple and concise without literary or oratorical extravagances but neither inelegant nor barbarous. Bouquillon points out the differences between the Thomistic approach and the Scotistic with the Thomistic insisting on morality being determined by the nature of things and the intrinsic end of actions rather than the free will of God. The most important characteristic of moral theology at this time was its being an integral part of the one theology and not a separate discipline as illustrated by the *Summa* of Thomas Aquinas.[89]

What happened to theology in general and moral theology in particular in the second period of this epoch including most of the fourteenth century until the sixteenth? These years were an age of decline, primarily because of the influence of nominalism. Theology was less original, less elegant, less synthetic. Nominalism put the emphasis on the individual and the particular with many published works on particular topics and not on universal summas. Polemical, political, and practical questions were preferred to more theoretical questions. The abuse of overly subtle distinctions deformed the entire theological enterprise.[90]

In the epoch from the pseudo-reformation to 1830 Bouquillon again distinguishes two periods with the first extending to the rise of

Jansenism in 1660 but reaching its highest point from 1570 to 1630.[91] Theology in this period gave greater attention to its sources, moved away from the nominalism and Platonism of the previous period, and imposed its own method and form. At this time Thomas Aquinas became the common master of all. Commentators on the *Summa* of Aquinas now succeeded the commentaries on the *Sentences* of Lombard. In these commentaries on Aquinas and in other general works depending on Aquinas, moral theology was treated in a scientific and speculative way as part of the one theology. Bouquillon recognizes the very sharp divisions and acrimonious disputes between Banezianists and Molinists in the struggle about grace, but still praises the period especially from the perspective of moral theology.[92] Our author also points to the rise at this time of a practical and casuistic moral theology (as illustrated in the work of John Azor, Henry Henriquez, Thomas Sanchez, and many others) that was completely separated from dogmatic theology.[93] Bouquillon fails to point out that these *Institutiones theologiae moralis* constituted the beginning of the manual tradition which he opposes in his own writings. And, as a creature of his own time, he fails to recognize the defensive and one-sided approaches coming from a polemic against Protestantism.

Bouquillon is quite negative in his judgment of the second period of this epoch from 1660 to 1830. He describes it as a time of change and especially perversion and a progressive fall into ruin. General causes of this decline included a tedium and lassitude with regard to scholastic questions, the spread of Jansenism and Gallicanism as well as the beginning of Febronianism and Josephism within the church, and the rise of rationalism. A most potent cause of the perversion was the rise of new philosophical systems from the Cartesian to the Kantian which attacked the ancient Christian wisdom.[94]

Theology at this time became less speculative and ceased to be Thomistic as the Angelic Doctor lost his prominence. The *Summa* was no longer used as a textbook; fewer treatises attempted to discuss the whole of theology. The Latin language gave way to the use of the vernacular in some places. Theology often lost its universal character and was replaced by a theology of Lyons or the particular place in which it was written. Just as each diocese had its own breviary, missal, ritual, and catechism, it now gloried in its own theology. Notice the negative attitude with regard to anything particular detracting from the universal nature of theology. Moral theology at this time was rent with controversies and bitter disputes between the more rigid and the more benign positions called more specifically the antiprobabilists and the probabilists. The primary objects of concern were the tracts on conscience and on the administration of the sacraments. The Holy See had to intervene to condemn extreme positions on both sides which gave rise to the new genre of commentaries on the condemned propositions.[95]

Writers in this period generally developed moral theology as totally apart from dogmatic theology and with a different spirit and method.[96] It is precisely in this context that Bouquillon devotes one short paragraph of two sentences in his text to the work of St. Alphonsus Liguori. Alphonsus, free from any prejudices of the contending parties and intending only the glory of God and the spiritual salvation of human beings, found a safe middle way between the more rigid and the more lax positions. However, only after his death did peace finally come to moral theology.[97]

Catholic moral theologians are startled to find Alphonsus in the period of perversion and progressive fall into ruin in moral theology. Was Alphonsus not already canonized as a saint and made a doctor of the church? Bouquillon himself recognized that by the end of the nineteenth century Catholic moral theology could be called Alphonsian because of the widespread acceptance of his approach in moral theology.[98]

What does Bouquillon think of the work of Alphonsus? In the long footnote to his two sentence treatment of Alphonsus in the text on moral theology Bouquillon proposes his evaluation of Alphonsus. With regard to method, the founder of the Redemptorists is a commentator on the manual of Busenbaum, but his commentary is a truly personal work much like Aquinas's commentary on the *Sentences* of Lombard. With regard to doctrine, the theology of Alphonsus is derived from the earlier casuists especially the Salmanticenses, the seventeenth- and eighteenth-century Spanish authors of a six volume moral theology. With regard to his mind and spirit, Alphonsus finds a middle way between the extremes and his endorsement by the Holy See proves that he accomplished his purposes. With regard to his merits, the holy doctor stands out in his wise choice of opinions and in his extraordinary Christian perception rather than in profound learning or the orderly exposition of theology. In a word he stands out above most others in the prudential part of moral theology which was so dear to his heart, but he cedes to many others with regard to the strictly scientific aspect of moral theology which because of his many involvements he did not have the time to develop.[99] This judgment couched in careful terms thus recognizes Alphonsus as an outstanding casuist but not as a scientific moral theologian.

In an earlier section of almost six pages in his introduction to moral theology Bouquillon discussed the authority of St. Alphonsus for moral matters.[100] In this earlier discussion Bouquillon reviews and comments on the different documents commending the work of Alphonsus beginning with the decree of the Congregation of Rites in 1803 paving the way for his beatification (the first step to canonization) with the judgment that nothing deserving of censure was found in his writings. Bouquillon considers all the documents from the Sacred Penitentiary, the Holy Office, and the Congregation of the Council, as well as the papal documents when he was beatified, canonized, and made a doctor of the church. Bouquillon concludes that the doctrine of St. Alphonsus taken as a whole is eminent especially in its moral part. Salutary effects have come from this teaching. There is a presumption of truth in favor of the positions he proposes, but that presumption sometimes can be wrong. But nowhere have official documents said that the teaching of Alphonsus is eminent in all its parts or that his teaching is the equal of the teaching of any other doctor of the church or that his teaching is more eminent than the teaching of noncanonized writers. The authority of St. Alphonsus is rightly such that it does not need to be exaggerated. It is an exaggeration, for example, to say that Alphonsus is the greatest among moral theologians or that Alphonsus has the same eminence in moral theology as Aquinas in dogmatic theology as if Aquinas were not eminent in both sciences.[101]

Without doubt Bouquillon recognizes the contribution of Alphonsus but he limits the role of Alphonsus especially to the area of casuistry and the prudential aspects of morality and does not want to make Alphonsus the model for all moral theology. Thus the Catholic University professor's treatment of Alphonsus prepares the way for a very significant aspect in his approach to moral theology—his dissatisfaction with the manuals. The eminence of Alphonsus is limited to the area of casuistry and does not extend to profound erudition in the field in general or to a systematic ordering of moral theology. Bouquillon's opposition to the genre of the manuals of moral theology will be developed in a subsequent section.

Bouquillon sees the third stage of moral theology beginning in 1830 as an age of renewal following the falling into ruin at the end of the second epoch. The centerpiece of this renewal is the reclamation of the philosophy and theology of Thomas Aquinas. During this time the founts or sources of theology have been studied and new editions of classical authors have appeared. Christian philosophy as the instrument of theology has happily been restored in the schools replacing false doctrines and philosophies. Church history as a help to theology has been perfected. Practical theology has been purged of the negative effects of Jansenism and Gallicanism. In speculative theology Thomas Aquinas has been restored as its teacher, and in casuistic theology Alphonsus has put an end to the contentions that so long plagued the church. All this has been done by scholars but especially by the powerful actions of the Roman pontiffs.[102]

With these developments the church is better able to meet the more urgent necessities of the times. Philosophically, the church must refute three philosophical systems opposed to Christian faith and morals—the critique of Kant, the pantheism of Hegel, and the positivism of Comte. Politically, the church must oppose the liberal political systems with their modern liberties of thought, religion, the press, and the secularization of government emphasizing the separation of church and state and the secularization of marriage and the schools. Economically, the problems of the workers need to be addressed. Likewise the church must respond to the popular sects that have arisen in these contexts—communism and socialism. Finally the church must respond to the diffusion of rationalism in all its forms and to the pretensions of many of the new sciences such as biology, psychology, and sociology that vie with moral theology.[103] Notice his strong opposition to the Enlightenment.

In describing the new epoch with its developments and needs Bouquillon does not review what has been done, but rather proposes his idea of what should be done. To respond to the necessities of the disturbed present times, Bouquillon sees two main thrusts that Catholic theology should take. First, theology must stress the supernatural character of religion and the church against naturalism, rationalism, and liberalism. Second, theology must show the necessary coherence that God wills between the natural and the supernatural orders. With regard to the work of moral theology the Catholic University professor proposes three tasks: First, to accurately establish reason and authority as the immutable principles of divine and natural law. Second, to apply these same principles to the grave psychological, economic, and political questions of the day and especially to oppose that most pernicious separation of the political and legal orders from the moral order. Third, to show the efficaciousness of Christian morality for attaining not only supernatural happiness but also natural happiness—an approach exemplified in the encyclicals of Leo XIII dealing with marriage, politics, and the Christian constitution of states.[104]

However, Bouquillon continues, only a few in our time have attempted to establish an integral, theoretical, and practical approach. Joseph Kleutgen, who was an excellent theologian equal to the task, recently began such a work but died after publishing the first volume. Many have continued to publish works in moral theology but the works published up to now are either manuals for the use of students or compendia for confessors and generally just practical works some of which have even been published in the vernacular.[105]

The history of moral theology proposed for the later edition of Bouquillon's fundamental moral theology illustrates his great interest in history as well as in bibliography. For our purposes it also calls attention to two other important elements in his theology—his support for neoscholasticism as mandated by Leo XIII and his downplaying of the manuals or compendia of moral theology. Both of these elements will now be explored in greater detail.

BOUQUILLON AS A NEOSCHOLASTIC

The Belgian-born professor interprets moral theology as having reached its high point in the work of the earlier scholastics especially Aquinas, going downhill under the influence of nominalism, returning to a better condition with the emphasis on Aquinas in the sixteenth century, but then falling into ruin with the controversies over probabilism. However, the rise of neoscholasticism after 1830 helped moral theology reach a better state. The first name Bouquillon mentions in describing the restoration after 1830 is Joseph Kleutgen, described as a theologian of outstanding merit. Kleutgen was the primary leader of neoscholasticism. Bouquillon is opposed to modern philosophical developments as well as to the political and economic developments associated with the Enlightenment. He accepts the importance of the faith-reason, grace-nature, supernatural-natural distinctions of neoscholasticism to deal with the theoretical and the practical problems of the times.

From what American church history has remembered of Bouquillon, one would never suspect that he was a committed neoscholastic. He was identified with the liberal wing of American Catholicism in opposition to the Jesuits and others. His great interest in history seemed to indicate an appreciation for historical consciousness which was buttressed by his support of the newer sciences such as sociology and economics. In his history of moral theology, however, he insists on the need for moral theology to establish the immutable principles of the divine and natural law and to apply these principles to the grave economic, psychological, and sociological questions of our age.

His deep interest in history does not mean that he also accepts historical consciousness. Neoscholasticism embraced a classicism that emphasizes the eternal, the unchangeable, and the immutable. Bouquillon sees neoscholasticism as the perennial philosophy seemingly unaffected by historical development and change. Moral theology proposes the immutable principles of divine and natural law which are then applied to the different historical and cultural contexts. The sciences do not contribute anything to the principles of moral theology, but they provide the knowledge of the conditions and circumstances in which these principles are applied. This history also reveals that Bouquillon sees the theological and philosophical approach of Thomas Aquinas as understood by the leaders of nineteenth-century neoscholasticism such as Joseph Kleutgen to be the only true and adequate method and this method alone as the only one that can properly address the many problems facing the contemporary world. Such was the program which Pope Leo XIII authoritatively proposed for the church. This section will now show from his other writings Bouquillon's wholehearted support for Leo XIII's neoscholasticism.

Thomas Bouquillon was a firm supporter and follower of Pope Leo XIII's program of renewal. He published an edition in two volumes of the allocutions, letters, constitutions, and other principal acts of Leo in Bruges in 1887.[106] From January to December 1888 he published six articles in the *Messager des Fidèles de Maredsous* dealing with various aspects of Leo's thoughts.[107]

In assessing the first ten years of the pontificate of Leo XIII, our author points out that the major preoccupation of the pope is the salvation of modern society through religion. This preoccupation involves repairing the evils caused to the church by secularism and impiety and showing how the influence of Catholicism can benefit society by reestablishing peace and concord in the intelligences and the hearts of people. Above all, the action of the church must be at the level of the intellectual because it is here that the problems lie.[108] In another article that same year Bouquillon interprets Pope Leo XIII as seeing naturalism as the greatest problem of our age because it denies the sovereign reign of the creator over the creature and puts the author- ity of humans in place of God. The two principal forms of this natural- ism are rationalism and liberalism.[109]

Rationalism refers primarily to science and preaches the indepen- dence of human reason from the divine. Atheists and deists embrace complete rationalism. Protestantism is an incomplete rationalism in that it admits the divine but not the doctrinal authority given by God to the church and submits all to private judgment. A mitigated rationalism in Catholicism does not deny but diminishes doctrinal authority by submitting only to *ex cathedra* statements and by not taking account of the decisions of the Roman congregations. Pius IX opposed this miti- gated rationalism in *Tuas libenter*, his famous letter to the archbishop of Munich in 1864. Such mitigated rationalism was also disowned in the *Syllabus of Errors* and in the constitution *Dei filius* of the First Vatican Council.[110] Notice the expansive understanding of rationalism.

Likewise liberalism has its degrees. Complete liberalism rejects the divine law both supernatural and natural, for example, the positiv- ists and the Kantian partisans of the autonomous will. A less radical liberalism rejects the supernatural divine law while admitting the natu- ral law and thus repudiates any role for the church in civil society. There is also a mitigated liberalism that does not deny but restricts the authority of the church either in terms of its instrumentality (only an ecumenical council and not the pope) or in terms of its object (only matters of faith and morals in the strict sense) or in terms of action (making the obligatory force of ecclesiastical prescriptions depend on the acceptance by the faithful or by governments).[111]

Bouquillon sees the approach of the popes primarily on the intel- lectual level. Unfortunately some divisions exist here even among Cath- olics so that it makes it harder for the church to speak and act against the evils of the day. Leo therefore recalls that according to its divine constitution the government of the church belongs to the pastors and the clergy, and laity ought to be united in following the direction of the pope.[112]

Implicit in Bouquillon's article assessing the first ten years of Leo XIII's pontificate is his notion that Leo and the church have used the philosophy and theology of Thomas Aquinas to condemn errors in the church and to achieve unity especially on the intellectual level. Bouquillon explicitly recognizes and strenuously defends the need for authoritative teaching by the pope. Elsewhere that year the Belgian priest residing at Maredsous pointed out the need for the church to condemn Catholic liberals such as Lamennais and Catholic rationalists such as Hermes on the basis of the renewed Thomism or neoscholasticism of the times.[113] Some tried to defend Antonio Rosmini as being in accord with Thomas. But Bouquillon replies that Rosmini's concept of ideal being is not in accord with Aquinas's thought so that finally in 1887 forty propositions of Rosmini were rightly condemned by the Congregation of the Inquisition.[114] Thus the Catholic church needs both the philosophy of Thomas Aquinas and authoritative papal teaching to achieve internal unity within the church so that it can better deal with the problems of the modern world through that same Thomistic philosophy.

To address the problems of the modern world on an intellectual plane the church in Bouquillon's interpretation of Leo XIII's pontificate needed to employ four instrumentalities—philosophy, history, natural science, and literature. Philosophy furnishes the basis for establishing the Christian principles for governing society and gives to human intelligence the ability to know and appreciate these principles. This need explains the measures taken by Leo XIII in his encyclical *Aeterni Patris* for teaching the philosophy of Thomas Aquinas in seminaries and universities. Since history shows the proper role of the church and the pope and their positive influence on society, Leo XIII has encouraged the development of the historical sciences and the publication and use of ancient documents. Since natural sciences have points of contact with dogma and morals and can be a source of strength for faith rather than an obstacle to it, the pope has encouraged the study of the natural sciences. Likewise the pope has stimulated the study of literary culture to make the church's teaching so much more appealing.[115] Leo XIII's program on the intellectual level employs Thomistic thought to unify the church within and to give it the principles to deal with the major problems of liberalism and rationalism affecting the world at the end of the nineteenth century.

In an article commenting on Pope Leo XIII's encyclical to Bavaria, Bouquillon contrasts the position of the pope with that of Joseph Ignatius von Döllinger especially in the latter's address to the famous meeting of intellectuals in Munich in 1863. The first difference concerns the philosophy of Thomas Aquinas. Bouquillon quotes Döllinger as saying that the old theological edifice constructed by the scholastics has fallen into ruin and there is no way to repair it because it does not correspond to modern needs. One must build a new edifice which will be based on a better philosophy and especially on history which alone is capable of inculcating and appreciating religion. In fact, Döllinger claims that through the science of history we shall arrive at the greatly desired union of all the Christian communions. Bouquillon cites the papal nuncio to Munich as pointing out that for these thinkers the theology of Thomas is only a historical reality corresponding to the culture of its own times but not adequate for the present time.[116]

Bouquillon supports the approach of Leo XIII in opposition to Döllinger. The encyclical to the church in Bavaria provides a magnificent supplement to the encyclical *Aeterni Patris* and the *motu proprio* that proclaimed Aquinas the patron of Catholic schools. The pope here clearly sets out what Aquinas can contribute to the students of theology and the future clerics. In a footnote Bouquillon cites one significant sentence of that document—"Indeed the method of the Angelic Doctor is admirably adapted for training minds, wonderfully fitted for use in making comments, in philosophizing, in discoursing forcibly and incontrovertibly, for it shows clearly each subject connected one with another in a continuous series, all however joined together and fitting into each other, all leading to the highest principles."[117]

Bouquillon's second contrast between Döllinger and Leo XIII concerns authority in the church and the role of intellectual freedom. Döllinger maintained that among the Hebrew people prophets existed side by side with priests. So too in the church; in addition to the ordinary powers one finds the extraordinary power of public opinion by means of which theology does its work and to which all must pay attention. So too in the middle ages the church reposed on three columns—the papacy given to the Italians, the empire accorded to the Germans, and the science of the French.[118]

On the contrary, Leo XIII points out that the masters of doctrine are the bishops with their auxiliaries the priests who have received from Christ the mandate and power to teach all nations.[119] (Bouquillon does not cite the part of the encyclical that claims, "But whosoever severs himself in thought or will from his shepherd and from the chief of shepherds, the Roman pontiff, is in no way joined to Christ," or "One that heareth you heareth Me, and he that despiseth you, despiseth Me."[120])

Bouquillon believes it necessary to call special attention to the passage in the encyclical to Bavaria in which Leo, while recognizing the legitimate freedom of inquiry, indicates the limits within which this freedom must be exercised. Liberty that merely scatters opinions according to its own will and pleasure is the vilest license, lying and false science, a disgrace and slavery of the mind. The true doctor is one like Aquinas who not only never differs from God but who no less piously listens to the Roman pontiff when speaking, reveres in him the divine authority and firmly holds in the very words of Aquinas that submission to the Roman pontiff is necessary to salvation.[121] No one can doubt that Bouquillon is both a neoscholastic and an ultramontanist.

One should not judge Bouquillon by today's standards and approaches, but his praise of Leo XIII borders on the extreme. The future Catholic University professor concludes his article on liberalism by claiming that immortal thanks should be given to this wise pontiff who has put the truth in a new light, dissipated misunderstandings, assured peace among all Catholics, and established harmony in political action.[122] He closes his discussion of the first ten years of Leo's papacy with a quote from the bishops of Gaul to Leo the Great—"We thank God who has given to the Apostolic See a pontiff of such great sanctity, of such great faith, and such great doctrine."[123] In closing his article on Rosmini, Bouquillon laments the number of theologians who have gone astray from the Catholic tradition. His very last sentence thanks the pope who has brought us back to the sure ways of Christian philosophy, pointed out the dangers to be avoided, and given a supreme warning to those embarked on dangerous ways.[124]

Some want to contrast the work and pontificate of Leo XIII to that of a conservative and reactionary Pius IX his predecessor,[125] but not Bouquillon. Yes, there are differences of character and circumstances, but we find the most complete harmony between the two popes. Leo has given to the study of Christian theology a powerful direction, but Pius IX encouraged the first restorers of scholasticism and strongly criticized those who claimed that Thomas was not suited for our times. Leo XIII has given us the most complete and luminous explanation of the Christian teaching concerning the political and social orders, but Pius IX condemned the errors that were opposed to it.[126] Bouquillon was a most exuberant, enthusiastic, and loyal supporter of Pope Leo XIII and his neoscholastic approach.

In his history of moral theology, Bouquillon strongly endorses the approach of Thomas Aquinas. In 1882 he gave the address at the Catholic University of Lille on the occasion of the feast of Thomas Aquinas. The occasion obviously calls for lavish praise and the professor of moral theology rose to the occasion in lauding Thomas for his moral theology. Aquinas is the most perfect (*absolutissimum*) teacher in the science of the moral order and the most accomplished (*perfectissimum*) exemplar in execution. Aquinas proposed a marvelous synthesis of the moral life in the second and third part of the *Summa*. He brought all these disparate parts together into an integral system, harmoniously relating all the parts in accord with full scientific rigor. In Aquinas you will not find different parts of the same material separated from each other like scattered parts of the body. Nor will you find in Aquinas conclusions disconnected from their principles, nor applications destitute of any foundation. However, our orator warns against a mechanical and dead restating of the words and formula of the Angelic Doctor. We need to be imbued with the spirit of Aquinas.[127]

Bouquillon frequently cites and has a great appreciation for those who spearheaded the renewal of neoscholasticism in the nineteenth century. His history of moral theology singled out Joseph Kleutgen for special praise.[128] Our author points out that Matteo Liberatore refuted Rosmini's philosophical system in his great work on intellectual knowledge.[129] Taparelli d'Azeglio is described as one of the great Christian philosophers of our time.[130] Bouquillon strongly supported and relied on the proponents of neoscholasticism.

His contemporaries recognized not only his adherence to the philosophy and theology of Aquinas but also his faithfulness and loyalty to the pope. His student William Kerby pointed out, "His loyalty, devotion, love; his thought, his energy, were consecrated to the concrete church; to the persons in whom the providence of God has vested authority; to the church entire; to no party, view or school other than that of the church itself." [131] His Catholic University colleague, Thomas Shahan, remarked at the time of his death: "As becomes a Roman student, he was devoted to the Roman church. His writings gave ample proof of this attachment which his teaching and habitual discourse emphasized." [132]

Rommel pointed out that accusations about Bouquillon's orthodoxy in connection with the school controversy were very troubling for those who knew his inviolable attachment to the Catholic tradition and his propensity for drawing inspiration from the spirit of the Roman church. If someone loves the church it is certainly the editor of that beautiful work of Stapleton's *De magnitudine romanae ecclesiae*, that author of the *Acta Leonis XIII*, that admirer of the gloriously reigning pope whose magnificent encyclicals he has studied, praised and explained.[133]

Laurent Janssens writing after Bouquillon's death pointed out why the fear of being condemned over the school controversy was such a cruel test for the Belgian-born professor. Bouquillon who was so plainly orthodox, so Roman, saw himself accused of statolatry and liberalism in the most authoritative journal in the Catholic press in the very city of Rome under the eyes of Leo XIII for whom he had always professed the most profound admiration.[134]

Thomas Bouquillon's own words and the testimony of others shows that he was an ultramontane supporter of Pope Leo XIII and his neoscholastic program as the best way of assuring unity within the church and of providing a sure way for the church to address the needs of the modern world.

BOUQUILLON AS CRITIC OF
THE MANUALS OF MORAL THEOLOGY

The discussion of Bouquillon's history of moral theology and his adherence to neoscholasticism has hinted at his strong opposition to the manuals or compendia of moral theology. The most systematic and sustained criticism of the manuals in his work is found in one of his last articles written in 1899 on "Moral Theology at the End of the Nineteenth Century."[135] However, the careful reader will note the same criticism of the manuals in a somewhat muted form in the introduction to his moral theology.[136] At the very beginning of his teaching career at the seminary in Bruges he was so dissatisfied with the manuals of moral theology that he decided to write his own book.[137]

His neoscholastic adherence to Thomas Aquinas served as the ultimate basis for his criticism of the manuals. The genius of the theologian is to bring out the unity of theology to so analyze, subordinate, and coordinate religious truths that the parts and their relationship to one another and to the whole may be clearly seen. Such a genius was Aquinas whose *Summa* admirably accomplished this task. To separate the partial truths that are the subject of moral science from the theoretical, the theological, and the social is disastrous. Moral theology cannot be separated and isolated from dogmatic theology. Here the Catholic University professor quotes Kleutgen to reinforce his point.[138] Bouquillon's plea for a holistic moral theology thus calls for moral theology not to be separated from dogma.

Any study of moral theology must be complete and include all the pertinent perspectives. The positive aspect of moral theology studies the sources of religious truths. The strictly dogmatic perspective explains moral truths in relation to the definitions of the church and their degree of certainty. The speculative side includes the systematic exposition and comparison of truths. The polemic or apologetic perspective defends truth and exposes error. A moral theology which is complete must include all these perspectives. The great scholastics of the middle ages employed such an approach as is evident from reading the *Summa* of Aquinas or the *De legibus* and *De religione* of Suarez.[139]

Bouquillon severely castigates the present state of Catholic moral theology in the light of the *Summa* of Aquinas. The treatise on the ultimate end and destiny of human beings, the very foundation of the science, is found only in exceptional cases. The study of human acts is much too jejune and usually deprived of its ontological, psychological, and supernatural aspects. The treatise on the passions to which Aquinas devotes twenty-seven questions never appears. Nothing is written about habits with the twofold aspects of vices and virtues. The essential theological aspect of the law of God is most often omitted. God's law is studied in a superficial way while canon law is most insisted upon. The treatise on conscience is reduced to a minimum and almost totally absorbed into the question of probabilism. The virtues, vices, and sin are incompletely treated.[140]

The portion of the manuals relating to the *Secunda secundae* is not any more satisfactory. The theological virtues constitute the alpha and the omega of the Christian life and give to Christian ethics its distinctive character, yet the manuals devote no more than fifty pages to these virtues. Faith as the door to the whole theological enterprise and charity as the source and the queen of the virtues are not properly discussed. At first glance one might think that the cardinal virtues receive a better treatment in the manuals, but such is not the case. Thus the individual treatises in the manuals are quite deficient in the light of the *Summa*.[141]

What explains the impoverished state of the manuals of moral theology? Moral theology as a subject became separated from dogmatic theology and other related disciplines. Ascetical theology dealt with the law of Christian perfection. Liturgical science treated the laws of religious life. Moral theology lost contact with its related sciences—ethics, sociology, politics, economics, and law. Laws governing the public life were given over to the science of law. Moral theology was forced to confine itself only to the laws of private life. But the primary interest was in conclusions and applications not in the principles of morality. As a result of the probabilism controversy great emphasis was placed on assessing whether or not an opinion was probable by citing the number of authors who supported it. Truth was no longer the driving force of moral theology. The test of scholarly moral theology today seems to be the ability to collect opinions of the theologians of the last three centuries. Casuistry has become a lifeless form intended primarily for teaching and not a living reality directing human life. Moral theology has been reduced to a mere compendium of 500 pages.[142]

Instead of reigning among the sciences as a queen, moral theology is hardly recognized as an equal. Instead of being consulted by those who deal with human activity and its different spheres, the very existence of moral theology is all but ignored. Modern civilization has raised important problems, but moral theology has not provided any guidance for these issues. Even the clergy do not seek solutions for the important questions of wages, property, and education in the principles of moral theology but see in moral theology only what is needed to administer the sacrament of penance. Bouquillon cites many others who also lament this present condition of moral theology.[143]

The Belgian-born professor, with his interest in and knowledge of history and in keeping with his approach of examining all aspects of the problem, also points out some of the historical factors that have influenced the decline of moral theology. With the movement toward secularization in the political realm came a parallel movement of secularization in the world of science. Theology was driven from the universities and relegated to the seminaries and sacristies. In a country as solidly Catholic as Belgium the principle of the separation of church and state excludes theology from every one of the state universities. France, Italy, and Spain are in the same boat. The vicissitudes to which the church has been subjected during the last few centuries such as restrictions, persecutions, confiscation of church property, suppression and expulsion of religious orders, and the destruction and scattering of libraries have not been conducive to the doing of good theology. The weakening and decadence of some nations especially Spain which formerly stood at the forefront of Catholic science have negatively affected theology. The Reformation, Jansenism, and rationalism occasioned the need for polemical literature but as a result destroyed the synthesis of theology and the proportion, order, and balance of the parts of theology.[144]

The Catholic University professor thus presents a devastating critique of the state of moral theology at the end of the nineteenth century. There is no doubt about his target—the manuals of moral theology of which Busenbaum's *Medulla* is a type.[145]

Two comments about this criticism are in order. First, Bouquillon recognizes that moral theology has been limited to training confessors for the sacrament of penance, but he does not emphasize the narrow purpose of moral theology as one of the reasons for the decline of the discipline.[146] Surely the purpose and scope of moral theology deserve more importance and discussion in his critique. Second, Bouquillon does not criticize the legal model of the manual which sees morality primarily in terms of obedience to the different types of law. Thomas Aquinas does not emphasize or employ such a method but Bouquillon readily accepts it as indicated by his frequent talk about laws even in this article condemning the present state of moral theology. These two comments have a common root. These problems, as I will later develop them, come from the very discipline of moral theology itself and from the internal life of the church. Bouquillon's criticisms of the manuals often stressed circumstances extrinsic to the discipline of moral theology and the life of the church, but he needed to focus more on the problems inherent in the development of Catholic moral theology itself.

Despite this severe criticism of the present state of moral theology, Bouquillon believes that moral theology can be renewed by reversing the causes that have led to its downfall. In summary form he mentions the following points—use of the philosophy of Thomas Aquinas, a more intimate union with the theoretical truths of revelation, critical study and research into the fundamental ideas and principles of the moral life; and the consistent application of these principles to the problems of modern individual, social, and religious life through contact with the other social sciences. Bouquillon had reason to hope that the coming century would see such a resurgence, for the impetus had already been given in the admirable encyclicals of Pope Leo XIII.[147] This background should help us to understand, analyze, and criticize Bouquillon's moral theology.

NOTES

1. Thomas Joseph Bouquillon, *Institutiones theologiae moralis fundamentalis* (Bruges: Beyaert-Defoort, 1873); *Theologia moralis fundamentalis*, 2nd ed. (Bruges: Beyaert-Storie, 1890); *Theologia moralis fundamentalis*, 3rd ed. (Bruges: Car. Beyaert, 1903).

2. The best source for Bouquillon's biography is H. Rommel, *Thomas Bouquillon . . . — bio-bibliographique* (Bruges: Louis de Plancke, 1903). Since this small booklet was written immediately after his death, it tends to be a eulogy for Bouquillon and is not that critical. For the best available information on Bouquillon in English, see C. Joseph Nuesse, "Thomas Joseph Bouquillon (1840–

1902): Moral Theologian and Precursor of the Social Sciences in the Catholic University of America," *Catholic Historical Review* 72 (1986): 601–619.

3. Rommel, *Thomas Bouquillon*, pp. 13–23.

4. For further details of Bouquillon's life at Maredsous, see Laurent Janssens, "Maître Thomas Bouquillon," *Revue Bénédictine* 20 (1903): 2–6.

5. Thomas Joseph Bouquillon, *Theologia moralis fundamentalis*, 2nd ed. (Bruges: Beyaert-Storie, 1890).

6. Patrick Henry Ahern, *The Catholic University of America 1887–1896: The Rectorship of John J. Keane* (Washington: Catholic University of America Press, 1948), pp. 22–23.

7. Rommel, *Thomas Bouquillon*, pp. 23–24.

8. Ibid., p. 33.

9. Ibid., pp. 5–6.

10. Daniel F. Reilly, *The School Controversy 1891–1893* (Washington: Catholic University of America Press, 1943).

11. Robert D. Cross, *The Emergence of Liberal Catholicism in America* (Cambridge: Harvard University Press, 1958); Gerald P. Fogarty, *American Catholic Biblical Scholarship: A History from the Early Republic to Vatican II* (San Francisco: Harper and Row, 1989), pp. 27–42.

12. Reilly, *School Controversy*, pp. 26–38.

13. Ibid., pp. 67–105.

14. Thomas Bouquillon, *Education: to Whom does it Belong ?* (Baltimore: John Murphy and Co., 1891).

15. Reilly, *School Controversy*, pp. 89–90.

16. Ahern, *Catholic University*, pp. 122–123.

17. Kauffman, *Tradition and Transformation*, pp. 150–168.

18. Bouquillon, *Education*, p. 3.

19. Ibid., pp. 5–31.

20. E. G. Ryan, "Bouquillon Controversy," *New Catholic Encyclopedia*, 2, pp. 731–732.

21. Holaind, *The Parent First*.

22. Reilly, *School Controversy*, p. 113; for the entire history, see pp. 112–133.

23. Thomas Bouquillon, *Education: to Whom does it Belong? A Rejoinder to Critics* (Baltimore: John Murphy and Co., 1892).

24. Reilly, *School Controversy*, pp. 114–115.

25. Brandi, *Education: to Whom does it Belong? A Review*.

26. Thomas Bouquillon, *Education: to Whom does it Belong? A Rejoinder to Civiltà Cattolica* (Baltimore: John Murphy and Co., 1892).

27. Reilly, *School Controversy*, p 131.

28. Bouquillon, *Rejoinder to Civiltà Cattolica*, p. 7.

29. Bouquillon, *Rejoinder to Critics*, pp. 41–42.

30. Ibid., p. 30.

31. Ibid., pp. 35–36.

32. Bouquillon, *Rejoinder to Civiltà Cattolica*, pp. 24–26.

33. Bouquillon, *Education: to Whom does it Belong?* pp. 30–31; *Rejoinder to Civiltà Cattolica*, pp. 28–29.

34. Bouquillon, *Rejoinder to Civiltà Cattolica*, p. 29.

35. Ahern, *Catholic University*, pp. 122–133.

36. Rommel, *Thomas Bouquillon*, pp. 48–49.

37. Ahern, *Catholic University*, p. 132; Rommel, *Thomas Bouquillon*, p. 55.

38. Rommel, *Thomas Bouquillon*, p. 51.

39. E. H. Smith, "McGlynn, Edward," *New Catholic Encyclopedia*, 9, pp. 18–19; Gerald P. Fogarty, *The Vatican and the American Hierarchy* (Wilmington, Del.: Michael Glazier, 1985), p. 114.

40. Nuesse, *Catholic Historical Review* 72 (1986): 604.

41. Nuesse, *Catholic University of America*, pp. 3–104.

42. Ahern, *Catholic University*, p. 130.

43. Bouquillon, *Rejoinder to Civiltà Cattolica*, p. 6, fn. 1.

44. Nuesse, *Catholic Historical Review* 72 (1986): 604.

45. Ahern, *Catholic University*, p. 71. See Nuesse, *Catholic University of America*, p. 49, fn. 66; p. 108.

46. John A. Ryan, *Social Doctrine in Action: A Personal History* (New York: Harper and Brothers, 1941), p. 63.

47. For my assessment of Ryan's contribution, see my *American Catholic Social Ethics* (Notre Dame, Ind.: University of Notre Dame Press, 1982), pp. 26–91.

48. Nuesse, *Catholic Historical Review* 72 (1986): 607.

49. "Discourse of Rev. Dr. Kerby," *Catholic University Bulletin* 9 (1903): 161.

50. Nuesse, *Catholic Historical Review* 72 (1986): 609.

51. Ibid., p. 616. This report was published in C. Joseph Nuesse, "Before *Rerum novarum*: A Moral Theologian's View of Catholic Social Movements in 1891," *Social Thought* 17, n. 2 (1991): 5–17.

52. Thomas Bouquillon, "European Congresses of 1897," *Catholic University Bulletin* 4 (1898): 234–248.

53. Nuesse, *Catholic Historical Review* 72 (1986): 619.

54. Rommel, *Thomas Bouquillon*, pp. 18–25.

55. Cited in Ahern, *Catholic University*, p. 36.

56. Ibid., pp. 37ff.

57. Ibid., p. 104; Nuesse, *Catholic University of America*, p. 110.

58. Cited in Ahern, *Catholic University*, p. 71, fn. 173.

59. For the most complete bibliography of his works, see Rommel, *Thomas Bouquillon*, pp. 75–79.

60. Nuesse, *Catholic Historical Review* 72 (1986): 607–608.

61. Ibid., pp. 613–615; Rommel, *Thomas Bouquillon*, p. 34. As a result of the 1895–1896 seminar, Bouquillon with the collaboration of his seminar students published "Catholicism vs. Science, Liberty, Truthfulness: A Reply to the Dudley Lecture," *Catholic University Bulletin* 2 (1896): 356–387.

62. Thomas J. Shahan, "Thomas Joseph Bouquillon," *Catholic University Bulletin* 9 (1903): 152–156; Nuesse, *Catholic Historical Review* 72 (1986): 613. The Shahan article appears as a necrology and is unsigned, but Rommel (*Thomas Bouquillon*, p. 3) attributes it to Shahan.

63. Janssens, *Revue Bénédictine* 20 (1903): 3.

64. Thomas Bouquillon, "The University of Paris I," *Catholic University Bulletin* 1 (1895): 349–364; "The University of Paris II," *Catholic University Bulletin* 1 (1895): 491–512; "The University of Paris III," *Catholic University Bulletin* 2 (1896): 11–20.

65. Thomas Bouquillon, "Theology in Universities," *Catholic University Bulletin* 1 (1895): 25–34.

66. Kerby, *Catholic University Bulletin* 9 (1903): 161.

67. Shahan, *Catholic University Bulletin* 9 (1903): 153.

68. Rommel, *Thomas Bouquillon*, pp. 42–47.

69. Ahern, *Catholic University*, p. 83; Shahan, *Catholic University Bulletin* 9 (1903): 154–155.

70. Thomas Bouquillon, "The Ambrosiana Library at Milan," *Catholic University Bulletin* 1 (1895): 567.

71. Kerby, *Catholic University Bulletin* 9 (1903): 159–160.

72. Shahan, *Catholic University Bulletin* 9 (1903): 154.

73. Thomas Bouquillon, "De l'ignorance invincible des conclusions eloignées de la loi naturelle," *Revue des sciences ecclésiastiques*, 4th series, vol. 8 (1878): 257–268; 545–558; 4th series, vol. 9 (1879): 355–362.

74. Thomas Bouquillon, "The Science of Bibliography and Some Recent Bibliographies," *Catholic University Bulletin* 4 (1898): 37–49.

75. Rommel, *Thomas Bouquillon*, p. 56.

76. Shahan, *Catholic University Bulletin* 9 (1903): 153.

77. Kerby, *Catholic University Bulletin* 9 (1903): 161.

78. Thomas Bouquillon, "Coup d'oeil sur l'histoire de la théologie," *Revue des sciences ecclésiastiques*, 5th series, vol. 8 (1883): 298–337.

79. Thomas Bouquillon, "Coup d'oeil sur l'histoire de la théologie II," *Revue des sciences ecclésiastiques*, 5th series, vol. 8 (1883): 395–423.

80. Janssens, *Revue Bénédictine* 20 (1903): 2–3.

81. Bouquillon, *Institutiones theologia moralis fundamentalis*.

82. Bouquillon, *Theologia moralis fundamentalis*, 2nd ed., pp. 49–140.

83. Bouquillon, *Theologia moralis fundamentalis*, 3rd ed., 71–167. Subsequent references will always be to the third edition unless noted to the contrary.

84. Bouquillon, *Theologia moralis fundamentalis*, pp. 75–80.

85. Ibid., p. 72.

86. Ibid., p. 92.

87. Ibid., pp. 92–167.

88. Ibid., p. 93.

89. Ibid., pp. 93–97.

90. Ibid., pp. 94–95.

91. Ibid., pp. 111–128.

92. Ibid., pp. 111–115.

93. Ibid., pp. 121–127.

94. Ibid., p. 129.

95. Ibid., pp. 130–132.

96. Ibid., pp. 137–140.

97. Ibid., p. 140.

98. Ibid., p. 157.

99. Ibid., p. 140, fn. 7.
100. Ibid., pp. 46–51.
101. Ibid., p. 51.
102. Ibid., pp. 154–155.
103. Ibid., p. 155.
104. Ibid., pp. 155–156.
105. Ibid., pp. 156–157.
106. Thomas Bouquillon, ed., *Leonis Papae XIII allocutiones, epistolae, constitutiones aliaque acta praecipua,* 2 vols. (Bruges: Desclée De Brouwer, 1887).
107. The following six articles of Thomas Bouquillon appeared in *Le Messager des Fidèles de Maredsous* 5 (1888): "Dix années de pontificat," pp. 4–9; "Léon XIII et la Bavière," pp. 74–87; "Condamnation des doctrines Rosminiennes," pp. 199–207; "Le libéralisme d'après l'Encyclique *Libertas*," pp. 361–370; "La liberté chrétienne d'après l'Encyclique *Libertas*," pp. 399–404; "Les droits de l'Église," pp. 533–546. This journal began in 1884–1885 with the subtitle *Petit Revue Bénédictine.* Vol. 3 (1886–1887) changed the subtitle to *Revue Bénédictine.* Vol 4 (1887) started the system of having the volume number coincide with just one year. Vol. 7 (1899) changed the name to *Revue Bénédictine.* Subsequent references will use this title.
108. Bouquillon, *Revue Bénédictine* 5 (1888): 4.
109. Ibid., p. 362.
110. Ibid., pp. 362–363.
111. Ibid., pp. 363–365.
112. Ibid., p. 4.
113. Ibid., pp. 368–369.
114. Ibid., p. 205.
115. Ibid., pp. 4–5.
116. Ibid., p. 81.
117. Ibid., p. 80, fn. 1.
118. Ibid., p. 82.
119. Ibid., pp. 81–82.
120. Pope Leo XIII, *Officio sanctissimo,* par. 9, in *The Papal Encyclicals 1878–1903,* ed. Carlen, p. 151.
121. Bouquillon, *Revue Bénédictine* 5 (1888): 82 and fn. 3.
122. Ibid., pp. 369–370.
123. Ibid., p. 9.
124. Ibid., p. 207.
125. Philip Hughes, *A Popular History of the Catholic Church* (Garden City, N.Y.: Doubleday, Image, 1954), p. 255. C. Joseph Nuesse in his commentary on the memorandum on Catholic social movements prepared for Bishop Keane, the rector of Catholic University, in 1891 finds it difficult to interpret Bouquillon's position that Pius IX had greatly promoted and encouraged these movements. See Nuesse, *Social Thought* 17 n. 2 (1991): 10.
126. Bouquillon, *Revue Bénédictine* 5 (1888): 8–9.
127. Thomas Bouquillon, "Oratio in laudem S. Thomae Aquinatis," *Revue des sciences ecclésiastiques,* 5th ser., vol. 5 (1882): 345–350.
128. Bouquillon, *Theologia moralis fundamentalis,* p. 156.

129. Bouquillon, *Revue Bénédictine* 5 (1888): 202.
130. Bouquillon, *Revue Bénédictine* 6 (1889): 157.
131. Kerby, *Catholic University Bulletin* 9 (1903): 162.
132. Shahan, *Catholic University Bulletin* 9 (1903): 155.
133. Rommel, *Thomas Bouquillon*, p. 50.
134. Janssens, *Revue Bénédictine* 20 (1903): 4.
135. Thomas Bouquillon, "Moral Theology at the End of the Nineteenth Century," *Catholic University Bulletin* 5 (1899): 244–268.
136. Bouquillon, *Theologia moralis fundamentalis*, especially pp. 12–22.
137. Rommel, *Thomas Bouquillon*, p. 18.
138. Bouquillon, *Catholic University Bulletin* 5 (1899): 250–251.
139. Ibid., pp. 252–253.
140. Ibid., pp. 260–261.
141. Ibid., p. 262.
142. Ibid., pp. 258–259; *Theologia moralis fundamentalis*, pp. 20–21.
143. Bouquillon, *Catholic University Bulletin* 5 (1899): 244–248.
144. Ibid., pp. 256–264.
145. Ibid., p. 265.
146. Ibid., pp. 246; 259.
147. Ibid., pp. 267–268.

6

Bouquillon's Fundamental Moral Theology

Without doubt Thomas Joseph Bouquillon's most important and significant book is his *Theologia moralis fundamentalis*, the third edition of which he finished just before his death. This was the only book published by him after he came to the United States. It appeared thirteen years after the second edition. A brief overview of his fundamental moral theology is in order.

OVERVIEW

In the preface to the second and third editions Bouquillon uses the analogies of the atrium and the foundation of the moral theological building. The atrium is the place from which you are led into the building and from which you can contemplate the various parts. The foundation serves as the basis for the whole edifice. The atrium is the introduction to moral theology which consists of three parts—the nature of moral theology, the study of moral theology, and in the largest part the history of moral theology. The foundation is the major section of the book—fundamental moral theology itself.[1]

Fundamental moral theology deals with the principles of moral theology, not its presuppositions and preambles. The presuppositions are those dogmas on which moral theology depends such as the existence of a personal God, creation, and redemption. The preambles of the science of moral theology are those psychological notions which serve the understanding of moral realities such as the concept of action or of human powers and faculties. The proper principles of the science are those general moral truths that are necessary for the solution of particular moral questions such as the idea of morality, virtues, vices, sin, obligation, and conscience. The purpose of fundamental moral theology is to explain and expound these principles. Note that "princi-

210

ple" here does not just mean standard or rule but the basic foundations of the discipline which in a certain sense are the first principles from which everything else develops. The definition of moral theology serves to determine the material to be treated. Moral theology is the science of the means and the laws by which the human being is helped and directed to come to one's supernatural end. As a result of this understanding the Catholic University professor divided his fundamental moral theology into five tracts dealing with the ultimate end of human beings, the means to the end, the rules directing one to the end, the acts by which we attain the end, and finally the attainment or loss of the end itself.[2]

The first treatise on the ultimate end of human beings considers the end from the perspective of the external end (the glory of God) and the internal end (the supreme good or happiness of the human being) as well as from the perspective of the natural and supernatural ends.[3] Since God who assigned the end for human beings has also given us the aptitude and the means to attain this end the second treatise discusses the means to attain the twofold natural and supernatural end of human beings—nature and grace, reason and faith, the will and its helps, and Christ and the sacraments.[4]

The last part of the second treatise on means to the end deals with the religious and civil societies to which human beings belong. One can readily see here Bouquillon's recognition of the social nature of human beings and the problems of individualism and privatism that too often characterize the manuals of moral theology. Human beings are by nature social not only because they are ordered to society as an end but also because they need society in order to attain that end. These two societies are the religious society and the civil society.[5] Bouquillon mentions the family in passing as one of the three principal societies established by God for human beings, but does not develop specific ideas about the family which seems strange in the light of the fundamental role and importance of the family in moral formation and education.[6] Our author does briefly discuss the family in his discussion of domestic law under the section on law.[7]

The third treatise deals with the rules directing human beings to their end. All beings are moved by God to their end in accord with their nature. Irrational creatures necessarily achieve their end but rational creatures have freedom and can go against their God-given end. God freely moves human beings to their end by imposing their end upon them and directing them by efficacious rules to attain the end. These rules which are the complement and remedy of freedom are two. Law is the *in se*, objective, and remote rule of human actions. Conscience as the subjective and proximate rule applies the law to practice.[8]

The third treatise of the book on the rules of law and conscience comprises sixty percent of the pages dedicated to fundamental moral theology with only forty percent given to the other four treatises. Six types of law are considered in great detail—eternal law, the natural law of God, the supernatural law of God, domestic law, ecclesiastical law, and civil law. The section on conscience discusses the definition and obligatory force of conscience, general notions, qualities of a true conscience and formation of a true conscience.[9]

Since human beings attain their ultimate end by their acts, the fifth treatise considers human acts under three headings—as free, moral, and salutary.[10] The final, very short fifth treatise briefly treats the attaining and losing of the ultimate end.[11]

THE INFLUENCE OF NEOSCHOLASTICISM AND THE MANUALS

An earlier section has demonstrated the Catholic University professor's support for neoscholasticism. How did this support affect his moral theology? Bouquillon shows the Thomistic influence in his fundamental moral theology by beginning with the consideration of the ultimate end of human beings. The Catholic University professor explicitly ties this move to Aquinas. Humankind must constantly raise a twofold issue—where do human beings come from and where are we going? Catholic truth solves the problem by its *"exitus-reditus"* theory. We come from God as the first principle of our being, and return to God as our ultimate end. This theory explains why Thomas Aquinas in the first part of the *Summa* treats of the production, distinction, conservation, and providence of creatures and in the second part treats of the ultimate end of human beings and the way to attain it.

In accord with the Thomistic understanding the internal ultimate end of human beings consists in happiness. The supreme good is that which fully perfects one's nature, and in attaining this supreme good one finds happiness which according to Aquinas is the ultimate perfection of the rational or intellectual nature.[12] Bouquillon does not follow the treatment on the ultimate end and happiness exactly as it is found in the *Summa*. He brings into the discussion a distinction found elsewhere in Aquinas but explicitly developed at great length by Kleutgen between the external ultimate end of human beings and the internal ultimate end of human beings. The external ultimate end of human beings is the formal glory of God whereas the internal end is the happiness of human beings, but both ends consist in one and the same reality.[13] Thus in the discussion of the ultimate end one clearly sees the influence of Thomas Aquinas and neoscholasticism.

The discussion of the ultimate end not only follows the teleological method of Aquinas but from the very beginning also points out the intrinsic nature of morality which is such a distinctive characteristic of the Thomistic approach. Bouquillon accepted Thomas Aquinas's understanding of happiness as the ultimate perfection of human beings as rational creatures.[14] Bouquillon explains this notion by saying that the supreme good of any being is known from its nature, faculties, apprehensions, and ordered tendencies. The most wise Creator could not act properly without providing a proportionate object for this nature and its tendencies. Augustine has reminded us that God has made us for God's self and our hearts will not rest until they rest in God. But God the supreme good can only be attained by acts of the intellect and will—the highest two powers or faculties of human beings.

In knowing and loving God we come to the fulfillment of our own nature and hence to our beatitude. For Bouquillon happiness is the ultimate internal end of human beings, while the glory of God is the ultimate external end of human beings but these two ends consist in one and the same reality.[15] We see here an illustration of the Thomistic notions of participation and mediation. The glory of God and human fulfillment are the same reality. The same basic emphasis on participation comes to the fore in the discussion of natural law. Bouquillon ends his discussion of natural law by comparing it with the eternal law and concluding that the natural law is not something diverse from the eternal law but its participation in the rational creature in accord with the teaching of Aquinas.[16] This notion of participation thus does not see the divine and the human at odds with one another but brings them together in harmony so that the glory of God and the happiness of the human person are one and the same reality and the eternal law of God and the natural law point to the same basic reality.

In the discussion of the ultimate end Bouquillon deals with the relationship between the supernatural and the natural end of human beings. The human being, by nature a servant who through the immense goodness of God is raised up to the supernatural order of divine sonship is destined to know God in this world through faith, hope, and charity and in the consummation of glory and happiness to possess God as an heir of divine goods, being made similar to God. This supernatural end does not differ from the natural end in its object but only in its manner. Both involve knowledge and love of God and being joined with God; but the natural end involves knowledge through creatures, the supernatural involves faith and the intuitive vision of God. The natural involves natural law, the supernatural, charity; the natural involves most worthy servanthood, the supernatural heredity and the reign of God. However, this call to the supernatural has very significant repercussions for life in the temporal order in this world. One sees here how the distinction between the supernatural and the natural holds on to the gratuitousness of God's gift of saving love but at the same time has beneficial consequences in the natural or temporal order. The hope of attaining eternal union with God is not only a great consolation for the individual but also a spur to promote virtue and morality. Thus the Christian philosophy and theology stand out in their truth and dignity against the proponents of modern liberalism, the pantheistic believers in indefinite progress, and the naive dreams of the socialists.[17]

From the first pages of the introduction Bouquillon points out the difference between natural moral science or philosophy pertaining to the natural moral order and the supernatural moral science or moral theology pertaining to the supernatural order but also including the natural.[18] In the second treatise discussing means to the ultimate end, he considers in order nature and grace, reason and faith, and the will and its helps. The human being by nature is apt and fit for attaining its natural end. Nature is the substantial principle of operation in every created thing by which each is attracted to and directed to its proper end. The instrument for moving human nature to its end involves the powers and faculties that are modified by habits. The four cardinal virtues are good habits that modify the four faculties—prudence in the intellect, justice in the will, fortitude in the will and irascible appetites, and temperance in the will and concupiscible appetites. In order to become apt and fit to obtain the supernatural end, the human being receives a new supernatural existence—grace together with the infused supernatural virtues of faith, hope, and love—which will dispose her to act on the supernatural level. Bouquillon agrees with the Thomistic thesis about the existence of infused moral virtues as well as the theological virtues mentioned above. The gifts of the Holy Spirit, which render the powers docile to the urgings of the spirit, are added to grace and the infused virtues.[19]

The next question concerns the roles of reason and faith. Not only in the possible state of pure nature (without the supernatural ordering and without sin) but also in the present state of fallen and redeemed nature, the human being by the light of reason is physically capable of knowing her natural end and the way to it. This is the teaching of Vatican Council I. However, in the present state of fallen nature the human race by the sole force of intellect is impotent for knowing its natural end and the way to it with due fullness, facility, and purity. In no way by reason alone can the human being know her real destiny to the supernatural end and the means of attaining it. In its present state of fallen and repaired nature, the human being receives from revelation, to which faith corresponds, both the necessary knowledge of the supernatural end and the way to it and the fitting knowledge of the natural end and the means to it. Note here the typical neoscholastic approach sanctioned by the First Vatican Council about the role of reason. Sin does not destroy the power of reason to know the natural end and the way to it, but sin does make such knowledge in its fullness and purity morally impossible for humankind. The same basic possibilities and limitations confront the will.[20] Bouquillon thus shows himself to be following very clearly the distinctive approach of neoscholasticism about the natural and the supernatural order and the powers corresponding to these orders.

No one can deny the influence of neoscholasticism in Bouquillon's approach to moral theology but for some reason Bouquillon did not follow the Thomistic approach on what we call fundamental moral theology. The Catholic University professor knowingly departed from Thomas's outline and schema, but gave no reason for so doing.[21]

After discussing the ultimate end of human beings Thomas Aquinas considered human acts, first those that are proper to human beings and then those that are common to human beings and animals. The *Prima secundae* then discussed the intrinsic principles of human acts—the powers and the habits that are either good (virtues) or bad (vices) that modify the person and the external principles of human acts—the devil and God who instructs with the law and helps by grace.[22]

What is missing in Bouquillon's fundamental moral theology is the emphasis on the intrinsic principle of human acts—the powers and the habits that modify them. Thomas Aquinas gave primary importance to the virtues in his moral theology. One might maintain that the failure to consider these aspects is somewhat minimal but I think not.

Contemporary ethical theory sometimes contrasts the virtue approach to ethics with an obligational approach. In reality Aquinas proposes both aspects but gives primary emphasis in terms of prior treatment and length of treatment to the virtues in his discussion of what we call fundamental moral theology. So significant is the role of the virtues in Aquinas's fundamental moral theology that the virtues become the basis for his whole discussion of particular human acts in what we call special moral theology. Thomas develops his ethical discussion of particular acts around the three theological virtues (faith, hope, and charity) and the four cardinal virtues of prudence, justice, fortitude, and temperance.[23] Thus by leaving out the section on habits, virtues, and vices Bouquillon loses a very characteristic aspect of the Thomistic approach to moral theology. Recall also that Bouquillon had criticized the manuals of moral theology for not treating the habits and passions,[24] but his fundamental moral theology likewise does not treat the habits and the passions in any depth.

Not only does Bouquillon leave out the important section on habits; he also gives disproportionate place to the treatise on law and conscience which takes up about sixty percent of his entire fundamental moral theology. Aquinas had no separate section on conscience, which came into existence in the manuals of moral theology especially in the light of the controversies over rigorism and probabilism. Bouquillon's long third treatise discusses the rules directing human beings to their end, which are law as the objective and remote rule and conscience as the subjective and proximate rule of human action. The discussion on law alone involves one-half of the entire fundamental moral theology.[25] The discussion of law becomes the most central, lengthy, and important consideration in Bouquillon's fundamental moral theology.

Ironically Bouquillon's negative criticism of the manuals tends to accentuate the length and importance of his treatise on laws. The Catholic University professor criticizes the manuals for not giving enough importance to establishing the principles and the basis of their moral theology. To rectify such an approach he has to devote much more space to such considerations. Aloysius Sabetti in his *Compendium*, for example, devoted one page to natural law.[26] Bouquillon devotes over twenty-five pages to natural law.[27]

On the other hand, despite Bouquillon's strong negative criticism of the manuals, he does not disagree with one important characteristic of the manuals—the close relationship between moral theology and canon law. His 1899 article mentioned that the manuals insist on the external canonical character of law while studying civil law only in a superficial manner.[28] In his own volume, Bouquillon does not object to the insistence on canon law, but in fact clearly endorses it. Our author spends over 150 pages of his fundamental moral theology discussing ecclesiastical laws.[29] Such an approach is totally foreign to Aquinas.

Despite his strong neoscholastic perspectives, Bouquillon in reality departs from the Thomistic approach to fundamental moral theology. For all practical purposes he accentuates the legal model for the structuring of moral theology at least as far as fundamental moral theology is concerned. The discussions about the ultimate end are quite short and do not seem to influence the heart of the material which deals with the objective and subjective norms of human action. There is no discussion of the virtues.

Bouquillon might object to our characterizing his approach as a legal model. The Catholic University professor never did write a complete special moral theology, but he did discuss the various ways in which special moral theology might be structured. Special moral theology involves three parts. The first part expounds the rules of theological acts that come from faith, hope, and charity, the three theological virtues. The second part considers the rules of the moral acts common to all human beings regardless of their state and circumstances. The third concerns the rules for actions of certain particular persons.

Three possible formats exist for developing the very large section on the rules for human acts common to all human beings. Some theologians such as Thomas Aquinas attend to the diverse species of goodness or rectitude in the acts and employ the schema of the four cardinal virtues; this format favors a scientific exposition and is helpful for preachers. Others such as St. Alphonsus and many more recent moral theologians follow the schema of the commandments of God and the church; this approach is helpful for catechists and confessors but does not present a sufficient explanation of the virtues. Bouquillon himself presents a schema based on the threefold reality of the human being as an individual being, a religious being, and a social being because such an approach is clearer, responds to the natural order of love and the supernatural order of charity, and brings together the benefits of the two other approaches.[30]

Although the Catholic University professor explicitly rejects the legal model as an outline for special moral theology, still his basic understanding puts a heavy emphasis on the legal aspects in his own outline. Recall that his heading for the entire discussion of the moral actions common to all human beings is the *"regulae"* or rules of human acts. The primary emphasis on rule indicates a strong legal strain. An evaluation of his fundamental moral theology itself must recognize the predominance of the legal model. True, the book does have a broad teleological approach on the basis of the ultimate end and the way to attain it. But the longest and most significant section deals with the rules of attaining this ultimate end. The very short discussion of grace and the sacraments in the section of means to the end is illuminating. The obligations of the Christian life do not come from grace, Christ, and the sacraments as such but rather from the rules to be developed at great length in the following treatise.[31] The implication remains that grace, Christ, and the sacraments are means to obey the laws by which we arrive at our end. The primary reality in this one volume remains the discussion of law and conscience as the objective and subjective rules of human action. The centrality, length, and the importance of this discussion on law and conscience is not Thomistic and seems to give a priority to the legal model even though the section on law exists within the parameters of a more teleological model.

Why does Bouquillon go against a Thomistic approach and give such an importance to the legal model? Three reasons suggest themselves. His criticism of compendia and the manuals did not explicitly reject their emphasis on the close connection between canon law and morality. His fundamental moral theology strongly emphasizes such a relationship. Second, Bouquillon never abandoned the purpose of the manuals which was to prepare confessors. His *Theologia moralis fundamentalis* originally began in the context of teaching moral theology to seminarians. This location and purpose of the course put heavy emphasis on the training of confessors. The subsequent editions, especially the second, made substantial additions such as the long historical section, but the last two editions still show the book's original purpose and context. In reality Bouquillon made comparatively few changes between the second and third editions. His thirteen years in the United States were so busy with other teaching and writing activities that he had no time to thoroughly revise his fundamental moral theology. On the basis of his 1899 article criticizing the manuals it seems he might have published a different book in 1903 had he been conceiving and writing the book for the first time. But he was working with a text that he had originally written for seminarians preparing for priestly ministry.

Third is the influence of Francis Suarez (d. 1617). Suarez is known for his treatise on laws and for having introduced a heavy emphasis on law in general and canon law into moral theology.[32] In the preface to his fundamental moral theology, Bouquillon mentions that he has three principal masters and teachers—Thomas Aquinas from whom he has received the firm principles of moral science, Suarez from whom he has received the learned exposition and vindication of principles, and finally St. Alphonsus from whom he has received the prudent application of the same principles.[33]

Thus Bouquillon recognizes his dependence on Suarez precisely with regard to those principles that deal with law. In fact, in his criticism of the manuals of moral theology he prefers some of the older approaches to moral theology and includes not only Aquinas but also the *De legibus* and *De religione* of Suarez. With regard to the speculative side of moral theology, Bouquillon mentions just two authors—Aquinas, whose *chef d'oeuvre* is the second part of the *Summa* and Suarez who is at his best in *De legibus*.[34] His appreciation for Suarez also comes through in his earlier work on religion, another area in which Suarez made a significant contribution.[35] The Suarezian influence definitely shows itself in the length and importance given to the role of law in Bouquillon's fundamental moral theology.

Thus despite his strong neoscholastic approach and his stinging criticism of the manuals, the basic structure of Bouquillon's fundamental moral theology does not follow the Thomistic approach or schema but like the manuals makes law and conscience the primary and most important considerations. While the overall format of his ethical model is teleological the legal model appears as the most significant and operationally primary.

His discussion of law differs greatly from the manuals, however, in terms of the depth and breadth of his considerations. Bouquillon truly tries to develop in a scientific way the basic principles and ideas of morality. An analysis of some aspects of his teaching on law will show both his in-depth approach and how his own positions differed from others.

In his brief discussion of law in general our author refers to the "magisterial definition" of Aquinas on the ordering of reason for the common good promulgated by the one who has charge of the community. However, according to Bouquillon this definition has some defects and some aspects that need further elaboration. The first defect consists in not giving enough importance to obligation. The ordering to the common good comes about by commanding, prohibiting, permitting, punishing, or irritating. However, this defect can be rectified from other places in Aquinas in which he points out that it is the very nature of law that it be a rule of human acts and it must be coercive in order to achieve its purpose.[36]

In reality, Bouquillon here is depending more heavily on Suarez with his insistence on obligation and the will of the legislator than on Aquinas's insistence on law as an act of practical reason.[37] Our author does not explicitly mention his dependence on Suarez but rather attempts to correct the defects in Aquinas's "magisterial definition" from other Thomistic texts. However, Suarez himself appealed to other texts in Aquinas to support this approach to law.[38]

Bouquillon's very first comment on the concept of natural law comes from Suarez. One must distinguish a threefold norm in the natural law: the norm as discriminating good actions from bad actions (human nature); the norm as obliging (the divine command); and the norm as declaring the obligation (the light of reason). The obliging norm is the divine will ordering the natural order to be conserved and forbidding it to be disturbed. The natural order in this case is human nature completely and adequately understood in its constitution, its relationships, and its end.[39]

This understanding of natural law based on Aquinas with a Suarezian interpretation differs from a number of other ethical approaches. The natural law is not merely the light of reason as many scholastics held. The dictates of practical reason do not make the obligation but declare it. The natural law is not only the free will of God as the Nominalists assert, and a fortiori it is not the formal and universal dictate of practical reason or the categorical imperative of the autonomous will of Kant. The Kantian understanding cannot be reconciled with the idea of true moral obligation and is based on the false premise that the human being is its own end.[40]

Having discussed the concept of natural law, Bouquillon considers the existence, dictates, properties, promulgation, and knowledge of natural law as well as its social and political character and its sanction.[41] By definition these discussions cannot be in-depth but they are solid presentations that show Bouquillon's familiarity with the sources and the historical development exemplified in the discussion of invincible ignorance of the natural law.[42] In contradistinction to the manuals Bouquillon explicitly calls attention to the social and political character of natural law which cannot be simply reduced to regulations guiding the actions of private individuals. Yet Bouquillon does not develop these aspects.[43]

The classicist understanding of natural law with its implicit opposition to historical consciousness comes through in Bouquillon's discussion of the properties of natural law. The fundamental property of natural law is its necessity based on creation and from which three other properties are derived—universality, perpetuity, and indispensability. Above all, natural law embraces all those who have rational nature and is the same among all. The natural law cannot be changed from the inside because it is grounded in the nature of things and the divine essence. Natural law prohibits those things that are essentially evil. But what about the older scholastics who said that the more remote conclusions of the natural law could change? The change does not refer to the precepts themselves but to their expression and application. Often the precepts are formulated in a general and abstract manner such as "thou shalt not kill" without added restrictions such as "on one's own authority" or "outside the case of self-defense." In this sense the more abstract precept is said to admit exceptions. But when the precept is spelled out with all its restrictions it does not admit exceptions.[44] Some contemporary commentators interpret Thomas as being more open to exceptions.[45]

Bouquillon also insists on the universality of the natural law from the outside, either by abrogation or dispensation. Again, the fundamental reason remains that neither God nor an inferior authority can change the natural law. However, Bouquillon recognizes that some older scholastics admitted the possibility of dispensation or abrogation. Careful attention to what they wrote shows that they did not admit change properly so called through dispensation or abrogation. Strictly speaking, these authors dealt with additions to the law, the changing of the conditions which are supposed for the application of the laws, or at most a change in what the natural law demands as more fitting but not strictly required. The older scholastics had dealt with the biblical incidents of Abraham intending to kill Isaac, Israelites taking things from the Egyptians that did not belong to them, or Hosea having relations with a prostitute. These did not involve dispensations from the law but rather the introduction of circumstances that made these actions no longer against the law. God as the supreme Lord of life and of all things could dispose of the life of Isaac and the goods of the Egyptians so that the actions in these cases are no longer murder or stealing. Likewise God has disposition over human bodies so that an act is now licit which without this divine concession would have been fornication.[46] Some contemporary commentators interpret these texts in a much more expansive manner.[47]

Bouquillon continues to propose what has been called the ontological and gnoseological aspects of natural law.[48] The ontological aspect consists of the essential inclinations of human nature. According to Aquinas natural reason apprehends as good all things to which the human being has a natural inclination. These essential inclinations are properly ordered and contrasted with the inordinate inclinations or concupiscence. Bouquillon follows Thomas in distinguishing a three-fold aspect of human nature with corresponding inclinations. Human beings share the nature of a substance and hence like all substances seek the conservation of their own being. Human beings share the nature of animals and according to this nature whatever nature teaches humans and all the animals constitutes natural law such as the inclination to the union of male and female and the education of children. Third, human beings have their own proper rational nature with its inclination to know God and to live in society with other human beings.[49]

In my opinion such an understanding of the natural inclinations of human nature, especially animal nature, tends to absolutize the physical and biological aspects of the human preventing any interference in them. Thus one cannot interfere with the conjugal act for the purpose of responsible parenthood. Such physicalism absolutizes the biological and physical aspects to the detriment of the fully human.[50] In his discussion of natural law Bouquillon illustrates the neoscholastic emphasis on the universal, immutable, and unchanging aspects of morality with little or no attention to historicity. Unchangeable human nature and not history serve as the basis for morality.

Bouquillon's acceptance of neoscholasticism and his criticism of the manuals affect his own approach to fundamental moral theology, with some unexpected and surprising effects. His neoscholasticism comes through in his heavy dependence on Aquinas and his classic emphasis on the universal, the absolute, and the unchanging. However, the Catholic University professor puts a strong Suarezian spin on his neoscholasticism and also fails to follow the Thomistic schema and outline for moral theology. As a critic of the manuals he presents a more substantive development of the principles of moral theology, but in reality Bouquillon agrees with the purpose of the manuals and continues to give primary significance to the reality of law as the guiding model of morality.

THE SOURCES OF MORAL THEOLOGY

In his more scholarly approach to fundamental moral theology Bouquillon reflects on the discipline itself and devotes about fifty pages to the founts and sources of moral theology.[51] In keeping with his neoscholastic emphasis on the natural and the supernatural orders, his treatment considers only two sources—the use of reason in moral theology and the use of revelation.

REASON. In this context Bouquillon discusses reason solely as a source for moral theology insofar as moral principles are contained in reason and conclusions are deduced from it. Human reason in this context is the reason existing in the state of fallen and redeemed nature directed by the authority of the church. All theologians agree that the principal truths of the natural moral order are explicitly or implicitly contained in revelation, but theologians disagree whether all the truths of natural law are so contained in revelation. Even if all natural law truths are part of revelation, still moral theology has often discussed these in the light of human reason alone. Thus reason is a source of moral theology but secondary and subordinate to revelation. Moral theology is distinguished from moral philosophy but not separated from it.[52]

The narrow focus of the discussion means that many issues about human reason and how it functions in moral theology are not discussed, but one aspect developed by Bouquillon is most interesting. Reason as a source for moral theology is either individual (which can be either common or scientific) or social. Our author mentions that difficult questions can be asked about the origin and value of common individual reason. Scientific individual reason must also be subject to analysis and verification. Social reason is expressed in the customs and laws of the people. A knowledge of secular history is necessary to understand and critically interpret these customs. Moral theology also cannot forget the social reason expressed in the rites and religions of primitive people although moral precepts and practices can and do appear together with superstitions and crude practices in these religions.[53] Implicit in such an understanding is the need for moral theology to be in constant dialogue with human reason in all its different manifestations. Moral theology cannot be limited only to reason as developed within the church. The explicit mention of the moral truths found in primitive religions is most surprising. Such an expansive understanding of reason also includes human experience, but the text does not develop this opening to experience.

Other significant questions about human reason need to be explored, and Bouquillon elsewhere in his fundamental moral theology addresses some of these issues. First, how does reason function in terms of morality? Without doubt Bouquillon uses a deductive and discursive reasoning process going from the more general to the more specific. The emphasis throughout the book is on the application of norms or laws to particular cases. In discussing the natural law Bouquillon follows the Thomistic tradition in stating that the natural law consists in a supreme universal principle in which are contained and from which are derived various obligations that are called the dictates, precepts, or articles of the natural law. But in describing the supreme principle of the natural law the Catholic University professor moves away from the Thomistic version of "do good and avoid evil" to one more in keeping with his Suarezian emphasis on obligation—observe the right order of natural reason sanctioned by God. Some principles are immediately formed from the first principle, for example, God is to be adored. Others are derived mediately in a discursive way from the first principles but with certitude while others are deduced from the principles only through a more subtle reasoning process and are only probable and not certain.[54] One thus moves from the more general to the more specific principles using discursive reasoning and deduction to discover those principles that are mediately derived from the first principle. In this context Bouquillon frequently speaks of deduction.[55]

Conscience as the proximate and subjective norm of morality also works by deduction. Conscience is the application of the habitually known objective moral rule to a particular case. Thus conscience is nothing other than the conclusion of a syllogism. The major contains the known general principles or precepts or prohibitions of the law. The minor is a statement of the fact by which this or that act or omission now proposed to the will is judged to be under the law or not.[56] Bouquillon clearly understands moral reasoning to work in a deductive manner both with regard to the objective and the subjective norms of human actions.

In the light of Bouquillon's emphasis on the importance of the other sciences such as economics, law, anthropology, and sociology one would expect a thorough discussion of their role in moral theology. However, for all practical purposes these sciences are not developed at any length in the entire volume on fundamental moral theology. Why not? Perhaps the very nature of fundamental moral theology as a general and universal discipline is the reason that the other sciences are not mentioned. In his brief discussion of the nature of moral science in the introduction, our author recognizes a greater role for these sciences in the various discussions or parts of moral theology as distinguished from universal or general moral theology. The further divisions of moral science include the ethico-religious, the ethico-social, the ethico-political, the ethico-juridical, and the ethico-economic. Therefore religion, sociology, politics, jurisprudence, and economics pertain to moral science, for they have the same object—free human activity. But these sciences study free human activity from the viewpoint of utility and a proximate end, whereas moral science considers such an activity from the perspective of rightness and the ultimate end. These sciences are not complete without moral science and depend on moral science as the more superior science. Moral science receives data from these other sciences.[57]

But Bouquillon's understanding of fundamental moral theology also helps to explain why the sciences have little or no place in his book. Moral principles and rules are derived deductively. The other sciences do not enter directly into the establishment of these principles. In a more inductive approach the sciences would play a much more significant role in moral theology. From Bouquillon's great insistence on the sciences I thought he might give them a greater role in moral theology, but his deductive approach lessens the role of these sciences. Bouquillon attaches great importance to the other sciences but sees their role as necessary for a proper application of the principles of moral theology to the different areas of moral concern.

A third important question concerns the differences between the supernatural law and the natural law. Does faith propose a moral content different from that proposed by reason? Bouquillon addresses this significant question in his discussion of the supernatural law. The supernatural law comes from God the author of grace, is known by revelation, is given to human beings elevated to divine sonship, prescribes supernatural acts, is fulfilled by supernatural power, and intends a supernatural end. Such an assessment certainly stresses the differences of the supernatural from the natural law. The supernatural rule of actions, although it is externally promulgated and proposed, is rightly called internal since it is written on the heart, placed in the mind because it is received in faith, and taught by the illumination of the Holy Spirit; likewise it is set in the will because it is fulfilled by the abundance of love and grace sweetly attracting us.[58]

This understanding of the supernatural law is quickly set aside as the discussion centers on the precepts of the supernatural law. Bouquillon's basic thesis which is common among the scholastics maintains that the supernatural law with regard to its substance basically agrees with the natural law. The great difference that seemed to exist between the supernatural and the natural laws does not exist on the level of precepts. The supernatural end does not differ from the natural end by reason of its object but only by the means of attaining it. Besides including the precepts of the natural law, the supernatural law contains those precepts which, given a certain fact, arise from the nature of things such as precepts of faith, hope, charity, penance, and reverence of holy things. The supernatural law also contains some precepts that determine what is left indeterminate by the natural law or precepts which propose as necessary what according to the natural law is fitting. These precepts refer, for example, to laws about worship and fasting.[59] Our author earlier distinguishes two kinds of supernatural acts: theological, such as acts of faith, hope, and charity; and moral acts. The theological acts commanded by the supernatural law are different but the moral acts are basically the same as the moral acts required by the natural law.[60]

The Catholic University professor goes on to point out that the substance of the supernatural law is expressed in the decalogue. Note here the reduction of the internal grace and gift of the Holy Spirit to the decalogue. This comes from the fact that Bouquillon understands the supernatural law in terms of precepts that are universal, immutable, and indispensable. In keeping with this understanding our author insists on the distinction between counsels and precepts with a counsel being a moral rule generally recommended, not required, for human beings to live more perfectly and more fully and to attain expeditiously their ultimate end. The precepts of the decalogue can be reduced to the love commandment with its twin precepts of love of God and neighbor. Thus with regard to the strictly moral precepts required for all human beings living in this world, the natural law, the decalogue, and the love command of Jesus propose basically the same precepts.[61]

REVELATION. Bouquillon's understanding of revelation as the second source of moral theology mirrors the Catholic approach generally held at the time. Revelation involves either scripture or tradition thus indicating his acceptance of the so-called two sources of revelation. The written scriptures are contrasted with the unwritten tradition as accepted by the apostles from the mouth of Jesus or given to the apostles by the Holy Spirit and handed on to us. The principal source of moral theology is divine revelation whether in inspired scripture, handed down in tradition, or entrusted to the church.[62] This understanding grounds the threefold division of the exposition—the use of the scripture in moral theology, the use of tradition, the use of the authoritative magisterium. The amount of space given to the three aspects indicates the importance of their role in moral theology. The book devotes three times as many pages to tradition[63] and to the magisterium[64] as it does to scripture.[65]

The consideration of scripture is divided into the use of the Old Testament and the use of the New Testament. A progressive and developing revelation occurs in the Old Testament so that much interpretation is required. The Old Testament deals first with the primitive and universal economy of salvation and then with the Mosaic economy which was external, material, figurative, temporal, and characterized by fear and subjection in comparison with the Christian economy. However, the difference between the two testaments or economies should not be exaggerated. Legal, sapiential, prophetic, and historical books comprise the Old Testament. The Catholic University professor uses the well-known distinction of moral, juridical, and ceremonial precepts to determine what is of permanent significance for Christians. Only the truly moral precepts continue to be binding for Christians today. In this way the treatment of divorce, polygamy, slavery, and war are relegated to the category of the juridical and are not applicable today.[66] Here one sees the primary focus of the short discussion of the Old Testament—a defensive posture maintaining that one cannot appeal to the Old Testament to disagree with some of the existing moral teachings in the church. This defensive posture comes to the fore in the discussion of the historical books which narrate events and actions that are not acceptable in church teaching today. Bouquillon refuses to admit anything from the Old Testament that raises questions about the intrinsic morality of particular actions or the absolute obligation of the divine law.[67]

The discussion of the New Testament comprises two pages and is even shorter than the discussion of the Old Testament, but the narrow and defensive focus on absolute precepts remains.[68] This section points out that although revelation was closed with the apostles, not all was contained clearly, explicitly, and distinctly in the scriptures either with regard to the theoretical principles or especially the practical truths of the moral life. Nothing more is said about the principles but the ensuing discussion centers on precepts—whether something is truly a precept or only a counsel, whether the precept is absolute or adaptable, whether the precept is general and indistinct or distinct and precise, whether the precept regards the substance of the reality or only its mode and form. Such distinctions are made to help solve the difficult practical questions of the biblical teaching about the nature of sacrifice, taking oaths, the forgiveness of sin and penance, contrition and absolution, communion under both species, duties in the family, property, loans, military service, and slavery.[69] In an earlier work on the virtue of religion Bouquillon discussed in greater detail the biblical teaching on taking oaths in light of the practice of the church. Bouquillon explains together the two texts of Matthew. Matthew 23:16–22 relates Jesus' reaction to the way in which the Pharisees understood oath-taking. Matthew 5:33–37 contains Jesus' admonition not to swear but simply to say yes or no since anything else comes from evil. Bouquillon explains these texts in the following way. Christ corrected the twofold error of the Pharisees and indicated that the simple affirmation or negation is more in keeping with Christian sincerity. Basically the saying of Jesus in the Sermon on the Mount is interpreted in the light of some other passages in the New Testament allowing oaths and is thus treated as a counsel.[70] This very short discussion of the use of the scripture in moral theology deals almost exclusively with the question of the morality of acts and then from the apologetic standpoint of making sure that appeals to scripture do not change existing church teaching.

Bouquillon's explicit treatment of scripture as a source of moral theology coheres with the way in which he employs scripture in his fundamental moral theology. The scriptures have not influenced the basic outline of the book itself. *Theologia moralis fundamentalis* follows a combination of Thomistic and manualistic outlines and approaches. Bouquillon's outline of the ultimate end and the means to attain it comes not from the scripture but from the twofold problem that the human race has constantly grappled with—where have I come from and where am I going? Catholic doctrine solves the problem by saying we have come forth from God and are destined to return to God. Thomas Aquinas developed his *Summa theologiae* on this model.[71] Likewise the scripture has not influenced Bouquillon's emphasis on the legal model and its significant use throughout the volume.

Neither the general outline of the book nor the development of the particular parts (e.g., the section on the ultimate end of human beings or on law or conscience) is based primarily on the scripture. Scripture is often used as a proof text to further support positions that are primarily derived from theological and philosophical sources. The external end of human beings and all creation is to glorify God. Bouquillon brings together a number of scriptural quotations (e.g., the heavens proclaim the glory of God; do all things for the glory of God) to support the position that has been strongly rooted in the Catholic theological tradition.[72] The ultimate internal end of human beings is happiness. Here Bouquillon can find only one scripture text—John 3:16 to support his point. According to this passage God so loved the world that he sent his only begotten Son so that we who believe in him would not perish but have eternal life. However, such a passage does not necessarily prove that happiness is the internal ultimate end of human beings. At best it indicates that human beings will find eternal life and, with it, happiness through believing in Jesus.[73]

The consideration of natural law also illustrates this use of the scriptures. The whole section depends heavily on theologians especially Thomas Aquinas and Suarez among many others.[74] References to the scriptures are very rare indeed. Bouquillon holds that one can be invincibly ignorant of the mediate or more remote conclusions of the natural law. Some theologians have denied such ignorance arguing from the axioms that God does not deny grace to one who is trying and the precepts of God are not impossible. In regard to the latter our author contends that the axiom refers to the matter of the commandment and not its knowledge. A footnote refers to Saint Hilary and Saint Augustine but begins by referring to Matthew 11:30 (my yoke is easy and my burden light) and 1 Corinthians 10:13 (God will not allow you to be tempted beyond your strength). These two citations do not really prove the point but themselves need to be interpreted in the light of his distinction between the matter of the precept and the knowledge of the precept.[75]

In the section on the existence of natural law, one would expect to find a discussion of the famous pericope of Romans 2, and such is the case. But even here the scriptural support for the existence of natural law is comparatively sparse and not controlling. The existence of the natural law is first proved by the intimate experience of human beings, then by the unanimous consent of all people before the first appeal to the scriptures in an even shorter paragraph. The footnote reference is to Romans 2:12–16 with a reference to the outstanding interpretation of Cardinal Franzelin, but this interpretation is not elucidated. The biblical text affirms that the gentiles naturally do the work of the law which is written on their hearts. The footnote also mentions that some authors including Aquinas appeal to Psalm 4:7—"the light of your countenance has been marked on us," but Bouquillon does not accept such an interpretation of that text.[76]

The section on the use of tradition in moral theology begins with a paragraph explaining that this source of moral theology has been handed down to us as accepted by the apostles from the mouth of Christ or as coming from the apostles through the work of the Holy Spirit. The church as the living and indefectible mystical body of Christ (note the terminology "mystical body" which is more apt than the legal and hierarchical metaphors for the church) is the instrument or organ of tradition. The paragraph concludes by maintaining that tradition is manifested in the life of the church especially by its signs and actions and in its doctrines or teachings, observances, and prayers which will now be discussed.[77]

The above discussion with its concluding sentence does not pre- pare the reader for what follows. The entire following section on tradi- tion comprises eighteen pages and considers only the writings of schol- ars and none of the other sources mentioned by our author. These scholars include three groups—the teachers or doctors, the legal schol- ars, and the liturgical scholars with the first group receiving almost all the attention in this section.[78] The teachers or doctors are all those who constitute the doctrinal magisterium and are helpers of the authoritative magisterium. The work of such doctors or teachers under the direction of the authoritative magisterium involves polishing, evolving, and adapting the revealed teachings. The Catholic University professor uses the word "fathers" to refer to those who wrote from the apostolic age to the time of St. Bernard and the term "theologians" to refer to the sacred writers from the middle ages to the present.[79]

Bouquillon here gives a very high place to scholars and theolo- gians seeing them as belonging to the magisterium of the church. Authors writing in the twentieth century before Vatican II did not ordinarily see theologians as belonging to the magisterium of the church. However, the medieval scholastics did recognize such a role for theologians,[80] and Bouquillon was probably familiar with such ap- proaches. Bouquillon distinguishes the magisterium of the theologians from the authoritative magisterium, or what I refer to as the hierar- chical magisterium, which is described in the following section. The theologians work under the direction of the authoritative magisterium. However, Bouquillon never discusses the tensions and perhaps even disagreements that might exist between theologians and the authorita- tive magisterium.

A primary concern in this section involves the authority to be given to such teachers. Their authority depends on many factors but especially on approbation by the church.[81] This section just mentions the eminent authority of Thomas Aquinas,[82] but contains a six page appendix on the authority of St. Alphonsus[83] which has already been discussed in this book.

Bouquillon's *Theologia moralis fundamentalis* coheres very well with his explicit discussion of the role of scholars with regard to revealed truth. His work belongs to the tradition of Catholic theology as developed by scholars over the years. He is familiar with and in dialogue with past authors attempting to evolve and accommodate their thought to the present realities. As mentioned previously he is thoroughly familiar with the scholars in the tradition but gives great authority especially to Aquinas and Suarez.

The third article under the sources of moral theology deals with the authoritative magisterium of the church.[84] Bouquillon uses the Latin word *"authenticum seu auctoritativum"* which rightly indicates that the proper understanding of the Latin word *authenticum* is not authentic but authoritative. At one time authentic in English did have the meaning of authoritative but it now usually means genuine.[85] This authoritative magisterium of the church is exercised by the pastors and distinguished from the doctrinal teaching magisterium discussed in the previous section which is exercised by private scholars and writers. The authoritative magisterium is either ordinary, that is, instituted by Christ, or delegated, that is, given by one who has the ordinary magisterium. The ordinary magisterium is exercised by the whole teaching authority through the pope or a general council (called adequate) or only by a partial authority such as an individual bishop or particular council.[86]

Bouquillon first discusses the acts of the pope and carefully distinguishes different levels of teaching. Infallible or irreformable teachings about faith and morals must fulfill the necessary conditions with regard to the matter involved, the intention of the pope, the manifestation of the intention, and the object of the definition. The short discussion never gives an illustration of an infallible teaching and does not bring up the subject of whether or not the natural law can be taught infallibly.[87] Today most Catholic moral theologians maintain that the specific norms of the natural law cannot be taught infallibly.[88] A second level (my word) involves the pope "efficaciously teaching a doctrine" but not proposing it as infallible. This is an authoritative statement although not infallible and demands internal and religious assent. Here Bouquillon cites the letter *Tuas libenter* of Pope Pius IX to the Archbishop of Munich in 1863. He also cites more fully the encyclical *Quanta cura* of

Pope Pius IX claiming that one cannot deny assent and obedience from acts of the pope that are not infallible.[89] Joseph Komonchak has pointed out that the earliest references in the nineteenth-century manuals of moral theology to the internal religious assent due to noninfallible teaching are to this letter of Pius IX.[90]

Other levels of papal teaching are also mentioned—when the pope recalls to mind important aspects of teaching as often occurs in encyclicals, or when the pope directs a document to a particular local church. Other acts differ from the proposing of a teaching such as proposing a precept or a prohibition of teaching, the proscription or commendation of a book, disciplinary laws, and liturgical laws.[91]

Under the delegated authoritative magisterium, the Catholic University professor discusses the acts of the Roman congregations. He first mentions three congregations. The Congregation of the Holy Office judges about doctrine. The Congregation of the Index censures books. The Penitentiary looks at the prudent application of principles and proposes a safe way of acting, solving practical difficulties rather than doctrinal controversies. The responses of these three congregations are to be treated as a pronouncement of the pope himself even if they are issued in the name of the congregation with the approval or confirmation of the pope. A sincere obedience is due to these responses. An irreformable assent is not due to these teachings if they are doctrinal because the matter is not infallible, but a true, internal, and religious assent is required because the matter deals with the security of Catholic doctrine. Here again Bouquillon cites the famous letter of Pius IX *Tuas libenter.*[92]

Our author recognizes the very frequent and important use of the decrees of the congregations in the work of moral theology. He provides significant directions for the proper interpretation of such statements. Responses from the Holy Office deal with doctrinal matters, but not responses from the Penitentiary. The object and the formula of the response must be carefully stated. One must be very cautious in deducing conclusions from these documents and not conclude to more than was said.[93]

The last edition of his fundamental moral theology does not repeat what he had said a few years earlier in his discussion of the state of moral theology. In the earlier article he criticized the abuse of having recourse to the Roman congregations for decisions when there was no reason to do so. However, the criticism was not directed at the congregations as such. In fact the congregations show that they appreciate the problem by often responding that the approved authors should be consulted. When the congregation replies that people should not be disturbed, too often the petitioners and moral theologians in general are satisfied and do no more work or research to arrive at the truth.[94] Such a criticism is in keeping with his contention that the manualists often merely list the number of authors or authorities who maintain a certain position and do not attempt the hard work of discovering the moral truth.

Bouquillon also briefly discusses the acts of general councils under the rubric of the authoritative, ordinary, adequate magisterium and the acts of bishops and particular councils under the category of the authoritative, ordinary, inadequate magisterium.[95] However, a deeper consideration of these aspects is not necessary here.

The Catholic University professor recognizes a twofold magisterium—the doctrinal magisterium of private teachers and the authoritative magisterium of the pastors of the church. The obvious question arises about the relationships between them. Contemporary Catholic moral theology is much more aware of the question in terms of the role of theologians in the church today and the issue of dissent from authoritative noninfallible teaching of the popes.[96] Bouquillon never raises the contemporary issue of dissent, but he does discuss the different roles of theologians and the hierarchy.

In general the doctrinal magisterium is described as helping the authoritative magisterium. These teachers work under the direction of the authoritative magisterium.[97] Bouquillon carefully recognizes various levels and types of authoritative papal teaching going from the more authoritative and doctrinal to the less, but he never explicitly recognizes that papal teachings or even replies of Roman congregations can be wrong. On the other hand, our author explicitly recognizes that particular councils authoritatively teach the law of God although they are able to err and as a matter of fact have erred.[98] While insisting that the replies of Roman congregations dealing with doctrine require true, internal, and religious assent because they come from a delegated power and deal with the security of Catholic teaching, Bouquillon calls for a discreet and prudent interpretation of such responses.[99]

The Catholic University author's other writings generally point in the same direction of denying the possibility of error in authoritative papal teaching. As mentioned earlier he fully subscribes to the neoscholastic agenda authoritatively proposed by Leo XIII including the condemnations of Rosmini, Gioberti, Ventura, Hermes, Gunthor and others. Most of Bouquillon's articles in support of Leo XIII were written before he came to the Catholic University of America, but in the first volume of the *Catholic University Bulletin* Bouquillon again praises at great length the work of Leo XIII in preserving Catholic truth especially by explaining the true principles that refute the modern errors. Bouquillon here notes that the encyclicals do not contain infallible definitions of faith (although the pope could use them for infallible pronouncements if he so intended), but Catholics are obliged to receive these teachings and accept them as rules of conduct.[100] Even in his so-called liberal position on education, Bouquillon took great pains to point out that such a teaching is solidly based in the Catholic tradition. In the light of the spirit of the times, his own exaggerated praise for the papacy in the persons both of Pius IX and of Leo XIII, his strong support of neoscholasticism, and his agreement with the condemnations of liberalism and modern errors, one can understand why Bouquillon does not mention any possibility of error in the authoritative teaching of the pope and the Roman congregations. Bouquillon was an ultramontanist.

Bouquillon discussed the Catholic teaching on slavery in an 1889 article, commenting on the 1888 encyclical of Leo XIII to the bishops of Brazil on slavery.[101] This article provides an obvious place to see if our author acknowledges any error in the teaching of the church, but in fact the article strongly defends the teaching of the church on the question of slavery. The tone of the article is heavily triumphalistic and defensive.[102]

The first part of the article indicates that the church has worked for 1800 years for the abolition of slavery. The Protestant heresy and the rationalism which comes from it have tried to exploit the question of slavery. These enemies of the church have directed calumnies against her. Even Alexis deTocqueville joined in these calumnies. The Catholic church, however, teaches today what it has always taught; and rationalists, Protestants, and schismatics are forced to recognize the leadership role of the Catholic church in this question of slavery.[103]

Bouquillon considers three aspects of slavery, beginning with the older slavery that was in existence at the beginning of the Christian era. Since the small nascent church could not immediately change this entrenched social institution, the church tolerated the reality but, at the same time, tried to transform slavery. Over three hundred church documents sought to safeguard the slaves and improve their lot. Our author cites only one illustration—Pope Alexander III in 1167 solemnly decreed that all Christians should be exempt from slavery.[104] Bouquillon does not advert to the implications of this document for those who are non-Christian!

With regard to Indian slavery in the Americas, the greedy colonists found many excuses to justify slavery, but they ran into opposition from the church. The whole world knows the name of Las Casas. Bouquillon cites Pope Leo X's declaring that nature as well as religion condemns slavery.[105] However, the contemporary Catholic author, John F. Maxwell, contends that Pope Leo X in 1514 in the brief *Praecelsae devotionis* followed the example of three of his predecessors in authorizing the kings of Portugal to invade and conquer the newly discovered territories of the New World, to reduce the non-Christian inhabitants to perpetual slavery, and to expropriate their possessions.[106] According to Bouquillon Spain at this time was governed by some truly Catholic monarchs and he renders special homage to Charles V who was Flemish by birth, education, taste, and affection. Charles V proposed a code of law which explicitly declared the freedom of the Indians and forbade them to be reduced to slavery for any motive whatsoever.[107] However, Maxwell in his contemporary study of the Catholic church and slavery points out that this antislavery policy unfortunately did not last long. On February 20, 1534, Charles V revoked this edict and once more authorized the slavery of Indian prisoners captured in just warfare.[108]

With regard to the slavery of blacks and the slave trade originating in Africa, Bouquillon recognizes that the first explorers from Portugal went along with the slave trade and greatly profited from it. Although governments tolerated this scandal, the church was not silent. One must also remember that the slave trade grew enormously in the seventeenth century when the slave trade fell into the hands of Dutch and English heretics and even more so in the eighteenth century when the influence of the church waned and the Encyclopedists flourished. The French Revolution despite its claims of liberty, equality, and fraternity maintained the slave trade and slavery as long as it could. During this time what the church could not impede by its teaching it tried to soften by its charity.[109]

Bouquillon's approach is much different in tone and content from the contemporary study of John F. Maxwell. Maxwell concludes that from the sixth century Catholic teaching accepted the moral legitimacy of the legal institution of slavery provided that the master's title of ownership was valid and that the material and spiritual welfare of the slaves was provided for. The institution of genuine slavery whereby one human being is legally owned by another and is forced to work for the exclusive benefit of the owner in return for food, clothing, and shelter, and can be bought, sold, donated or exchanged, was not merely tolerated but commonly approved of in the Western Church for over 1400 years.[110] The carefully worded understanding of slavery in the above conclusion implies the distinction between chattel slavery which the church rejected and an ameliorated slavery which the church accepted. This distinction came to the fore in Catholic circles after 1633. In unjust chattel slavery the master has full right of ownership over the slave as his personal property. In the ameliorated type of slavery accepted by the church the master has a right of use and of disposing of the work of the slave for his own benefit, but Christian masters must respect the life, marriage, personal property, and reputation of their slaves.[111] As late as 1866 the Holy Office appealed to this ameliorated understanding to justify slavery.[112]

Bouquillon prided himself on his interest in and knowledge of history. However, there were stronger forces at work in his consideration of slavery. This short essay clearly shows his triumphalistic and apologetic approach to the teaching and the role of the Catholic church with regard to slavery. The Catholic church always acted correctly in its approach to slavery. He could not admit any error in the Catholic church's teaching on slavery.

However, Bouquillon raises the question about authoritative church teaching again in his discussion on the formation of conscience. One footnote in this consideration differs from the position he took under the sources of morality. Since conscience is the conclusion of a syllogism whose major is a principle of law and whose minor is the fact to which the law is applied, two things are required for the formation of a correct conscience—sufficient understanding of the law and a just and impartial judgment of the facts. This understanding and judgment require first of all proper consideration by the agent but also the consultation of experts and the seeking of counsel. In obscure matters, the individual faithful may safely follow the judgment of the pastor or confessor. The pastor or confessor often follows the opinion of an approved author without having to study the matter oneself. But it is not permitted to follow any teacher or author whatsoever. However, things are different with the authoritative magisterium of the pastors of the church from which all Christians, the learned as well as the uninstructed, are held to seek the solution of moral difficulties and to which they must faithfully submit themselves.[113] This exposition seems to be in accord with what was said in the discussion of the authoritative magisterium in the section on the sources of moral theology, but Bouquillon adds a fascinating and somewhat ambiguous footnote.[114]

The footnote refers the reader to the earlier discussion of the authoritative magisterium and especially to the paragraph discussing the Sacred Penitentiary. From this discussion it follows that the conscience of the faithful should be directed by the authoritative magisterium through the sound explanation of the objective rule and through its prudent application, and that is done sometimes infallibly and sometimes noninfallibly. When the individual conviction is opposed to the authoritative direction or teaching, check to see if the authoritative teaching is infallible or not. The individual conviction must truly cede to infallible teaching. If it is noninfallible teaching, and the individual conviction is not altogether firm and certain, the authoritative direction prevails. However, if the individual conviction is certain and firm, it should be seen if the conviction can be practically put aside by a consideration of those things that ought to beget a lack of confidence in one's own judgment. If such a test does not cause one to put aside the conviction, then the individual judgment will prevail in the formation of conscience.[115]

One must understand the teaching in general and the footnote in particular in the context of the traditional Catholic teaching on conscience as found also in Bouquillon. In no way does this tradition hold that it is always good to follow one's conscience. The reality is much more complex than that. Conscience is the subjective and proximate norm or rule of acting; law is the remote and objective norm of acting. In this light, the obliging force of conscience comes from the fact that it applies the remote and objective norm of morality. Conscience does not make something right or wrong but applies the objective norm to the particular question. The human being does not make or create the law for oneself. From this follows the proper understanding of the inviolability of conscience. It is always licit to follow conscience if the due qualities are present and it is never right to act against what conscience commands or prohibits. The first assertion is based on the reason that to act according to conscience indicates the good will to do what we judge God wants us to do. However, the phrase, "if the due qualities are present," is added because not every conscience is a correct (*recta*) norm of action. The reason for the second assertion is that to act against conscience involves a bad will for it means we act against what we judge to be the case.[116]

What are the due qualities that conscience must have if it is to be correct? Only a true conscience is the unqualified, legitimate norm of action. Such a conscience truly proclaims the will of God for us. An invincibly erroneous conscience (without one's fault) is not simply and absolutely a legitimate norm of action; it is, however, legitimate *per accidens* and *secundum quid*. It is not simply and absolutely legitimate because it does not coincide with the law or the will of God; but it is accidentally and in some way legitimate because the defect or lack of conformity with the law or the fact is not imputable. Acting with an invincibly erroneous conscience involves a material evil since the act is not in conformity with the law, but is always formally good because the object is judged to be good and is pursued by the will as such. On the other hand, the vincibly erroneous conscience (one should have known the truth) is not per se and as such a legitimate norm of acting. The lack of conformity with the truth in this case cannot be excused.[117] The approach of Bouquillon thus equates a true (*vera*) and correct (*recta*) conscience. Some Catholic moral theologians distinguish between a true conscience which conforms to the objective order and a sincere (a better English word in this context for the Latin *recta*) conscience as exemplified in the case of an invincibly erroneous conscience.[118]

Bouquillon's understanding of conscience serves as the background, context, and basis for his discussion of the formation of the correct conscience in what he considers the conflict between one's individual conviction of conscience and the objective explanation of the rule or its application to the facts by the authoritative magisterium. No appeal is made in this footnote to an invincibly erroneous conscience which if it were appropriate in this discussion would have logically and easily fit into the discussion. The text had just talked about the invincibly erroneous conscience in great detail. In the precise section and footnote under discussion, Bouquillon considers the formation of a correct conscience. The only logical conclusion is that the individual conscience judgment in this case is a true or correct conscience mediating the will of God and the objective moral truth. Although the author does not explicitly say so, the logical conclusion that he holds is that the authoritative teaching in this case is in error. One can readily speculate about the reasons why Bouquillon did not explicitly conclude that the authoritative teaching was in error, but such is his position.

However, another question immediately arises. What type of authoritative magisterial teaching is involved here? The footnote refers to the earlier treatise on the authoritative magisterium but especially the discussion in number 113 about the Sacred Penitentiary. The problem arises from the specific nature of the Penitentiary and its relationship to the other offices in the Roman Curia and their work. Whereas the Holy Office deals with doctrine and teaching, the Penitentiary deals with the prudent application of principles, proposing a safe rule of acting. In a word, the Penitentiary deals with practical difficulties rather than intending to resolve doctrinal controversies. Sincere obedience is due to these acts of congregations and internal religious assent is due if the matter deals with doctrine or teaching.[119] One could properly conclude from this that the responses of the Penitentiary do not deal with doctrine or teaching and thus do not require internal religious assent.

In his discussion on conscience then is Bouquillon talking only about responses from the Penitentiary and not the doctrine or teaching of the authoritative magisterium in either its ordinary or delegated form? The very fact that his footnote on conscience in which this matter is discussed refers explicitly and only to the Penitentiary lends support to such a narrow interpretation. However, an analysis of the entire footnote shows that Bouquillon is referring to the teaching and doctrine of the authoritative magisterium and not just to the practical and prudential decisions of the Penitentiary. First, the footnote refers "especially" to what was said about the Penitentiary earlier, but not exclusively. Second, the object or what is talked about here is either the sound explanation of the objective norm or its prudent application which the authoritative magisterium proposes sometimes infallibly and sometimes noninfallibly. The earlier discussion of the Penitentiary limited its function to the application of the norm but here Bouquillon is talking about the explanation of the norm itself which clearly implies teaching and doctrine. But the totally convincing argument comes from Bouquillon's description that such a teaching can be taught either infallibly or noninfallibly. All admit that the responses of the Sacred Penitentiary could never be taught infallibly. Bouquillon explicitly says that the teachings of the Holy Office and the congregations as such are not infallible.[120] Thus this footnote deals with the authoritative, noninfallible magisterium in general and not just with the Penitentiary or only with the teachings of the Roman congregations as such. Under the carefully nuanced conditions proposed here, Bouquillon recognizes that an individual Christian can dissent in theory and in practice (to use contemporary terminology) from the authoritative, noninfallible magisterium.

Bouquillon discusses this possibility in a footnote under conscience and not in the text itself in his discussion of conscience or in his earlier and lengthier discussion of the authoritative magisterium.

He certainly does not want to call attention to his position and its important ramifications which he never develops. Such a low key and understated manner of dealing with the question is also found in other nineteenth and early twentieth century authors.[121] Bouquillon, despite his commitments to neoscholasticism and to the increased role of the papacy in Catholic thought and practice, still implicitly admits in one footnote the possibility of dissent from authoritative, noninfallible church teaching.

HUMAN ACTS

Bouquillon's discussion of human acts in *Theologia moralis fundamentalis* shows the characteristics of his approach which have already been discussed—his opposition to the manuals of moral theology, his acceptance of neoscholasticism, and his tendency to be more influenced by the manual tradition than his criticism on face value would seem to allow.

The comparison with Sabetti's treatment of human acts well illustrates Bouquillon's differences with the manualistic approach. Since Sabetti as a manualist deals primarily with the practical question of the morality of particular acts, he logically begins his entire book with a discussion of human acts. In terms of style, Sabetti's brief, twenty-page discussion of human acts epitomizes the manualist at work. The presentation is concise, practical, geared for the student, but avoids theoretical or in-depth considerations. The entire discussion involves four sections which are quite short and eminently concise—the notion of human acts; what constitutes a human act (which is reduced to a consideration of the voluntary act); realities that modify the human act—ignorance, concupiscence, fear, force, and violence; and the morality of human acts which includes the sources of morality and the threefold sources or founts of object, end, and circumstances.[122]

The Catholic University professor considers all these aspects but in greater depth and length and especially in a very different context. *Theologia moralis fundamentalis* considers human acts after having considered the ultimate end, the means to come to the ultimate end, and the objective and subjective norms for the act. The ninety-eight page discussion of human acts is entitled "Acts toward the End."[123] Thus human acts are seen in the general context of a teleological model but as pointed out earlier with a very strong emphasis on the deontological aspects of the objective (law) and subjective (conscience) norms of human acts.

The very framework of the discussion of human acts shows the same characteristics. Since the ultimate end is attained as a crown and supernatural reward, and since it is lost through deviation, it follows that the acts by which the ultimate end is obtained must be free, morally good, and supernatural. These three aspects form the outline for the entire discussion of human acts.[124] Sabetti basically treats the first two aspects but in a much more superficial fashion.[125] Sabetti never even discusses in a separate section the salutary aspect of the human act apparently just presuming that aspect and putting all his attention on the morality of particular actions. On the other hand, Bouquillon develops the salutary aspect of the human act in the context of the neoscholastic emphasis on the distinction between the supernatural order and the natural order.[126]

The discussion of particular questions such as the essence of morality also shows the various characteristics of Bouquillon's approach at work. The essence of morality in terms of its moral quality consists in its relationship to a norm or rule. But what is the norm? The supreme, absolute, and necessary norm of human action is the ultimate end. The ultimate end determines the goodness of all things. That is, the supreme norm of human acts is the order established by God for God's glory and the happiness of human beings. Another way to phrase the same reality is that the norm of human acts is the divine will. The norm of human action in particular is twofold—the remote norm or law and the proximate norm or conscience.[127] Bouquillon first appeals to the teleological aspect and its framework, then quickly and practically develops this framework in terms of the deontological model.

Three issues discussed in Bouquillon's consideration of human acts call for further comment—the question of indifferent acts, sin, and virtue. First, the issue of indifferent acts. The Catholic University teacher raises the question of indifferent acts in a discussion of what he calls the principles of morality, but what the manuals describe as the founts or sources of morality—the object, end, and circumstances.[128] These three elements determine the morality of an act or its conformity or deformity with the norm.[129] These three principles or sources of morality have traditionally been proposed in Catholic moral thinking.[130]

However, Bouquillon's understanding of the object differs from the usual approach of the manuals as illustrated by Sabetti. The human act is a movement proceeding from the deliberate will. Every movement per se and by its very nature tends toward something by which it is terminated and finished. The object is that to which the action per se and by its nature tends and which is the proximate terminus of the act or the intrinsic end of the act. Thus the act of giving money does not yet have an object to which it tends. It could be a donation, an alms, a payment of a debt, restitution, or recompense. The object of the act is the *finis operis*, the end of the act.[131]

Theologia moralis fundamentalis then raises the question whether because of the object all acts are either good or bad or are there actions that are indifferent by reason of their object. In the light of his understanding of the object of the act, Bouquillon cannot admit indifferent acts; but he recognizes that most theologians maintain that there are actions which are indifferent by reason of their object such as walking or plucking a piece of grass. Those who maintain there are indifferent moral acts by reason of the object refer to indeterminate acts without any special direction, but in reality such acts cannot occur. Nobody walks except for a particular reason. If the end is necessary for the act to be complete in itself, then the end is not something added on to the act but constitutes the complete and proximate object of the act. To give an alms is the complete and proximate object of the act. The fundamental, principal, and primary morality comes from the object understood in this way.[132]

Does the position of denying the existence of indifferent acts by reason of the object have any consequences for judging the morality of particular acts? The twentieth-century manualistic understanding of the principle of double effect immediately comes to mind. This principle has exerted a wide influence in Catholic moral theology as the means of solving conflict situations when there exist both good and bad effects of an act. Sabetti, for example, stated the now traditionally accepted four conditions of the principle of double effect with the first condition that the act must be good or at least indifferent. The third condition insists that the good effect cannot be achieved by means of the evil effect. The physical causality of the act is determinative of the morality of the act.[133]

Bouquillon considers the morality deriving from the effect in a special appendix after considering the three principles of morality—object, end, and circumstances. Is the act able to receive its morality from the effect—either good or bad?[134] In this consideration and some others,[135] he sometimes accepts but never concedes the existence of indifferent acts because so many authors do maintain their existence. For an act to be good by reason of its good effect, the act itself must be free and good or indifferent, while the good effect must be foreseen and intended. For an act to be morally bad by reason of the bad effect the act must be free while the effect must be foreseen and the agent must have a responsibility to impede that evil effect. The latter consideration of having an obligation or responsibility to impede the bad effect receives further elucidation in responding to the question: when is it licit to permit (not intend) the evil effect. Six things must be considered: the morality of the act, the causality of the act, the connection of the effect with the act, the utility or the necessity of the act, the gravity of the evil effect, and the condition of the agent.[136]

To the above question, the Catholic University professor attaches the question of the double effect—whether and when is it licit to place an act which has two effects: one good and one bad. As mentioned above the general answer maintains that the act is good if one has a right to place the act despite the fact that an evil effect will follow. The text goes on to point out that it scarcely needs to be mentioned that in this case the act or cause is not bad itself and the two effects are directly caused by the act. The action is not morally acceptable if the cause or act itself is bad or if the good effect is attained indirectly by means of the evil effect.[137] Thus Bouquillon endorses what has become the accepted understanding of the principle of double effect in Catholic moral theology in the twentieth century.

Thomas Bouquillon shares with some contemporary revisionist moral theologians a problem with the way the object of the act is described by many in the manualistic tradition of Catholic moral theology. The full object of the act cannot be identified with the material aspect or the remote object of the act.[138] At first sight this position seems to indicate that he might not accept the principle of double effect with its understanding of direct effect based on the physical causality or structure of the act.[139] However, the Belgian-born theologian supports the principle whose heart and soul is the third condition that the good effect cannot be attained by means of the evil effect. Bouquillon in this case logically would have to conclude that the material act itself which produces the good effect by means of the evil effect is actually a morally bad action. The physical structure of an act which achieves the good effect by means of the bad effect tends per se and by its very nature to the bad effect. Hence it is a morally bad act.

But there exists some ambiguity in Bouquillon's understanding of the object of the act so that he might be interpreted as somewhat open to agreeing with the charge of physicalism made by contemporary revisionist Catholic moral theologians. Physicalism refers to the a priori and total identification of the human moral act with the physical or material structure of the act. Some revisionist Catholic moral theologians claim that artificial contraception is a physical act that can be justified for a proportionate reason. Sometimes directly doing a physical evil can be justified for a proportionate reason. Taking something belonging to another is not always the moral act of stealing.[140]

In his discussion of the human act our author often denies that the full object of the act is identified with the material structure of the act itself. He frequently makes the point that the same material act can have different moral meanings. The true object of giving money is very different if it is a gift, an alms, or a payment. The object of the act properly speaking is not the matter of the act such as the giving of money. Sometimes the material aspect is called the remote object of the act.[141] To walk, to love, to pluck grass, to give money, to take something belonging to another all indicate the matter of the act or the remote object but not the full object properly so called. To give an alms, to perpetrate a theft, and to utter a blasphemy in addition to the matter of the act indicate the proper object of the act or that to which the act tends. Bouquillon insists that in these cases the end is not extrinsic (*finis operantis*) but intrinsic (*finis operis*) because the end is necessary in order that the act is complete.[142]

Here is the important condition that makes Bouquillon's positions logically consistent. If the end is necessary in order that the act is complete, then the matter or physical structure of the act is not morally normative. But if the act is already complete (e.g., directly causing evil or even contraception, although he does not discuss this issue) then the matter or physical structure of the act is morally normative. In the total picture Bouquillon is thus consistent, but he seems inaccurate from the perspective of his own positions by saying that the matter or physical structure of the act is only the remote object of the act. When the act is already complete in itself, the remote object is the full and proper object of the act.

However, Bouquillon's bold statement that the proper object of the moral act is not determined by the matter of the act itself does support the revisionist position. The moral object of the act according to contemporary revisionists cannot be understood solely in terms of the physical aspect of the act. (Note that Bouquillon uses the term "material" and not "physical.") Other aspects such as the end or circumstances must also be a part of the moral object. But recall that because of other additions to his understanding of the object of the act, Bouquillon remains firmly committed to the Catholic approaches of his day.

The teaching on human acts involves the discussion of sins and some aspects of virtues. There is no separate treatise on these two subjects as there is in Aquinas's *Summa*.[143] As mentioned earlier the lack of a separate treatise on the virtues is most surprising especially in the light of Bouquillon's strong criticism of the manuals and his adherence to Aquinas and neoscholasticism. His position here helps to clarify and underscore the precise nature of his criticism of the manuals. He basically accepts the fundamental purpose of the manuals with their emphasis on the conformity of human acts with law, the objective and remote norm of morality, and conscience, the subjective and proximate norm of morality. His criticism of the manuals focuses on how they treat these topics—the superficial way in which the matter is discussed with no sustained, in-depth development.

Bouquillon's discussion of the virtues in his fundamental moral theology occurs only in the section on human acts and is really not a consideration of the virtues as such but of the species of the moral goodness of actions. The different ways or means of conforming with the ultimate end as the will of God depend upon the object of the act. Thus the act takes its species of moral goodness from the object. Good acts exist in two different orders of goodness—the theological and supreme goodness which embraces acts that directly and immediately tend to the ultimate end, and the moral and inferior goodness which characterizes actions only mediately tending to the ultimate end. Theological goodness is threefold—acts of faith, hope, and charity which deal directly with God the ultimate end.[144]

Moral goodness is fourfold and here our author follows the fourfold cardinal virtues. Acts of prudence apply the universal principles to the specific conclusions of what is to be done. Note here the reduced role of prudence and how it is interpreted to fit in with a legal model. In the only other sentence dealing with the cardinal virtue of prudence Bouquillon espouses the Thomistic and teleological approach—prudence consists in ordering acts properly to a good end. Apparently he saw no contradiction in these two sentences. Acts of justice render to each what is due. Acts of fortitude intrepidly undergo labors and dangers. Acts of temperance moderate the sensual proclivities in accord with the demands of reason. He then discusses the secondary, annexed, subordinate, or potential virtues that fall under the principal category of each of the four cardinal virtues.[145] Thus the virtues as virtues are not discussed in this volume but only the virtues insofar as they determine the specific moral goodness of human acts.

Bouquillon had published an earlier book on the three theological virtues so one would not expect this treatise to be repeated here.[146] But from a professed follower of Aquinas one would expect a fundamental or independent and significant section on the role of the virtues in the moral life.

In addition to virtue, Bouquillon also discusses sin in his consideration of human acts. By definition such an approach sees sin primarily as an act—a morally bad act which in some way stands in the way of attaining the end.[147] This approach fails to recognize sin as a power inhering in the person and tending to sinful actions. Catholic theology does have an understanding of the state of sin which corresponds somewhat to this notion of the power of sin existing in the human person, but this receives no recognition in these pages. In addition, just as there is no discussion of virtue, there is no discussion of vices as the bad habits that incline the agent to bad actions. Sin thus refers only to actions. Such a narrow and one-sided approach is in keeping with the Catholic manualistic tradition but does not do justice to the full reality of sin and its role in the moral life.

Bouquillon discusses sin in two different contexts—first, with regard to the specific distinction of bad acts under the moral aspect of human acts, and later under the salutary aspect of human acts. In the discussion of the specific distinction of bad acts sin is defined as an act deviating from its due end, contrary to the order and nature of things, mediately or immediately opposed to the divine will; in one word, not in conformity with the rule. The nature of sin consists in its aversion from the end, disturbance of the order, transgression of the divine will, and violation of the law. Thus sin is in opposition to God as the final, exemplary, and efficient cause.[148] Note how the consideration of end, order, law, nature, and reason are all reduced to the same reality.

The specific distinction of sins is derived primarily from the object, end, and circumstances. Secondarily, some theologians claim the specific distinction of sins comes from the diversity of goodness or virtue to which the act is opposed and from the different ways (excess or defect) in which the goodness is opposed. Others see the specific distinction secondarily based on the formal diversity of laws which are violated. Bouquillon cites a number of authors to prove his thesis that the difference between these two approaches is only verbal and not real.[149] Again, in my judgment such an understanding gives too much primacy to the legal model which is so evident throughout Bouquillon's fundamental moral theology.

Bouquillon's discussion of sin in the section on salutary acts gives less emphasis to the legal model and more to the teleological model, although the emphasis still falls on the morality of particular acts. Such an emphasis on teleology and finality in discussing sin in the light of salutary acts has a twofold basis. The first basis comes from the very nature of the reality being discussed—acts which stand in the way of achieving the end. Every bad act by definition stands in the way of achieving the end. Mortal sin goes against the ultimate end because it tends toward a contingent and changeable good which is incompatible with the absolute good, because it disturbs God's order in a substantial way, and because it violates an essential rule. A venial sin does not tend directly against the ultimate end and the habitual conversion to good remains, but God's order is disturbed in accidental matters and secondary rules are violated. The second basis for the insistence on the teleological model for understanding mortal sin comes from the heavy emphasis on Aquinas who is quoted at very great length in this section. However, even here the teleological aspect of being against the end (*contra finem*) in mortal sin and beside the end (*praeter finem*) in venial sin still becomes identified with the legal—essential rules and secondary rules.[150]

CONCLUSION

United States Catholic history knows Bouquillon as a supporter of American Catholic liberalism at the end of the nineteenth century. However, his fundamental moral theology shows no traces or influence of his life in the United States. His is a moral theology proposed for the whole church and purposely does not give that much attention to the particular characteristics and culture of an individual country. He sharply criticizes the particularization of theology in the seventeenth and eighteenth centuries because of the need for a universal moral theology.[151] His fundamental moral theology is devoid of references to the United States. In his short discussion of the relationship between the spiritual society (the church) and the temporal society (the state) he is content for the most part to cite Pope Leo XIII's encyclicals to support the position that the state is ordered to and subordinated to the church. He never even mentions the possibility of tolerating a separation of church and state (which he defends elsewhere), let alone focuses on the practice and theory in the United States.[152]

United States Catholic history knows Bouquillon as a strong supporter of the social sciences and his own essays show his interest in and knowledge of these social sciences. However, little or nothing from the social sciences appears in his fundamental moral theology. His deductive neoscholastic methodology leaves no room for the social sciences to contribute to the principles of moral theology. The social sciences come into play in the application of principles but such application lies beyond the scope of fundamental moral theology.[153] In addition his deductive, essentialist, and classicist approach did not appreciate the important role of prudence in the moral life which was recognized by a more authentic Thomism. Like all of us Bouquillon was strongly influenced by the thought and accepted understandings of his day. Nowhere is this more evident than in his understanding of the role of women. In his short discussion of domestic society the Catholic University professor recognizes the natural law authority of the husband over the wife but understands this authority to be more directive than coercive since the wife is not a slave but a partner.[154] As a bibliophile greatly interested in bibliography our author frequently gave long bibliographies but only very rarely are women mentioned. Obviously there were comparatively few women authors at work in the sacred sciences in Bouquillon's time, but there were more female ascetical writers than Theresa of Avila who is the only one mentioned by Bouquillon.[155] The Catholic University professor shared the predominately negative Catholic attitude toward Protestantism. In his fundamental moral theology Bouquillon, unlike Kenrick, has no dialogue with non-Catholic theologians. The entire discussion takes place within the Catholic household. For Bouquillon, the late nineteenth-century neoscholastic and ultramontanist, the one true religion is the Catholic religion; Protestants are heretics; and the Reformation is the pseudo-reformation.[156]

The greatest unresolved tension in Bouquillon concerns his strong neoscholasticism and stinging criticism of the manuals in comparison with what appeared in the third edition of his fundamental moral theology which was finished just after his death in 1902. Bouquillon's *Theologia moralis fundamentalis* accepts the basic purpose of the manuals to train confessors as judges, follows for all practical purposes a corresponding legal model, and gives no role to the virtues. On the other hand the book had no chance of ever being used as a manual or textbook. The Catholic University professor showed his neoscholastic tendencies by including a section on the ultimate end and a more developed discussion of human acts than found in the manuals. In addition his teaching on law and conscience is much more thorough and scholarly than the manualistic treatment. His almost one hundred pages on the history of the discipline flies in the face of the practical intent and purpose of the manuals. In a sense this book falls between the cracks. It is neither a consistent neoscholastic development of moral theology nor is it a manual. As a result one is not surprised that the book was really not used as a textbook or even reedited after the author's death.

The basic reality was that he did not and perhaps could not break away from the fundamental purpose of the manuals—the training of confessors to be judges in the sacrament of penance. This would have been a very revolutionary change and not just a development in the discipline itself. In his time and circumstances such a break with the existing tradition was well nigh impossible. If he were starting out to write a fundamental moral theology in 1899 (the year he published his severe criticism of the manuals) and had the time and the energy, there is a greater possibility that he might have been able to write a different book. However, in reality Bouquillon was not starting anew in 1899. He was working with the second 1890 edition of a textbook first published for seminarians in 1873. His second edition had made extensive and significant changes in the textbook including the introduction of the long historical section.

In reality Bouquillon did not spend much time revising the third edition. We know that during his thirteen years in the United States he published in a number of different areas, but with a few exceptions such as his 1899 criticism of the manuals of moral theology his essays and articles did not deal with issues of fundamental moral theology. There were no seminarians to teach at Catholic University so he never used the textbook in class and did not have the opportunity to modify and change it in the light of his experience teaching a course in fundamental moral theology. As a matter of fact the third edition is almost exactly the same as the second edition. The same basic table of contents is followed and the new edition is less than thirty pages longer than the second edition.

Questions abound. Why did he bother to put out a third edition that was fundamentally the same as the second? Did he personally experience any tension between his neoscholastic perspective and the approach of his textbook? We do not know the answers to these questions.

In one sense what he did write was probably the most change he could achieve. The basic purpose of the discipline of moral theology involved the training of future confessors as judges in the sacrament of penance. He could not back away from that approach and still be writing a textbook to be used in seminaries. He probably went as far as he could to change the approach given the nature and purpose of the discipline at that time.

However, his own critique of the manuals and his neoscholastic commitments pointed the way to a much more radical change in moral theology that would truly modify the nature and purpose of the discipline itself. Thus he must have experienced to some degree the severe constraints that militated against more substantial change. His writings at this time, show that criticism and change were in the air. The situation was somewhat fluid and greater changes might come about in the future. But in reality the conditions were not conducive to changed approaches to Catholic theology in the beginning of the twentieth century. The manualistic approach remained the norm until Vatican II.

The testimony of his contemporaries shows that Bouquillon was an important figure in Catholic moral theology in the United States and even in the world at the end of the century. In the light of the other aspects of Bouquillon's life and thought *Theologia moralis fundamentalis* is somewhat surprising and disappointing. On the other hand, his criticisms of the manuals remain even though he did not radically change the focus and purpose of the seminary course in moral theology.

N O T E S

1. Bouquillion, *"Praefatio,"* *Theologia moralis fundamentalis,* pp. vii–viii.
2. Ibid., pp. 169–171.
3. Ibid., pp. 172–184.
4. Ibid., pp. 185–201.
5. Ibid., pp. 201–215.
6. Ibid., p. 202.
7. Ibid., pp. 276–283.
8. Ibid., p. 216.
9. Ibid., pp. 216–612.
10. Ibid., pp. 613–711.
11. Ibid., pp. 712–718.
12. Ibid., pp. 172–173.

13. Ibid., pp. 173–181.
14. Ibid., p. 173.
15. Ibid., pp. 178–181.
16. Ibid., pp. 224–229.
17. Ibid., pp. 183–184.
18. Ibid., pp. 6–10.
19. Ibid., pp. 185–191.
20. Ibid., pp. 192–196.
21. Ibid., p. 170.
22. $I^a II^{ae}$, q. 6–114.
23. $II^a II^{ae}$, q. 1–170.
24. Bouquillon, *Catholic University Bulletin* 5 (1899): 261.
25. Bouquillon, *Theologia moralis fundamentalis*, pp. 217–492.
26. Sabetti, *Compendium*, nn. 108–109, p. 75.
27. Bouquillon, *Theologia moralis fundamentalis*, pp. 224–251.
28. Bouquillon, *Catholic University Bulletin* 5 (1899): 261.
29. Bouquillon, *Theologia moralis fundamentalis*, pp. 283–439.
30. Ibid., pp. 15–16.
31. Ibid., pp. 197–201.
32. Mahoney, *Making of Moral Theology*, pp. 226–242. For the greater emphasis on the will in Suarez and its effect on the demise of prudence, see John L. Treloar, "Moral Virtue and the Demise of Prudence in the Thought of Francis Suarez," *American Catholic Philosophical Quarterly* 65 (1991): 387–405.
33. Bouquillion, *Theologia moralis fundamentalis*, p. viii.
34. Bouquillon, *Catholic University Bulletin* 5 (1899): 252–253.
35. Thomas Bouquillon, *Institutiones theologiae moralis specialis: Tractatus de virtute religionis* (Bruges: Beyaert-Storie, 1880).
36. Bouquillon, *Theologia moralis fundamentalis*, pp. 218–221.
37. Mahoney, *Making of Moral Theology*, pp. 226–228.
38. F. Suarez, *De legibus et legislatore Deo*, Book 1, cap. 6, n. 24, p. 22.
39. Bouquillon, *Theologia moralis fundamentalis*, pp. 224–225.
40. Ibid., pp. 228–229.
41. Ibid., pp. 229–251.
42. Ibid., pp. 244–248.
43. Ibid., pp. 248–249.
44. Ibid., pp. 237–238.
45. For example, Franz Scholz, "Problems on Norms Raised by Ethical Borderline Situations: Beginnings of a Solution in Thomas Aquinas and Bonaventure," in *Readings in Moral Theology No. 1: Moral Norms and Catholic Tradition*, ed. Charles E. Curran and Richard A. McCormick (New York: Paulist, 1979), pp. 158–183.
46. Bouquillon, *Theologia moralis fundamentalis*, pp. 239–240.
47. E.g., John Dedek, "Moral Absolutes in the Predecessors of St. Thomas," *Theological Studies* 38 (1977): 654–680; "Intrinsically Evil Acts: The Emergence of a Doctrine," *Recherches de théologie ancienne et médiévale* 50 (1983): 191–226.
48. Jacques Maritain, *Man and the State* (Chicago: University of Chicago Press, 1951): pp. 84–94.

49. Bouquillon, *Theologia moralis fundamentalis*, pp. 225; 235–236.
50. Charles E. Curran, *Directions in Fundamental Moral Theology* (Notre Dame, Ind.: University of Notre Dame Press, 1985), pp. 127–144.
51. Bouquillon, *Theologia moralis fundamentalis*, pp. 22–70.
52. Ibid., pp. 23–27.
53. Ibid., pp. 27–28.
54. Ibid., pp. 233–234.
55. For example, ibid., pp. 6–22.
56. Ibid., pp. 494–496.
57. Ibid., p. 7.
58. Ibid., pp. 254–256.
59. Ibid., pp. 258–260.
60. Ibid., p. 15.
61. Ibid., pp. 260–268.
62. Ibid., p. 29.
63. Ibid., pp. 35–53.
64. Ibid., pp. 53–70.
65. Ibid., pp. 29–35.
66. Ibid., pp. 30–31.
67. Ibid., pp. 32–33.
68. Ibid., pp. 33–35.
69. Ibid., pp. 34–35.
70. Bouquillon, *Tractatus de virtute religionis*, pp. 339–346.
71. Bouquillon, *Theologia moralis fundamentalis*, p. 172.
72. Ibid., p. 174.
73. Ibid., p. 179.
74. Ibid., pp. 224–251.
75. Ibid., pp. 245–246, fn. 1.
76. Ibid., p. 230 and fn. 6.
77. Ibid., p. 35.
78. Ibid., pp. 36–53.
79. Ibid., pp. 37–38.
80. Yves Congar, "A Semantic History of the Term 'Magisterium' " and "A Brief History of the Forms of the Magisterium and its Relations with Scholars," in *Readings in Moral Theology No. 3: The Magisterium and Morality*, ed. Charles E. Curran and Richard A. McCormick (New York: Paulist, 1982), pp. 297–331.
81. Bouquillon, *Theologia moralis fundamentalis*, pp. 36–37.
82. Ibid., p. 45.
83. Ibid., pp. 46–51.
84. Ibid., pp. 53–70.
85. Francis A. Sullivan, *Teaching Authority in the Catholic Church* (New York: Paulist, 1983), p. 27.
86. Ibid., p. 53.
87. Ibid., pp. 54–55.
88. William Levada, "Infallible Church Magisterium and the Moral Law," (S.T.D. diss., Gregorian University, Rome, 1970).

89. Bouquillon, *Theologia moralis fundamentalis*, p. 55.

90. Joseph A. Komonchak, "Ordinary Papal Magisterium and Religious Assent," in *Readings in Moral Theology No. 3*, ed. Curran and McCormick, pp. 76–77.

91. Bouquillon, *Theologia moralis fundamentalis*, pp. 55–57.

92. Ibid., p. 64.

93. Ibid., pp. 64–65.

94. Bouquillon, *Catholic University Bulletin* 5 (1899): 267.

95. Ibid., pp. 59–63.

96. See Curran and McCormick, eds., *Readings in Moral Theology No. 3*, and *Readings in Moral Theology No. 6: Dissent in the Church* (New York: Paulist, 1988).

97. Bouquillon, *Theologia moralis fundamentalis*, p. 36.

98. Ibid., p. 61.

99. Ibid., pp. 64–65.

100. Thomas Bouquillon, "Public Writings of Leo XIII," *Catholic University Bulletin* 1 (1895): 300–306.

101. Leo XIII, *In plurimis*, in *The Papal Encyclicals 1878–1903*, ed. Carlen, pp. 159–167.

102. Bouquillon, *Revue Bénédictine* 6 (1889): 157–169.

103. Ibid., pp. 157–160.

104. Ibid., pp. 160–163.

105. Ibid., p. 163.

106. John Francis Maxwell, *Slavery and the Catholic Church* (London: Barry Rose, 1975), pp. 181 and 54.

107. Bouquillon, *Revue Bénédictine* 6 (1889): 163–164.

108. Maxwell, *Slavery and the Catholic Church*, p. 58.

109. Bouquillon, *Revue Bénédictine* 6 (1889): 165–168.

110. Maxwell, *Slavery and the Catholic Church*, p. 10.

111. Ibid., pp. 86–87.

112. Ibid., pp. 78–79. In his *Theologia moralis fundamentalis* Bouquillon recognizes this same distinction and says that the ameliorated form of slavery is not absolutely against the natural law; but because of its nature and the circumstances connected with it such slavery is very imperfect and must be judged one of the principal miseries of our fallen human nature. Consequently the constant care of the church was little by little to impede or abolish this institution among Christians. Chattel slavery was truly opposed to both nature and religion. In this connection Bouquillon cites a number of other articles but does not mention his own (*Theologia moralis fundamentalis*, pp. 278–279).

113. Bouquillon, *Theologia moralis fundamentalis*, pp. 524–525.

114. Ibid., p. 525, fn. 1.

115. Ibid.

116. Ibid., p. 498.

117. Ibid., pp. 518–523.

118. Zalba, *Theologiae moralis summa*, 1, p. 246.

119. Bouquillon, *Theologia moralis fundamentalis*, pp. 63–64.

120. Ibid.

254 Notes to Chapter 6

121. Komonchak, in *Readings in Moral Theology No. 3*, ed. Curran and McCormick, pp. 70–78.

122. Sabetti, *Compendium*, pp. 1–20.

123. Bouquillon, *Theologia moralis fundamentalis*, p. 613.

124. Ibid.

125. Sabetti, *Compendium*, pp. 2–20.

126. Bouquillon, *Theologia moralis fundamentalis*, pp. 698–711.

127. Ibid., pp. 646–647.

128. Sabetti, *Compendium*, pp. 16–20.

129. Bouquillon, *Theologia moralis fundamentalis*, p. 649.

130. $I^a II^{ae}$, q. 18., a., 2–4.

131. Bouquillon, *Theologia moralis fundamentalis*, pp. 649–650.

132. Ibid., pp. 651–653.

133. Sabetti, *Compendium*, p. 506.

134. Bouquillon, *Theologia moralis fundamentalis*, pp. 672–675.

135. E.g., ibid., p. 665.

136. Ibid., pp. 673–674.

137. Ibid., p. 674.

138. For a short textbook summary of revisionist Catholic moral theology on the human act, see Richard Gula, *Reason Informed by Faith: Foundations of Catholic Morality* (New York: Paulist, 1989), pp. 265–282.

139. For the principle of double effect and revisionist reaction to it, see in addition to Gula, Richard A. McCormick, *How Brave a New World? Dilemmas in Bioethics* (Garden City, N.Y.: Doubleday, 1981), pp. 413–429; James F. Keenan, "The Function of the Principle of Double Effect," *Theological Studies* 54 (1993): 294–315.

140. For my development of the problem of physicalism in the Roman Catholic tradition, see my *Directions in Fundamental Moral Theology*, pp. 127–137.

141. Bouquillon, *Theologia moralis fundamentalis*, pp. 649, fn. 2; 652.

142. Ibid., pp. 651–653.

143. $I^a II^{ae}$, qq. 55–67; 71–89.

144. Bouquillon, *Theologia moralis fundamentalis*, pp. 687–688.

145. Ibid., pp. 688–692.

146. Thomas Bouquillon, *Institutiones theologiae moralis specialis: Tractatus de virtutibus theologicis*, (Bruges: Beyaert-Storie, 1890).

147. Bouquillon, *Theologia moralis fundamentalis*, pp. 692–698; 703–711.

148. Ibid., pp. 692–693.

149. Ibid., pp. 694–696.

150. Ibid., pp. 703–711.

151. Ibid., p. 130.

152. Ibid., pp. 213–215. For Bouquillon's defense of religious freedom in the United States but only on the basis of tolerating evil, see Bouquillon, *Rejoinder to Civiltà Cattolica*, pp. 28–31.

153. Bouquillon, *Theologia moralis fundamentalis*, p. 18.

154. Ibid., pp. 280–283.

155. Ibid., p. 128

156. Ibid., pp. 14, 92, 111.

PART FOUR

John B. Hogan: An Historically Conscious Approach

7

Hogan's Approach to
Moral Theology

John Baptist Hogan proposes a third distinctive approach to moral theology at the end of the nineteenth century in the United States. Hogan, like Sabetti, found his ministry in the seminary and not in the university, but he was much more of an intellectual than his Woodstock colleague. While both Hogan and Bouquillon were strongly committed to the intellectual life and shared an interest in history, Hogan opposed neoscholasticism and was clearly identified with moderate Modernist approaches. Hogan's intellectual life was not devoted only to moral theology. He never wrote a textbook or monograph dealing with moral theology but only a long programmatic essay.[1] From this one can readily discern the general approach he takes to moral theology even though he did not develop his thought in a systematic and scientific way.

HOGAN'S LIFE AND BACKGROUND

Hogan was born in County Clare, Ireland, in 1829. Through the influence of an uncle who was a French priest he entered the seminary in Bordeaux at fifteen. He later joined the Society of Saint Sulpice which is dedicated to the training of seminarians for the priesthood. Ordained a priest in 1852 at age twenty-three, he was immediately appointed professor of fundamental theology at the seminary of St. Sulpice in Paris. In 1864 he became professor of moral theology. In the context of the seminary system of the time professors tended to have no advanced degree and often taught various subjects in the curriculum. However, Hogan's life indicates a deep interest in the intellectual aspects of theology and the life of the church. Hogan came to the United States in 1884 as president of St. John's Seminary in Brighton, Massachusetts, the official seminary of the archdiocese of Boston. After one term there he became the president of Divinity College, the residence for graduate priests studying at the Catholic University of America (1889–1894). Hogan, who was known in the United States as the Abbé Hogan, returned for a second term as president of St. John's Seminary in 1894, but his health failed and he died in France in 1901.[2]

Hogan was not a prolific writer nor did he publish original research. In this sense he was not a publishing scholar. However, his writings indicate he was a true intellectual with a broad and deep knowledge of church-related disciplines and of contemporary culture. All admit that he was a superb pedagogue who employed a Socratic method often jettisoning the textbook and challenging his students to understand and not just memorize the materials. The temptation at the time was simply to memorize the textbook.[3]

During his time in the United States, Hogan wrote two books— *Clerical Studies*, published in Boston in 1898 which originated as a series of articles published in the *American Ecclesiastical Review* from 1891 to 1895, and *Daily Thoughts for Priests*, short meditations for seminarians and priests.[4] The Abbé also contributed articles belonging to the genre of *haute vulgarisation* to a number of Catholic journals such as *American Catholic Quarterly Review*, and *Donahoe's Magazine*.[5] Just before his death he was working on an eleven-part series on "Church Building" for the *American Ecclesiastical Review*.[6] At that time he was also planning a book for the guidance of seminary students.[7] Many of his publications were intimately connected with his seminary work.

Clerical Studies, which was later translated into French, constitutes his most theological work and in these pages he discusses his ideas about moral theology. Hogan assisted the committee of United States bishops that proposed a plan of studies for American Catholic seminaries in 1885 in accord with the directions given by the Third Plenary Council of Baltimore.[8] The purpose of his book is to show how the program laid out in the light of Baltimore III may be pursued with the greatest advantages.[9] In thirteen chapters the book deals with the subjects of the seminary curriculum. More pages are devoted to moral theology than any other subject.[10] *Clerical Studies* indicates that although Hogan did not publish original theological research he was an intellectual with a broad and deep knowledge of all the facets of the disciplines involved in the seminary curriculum. He himself had taught a number of these disciplines. In this sense his knowledge is encyclopedic. In practically every discussion he reviews the history of the discipline and refers to the most significant literature in its development as well as to contemporary approaches. His class notes reveal this same broad and deep grasp of philosophy, theology, church history, and exegesis. Likewise his correspondence shows him in dialogue with many of the most advanced thinkers of the day in Catholic circles especially in Europe.[11]

Daily Thoughts for Priests is a very different genre of book. Hogan provides fifty short meditations for the busy priest. The meditations are heavily biblical starting with a particular biblical text which the priest can use when he has missed his regular morning meditation.[12] The book is obviously spiritual in nature and not primarily theological.

Four formative influences affected the intellectual positions adopted by the Abbé Hogan—the milieu of French liberal Catholicism; the tradition of the Society of St. Sulpice; the role of the Sulpicians in the United States with the running of theological seminaries beginning with St. Mary's Seminary in Baltimore; and his role as a seminary professor and rector.

Liberal French Catholicism in the nineteenth century was identified with the names of Charles Montalembert and Felix Dupanloup. This position supported a liberal political agenda with an emphasis on a free church in a free state. One of the issues in France in the middle part of the century concerned the question of church schools. Here the liberal Catholics worked for some type of compromise with the anticlerical liberal government with regard to the role of the state and the church in education. As the century went on liberal Catholicism in France became associated with Americanism and with some aspects of Modernism.[13]

The Society of St. Sulpice was not totally in agreement about French Catholic liberalism, but Hogan definitely supported it. The Sulpicians, like many others at the time, generally embraced the moderate Gallicanism which recognized the primacy of the bishop of Rome but wanted to give an important role to national and local churches. Hogan shared such sentiments. In the beginning of the nineteenth century the French Catholic liberals were often known as ultramontanists but after 1830 the more conservative forces in the French church became strongly identified with Rome and the liberal group became more associated with Gallicanism.[14] An important philosophical influence on Hogan came from Louis Branchereau, a Sulpician philosopher who extolled the role of intuition, had affinities with ontologism, and whose book was later labeled as dangerous by Rome.[15]

The Sulpicians at Baltimore, who had come from France, were accused by some in this country of being too foreign and of not understanding the American ethos. However, with the leadership of Alphonse Magnien (1837–1902) and the scholarship of John Hogan the approach of the Sulpicians in the United States changed dramatically. Magnien came to Baltimore in 1869, taught various subjects, and became the superior of the seminary and of the Sulpician community in the United States in 1878. He became a confidant of Cardinal James Gibbons and a strong supporter of Americanism.[16] The Irish-born Hogan was in sympathy with the more liberal elements in France as exemplified by a moderate Modernism in scripture and theology. Some of Hogan's students became leaders in the more liberal approach to theology in France—Maurice d'Hulst (1841–1896), rector of the Institut Catholique; Exale Irénee Mignot, Archbishop of Albi; and Felix Klein, the French promoter of Isaac Hecker and Americanism. Hogan corresponded with John Henry Newman and Alfred Loisy who was later accused of Modernism.[17]

While Hogan accepted many of the positions of Modernism he would never have accepted the more radical aspects of it that developed after his own death.[18] Americanism and Modernism are quite broad terms, but Christopher Kauffman sees the two movements as clearly related and exemplified in the person of Hogan. Americanism focused on the evaluation of the social and political reality from the pastoral and ecclesiastical perspective, while Modernism focused on personal experience and the scriptural roots of faith from scientific, historical, and theological perspectives. The most inclusive term to embrace both movements is transformationist and Hogan well personifies such an approach which aims at a transformation of the church and of the world.[19]

Hogan's own ministry and *sitz-im-leben* also influenced his attitudes and approaches. The Abbé spent his life in the seminary work of training priests. In such a position he accepted the existing seminary system but tried to transform it. A person devoting his life to preparing future priests within a Sulpician institution almost by definition cannot be radical. The French-educated Irishman comes across in his writings as a judicious person trying to transform and change the church and the existing seminary structure and curriculum.

Hogan's discussion of moral theology in *Clerical Studies*, although not a systematic and constructive development of the discipline, clearly stakes out a different perspective from that proposed by either Sabetti or Bouquillon. To appreciate his approach to moral theology an understanding of Hogan's philosophical and theological presuppositions is most helpful.

PRESUPPOSITIONS

The Abbé's understanding of history in general and the nineteenth century in particular is quite different from that of many other Catholic thinkers at the time. As noted before he supports the political development of republican forms of government and does not hark back to the ideal of the union of church and state. Hogan maintains that the nineteenth century has been one of extraordinary mental activity. At no other time have so many scholars been involved in intellectual pursuits. About every subject that could awaken human curiosity has been examined. Whole regions entirely unknown to the human mind have been unveiled while familiar regions have had their boundaries indefinitely enlarged.[20] In the unparalleled intellectual activity of the nineteenth century spreading out in every conceivable direction nature and history have been the areas in which most study and progress have occurred.[21]

The church has nothing to fear from the natural sciences. The sciences are here to stay. The sciences stimulate the human intellect to seek fresh knowledge, to observe, to question, to test, and to look deeper into the reality of nature. The sciences have generally added to our understanding of the world having ennobled us with their intriguing theories and the extension of the mind in all directions.[22] Catholic priests must be familiar with these developments not only for their own liberal education but also to be able to dialogue with the contemporary world and explain and defend the Catholic faith today. The Catholic church has always been interested in promoting forms of knowledge including the advancement of the natural sciences. Ignorant or half-educated Protestants in this country often believe that the Catholic church is fearful of modern science lest it dilute faith. Such is not the case. Historically the church has defended and promoted science and must continue to do so in these days.[23]

The nineteenth century has witnessed an extraordinary growth in our knowledge of the bible just as it has in many other areas. Perhaps on no other subject has so much industry been expended. We may say without exaggeration that in the present age more has been done for the elucidation of the bible than in all preceding ages put together. Hogan mentions some of these areas of extraordinary development of our knowledge—biblical languages, biblical history, biblical archeology, biblical manuscripts.[24] In philosophy the Abbé did not believe the high point was reached in the thirteenth century. Although at times Hogan disagrees with Descartes, he describes him as leading the greatest philosophical revolution of modern times which is meant as high praise indeed. Despite radical opposition, Cartesianism grew and became acceptable to many Catholics.[25] Hogan welcomed the intellectual developments that had been occurring at such great pace in the nineteenth century and saw in them no threat to the church. How different from the approach of the neoscholastics of the time. However, Hogan never explicitly compared his approach to that of the prevailing neoscholastic orthodoxy.

On the other hand, the Irish-born Sulpician is not naive about inevitable progress and development. In his discussion of apologetics he faces some of the problems that modern developments have brought about. In fact, one reading only his discussion of apologetics might get the impression that he is quite negative about modern developments especially in the sciences and history. Modern science appeared to have set aside much of the supernatural and further progress will undoubtedly dispose of the rest of the so-called supernatural. Historical criticism has demolished many miraculous narratives of the scripture which have nourished faith for so many centuries. It is a sad but unquestionable fact that most of the leaders in the various branches of human knowledge at the present time are strangers to Christian faith.[26] No one can deny that we have entered a period of exceptionally deep and widespread unbelief. Christianity in great measure has ceased to be the basis of society and the common bond of civilized nations. Outside Catholicism the seeds of doubt sown by the Protestant Reformation have developed in the current climate into wholesale confusion and perplexity. Year after year prominent Protestant writers have less to say on positive Christian doctrine and commit themselves to as little as possible. A radical skepticism today tends to do away with the notions of God, the soul, and even human liberty and responsibility. Can Catholics escape the pernicious influence of an age so saturated with unbelief?[27]

Hogan takes a similar tack in the beginning of his discussion of dogmatic theology. The world has become largely indifferent to religious doctrines. The world eagerly investigates the material universe but tends to deny anything that cannot be empirically verified. Religion is a matter of feeling that can be helpful to people but doctrines do not really matter. Many Protestants have accepted this doctrinal indifferentism with pleas for an undogmatic Christianity. Such a notion is seductive to all who love broadness and liberality. We must be aware of the dangers of such approaches in Catholicism for they would destroy the very nature of Christianity coming from the doctrines and teachings of Jesus.[28]

Such a negative description of the times would seem to have come from a cultural conservative who was very suspicious of the latest developments. Such a description seems right at home with a defensive ghetto Catholicism portraying itself as the divine truth against the onslaught of the modern world. However, from his other discussions one realizes that Hogan is very positive about the intellectual developments of the nineteenth century in science and in history. Perhaps he is exaggerating in this discussion in order to emphasize the importance of the role of apologetics today. However, his solution to the problems does not consist in a countercultural approach to these developments or a harkening back to an earlier and more positive historical moment. Hogan insists that there can be no true conflict of science and history with Catholic faith and tries to prove it in his response to the problems he has raised. Our author insists that Catholic seminarians and priests became familiar with all these contemporary developments of science, history, and philosophy and use them in the defense of the faith.[29] At the very minimum then Hogan cannot be accused of a sanguine attitude toward all nineteenth-century developments, but there is no doubt that he basically accepts the new intellectual approaches to natural science, history, philosophy, and biblical studies and sees them as totally compatible with Catholic faith and theology.

In his interpretation of history and especially from an intellectual perspective Hogan applauds the developments that have occurred since the Middle Ages and sees nineteenth-century developments as particularly significant. Such a view contrasts with the neoscholastic approach to intellectual history as illustrated in Bouquillon's history of moral theology which made the acceptance of Aquinas the basis for judging the vicissitudes of intellectual history.

Hogan puts a great emphasis on history. Practically every chapter of *Clerical Studies* reveals an intense interest in and wide knowledge of the history of various theological disciplines. Church history has always occupied an important place in clerical studies but it has never been more recognized and more significant than in the second half of the nineteenth century. Scholars are pursuing a deeper knowledge of every aspect of the Christian past. In this interest the church itself is following the general movement of the age with its great emphasis on history.[30] Even in such a practical discipline as canon law which the cleric needs in the practical exercise of ministry, the Abbé emphasizes the importance of historical study. The historical knowledge of canon law is essential to the full intelligence of almost every particular area of church legislation. To understand how law came to be and why it developed and was transformed over time is most important. The historical study of canon law becomes a school for learning and under-standing patience, moderation, and prudence. This study shows how inflexible firmness in essentials has been combined with consideration and compassion for human weakness. The church has consistently accommodated her discipline to the degree of civilization she meets often tolerating what circumstances seemed to require. Unfortunately some canonists who are more erudite than judicious tend to elevate church discipline above the natural and divine law making it something rigid and unbending. They distort the gentle, pliable, and in the highest sense of the word, the human rule of the church herself.[31]

Hogan's emphasis on history and its interpretation lead to an acceptance of historical consciousness which affects one's understand-ing of reality and the very knowing process itself. Historical conscious-ness sees reality in terms of the particular, the individual, and the changing as opposed to the eternal, immutable, and unchanging charac-teristics of the classicist mentality. On the other hand, as will be clear, Hogan avoids the danger of a sheer existentialism which tends to deny any continuity within history. Our author explicitly recognizes that the emphasis on history has brought about deep changes in the convictions of human beings and in their intellectual methods.[32] In his general approach to clerical disciplines Hogan's historical consciousness comes to the fore in three areas—an evolutionary understanding of dogmatic theology itself, an acceptance of historical criticism with regard to the bible, and the rejection of total a priori deductive reasoning in favor of more inductive methodologies.

First, Hogan accepted historical criticism as applied to the scrip-tures. The Abbé recognizes a tension here between Catholic biblical scholars who are more open to accepting historical criticism and Catho-lic theologians who tend to be more conservative.[33] (One sees here an exact parallel with what developed in Catholic theology in the 1950s and early 1960s.) Historical criticism basically recognizes that not all the bible is to be taken literally. The fundamental principle is that inspiration does not change the established literary habits of a people or a writer. God accommodates God's self to the human writer living in a particular milieu with a particular understanding of reality limited by the circumstances of time and place. The whole question resolves itself into the mind of the human author which has to be gathered from the nature of what is written, the literary methods of the time, and the understandings of the time.[34]

It becomes more and more difficult to say which statements of scripture are to be taken literally. We must know the literary habits of the times. At all times poetry and prophecy have had a freer scope and were less tied down to the more exact vocabulary of philosophy or narrative. Some people have interpreted history much more freely than we often do. Today questions are being asked about things in scripture which in an earlier era raised no problems. Very few today any longer concede the first chapter of Genesis to be strictly historical and the same holds true for the following chapters in Genesis and many other parts of the bible.[35] This understanding has significant consequences for the use of biblical arguments in theology. Without belaboring the point or directly criticizing others, Hogan points out what today is called the danger of using the bible as a proof text. As a result of our understanding of the literary composition of the bible it is almost impossible to build any doctrine or teaching solely on one single biblical passage. The true scriptural argument is cumulative and brings forth conviction only when the same truth emerges from several places and in different connections.[36]

The Catholic scholar or apologist should not engage in indiscriminate denunciation of higher criticism because at times it has led to unacceptable conclusions. Higher criticism is legitimate and necessary for a thorough study of scripture and has been used for constructive as well as destructive purposes. Abuses have been common so that vigilance is necessary. But the abuse does not negate the need to use such an approach. Theologians have to acknowledge that in the future much less can be built on the bible than in the past. Catholics can afford to contemplate this reality with perfect equanimity since our faith is based on the church.[37]

Historical consciousness in Hogan also calls for a recognition of the developmental and progressive character of Catholic dogmatic theology. The Abbé disagrees with a notion of theology as a science fixed long ago in all its parts and teachings to be learned once and for all like geometry or algebra.[38] Theology is revelation submitted to the normal processes of the human intellect. The human mind is the soil in which all new truth germinates and fructifies. The first impulse of the mind with regard to revelation will be to look at what is most vital in the divine message, to realize its full meaning, and to follow its consequences. The next step will be to reply to the many questions raised by revelation and thus try to perfect what God has left imperfect. Third and finally, the mind strives to establish order and consecutiveness and to bring forth from the unconnected elements of revelation an organic unity. Development has occurred in our understanding of the reality of Jesus and the Trinity and also in our understanding of grace, original sin, and the sacraments. Reflection makes more distinct the general conception of a divine truth that is substantially correct but vague or obscure or involved in some other truth in which it is only dimly perceived. Heresy has been the occasion at times for bringing precision and emphasis to orthodoxy. Most of what we call Catholic theology, however, came into existence not in response to heresy but to the craving of the Christian mind to know more about the divine economy and things unseen.[39]

This notion of the development of theology must be properly understood. Theology lives in a tension between two distinct and in some sense antagonistic forces—a progressive tendency and a conservative tendency. Theology appeals to what has been given in revelation in the past. Heretics are inevitably described as innovators. Theology as taught to seminarians must be especially conservative but this principle must always be balanced by the principle of progressivity.[40] One can see here how Hogan avoids the two opposite dangers of classicism and sheer existentialism.

The growth and development of theology resemble that of history and philosophy rather than the physical sciences. It grows as an organic body through the gradual expansion of what first appears in embryonic form. Theology develops by a process of assimilation by taking into its substance new vitalizing matter while dropping what proves worthless or devoid of vivifying power. The progress of theology comes from the dynamism of the human mind and from the object of theology which is the divine mystery that can never be completely known. However, such growth and progress are grounded in divine revelation.[41]

Our author sees the late nineteenth century as a period of great activity in Catholic theology. It is a time of universal criticism with a thoroughgoing independent investigation of origins, documents, and proofs. Such criticism has affected biblical, historical, and philosophical sciences and must likewise affect dogmatic theology. Unlike many of his neoscholastic contemporaries the Abbé is not defensive about this dialogue with the critical mind of the nineteenth century but warmly accepts such an invigorating challenge.[42]

In the dialogue, the Catholic theologian must recognize the great varieties of elements of very unequal value in theology—dogmas of faith, current doctrines, opinions freely debated, conjectures, and proofs of varying degrees of cogency from scientific demonstration down to intimations of the feeblest kind. Much liberty of opinion has always existed in Catholic theology. Defined doctrines themselves may still be far from determined in the full sense and the proofs alleged for them are not beyond question. For example, all agree that the inspiration of scripture is a dogma of faith, but many disagree about the implications of that fact. Human thought and human words might be able to enunciate dogmas in the future so that they will be more in harmony with a new and advanced state of the human mind and with the eternal truth.[43]

Hogan proposes some guidelines for Catholic apologetics in its dialogue with the contemporary world. The overriding principle is that from the Catholic perspective faith and reason cannot contradict one another. Often objections to Catholicism are based on misapprehensions. In dealing with potential conflicts three possible approaches are considered. If something is morally certain from a scientific viewpoint, it prevails over a theological opinion. A certain religious doctrine prevails over scientific speculation. In the case of conflicts between positions of religion and science neither of which can claim to be demonstrably certain one has to admit that the truth might be on either side. Theologians instinctively tend to be conservative but we know today how modern science has corrected some of our theological opinions such as the literal truth of Genesis. The Catholic apologist should not simply give in on all disputed points but carry on the discussion with the humility of knowing that at the present time there is no certitude on these issues. In uncertain matters Hogan proposes the Gamaliel principle from the Acts of the Apostles. Be patient and wait. If this work is of human beings, it will come to naught. But if it comes from God, you cannot overthrow it.[44]

Modern criticism can strengthen the main lines of the Catholic faith and sometimes certain secondary truths. But it has gradually weakened many positions long looked upon by many as safe from assault and quickly destroyed other acknowledged opinions. Such an understanding does not constitute a threat to Catholic theology and to the Catholic church. We are conscious today that we can no longer take all the biblical passages literally. Likewise we know more how some opinions arose as a result of the position taken by just one father in the past. We are aware that opinions based on abstract deduction do not always square with historical realities such as Thomas Aquinas's insistence that the deprecatory form of absolution in the sacrament of penance was invalid. In the past we theologians tended to think that we knew more than we should have known about the angelic world and about the events at the end of the world. At its best, however, Catholic theology has been humble in its understandings. Yes, modern criticism has brought about some changes in Catholic theology but the dialogue with modern criticism and modern science is necessary for the very life of theology.[45]

This historical consciousness also affects the mode and method of philosophical and theological inquiry. In a very logical manner Hogan opposes a deductive methodology and argues for a more inductive approach. The modern mind is different from that of ancient or medieval minds. We do not share their trust in abstract principles unless they are principles of the most obvious and definite kind. We do not rely on the unverified deductions spun out from these abstract principles. One whose training is deductive and scholastic can sit down in our time and draw endless conclusions from abstract principles with the serene confidence of the mathematician. But the modern person will demand testing and verification. The facts of history and the facts of human existence give religious doctrine and speculation a reality that abstract argument cannot impart.[46] In philosophy too our author opposes a priori theories and approaches.[47] In philosophy the inductive method which is universally prevalent should be used to establish necessary principles of demonstration that are not self-evident.[48] The Abbé ends his discussion of dogmatic theology with a paragraph including the phrase later made famous by the Pastoral Constitution on the Church in the Modern World of the Second Vatican Council—to discern the signs of the time. Divine truth is made for every age and every degree of culture and the primary question is to recognize which aspects of it best fit the intellectual, social, and moral needs of the people and times in which we live.[49]

This historical consciousness also affects the human knower. The human mind is fundamentally the same but ever changing. Consequently what recommends itself to the human mind in one period may fail to do so in another. Hence the need for historical and psychological methods.[50]

Such an understanding opposes a naive epistemological realism that would see the ahistorical human mind as corresponding to external reality. Hogan makes this point in his discussion of history. History is not merely a registering of documents, events, and facts. It is a living image of the past—an event of imagination. If history were merely a collecting of facts, then industry alone is what the historian needs. The historian, however, requires the critical faculty that Cardinal Newman calls "the illative sense"—a complex power of the mind by which from a multitude of data judgments are formed and conclusions reached.[51] Our author proposes a similar type of knowing process for philosophy and theology.

As is evident Hogan is not a scholastic or neoscholastic and strongly differs from such approaches. One can readily identify his position from the persons he cites. He never cites neoscholastic authors such as Kleutgen who is the favorite author of Bouquillon. He cites Cardinal Newman more than any other author and Newman was recognized as a strong opponent of neoscholasticism. However, the question then arises: how does Hogan's approach square with Leo XIII's encyclical *Aeterni Patris* which called for the restoration of Thomism in its neoscholastic form?

Before dealing explicitly with the encyclical Hogan mentions it in passing three times to support the positions he has taken on the use of philosophy by the fathers of the church, on the need to appeal to reason and philosophical arguments rather than authority in dealing with those who attack the church, and on the importance of philosophical study.[52] The references to Leo and the encyclical are all positive— "the learned Pontiff," "our great pontiff," "the memorable encyclical." His own remarks are only a "feeble echo" of the pope's.[53] In a true sense Hogan is here using the pope to support approaches which in this author's understanding really do disagree to some extent with the positions of the pope himself. Hogan's use of Leo is very affirming but also quite subtle and very nuanced.

In his discussion of philosophy the Abbé deals directly and at length with *Aeterni Patris*.[54] His commentary is always respectful, quite nuanced, and clearly minimalistic in its interpretation. Hogan begins his interpretation of *Aeterni Patris* by citing and developing two principles suggested by the pope—the need to engraft our philosophy on the wisdom of the past and the need to be loyal to revealed truth. On the first principle Hogan points out that although you have to disagree with the past occasionally you cannot break away from it totally. The second principle of loyalty to the church has always been present in the church but in different shapes as illustrated by the early church's use of Plato and the scholastics' use of Aristotle. Hogan even asserts that recent Catholic thinkers have welcomed the approach of Descartes, Malebranche, Leibnitz, Balmès, Rosmini, and others. Although such approaches are quite eclectic they truly constitute a Christian philosophy.[55]

According to Hogan, the pope now lays down a clear and strong recommendation to go back to the doctrine of Thomas Aquinas. The pope understands this to include the method, the truths, and the theories of Aquinas. Hogan points out that the pope speaks here in his directive capacity and not as the infallible teacher of Christians. Philosophy, apart from its connection with revealed truth, does not come under his authority any more than natural truths. The pope knows that outside the areas of religious belief and evident truth the mind is essentially free and cannot bend itself to what has failed to satisfy it. *Aeterni Patris* is interpreted as a recommendation and watered down in other ways. The pope himself recognizes that his approach does not extend to all the particulars of scholastic philosophy. The commendation of the philosophy of Aquinas cannot be interpreted more strongly than the commendation of his theology. Yet we know how broadly this commendation is taken by theologians of the highest repute and by religious orders including the Jesuits and the Dominicans who are committed to following the teaching of Aquinas. The continued existence of the Scotist school with its many differences from the Thomistic supports this understanding of the import and extent of *Aeterni Patris*. Limited to its true meaning, *Aeterni Patris* loses that seeming exclusiveness which made it objectionable to many.[56] At the time no one seemed to take any exception to this analysis proposed by Hogan. But after the condemnation of Modernism such an interpretation would have been recognized by church authorities as a red flag despite its calm, judicious, and respectful approach.

In another place, the Abbé gives his assessment of Aquinas. The Dominican friar knew all that was known in his age and in each department of knowledge discovered intimations, analogies, laws and principles by which to light up the dark places of divine revelation and accommodate it to the prevailing conditions of the human mind. If Aquinas were to return today, we would find him once more eager to take in all knowledge, busy with the most recent discoveries, alive to the great questions of the day, including the developments of minds and events, gathering light from everything and harmoniously blending it with the light from above.[57]

The ultimate success of neoscholasticism (Hogan never uses this term) will depend on two things. First, the intrinsic nature of the philosophy and not authority will be the basis for its success. Authority may have been necessary to originate this new movement but it cannot sustain it. Second, this philosophy must avoid the faults that had proved so harmful to scholasticism in history. Hogan claims, somewhat disingenuously, that he will devote his next article to showing how this can be done.[58] In fact Hogan really does not address the question in the following section.[59] Thus he avoids giving what logically he should have given—a negative answer to the question of how neoscholasticism can avoid the problems that brought about the demise of scholasticism. He obviously does not think that neoscholasticism will attract the whole Catholic intellectual community on the basis of its intrinsic merits. Nor can it really avoid many of the same problems that he describes as occurring to scholasticism in the past.

History has vindicated his judgment about the role of intrinsic value and authority. Neoscholasticism was authoritatively imposed on Catholic philosophy and theology and this imposition lasted for almost seventy-five years until the Second Vatican Council, but in the end the intrinsic merits of the system and not the authority proposing it became the most important consideration.

In his discussion of scripture Hogan had to deal with the 1893 encyclical of Leo XIII *Providentissimus Deus*. Recall that Hogan strongly supported historical criticism and saw no contradiction between the bible and science. Gerald Fogarty, the historian of American Catholic scripture studies, has called his approach daring.[60] According to Hogan *Providentissimus Deus* made the task of Catholic apologetics more difficult by insisting that error is not possible in any genuine passage of the scripture. But the pope has helped to lighten the difficulty by pointing out that the bible is written in popular rather than technical language. As a result Catholic scholars have found in the inspired pages loose and inexact statements, figurative language of all kinds, metaphors, hyperboles, rhetorical amplifications, facts veiled in poetic form, seeming narratives which are only allegories or parables, and all the literary approaches of Eastern people. Leo's principles are quite narrow and strict but Catholic scholars have never been bolder in their speculations and in applying historical criticism to particular parts of the scripture than since the encyclical itself was issued.[61] Hogan thus maintained his basic position and claimed to be in continuity with the encyclical of Leo XIII.

The seminary rector was more open in his writings to dialogue with Protestants than either Sabetti or Bouquillon, but one cannot judge him by our contemporary standards. Hogan credits the Reformation with leading to a more intelligent and popular study of the bible.[62] Protestants accepted historical criticism of the bible before Catholics.[63] On the other hand, the Reformation developed religious skepticism. The seeds of doubt sown by the Reformation have now come up and covered the whole surface of Protestant countries stifling everywhere the divine germs of revealed truth. Most prominent Protestant writers commit themselves to as little as possible.[64] Protestant studies seem to be moving in the direction of an "undogmatic Christianity."[65] Even in making such negative judgments Hogan avoids polemical and insulting language. In speaking of history he mentions that the main characters are a combination of good and evil. If authors emphasize only the good they do not depart from literal truth but leave a distorted picture. He then mentions that it was in this way that people such as Luther, Calvin, John Knox, Huss, and Wycliffe were made popular.[66] No other examples are given except these leaders of Protestantism! In describing Protestant writers Hogan is seemingly objective and always courteous. Professor Fisher's treatment of history presents in a learned and fair-minded way, naturally from the Protestant perspective, the main facts of church history.[67] Our author points out some good exponents of the Christian faith among his Protestant contemporaries.[68]

CONSISTENCY AND MINDSET

The previous analysis of Hogan's thought reveals a coherent and consistent understanding in his approaches to science, history, philosophy, scripture, and dogmatic theology. Only one question of possible discordance came to the fore. Specifically in the case of apologetics he was much more negative about contemporary intellectual and cultural realities than in his other discussions. Undoubtedly the very nature of the subject matter of apologetics meant that he had to stress the opposition between the church and the contemporary intellectual and cultural realities.

A greater problem of consistency arises in comparing his intellectual and theological approach in *Clerical Studies* with his approach to spirituality for priests in *Daily Thoughts for Priests*. This book was written to provide spiritual nourishment for the busy priest who for some reason might have skipped his morning meditation.[69] The general thrust of these fifty short meditations emphasizes how the priest is called out of the world. The very last meditation is entitled "Detachment." The priest is called to leave all things to follow Jesus. The priest abandons all worldly pursuits, interests, and projects. He belongs to his work and nothing else. The priest sets aside what he had hitherto enjoyed—family life, friends, intellectual pursuits, or the cultivation of some special gift.[70]

Similar themes frequently appear in this book. Self-denial like detachment is a means to make the priest freer for the service of God. He should deny himself the most natural and harmless enjoyments as did the saints who waged war fiercely on their flesh.[71] By a watchfulness in prayer the priest must avoid the worldly spirit which is in the air one breathes, in the numberless objects that strike the senses, and in every conversation.[72] The priest will have to choose between the present life and the future one just as Jesus suffered and died in this life.[73] On the basis of this book, one commentator has concluded that Hogan was a Jansenist.[74]

I do not think Hogan was a Jansenist. Sulpician spirituality built on the approach of their founder, Jean-Jacques Olier (1608–1657), a proponent of the so-called French school of spirituality or the Berullian school after Pierre Cardinal de Bérulle (1575–1629), its founder. In reality this school's approach to spirituality differed somewhat from the Jansenistic although there were some similarities. The French school emphasized the incarnation of the Word who offered perfect religion to God and the need for the priest to conform to and practice the interior dispositions of the Word Incarnate. Jansenism does not give the same importance to the incarnation and tends to see all in terms of the grace-sin dichotomy. The French school was firmly theocentric stressing the awe and adoration we should give to God through the practice of what was called religion as exemplified in the life of Jesus. Correlative to the awe before the triune God was the awareness of the nothingness of all creation in itself. The negative language of the French school was based on this comparison between the awesomeness of God and the nothingness of all else in comparison to it but not on the Jansenistic dualism between sin and grace.[75]

The nothingness of creation before the awe and wonder of God comes through in *Daily Thoughts for Priests*. In discussing the worldly spirit, Hogan recognizes that assuredly all is not evil in the natural human being. Such a person has a fund of integrity and nobleness and can perform many good actions. But without the gospel such a person belongs to Satan more than to God.[76] Detachment involves the willingness to leave everything for Christ even human affections however legitimate they may be.[77] Yes, Hogan, the Sulpician, is often quite negative in his judgments about human and worldly existence but his approach is not Jansenistic as such.

Elsewhere even in his more popular writings Hogan is not that negative about human nature and life in the world. In discussing the social aspects of religion Hogan recognizes that religion has a positive effect on human progress and is always supportive of the highest and best of the human.[78] In discussing the role of the priest in France at that time the French-trained Sulpician maintained that a priest has to remain to the end a man and a man of the people like the Son of Man who chose to embrace all human sympathies in his heart. Throughout his training the seminarian has to keep alive his first love for everything that is good and generous and hopeful in the age and in the people to whom he belongs. He must go back to them not as a foreigner. Just as French missionary priests have made themselves at home in missionary lands so they must accommodate themselves to the prevailing spirit of their own people.[79]

I think there is some inconsistency between Hogan's spirituality for priests and his theology. In the latter he is much more appreciative of the human in all its aspects whereas in the former the human seems to be nothing compared with the majesty of God. This spirituality was an intimate and integral part of his own life and something he tried to pass on to his students. He probably never realized the tension or unresolved dialectic between his theology and his spirituality. Many people experience similar unresolved tensions in their thinking and living.

This somewhat rigoristic spirituality and negativity with regard to the human might also have had a more practical side in Hogan's life. As president of Divinity College at the newly founded Catholic University of America Hogan was in charge of the religious life and discipline of the priest students. Some of the students resented the discipline of daily communal prayers and spiritual exercises similar to the regimen adhered to in seminaries. They thought they should be responsible for their own spiritual lives as other diocesan priests are. This seems to have been more of a problem of young priests no longer wanting to be treated as seminarians, but Hogan was tagged as a rigid and strict disciplinarian.[80] On the other hand, students from Boston picture him in a much more favorable light.[81]

Hogan's writings also reveal something of his mindset and how it affected his own approaches. He was irenic, nonconfrontational, tactful, and more of an incrementalist than a revolutionary. From what has been said there is no doubt that Hogan's approach to philosophy and theology was opposed to scholasticism, quite radical for the Catholicism of his day, and open to the ideas of moderate Modernism. If someone had written the same materials in 1920, the writings would have been officially censured or condemned. Alfred Loisy complained that Rome condemned in him what it approved in Hogan.[82] No doubts were publicly expressed in the United States about Hogan's orthodoxy, and *Clerical Studies* was very well received. However, the Roman authorities took a long time in 1900–1901 to process the request for an *imprimatur* for the French translation of *Clerical Studies*. Kauffman indicates that Hogan's irenic and tactful approaches made his positions more acceptable.[83]

The Irish-born Sulpician never directly attacked any contemporary Catholic authors or positions in his writings. He does not call attention to how much his positions may differ from others. Compare his *Clerical Studies* with the contemporary work of John Talbot Smith, *Our Seminaries: An Essay on Clerical Training*, which makes sharp attacks on the existing seminary system.[84] Hogan's theology is more radical than Smith's but his tone is entirely different. An earlier chapter pointed out how Bouquillon strongly disagreed with the manuals of moral theology.[85] As will be seen Hogan's approach to moral theology was much more opposed to the existing Catholic approaches than Bouquillon but he never directly attacked the manuals or any other authors. In his writings Hogan never directly disagreed with Leo XIII's encyclicals *Aeterni Patris* and *Providentissimus Deus* although he gave a very minimalist interpretation of them. However, in private correspondence he lamented the regressive character of *Providentissimus Deus*.[86]

The Sulpician's irenicism comes through even in his apologetics. Both Bouquillon and Hogan wrote attacks on the historical writings of Henry Charles Lea (1825–1909) and strongly disagreed with him. Bouquillon's approach involves a strong and unrelenting disagreement from the very beginning.[87] In his comments on Lea's work on auricular confession Hogan strongly disagrees with the American Protestant but his article is not an unrelenting attack. He begins by praising Lea. Dr.

Lea (Bouquillon refers to him as "Mr. Lea") is evidently above all things a scholar. By the wealth of his erudition and his evident love of learning he reminds one of those great Benedictine monks of the seventeenth and eighteenth centuries. Hogan also recognizes that much is obscure about the development of penance in the early church. He is still very negative in his conclusions about Lea's work, but his irenic approach appears in the praise that he also bestows on the author.[88]

Hogan's tactful and incrementalist approach comes through in his description of the different stages in the learning of dogmatic theology. Elementary theology is learned in the seminary but needs to be developed by the priest in his subsequent reading after ordination. Theology is instinctively conservative, but elementary theology has to be doubly so. Its function is to initiate the student into ascertained truths and the current teaching of the science. Scholastic vocabulary and forms (e.g., definitions, distinctions, divisions) have many weaknesses but they are in possession as the technical language of the science and should be learned. One can later develop newer forms of expression.[89] No one can be upset by such an approach.

Hogan often employs a literary genre of approaching a particular issue by condemning those (usually Protestants) who reject a particular Catholic position, but then nuancing the Catholic approach quite a bit in his development. His discussion of dogmatic theology in *Clerical Studies* follows such an approach. He begins by pointing out the indifference to doctrine in the contemporary religious world but the absolute need for it. In developing his understanding of dogma, however, he recognizes the progressive character of theology and ends by insisting that the deepest interest and highest usefulness of dogmatic theology is to watch the development of mind and events, gathering light from everything and harmoniously blending it with the light from above.[90] Dogmatic theology does not simply repeat what has been said in the past.

Hogan begins an article on miracles by pointing out that today rationalists and even some Protestants deny miracles. Hogan insists on the importance of miracles, but the great majority of the miracles we read of or hear about are merely probable. In dealing with them the Catholic is left to her own judgment. Church authority commits itself very sparingly to facts of any kind and especially to facts of this kind.[91]

Hogan's irenic, tactful, discrete, and incrementalist mindset and style tend to downplay the differences between his approach to Catholic philosophy and theology and most of the existing approaches. For example, Francis Connell, a prominent Catholic theologian who strongly identified with the pre-Vatican II church and conservative positions at the Second Vatican Council has nothing but praise for Hogan. He is a distinguished educator; *Clerical Studies* is justly regarded as a classic treatment of the subject. Each perusal of the essays in this book reveals a new and enriching aspect of the science of divine things.[92] In reality Hogan's approach to Catholic theology differs considerably from Connell's understanding.

MORAL THEOLOGY

Although Abbé Hogan never really developed moral theology in a systematic and scientific way, his programmatic essay in *Clerical Studies* gives more than a few hints of how he understood and approached moral theology. Our discussion will deal with three areas—his agreements with the general understanding of moral theology at the time, his differences, and finally a brief discussion of the irenic and tactful tone of his writings on the subject.

BASIC AGREEMENTS. The Abbé agrees with his contemporaries about the importance of moral theology. In fact, Hogan devoted more space to moral theology than to any other subject in his book *Clerical Studies*.[93] Moral theology and dogmatic theology are the two most important disciplines in the seminary and occupy the same amount of time in the curriculum. The preference of the majority of the students, however, goes to moral theology rather than dogmatic theology. Moral theology appeals because it is more practical and also because it is more directly and immediately related to priestly ministry. Throughout his book the seminary rector has insisted on the need for priests to continue their theological education after they leave the seminary, and this is even more true in the case of moral theology which is so significant in the daily practice of ministry.[94]

The first of five articles on moral theology is entitled "Importance of Moral Theology." The science of duty is the most necessary and therefore desirable form of knowledge. The chief excellence of human beings is to submit to one's duty. The pagan world and all history bear witness to the importance of the knowledge of one's duty. Church history reveals the same importance: Scripture calls for living a new life and following the law of God. The writers of the early church deal mostly with moral issues. The medieval schoolmen emphasize what we call dogmatic theology. At no time, was morality neglected though it was only later that moral theology took shape as a separate discipline geared for the practical uses of the ministry. With the growing complexity of modern life and the new questions that are constantly arising, moral theology has become even more important in our time.[95]

Hogan agrees with the basic scope and purpose of moral theology—the training of confessors for their ministry in the sacrament of penance. Hogan also mentions the importance of moral theology for other aspects of priestly ministry such as teaching and preaching.[96] Such an appraisal is not surprising from one who devoted his life to preparing students for the work of priestly ministry.

The emphasis on the morality of particular acts underscores the importance of casuistry. Casuistry is to moral theology what therapeutics is to medicine—the very end and object of the science. The priest confessor must know what is right and wrong.[97]

Criticisms are made against moral theology because it deals only with the minimum, but such a difficulty fails to understand the purpose of moral theology. As found in St. Alphonsus and as taught in the schools moral theology does not deal with the ideal but with what one is strictly bound to do. Moral theology is the science of the licit and illicit. The moral theologian thinks of the number of struggling persons who are willing in spirit but weak in the flesh striving to be faithful to God in the midst of many difficulties. The confessor knows the heroic struggle of some souls to do what many people can accomplish with little or no effort. Who in such circumstances would not try to bring the law within reach of these struggling souls and make it possible for them to hang on to God by fulfilling their basic obligations? True, such laws are far removed from the Christian ideal but strictness will not bring these people any closer to it.[98]

The moral theologian thus tries to limit moral obligations. Unscrupulous and ungenerous people may take advantage of such an approach and use it for their own purposes but such ends are foreign to the purpose of moral theologians and confessors. The public magistrates or popular feeling may be inclined to be somewhat scandalized by what the moral theologian says about a particular question of restitution or equivocation. But even the magistrate when considering a particular issue from the viewpoint of a human being recognizes the need to bend a point of law in order to show mercy to those who deserve it.[99]

The purpose and scope of moral theology, identifying it with the casuistry of the minimal, has thus limited and defined the nature of the discipline. In this respect Hogan recognizes and accepts the existing distinction between moral theology and ascetical theology. The Christian life admits of innumerable degrees from imperfect beginnings to the heights of holiness reached by saints. The first steps of the Christian life involve obligations; the later stages lead the soul from the realm of fear to freedom and love. Hogan here seems to have in mind the traditional distinction between precept and counsel. Moral theology could embrace the whole but as commonly understood it confines itself to what is obligatory whereas ascetical theology is the science of the higher Christian life.[100] A separate chapter devotes two articles to ascetical theology.[101] In this way Hogan also illustrates the comparatively minor place given to ascetical theology in the seminary curriculum.

Occasionally the Abbé indicates some uneasiness about this understanding of moral theology. The confessor also has the duty to point out what is higher and to encourage souls to do what is purest and noblest.[102] In light of some of his uneasiness about the scope of moral theology Hogan proposes that a new section might be added to the manuals of moral theology dealing with the casuistry of the higher Christian life. Such an approach would be beneficial to priests and people.[103] But Hogan has already claimed that such a role belongs to ascetical rather than moral theology. Our author accepts and encourages the scope of moral theology to prepare priests for knowing the limits of the basic obligations of the Christian life.

With such an understanding of the purpose of moral theology Hogan emphasizes the legal model in moral theology. His introductory description of moral theology at the very beginning of his chapter illustrates this approach. Divine revelation contains two kinds of elements—truths to be believed and precepts to be obeyed as the expression of the divine will. Moral theology comprises the divine law, the natural law, and at least in principle the laws of the church and the precepts of rightful authority binding on conscience. In a word moral theology covers the whole field of moral and religious duty.[104]

The seminary professor and rector logically recognizes that virtue has no place in such an understanding of moral theology. However, virtue has an important role to play in ascetical theology. Hogan is well aware that the medieval scholastics expounded the full plan of Christian holiness in its higher as well as in its humbler degrees. Nowhere can one find a more comprehensive plan of the spiritual life than in the *Secunda secundae* of St. Thomas where the individual virtues are discussed. It was only later and in the manuals of moral theology written especially for confessors that moral theology became confined to the study of strict duty.[105] Hogan chooses to follow that approach with its legal mode.

A legal model geared to discovering the basic limits of obligation gives great importance to casuistry. *Clerical Studies* sees casuistry as far and away the central aspect of moral theology. Casuist and moralist are used interchangeably. Moral theology deals with the precepts, duties, and laws directing moral conduct. These principles must then be applied to particular instances. The great law of charity, love one another, is quite general and needs to be formulated into more specific rules and applied to particular instances. To tell the truth is an acknowledged rule of human intercourse, but circumstances occur every day that raise questions about whether one can depart from the rule or whether certain modes of expression are truthful or not. Casuistry helps to clarify and specify the rules of moral conduct and at the same time deals with specific cases by applying the rules to them. Wherever there are laws or codes, casuistry is essential and necessary. Moral theology follows this same approach. Christ himself used casuistry as he discussed, for example, how to deal with the woman caught in adultery. St. Paul posed solutions to many issues arising in the early church. Casuistry has continued to flourish in the Catholic church. Casuistry is indispensable for the proper understanding and formulation of laws and principles and for dealing with particular issues. Unlike Bouquillon and many contemporary Catholic moral theologians, the Abbé praises the casuistry of the late nineteenth century. Casuistry today is the most living branch of the sacred science spreading out into the various areas of human activity, old and new, busy in applying the laws of Christian morality to every condition and every action of life.[106]

The Abbé recognizes that casuistry has been abused in the past. He recounts the laxism of the seventeenth century and the condemnations of Popes Alexander VII and Innocent XI. The very nature of moral theology dealing with the minimum of the duties of the Christian life occasions such laxity. Casuists and confessors with the best of intentions try to make duty as easy as possible with the concomitant danger of sacrificing what should never be given up. If one can kill the unjust aggressor who is stealing a significant amount of material goods, one can extend the rule of self-defense to include killing the slanderer because character is more precious than earthly possessions. Moral theology at the time knew the struggle between laxism and rigorism. It took some time to work out the proper limitations and restrictions in the theory of probabilism itself. Fortunately, St. Alphonsus helped to find a moderate way between the two extremes. Yes, abuses have occurred with regard to casuistry, but the abuse does not do away with the need for its proper use.[107]

By accepting the legal model and the need for casuistry to determine the limits of obligations for the confessor, Hogan not only endorses this manualistic approach to moral theology but with it also accepts the opposition between law and freedom. An obligation can have no hold on conscience until it attains to consistency or certitude in the mind either by inner development or by contact with reflex principles.[108]

In keeping with the generally accepted Catholic approach of his day the Irish-born, French-educated seminary president gave the primary and almost exclusive role to human reason in moral theology. The principles of moral theology are found primarily in the natural intelligence, in common sense, and in the moral sense of human beings. Almost all moral duties are natural duties connected in the Christian with a higher order but preserving all their original characteristic features. This is the teaching of the Catholic approach found in Aquinas, Suarez, and the tradition. According to Suarez, even the special positive duties of the Christian (e.g., participation in the Eucharistic liturgy or laws of fast and abstinence) flow *naturally* from the very fact of the supernatural order as it has been manifested to humankind. Beyond these obligations which are few in number everything forbidden to the Christian is forbidden by the natural law; whatever is prescribed is a command flowing from the moral nature of human beings.

As a consequence moral duty in all its parts lies within the sphere of human judgment and is subject to it. In keeping with the tradition of Catholic emphasis on participation and mediation but without explicitly invoking such an approach, Hogan cautions that reason is not the supreme arbiter or the first court of appeal but is the divinely appointed means of ascertaining moral truth in all its dimensions. In no part of sacred doctrine is human natural intelligence so much appealed to as in moral theology. Moral theology is essentially philosophical.[109] Our author does refer to natural law in his discussions, but the concept is never developed in any detail and the following section will show that his understanding of human reason operates in moral theology in a way quite different from the traditional natural law understanding.

In the light of the primacy of reason, scripture plays a comparatively minor role in the moral theology proposed by Hogan. Christians find their rules of conduct in many different sources, human and divine including of course the biblical sources such as Jewish law, the maxims of Jesus, and the teachings of the apostles.[110] But in their actual shape these rules are almost entirely due to the labor and thought of the schools throughout the ages.[111] The manuals of moral theology have often been criticized for using a single scripture text as a proof to support a position based on other considerations. Hogan does not bring up this criticism but his earlier discussion of sacred scripture pointed up the dangers of using an isolated scripture passage in this manner.

The Abbé also stresses the Catholic emphasis on the role of church authority in Catholic theology and life. Twice in his comparatively short discussion of moral theology Hogan appears to go out of his way to contrast the Catholic approach with the Protestant self-understanding. Hogan begins the first of his five articles on moral theology by pointing out that one of the most striking differences between the moral teachings of the Catholic church and those of Protestantism is found in the fullness and assurance of the former as compared with the habitual vagueness and hesitancy of the latter. The guidance of the Catholic church covers the whole ground of human conduct and offers peaceful serenity to those who follow it. But a closer examination reveals that much is unfinished and much remains to be discovered even in Catholic moral theology.[112] When a person is found with the rare occurrence of perplexity the Catholic has a way to solve the doubt by going to the priest. But other people in such perplexity are deserving of the sincerest sympathy because there is no way to overcome their perplexity. Here again Hogan recognizes that even within the Catholic church there are doubts and disagreements. He does not appeal to authoritative teaching to solve all problems.[113] In both cases Hogan starts out as is often his wont with a strong statement about the role of authority in general but then backs away from it and recognizes the great limits of authority in moral questions.

In fact, his discussion of church authority in these contexts is quite nuanced. The popes have never ceased to propose moral teachings and their decisions are carefully treasured and have become the practical rule of duty. These moral teachings over the years have been found in many different forms including the decisions of the Roman congregations. The more we consider the actions of the popes and the church the greater we find their influence in giving its distinctive, definite shape to the whole system of Christian life and conduct. However, here too the author backs away somewhat. Although the supreme regulative action always belongs to the popes, Christian ethics in its full development has been the work of the schools.[114] Since moral theology depends primarily on human reason, theologians while ever ready to listen to the suggestions of authority and bow to its decisions, constantly test everything by philosophical discussion weighing all in the balance of reason.[115] Yes, Hogan goes out of his way to insist on the role of authority, especially the popes in moral teaching, but he also seems to emphasize what nineteenth-century theologians did not usually point out—authority must conform itself to the true, the good, and the reasonable. Such an understanding has long been part of the best of the Catholic theological tradition.

Finally, in keeping with his acceptance of the scope and purpose of the manuals, Hogan has little or nothing to say about social morality in its political, economic, or cultural dimensions. Moral theology is geared to the sacrament of penance and the confession of the individual penitent. Thus questions of the political, social, and economic order and how these orders should be structured are not considered.

DISAGREEMENTS. Despite his agreement with many aspects of the Catholic tradition, Hogan proposes a radically different approach in two very important aspects—the very method of moral theology or casuistry and the understanding of the distinction between mortal and venial sin.

As in other areas of his thought, historical consciousness deeply affects Hogan's understanding of the method of moral theology which for all practical purposes centers on casuistry. His method thus differs considerably from that proposed in the manuals of moral theology, for his approach is much less deductive.

Each science has its own proper method. Wrong methods can create much havoc as illustrated by the use of a priori and deductive approaches rather than observation in the natural sciences. Moral theology is a practical science and follows the method proper to such sciences which try to shape human action in view of a specific end. Moral theology like all practical sciences comprises three types of elements— abstract principles, practical rules, and their application to specific cases. Logically principles come first, but in reality these are the last to be realized. Rules are only a generalization of a certain number of individual facts and are formulated slowly and tentatively. But it is in the form of rules as a code of law that ethics first presents itself. Rules are the most natural form of guidance in practical matters. Facts are too numerous to be considered individually. Abstract principles are too removed to deal with the concrete. Rules are midway between the two and form the core of ethics.[116] Hogan has not written a systematic monograph in these articles. At times there seems to be some imprecision but still one can easily understand his basic approach.

Logically one begins with the principles. The principles of moral theology are of two kinds—intuitive and discursive. Intuitive principles are supplied directly by the moral sense and rest on their own evidence. They need no proof and are incapable of receiving any proof outside themselves. Many positivists today question the existence of primitive moral intuitions. But the notion of right and wrong is primitive and irreducible as illustrated by certain elementary forms of duty such as benevolence, justice, or gratitude. They are not susceptible of proof and do not require any.[117]

Discursive or inferential principles have come to the human mind through a reasoning process either deductive or inductive. Here again Hogan gives a very great role to experience. These principles are held as duties because experience whether of the individual or the race has shown that an opposite course would prove seriously detrimental to the individual or to society. Our author does not explain in detail what these principles are but recognizes their basis in experience, thereby indicating a similarity with utilitarianism about the proximate reason and source of such duties but not their ultimate moral obligations. (The contemporary moral theologian would greatly appreciate seeing how that section would be elaborated.) In reality no sharp line divides the intuitive from the inferential principles of morality and it is not easy to determine in which category a particular principle belongs.[118]

Rules, the most important moral category, stand midway between abstract principles and concrete reality. Where do these rules come from? Christians originally gathered their rules of conduct from various sources, human and divine, including of course the scriptures, the fathers of the church, and the teachings of the popes and bishops.[119] These rules are often somewhat vague and need to be more specified. Take, for example, the biblical injunction, "Thou shalt not kill."[120] History reminds us how even this rule has changed over the years. In the early church some tended to make the counsels into precepts with regard to marriage, forbearance under injury, and self-defense, but these changed with a greater appreciation of our weakened human nature and the practical needs of society. Hogan also points out that some rules which at one time accepted a certain conduct are no longer acceptable today. Think, for example, of judiciary combats and dueling, the prohibition of usury or taking interest on a loan, the extent of parental authority, and slavery. All these and many others show the fluctuating and uncertain character of moral rules long unanimously accepted. Likewise, these changes suggest the possibility of more than one point, upon which there is present agreement, being reopened and discussed afresh.[121]

The rules of moral conduct are gathered from all manner of sources but in their actual shapes they come almost entirely from the schools. Their precision and authority come from the schools, but whatever their excellence in both respects they still remain human and consequently liable, more or less, to be reconsidered and recast.[122]

Casuistry tries both to formulate the rules exactly and to judge specific cases in the light of them. How does casuistry go about its work? In various places Hogan explains some of the process of such casuistry. First of all, one looks at the rules in the light of the more abstract principles. Whatever is prescribed is prescribed for a reason in view of an end to be attained. Moral theologians also seek the ultimate meaning and value of the rule in the light of their principles. Thus the understanding of the principle gives reason, meaning, and value to the particular rule or law.[123]

Rules stand midway between principles and specific cases and the ultimate formulation of and articulation of rules depends on a dialogue in both directions. Practice is as much a part of theory as theory is of practice. Many a principle (Hogan here seems to be talking more about rules than abstract principles) seems unquestionable until an attempt is made to carry it out. The practical impossibility of applying a rule gives warning that it has to be dropped or modified. The happy working of a rule is one of the surest signs of its correctness and truth.[124]

How precisely do theologians and others make their judgments in the matter of casuistry? The Abbé considers explicitly the case of an opinion running contrary to the teachings of the schools. These judgments are not infallible. We have seen that they may change. No absolute rule can be laid down. Speculation, principles, practical necessities, the judgment of theologians, the common sense of the Christian community, authority, and reason all have to be listened to.[125]

Principles have an important role to play but even principles can be extreme and need to be toned down. To love our neighbor as ourself needs to be limited. Common sense strengthened by experience has a considerable role to play in determining rules and duty, but it cannot be absolutized. One might argue that it is always best to follow the standard rules and authorities (meaning scholarly authorities), and leave no room for one's own personal experience or impressions. But such an approach is merely mechanical and fails to recognize the mistakes that the ablest authorities have made.[126] We are dealing with matters that can change.

Casuistry, after all, is much more an intuition of the cultured mind than a matter of applying or deducing from principles. The true casuist instinctively discerns what is right and what is wrong. The casuist appeals to argument not as much to satisfy oneself as to convince others. Practical judgments will often be more true than the ostensible premises. In one of his comparatively rare footnotes Hogan here cites Cardinal Newman on the origin of such moral conviction.[127] Moral judgments then are not made by logical deduction from the more abstract to the concrete.

This approach to moral theology logically coheres with Hogan's greater emphasis on evolution, induction, intuition, and the developing aspects of human knowledge. His whole approach to theology opposes a priori approaches and one-sided deductive demonstrations. In this connection it is interesting to take another look at his explanation of the rise of laxism in the seventeenth century. The desire to make the practice of religion more acceptable to all was one reason for its rise, but the other was the habit of following out blindly logical deductions regardless of what they led to. By following out logically certain general precepts incautiously admitted without restriction, casuists were betrayed into consequences utterly repugnant to the moral sense. As a mental process there is nothing new in this. All right conduct rests on principles but the difficulty is to formulate these principles accurately and precisely. Almost all the errors of political, economic, and social science are the logical consequences of the applications of principles which seem to be plausible. However, common sense and experience show the limitation of these principles. Ethical principles have similar tests and counterpoises.[128] Not only does Hogan reject an a priori totally deductive moral method, but he accuses such a method of causing great problems in the history of moral theology.

In addition to presenting an understanding of the method of moral theology that differs considerably from both manualistic and neoscholastic approaches, Hogan also challenges and downplays in his usual irenic manner the important distinction between mortal and venial sin which was so formative of the manuals. The manuals of moral theology prepared future ministers for their role in the sacrament of penance with special emphasis on the role as judge. The priest above all had to know what was sinful and its degree of sinfulness. The distinction between mortal and venial sin was all important. Mortal sin meant in the terminology of the times that one lost the state of grace, was in the state of sin, and as such doomed to the fires of hell. The manuals of moral theology began in response to the decree of the Council of Trent that once a year all Catholics had to confess their mortal sins according to their number and species. Recall that sin, the important distinction between mortal and venial sin, and the need to avoid mortal sin especially based on motives of fear constituted a distinctive characteristic of the Catholic ethos in the United States in the last half of the nineteenth century.

In this light Hogan's approach to the clear and distinct definitions of mortal and venial sin and the differences between them undermines a very important aspect of the manuals of moral theology and of Catholic piety in the United States. Hogan alludes to the catechetical importance of this distinction by hoping that priests would dwell less on such sharp distinctions than some do in their instructions to the faithful.[129] His arguing for a great deal of gray area also goes against both the manuals and the neoscholastic approaches with their emphases on clear and distinct concepts.

The Irish-born Sulpician begins his discussion of mortal and venial sin by insisting on the complexity and great variety of human good and human evil. Between the slightest obligation and the weightiest, between the faintest beginnings of evil and its lower depths, there are degrees without number. The varieties of good and evil are like the infinite varieties of color in reality as contrasted with the few basic colors in their original simplicity. The distinction between mortal and venial sin is at best rough and rudimentary, like dividing all human beings into good and wicked or rich and poor. The very theological distinction between mortal and venial sin involves some problems and difficulties. The category of mortal sin includes both an act of deep deliberate villainy and an act of transitory weakness, though a single case of the former may be worse than a hundred of the latter. In addition it is hard to see how the worst of venial sin and the lightest of mortal sins, with hardly a shadow of perceptible difference between them, should have consequences which are so disparate.[130]

Hogan indicates that the emphasis on mortal sin especially in the area of positive law has perhaps come from using the fear of hell to secure a more prompt and thorough obedience. Our author does not draw out the implications of this remark but they are obvious. According to the Catholic teaching of the time obligations such as Sunday mass and Friday abstinence bound under pain of mortal sin and obedience to these laws was often secured by the fear of committing a mortal sin and going to hell. Hogan points out that the fathers of the church were slow to make this distinction between mortal and venial sin. The distinction is serviceable only to coarse, weak, or ungenerous souls or to the priests who try to rescue them or preserve them from the worst.[131] Here Hogan's rhetoric is rather biting and negative. Recall that he had earlier justified casuistry with its goal of determining limits as a sign of God's mercy to the weak and the harassed. This is one of the few times that Hogan uses such rhetoric which certainly indicates his basic problem with the great emphasis on the distinction between mortal and venial sin.

Even accepting the theological distinction between the two kinds of sin, despite its many problems, the application of this distinction is extremely difficult. The basic question is how much of the evil does it take to constitute a mortal sin. Wasting how much time? Gambling how much money? Stealing how many possessions? Such considerations show the complexity of the problem and how conjectural are the solutions proposed by theologians for what constitutes mortal and venial sin.[132]

Hogan continues to build his argument even stronger and also raises the rhetoric. Even if it were possible to trace a distinct, clear-cut line of division between mortal and venial sin in every sphere of duty, this would deal only with the objective side of the issue. The moral value of human action is derived primarily from the subjective side— the mental and moral condition of the agent which can be ascertained only in a very imperfect way by another. Moral science cannot measure with any accuracy the moral value, positive or negative, of individual action. This is perhaps the principal limitation or weakness of moral science.[133] The outsider can never adequately judge the subjective dispositions and moral reality of the person who has acted.

IRENIC AND TACTFUL APPROACH. There can be no doubt that Hogan proposes an understanding of moral theology quite different from that of the manuals or of neoscholasticism. His historically conscious, inductive method brings together theory and practice and challenges the existing methodologies. His opposition to the clear distinction between mortal and venial sin calls into question a basic presupposition of the manuals of moral theology. His position logically recognizes the problem in the Tridentine requirement of the integral confession of sins according to number and species. His approach can be used today by proponents of other formats for the sacrament of reconciliation that do not involve such a confession of sins according to number and species. His pointing out the danger of using the fear of hell to secure more prompt obedience goes against one of the distinctive pastoral approaches of the time.

On the other hand, the Irish-born Sulpician with his irenic and tactful approach does not draw out the logical conclusions of his positions and thereby tends to soften his more radical approaches. He never really attacks or opposes a contemporary by name. Hogan even praises Catholic moral theology as he found it at the time. "Hence we find it [moral theology] today the most living branch of the sacred science, spreading out into the various parts of human activity, old and new, and busy in applying the laws of Christian morality to every condition and every action of life."[134] The author's development of the five articles on moral theology also illustrates his tendency not to call attention to the more radical aspects of his thinking. By his own description the first three articles have spoken only in terms of admiration of the great system of moral doctrine gradually elaborated in the Catholic church, but no human science is perfect and this is true also of moral theology.[135] The fourth article deals with the imperfections of moral theology and the fifth article with the limitations. The discussion of mortal and venial sin comes under the limitations of the discipline and thus appears to be a limitation within rather than attack on the moral theology found in the manuals.

In this comparatively short discussion Hogan does not develop in any detail his understanding of the role and limitations of the hierarchical magisterium in morality. In general he speaks appreciatively of the role of popes in moral teaching.[136] However, Hogan does insist on the need for verification and experience together with authority.[137] Clerical Studies never explicitly deals with the modern question of dissent from papal teaching on moral issues, but it does implicitly recognize the possibility of such dissent. The thrust of his argument is that specific norms by their very nature have changed and can change over time. In mentioning how moral law has changed he refers to the fact that theologians clung for many centuries to the condemnation of interest taking on loans.[138] However, with his understanding of history Hogan knew of the papal teaching proposing this condemnation and in another article specifically mentioned the papal teaching.[139] He confronts directly the issue of challenging decisions of casuistry which are supposed to rest on the immutable divine and natural law. If these decisions were infallible there could be no opposition. But they are not infallible and they might be wrong.[140] The logical conclusion is that the same holds for the noninfallible casuistry or rules of the hierarchical magisterium based on natural or divine law. Hogan thus makes his point but does not go out of his way to attack or antagonize others.

In an 1897 article Hogan explicitly recognizes that noninfallible papal teaching can be wrong. Andrew Dickson White, the first president of Cornell University, wrote a well-known book, *A History of the Warfare of Science with Theology in Christendom*, in which among other things he uses Catholic teachings on the literal interpretation of scripture, Galileo, and usury to attack and deny papal infallibility.[141] Hogan points out that infallibility was not involved in any of these decisions. Infallibility is a very limited concept. The only infallible teachings are those that popes, councils, or the collective voice of pastors and faithful solemnly proclaim as belonging to revealed truth. These are the only statements that bear the seal of inerrancy. Religious belief and theology comprise many different types of teaching. Besides the defined infallible dogmas, there exists an incomparably larger number of commonly accepted doctrines from which a Catholic rarely feels at liberty to depart, and on a lower plane a richer harvest of deductions, opinions, and speculations that really come and go. Hogan explicitly admits that Roman congregations are liable to be mistaken. Yes, the pope was involved in the Galileo controversy and in the condemnation of usury but not in an infallible way.[142] Hogan thus explicitly recognizes error in noninfallible papal teaching. However, within the context of his staunch defense of papal infallibility such a recognition of error in noninfallible papal teaching is in no way provocative.

John Baptist Hogan never developed a systematic moral theology but his long, programmatic essay points to an approach to moral theology sharing the purpose, focus, and model of the manuals but using a very different method and challenging the clear distinction between mortal and venial sin. His style and tone tended to downplay the extent of his differences with the manuals of moral theology and the regnant neoscholasticism of his day. One can readily see many similarities between his approach and that of revisionist Catholic moral theologians today.

Hogan and Bouquillon both criticized the manualist approach but from different perspectives. Bouquillon's neoscholasticism logically should have challenged the legal model of the manuals and insisted on the importance of the virtues. Hogan basically accepted the legal model and the importance of casuistry. In a sense, Bouquillon's position logically called him to a more radical disagreement with the approach of the manuals even though his own book did not live up to that understanding of moral theology. However, in another sense Hogan's approach was more radical. His historically conscious and more inductive method opposed the classicist and deductive approach of Sabetti and the other manualists as well as of Bouquillon's neoscholasticism. Hogan consequently recognized the possibility of error and change in some specific moral teachings. Although Hogan accepted the basic legal model of the manuals modified by his own historically conscious understanding of laws, principles and casuistry, he actually pointed out a problem that could undermine the whole purpose and function of the manuals. The Sulpician recognized that objectively it is very difficult to draw a line between mortal and venial sin. Subjectively it is basically impossible for someone to know the dispositions of the heart of another person. Such an understanding implicitly challenged the practice with regard to the sacrament of penance and the purpose of manuals based on that practice. Although Bouquillon and Hogan in different ways disagreed with the manual approach their differences with each other were even greater. Whereas Bouquillon emphatically supported neoscholasticism and its more classicist approach, Hogan strongly disagreed with neoscholasticism and in its place adopted a more historically conscious approach not only in moral theology but also in scripture and dogmatic theology. Their interpretations of nineteenth-century theology were almost diametrically opposed.

Serious tensions exist in Hogan's approach to moral theology. His irenic mentality and style tend to downplay these differences. Perhaps his temperament made it easier for him to live with these tensions. The newer approaches indicate the creativity of the times for moral theology and point to the possibility of a fruitful development in the very near future. Unfortunately the blanket condemnation of modernism in the first decade of the twentieth century, the continuing imposition of neoscholasticism, and the growing authoritarianism and defensiveness of the increasingly centralized Roman Catholic church prevented any such development from occurring.

NOTES

1. Hogan, *Clerical Studies*, pp. 197–262.

2. Hogan is occasionally mentioned in some of the American Catholic historical literature cited in chapter two. The best and most in-depth source for Hogan is Kauffman, *Tradition and Transformation*, especially pp. 168–177.

3. Kauffman, *Tradition and Transformation*, pp. 188–189; White, *Diocesan Seminary*, p. 248.

4. Hogan, *Clerical Studies*; *Daily Thoughts for Priests* (Boston: Marlier, Callanan, 1899).

5. Hogan's articles in the *American Catholic Quarterly Review* include "Church and State in France," 17 (1892): 333–355; "Pagan Virtue," 18 (1893): 1–19; "Marshall MacMahon—The Scholar and the Man," 19 (1894): 348–367; "Christian Faith and Modern Science," 22 (1897): 382–399; "The Miraculous in Church History," 23 (1898): 382–398; "Priests and People in France," 24 (1899): 123–136; "Penitential Discipline in the Early Church," 25 (1900): 417–437. Hogan's articles in *Donahoe's Magazine* include "Freedom of Thought in the Catholic Church," 30 (1893): 641–645; "Heroic Charity in Worldly Garb: The Story of an Ideal Sacrifice," 31 (1894): 135–141; "After Death: The Catholic Church and Cremation," 32 (1894): 17–22; "The Social Aspects of Religion," 33 (1895): 283–287.

6. John Hogan, "Church Building: The Priest and the Architect," *American Ecclesiastical Review* 20 (1899): 124–134, is the first article in this series of eleven. The last article is "Church Building: Stained Glass Windows," *American Ecclesiastical Review* 25 (1902): 361ff. This last article was published after his death.

7. "Necrology: Very Rev. J. B. Hogan, S.S.," *Catholic University Bulletin* 7 (1901): 508.

8. White, *Diocesan Seminary*, pp. 237–238.

9. Hogan, *Clerical Studies*, p. iv.

10. Ibid., pp. 197–265.

11. Kauffman, *Tradition and Transformation*, pp. 188; 169–177.

12. Hogan, *Daily Thoughts*, pp. v–viii.

13. Kauffman, *Tradition and Transformation*, pp. 155–157.

14. Ibid., pp. 156–160.

15. Ibid., p. 168.

16. Ibid., pp. 154–168.

17. Ibid., p. 168.

18. Ibid., p. 176.

19. Ibid., pp. 176–177.

20. Hogan, *Clerical Studies*, p. 430.

21. Ibid., p. 369.

22. Ibid., pp. 3–5.

23. Ibid., pp. 9–20.

24. Ibid., pp. 430–436.

25. Ibid., pp. 55–59.

26. Ibid., pp. 104–105.

27. Ibid., pp. 98–101.
28. Ibid., pp. 138–146.
29. Ibid., pp. 108–137.
30. Ibid., p. 369.
31. Ibid., pp. 316–320.
32. Ibid., p. 370.
33. Ibid., p. 470.
34. Ibid., pp. 472–475.
35. Ibid., p. 176.
36. Ibid., pp. 185–186.
37. Ibid., pp. 480–481.
38. Ibid., p. 152.
39. Ibid., pp. 156–161.
40. Ibid., pp. 152–155.
41. Ibid., pp. 162–166.
42. Ibid., pp. 165–166.
43. Ibid., pp. 166–168. See also Hogan, *Donahoe's Magazine* 30 (1893): 641–645.
44. Hogan, *American Catholic Quarterly Review* 22 (1897): 398; Hogan, *Clerical Studies*, pp. 115–120.
45. Hogan, *Clerical Studies*, pp. 170–179.
46. Ibid., p. 194.
47. Ibid., p. 33.
48. Ibid., p. 76.
49. Ibid., p. 196.
50. Ibid., pp. 193–194.
51. Ibid., pp. 405–410.
52. Ibid., pp. 24–25; 27; 31–32.
53. Ibid., pp. 24; 31–32.
54. Ibid., pp. 32–45.
55. Ibid., pp. 34–39.
56. Ibid., pp. 39–45.
57. Ibid., pp. 195–196.
58. Ibid., p. 60.
59. Ibid., pp. 60–78.
60. Fogarty, *American Catholic Biblical Scholarship*, p. 74.
61. Hogan, *Clerical Studies*, pp. 473; 476–477.
62. Ibid., p. 428.
63. Ibid., p. 477.
64. Ibid., pp. 97–98.
65. Ibid., p. 142.
66. Ibid., p. 417.
67. Ibid., p. 403.
68. Ibid., p. 95.
69. Hogan, *Daily Thoughts*, pp. vi–vii.
70. Ibid., pp. 198–202.
71. Ibid., pp. 93–94.

72. Ibid., p. 53.

73. Ibid., p. 131.

74. Donna Merwick, *Boston Priests, 1848–1910: A Study of Social and Intellectual Change* (Cambridge: Harvard University Press, 1973), p. 139.

75. William Thompson, ed., *Bérulle and the French School: Selected Writings* (New York: Paulist, 1989), pp. 3–96, especially footnote 5 on p. 90. See also Lowell M. Glendon, "French School of Spirituality," in Michael Downey, ed., *New Dictionary of Catholic Spirituality* (Collegeville, Minn.: The Liturgical Press, 1993), pp. 420–423.

76. Hogan, *Daily Thoughts*, pp. 50–51.

77. Ibid., pp. 198–199.

78. Hogan, *Donahoe's Magazine* 33 (1895): 285.

79. Hogan, *American Catholic Quarterly Review* 17 (1892): 352.

80. Ahern, *Catholic University of America*, pp. 39–43.

81. See the publication of the alumni of St. John's Seminary, *A Garland of Affectionate Tribute* (Boston, 1906).

82. Kauffman, *Tradition and Transformation*, p. 175.

83. Ibid., pp. 172–176.

84. John Talbot Smith, *Our Seminaries: An Essay on Clerical Training* (New York: William H. Young, 1896).

85. Bouquillon, *Catholic University Bulletin* 5 (1899): 244–268.

86. Kauffman, *Tradition and Transformation*, p. 172.

87. Thomas Bouquillon, "Henry C. Lea as Historian of Moral Theology," *Catholic University Bulletin* 1 (1895): 428–433; "Henry C. Lea as an Historian," *American Catholic Quarterly Review* 16 (1891): 131–159.

88. Hogan, *American Catholic Quarterly Review* 25 (1890): 417–437.

89. Hogan, *Clerical Studies*, pp. 180–182.

90. Ibid., pp. 138–196.

91. Hogan, *American Catholic Quarterly Review* 23 (1898): 382–398.

92. Connell, in *Essays on Catholic Education*, ed. Deferrari, p. 225.

93. *Clerical Studies*, pp. 197–262.

94. Ibid., pp. 203–205.

95. Ibid., pp. 197–207.

96. Ibid., p. 204.

97. Ibid., pp. 225ff.

98. Ibid., pp. 242–243.

99. Ibid., pp. 243–244.

100. Ibid., p. 263.

101. Ibid., pp. 263–290.

102. Ibid., p. 244.

103. Ibid., p. 246.

104. Ibid., p. 197.

105. Ibid., p. 278.

106. Ibid., pp. 223–227.

107. Ibid., pp. 236–242.

108. Ibid., p. 231.

109. Ibid., pp. 217–218.

110. Ibid., p. 211.
111. Ibid., p. 221.
112. Ibid., p. 250.
113. Ibid., p. 228.
114. Ibid., p. 214.
115. Ibid., p. 218.
116. Ibid., pp. 210–211.
117. Ibid., pp. 218–219; 250–251.
118. Ibid., pp. 219–220.
119. Ibid., pp. 212–214.
120. Ibid., p. 215.
121. Ibid., pp. 252–253.
122. Ibid., p. 221; 214.
123. Ibid., pp. 216–217.
124. Ibid., pp. 221–222.
125. Ibid., pp. 232–233.
126. Ibid., pp. 247–249.
127. Ibid., p. 247.
128. Ibid., pp. 240–241.
129. Ibid., p. 259.
130. Ibid., p. 257.
131. Ibid., p. 259.
132. Ibid., p. 258.
133. Ibid., pp. 260–261.
134. Ibid., p. 226.
135. Ibid., pp. 235–236.
136. Ibid., pp. 214; 236–240.
137. Ibid., pp. 247.
138. Ibid., p. 252.
139. Hogan, *American Catholic Quarterly Review* 22 (1897): 388.
140. Hogan, *Clerical Studies*, p. 233.
141. Andrew Dickson White, *A History of the Warfare of Science with Theology in Christendom* (New York: D. Appleton, 1896).
142. Hogan, *American Catholic Quarterly Review* 22 (1897): 386–388.

Epilogue

Scholars and students of moral theology especially in the United States need to have a better understanding of the historical development of the discipline in this country. Unfortunately, moral theology has not given enough attention to its own history. Sabetti, Bouquillon, and Hogan were not giants in their field, but they were well known in the church of their time not only nationally but also internationally. American Catholic history has known the work of these people especially Bouquillon and Hogan, but contemporary moral theology has not heard of their work and accomplishments. One of the purposes of this volume has been to make these people better known and to stimulate greater interest in the historical development of moral theology.

Moral theology has its own unique history and development. What is true of dogmatic or systematic theology is not necessarily true of moral theology. One must be careful of making judgments about moral theology on the basis of the history of dogmatic theology. The accepted wisdom has maintained that the manuals of moral theology like those of dogmatic theology are of neoscholastic inspiration. However, neoscholasticism did not really have that much influence on the late nineteenth-century manuals of moral theology. The genre of the manual was in place for a long time and was not sufficiently changed by the dominance of neoscholasticism in the nineteenth century.

Ironically, church authority itself played an important role in the fact that neoscholasticism did not substantially affect the manuals of moral theology. By making Alphonsus Liguori the authoritative figure in moral theology the papacy gave great weight to the manuals of moral theology and helped ensure that this genre would continue for some time without substantial change. Alphonsus deserves great praise for his pastoral approaches and for having adopted a sane middle position amid the severe controversies of his day. However, in the ultramontanist climate of the mid-nineteenth century his strong support of the papacy, especially infallibility, and of Marian doctrines and devotions, especially the Immaculate Conception, contributed enormously to his having been declared a doctor of the Church in 1871. Thomas Bouquillon correctly pointed out that one should not say that Alphonsus plays the same role in Catholic moral theology as Thomas Aquinas does in dogmatic theology as if Aquinas were not eminent in both dogmatic and moral theology. Bouquillon saw the great contribution of Alphonsus not in the speculative order but in the prudential aspect of his judgments. Despite the astute observation of Bouquillon, in reality papal approbation of Alphonsus tended to solidify and support the manualistic approach to moral theology which was not the method and approach of Aquinas.

History is full of surprises and this study has uncovered some fascinating developments in the nineteenth century. Most startling is the methodological pluralism that existed in moral theology in the United States at that time. The generally accepted wisdom maintained that Catholic moral theology before Vatican II was quite monolithic, but that was not the case. This methodological pluralism in the setting of late nineteenth-century United States Catholicism is quite surprising. Catholicism was at that time an immigrant church in this country facing huge practical problems of growth and adaptation but without a strong intellectual tradition especially in theology. In these circumstances one would not expect to find much intellectual ferment and theological diversity. But there it was.

This pluralism had some interesting features that raise some questions. The three theologians considered here were contemporaries and at one time lived within fifty miles of one another when John B. Hogan was president of Divinity College at Catholic University (1889–1894). Despite their obvious differences they never disagreed with one another in their writings. This seems strange. One can only conjecture about the reason. Their different approaches became more prominent and evident near the end of the lives of Bouquillon and Hogan. Sabetti had already died when Bouquillon published his article in 1899 strongly criticizing the manuals of moral theology. In that article Bouquillon never explicitly referred to Sabetti. Hogan died two years later. Bouquillon and Hogan knew one another at Catholic University during Hogan's time there. As mentioned, Hogan was a generalist and not a specialist scholar in moral theology but his approach to moral theology differed considerably from the method of Bouquillon. Precisely because Hogan dealt with many different areas he was unlikely to engage in extended discussions with those who had different approaches. In fact,

Hogan in his tactful way of proposing new approaches usually did not mention by name those with whom he was disagreeing.

One retains the impression that this ferment in moral theology was at a beginning stage at this time. The manuals of moral theology as represented by Sabetti were in possession. Bouquillon criticized these manuals from his neoscholastic perspectives. However, despite his strong opposition he basically followed the fundamental purpose and legal model of the manuals downplaying the overall teleology of Aquinas and leaving out entirely the discussion of the virtues. Hogan's moderate historical mindedness proposed an even more radical critique of the manuals but Hogan himself understood his own approach to be in continuity with the manuals and not in direct opposition. Both Bouquillon and Hogan appear to be feeling their way along in proposing their newer approaches. Neither worked out a totally synthetic and systematic presentation of their positions. However, the differences with the manuals were present and ferment was in the air.

In the light of the purpose and focus of the manuals, casuistry assumed a large role in moral theology. Here the differences in approach between Sabetti and Hogan are most interesting. Sabetti's manual and solution of cases followed the accepted approach of the manuals in solving cases by applying principles to acts and comparing the cases with other cases. The manuals definitely saw casuistry as an application of principles to cases with prudence reduced merely to the proper use of the principles. However, from other sources it appears that Sabetti often made an intuitive judgment about a particular act without seeing all the reasons justifying it. Hogan clearly recognized a reciprocal relationship in casuistry between the case and the specific principle which gives a more important role to human prudence. Principles can be modified and changed in the light of new cases. Such an approach to casuistry seems to be a more accurate understanding of what occurs in reality and is in keeping with a more historically conscious and inductive approach to moral theology.

The different approaches of the three authors to what today is called dissent or theological disagreement with noninfallible church teaching is most revealing. Sabetti embodied the approach that endured throughout the twentieth century before Vatican II—when Rome speaks, the matter is settled. Bouquillon reluctantly admitted the possibility of legitimate dissent or disagreement from such an authoritative teaching—a position similar to that taken in some manuals of dogmatic theology in the nineteenth century. Hogan with his more inductive and historically conscious approach explicitly recognized that specific norms can change and have changed. Noninfallible teaching could be wrong.

From today's perspective the major question concerns why the manuals of moral theology illustrated by Sabetti continued to be the way of doing moral theology in the United States (and in the world) until Vatican II. Bouquillon and Hogan from very different perspectives strongly criticized the approach of the manuals. These two were not marginal or insignificant figures in the Catholic church and its nascent intellectual life in the United States. Thomas Bouquillon was heralded as the leading intellectual figure at the Catholic University of America. He enjoyed an international reputation. Hogan was a teacher and administrator although not known as a specialist in moral theology. But he was well regarded in the Sulpician community and by the bishops of the United States. His *Clerical Studies* went through two editions in the United States and was translated into French. The criticism of moral theology came from very respected and mainstream figures in the Catholic Church in the United States. Why did their criticism have no effect?

This book has already pointed out several factors operating to prevent these different criticisms from having any effect, but one reason stands out. The climate in the Catholic church at the end of the nineteenth century was already moving in a more centralized and authoritarian direction associated with ultramontanism. The condemnation of Americanism in 1899 indicated the suspicion that the Roman authorities had with regard to what was occurring in the United States. Above all, the condemnation of Modernism in 1907 and its aftermath effectively closed the door on any questioning of the accepted approaches. In a defensive way the church after the condemnation of Modernism became even more authoritarian and centralized. Creative and newer theological approaches were no longer welcome. It is safe to say that someone writing after 1910 what Hogan wrote in the 1890s would have come under great suspicion and probably condemnation. Thus it was not until Vatican II and its aftermath that the earlier ferment present even in Catholic moral theology in the United States would again come to the surface.

Looking back at the history discussed in this volume from the perspective of a so-called revisionist moral theologian, four final observations are in place. First, John B. Hogan stands out as the precursor of much that has developed in Catholic moral theology in the United

States and in the world since Vatican II. Above all, his more historically conscious and more inductive method has been adopted by many contemporaries. This has important ramifications for method in moral theology, for casuistry, and for understanding the proper role and place of hierarchical teaching on specific moral issues.

Second, this history sheds some light on the contemporary discussion about the various approaches to moral theology. Virtues, principles, and casuistry are proposed as different approaches to moral theology today. In the light of the whole historical tradition discussed here I would maintain the need for all three approaches and point out the danger of excluding any one of them. The Catholic tradition has always emphasized a "both-and" or inclusive approach. Casuistry will necessarily have an important role in moral theology which must always consider individual cases and actions. Principles have consistently played an important role in the history of moral theology and will continue to do so insofar as they strive to direct our actions. Specific principles and norms, however, are open to change. Virtue or its equivalent has been downplayed and even forgotten by the manuals with their narrow focus of training confessors to judge the existence and the degree of sinful acts. If moral theology refers to the whole of the moral life and not just to the minimum of what is sinful, then virtue must play a wider role. Bouquillon was absolutely correct to criticize the manuals for their failure to give enough importance to virtues.

Although all three approaches must be part of a total and sound moral theology, the virtues are most important precisely because the virtues influence all the particular acts that the person places and also the virtues constitute the person as a moral agent and a moral subject. Even in the post-Vatican II era the virtues have not yet received the importance they deserve. Part of the contemporary problem comes from the fact that discussions have once again focused on particular acts but now in the light of the condemnation of these acts by the hierarchical magisterium and the attempt by some theologians to justify them.

Third, the question of theological model remains a very fundamental aspect of constructing any contemporary moral theology. The manuals by their nature followed a legal model. Despite Hogan's somewhat radical criticism of the manuals and their methodology, he still basically adopted the focus and purpose of the manuals with the accompanying legal model. Bouquillon also fundamentally accepted that model but his neoscholastic criticisms of the manuals pointed toward the need for a different type of model. In my judgment, the legal model is no longer an adequate model for moral theology. I have proposed a relationality-responsibility model as the most adequate approach.

Fourth, what will happen in regard to what John Paul II calls the genuine crisis in the church created by theological dissent from authoritative church teaching? The question of the relationship between theologians and the hierarchical magisterium is immense and very complex. The history studied in this volume is not able to supply a complete and detailed answer to this important question. However, Hogan's very astute observation in the debate over the imposition of scholasticism as the Catholic philosophy and theology in the late nineteenth century has an important bearing on our question. He said that the intrinsic nature of the philosophy and not authority will be the basis for its ultimate effect. In reality authority was able to keep Catholic theology and philosophy neoscholastic for over seventy-five years, but Vatican II opened up many new approaches and proved Hogan's contention. Such a contention is very much in keeping with the Thomistic tradition's insistence on an intrinsic morality—something is commanded because it is good and not the other way around. In my judgment, such an approach shows the way out of the contemporary crisis in the Catholic church in the relationships between authoritative magisterial teaching and theological discussions.

From a contemporary perspective the primary negative criticism of all three authors comes from their narrow understanding of moral theology as dealing primarily with acts and especially sinful acts in the light of the celebration of the sacrament of penance. In addition they did not give enough emphasis to the scriptural, theological, and sacramental dimensions. Contemporary moral theology must be life-centered and develop all the aspects of the Christian's multiple relationships with God, neighbor, and world within the context of the ecclesial and human communities.

Index

abortion, and acceleration of birth, 113–116; and craniotomy, 113, 115–116, 146–150; and ectopic pregnancy, 113–115, 146–150
Aertnys, Joseph, 54, 114
Albert the Great, 8
Alexander VIII, 25, 52, 55
Alexander of Hales, 8
Alexander VII, pope, 21, 52, 106, 107; and Forty-five Propositions, 21–22, 55
Alexander III, pope, 234
almsgiving, as penance, 6
Ambrose of Milan, 5
American Catholic Quarterly Review, 175, 258
American Ecclesiastical Review, 66, 88, 89, 112, 114, 140, 146, 176, 179, 258
Americanism, 25, 65, 67, 68–69, 70, 259, 299
analogy, 4, 149, 154
Aquaviva, Claudius, 134
Aquinas, Thomas, 8, 12, 78–79, 96, 116, 117, 118, 120, 132, 175, 177, 178, 188, 189, 193, 194, 196, 198, 204, 247, 263, 268, 270, 297, 298; and conscience, 32; and *exitus-reditus* model, 9; and freedom, 18; and grace and nature, 48; and habits, 10; and human acts, 17, 32, 48; and intrinsic and extrinsic principles of acts, 10–11; and natural law, 34, 108–109; and papal

approbation in nineteenth century, 8, 49–50, 55, 59, 118, 197–198; powers or faculties, 9; principle of finality, 9; principles of image and participation, 9; and *Summa theologiae*, 8–11, 12, 16, 55, 189, 190, 200, 201–202, 212–216, 228, 229, 245, 279, 281; and virtues and vices, 10–11, 162, 215, 217, 246
Aristotle, influence in Medieval universities, 7–8, 9, 189; and Aquinas, 50
Arnauld, Antoine, 23; and *The Moral Theology of the Jesuits Faithfully Extracted from Their Books*, 24
Arnauld, Mère Angélique, 23
Augustine of Hippo, 5, 10, 188; and ontologism, 48
Avanzini, Peter, 113
Avila Theresa, 248
d'Azeglio, Taparelli, 200
Azor, John, 15, 16, 19, 190

Badin, Stephen, 61, 64
Ballerini, Anthony, 54, 119, 120; and *Vindiciae Ballerinianae*, 58, 84, 119
Balmès, 270
Baltimore provincial and plenary councils, 61, 62–64, 66, 78, 81, 83, 97, 156, 160, 174, 258
Banezianist, 190
Barrett, Timothy, 82, 161

303